Modern Church History

SCM CORE TEXT

Modern Church History

Tim Grass

scm press

© Tim Grass 2008

The Author has asserted his right under the Copyright, Designs and
Patents Act, 1988, to be identified as the Author of this Work

British Library Cataloguing in Publication data

A catalogue record for this book is available
from the British Library

978 0 334 04062 0

First published in 2008 by SCM Press
13–17 Long Lane,
London EC1A 9PN

www.scm-canterburypress.co.uk

SCM Press is a division of
SCM-Canterbury Press Ltd

Typeset by Regent Typesetting, London
Printed in the UK by CPI William Clowes Ltd,
Beccles, NR34 7TL

Contents

Preface   ix
Abbreviations   x

1 **Introduction**   1
   About this book   1
   Key themes in modern church history   2
   Global Christianity in 1648   4

PART I   1648–1789   5

   Timeline: World Events, 1648–1789   6

2 **European Protestantism after 1648**   7
   The aftermath of war   7
   The state of the churches   8
   Reaction against confessionalization (i): Pietism   13
   Reaction against confessionalization (ii): Deism and the
   Enlightenment   19

3 **Roman Catholicism**   27
   The eighteenth-century papacy   27
   The Church in the Baroque era   29
   Church and state in the pre-revolutionary period   30
   Hierarchy and clergy   34
   Catholic devotion   35
   Catholic mission   37

4 **The 'Babylonian Captivity' of the Eastern Churches**   44
   East and West   46
   Russia   48
   Christianity under Ottoman rule   54

5 **The Churches in Britain, Ireland, and North America, 1688–1789**   59

   Timeline: Events in Britain, Ireland, and North America, 1689–1789   60

   England and Wales   61
   Scotland   73
   Ireland   75
   Christianity in the New World   76

6 **The Rise of Evangelicalism**   84
   What was Evangelicalism?   84
   The rise of Evangelicalism   88
   Evangelicalism and the churches   97
   The 'Great Awakening': early North American
      Evangelicalism   100

PART 2   1789–1914   107

   Timeline: World Events, 1789–1914   108

7 **Orthodoxy**   109
   Russia   109
   Ottoman domination and its legacy   112

8 **Rome, Revolution, and Reaction**   120
   Revolution   120
   Reaction   127
   Popular piety   133

9 **European Protestantism during the Nineteenth Century**   138
   The challenges of modern thought   138
   Biblical criticism   143
   Church and state   148
   Renewal movements   150

10 **The Churches in Nineteenth-Century Britain (I): Church and State in England and Wales**   155

   Timeline: Events in Britain and Ireland, 1789–1914   156

   Roman Catholicism   157
   Anglicanism   159
   From Dissenters to Nonconformists to Free Churchmen   169

11 **The Churches in Nineteenth-Century Britain (II): Growth
    and Division**   181
    The 1851 Religious Census   181
    The effectiveness of outreach   183
    The changing roles of women   187
    The growth of non-Anglican Christianity in Ireland   188
    Division and pluralism in Scotland   190

12 **Christianity in the United States**   197
    The development of religious pluralism   197
    The churches and the black community   198
    Adapting to the American context   200
    Theological developments   203
    American religious creations   206

13 **Western Christian Social Thought to 1914**   218
    Roman Catholic social teaching   218
    German and Scandinavian Protestantism responds to
        social need   219
    British Christian social thought   222
    The 'Social Gospel' in North America   229

14 **Nineteenth-Century Expansion Outside Europe**   233
    Where did Christianity expand?   233
    The main types of agency   235
    The missionaries   242
    Missionary strategy   242
    Missions and colonization   246
    The emergence of indigenous churches   251
    Edinburgh 1910   253

PART 3   **1914 to the Present**   257

    Timeline: World Events, 1914–2007   258

15 **The Impact of Two World Wars**   259
    World War I and the churches   259
    The rise of Neo-Orthodoxy   262
    Christians, Jews, and Nazis in inter-war Europe   263
    World War II, the Holocaust, and the churches   265

16 **The Eastern Churches from 1917**   270
    Communism and its impact   270
    East and West   281
    The churches in the Middle East   285

17 **Christianity in the West – Change or Decline?** 290
    Defining our terms 290
    The state of the churches 292
    Theological developments 297

18 **Pentecostalism and the Charismatic Movement** 306
    Pentecostal development 306
    The global spread of Pentecostalism 310
    The Charismatic Movement 314

19 **The Ecumenical movement** 318
    Roots 318
    Global ecumenical organizations 322
    The World Council of Churches 324
    Changing conceptions of ecumenism and its goals 328
    Other approaches to ecumenism 332

20 **Twentieth-Century Roman Catholicism** 336
    Papacy, church, and state 336
    Social and ethical thought before Vatican II 338
    Vatican II 339
    The Church since Vatican II 343

21 **The British Churches** 349

    Timeline: Events in Britain, 1914–2007 350

    The churches and society 349
    Institutional developments 354
    Ecumenism 356
    New traditions 359
    Changes in worship 365

22 **Global Christianity** 369
    The shift in the centre of Christian gravity away from the
        post-Christian West 369
    The churches and national identity 376
    The growth of regional theologies 377
    From missions to mission 378

23 **Conclusion** 382

Glossary 386
Suggested Further Reading 393
Index of Names and Subjects 399

Preface

This is a book I have wanted to write for a while now, the sort of book I wish I had had as a first-year student of Ecclesiastical History thirty years ago, and which I wished I could find in order to recommend to my students. Whether it fills the gap is for you to judge, but I hope that you will find yourself 'grabbed' by the story, as I have been.

Certain acknowledgements are in order. I have drawn on research undertaken in writing modules on Modern Church History and other related topics for Spurgeon's College and the Open Theological College, and thanks are due to these institutions for setting me on such an interesting project. I would also like to express my gratitude to the readers who have given considerable time to working through and commenting on my manuscript, Dr David Arnold and Dr Ian Randall. Barbara Laing's enthusiasm as commissioning editor has done much to move this project from wishful thinking to reality. Finally, I should like to dedicate this book to my wife, Ann, for without her long-suffering in allowing me to fill the house with musty history books this one would never have been written!

Tim Grass
September 2007

Abbreviations

ABCFM	American Board of Commissioners for Foreign Missions
AUCECB	All-Union Council of Evangelical Christians–Baptists
AIC	African instituted church
BCC	British Council of Churches
CELAM	Consejo Episcopal Latino-Americana (Latin American Episcopal Conference)
CHC	*Cambridge History of Christianity*
CIM	China Inland Mission
CMS	Church Missionary Society
CWC	Christian World Communion
EA	Evangelical Alliance
EBF	European Baptist Federation
IMC	International Missionary Council
LMS	London Missionary Society
NDT	Sinclair B. Ferguson and David F. Wright (eds), 1988, *New Dictionary of Theology*, Leicester: IVP
ODCC	F.L. Cross and E.A. Livingstone (eds), 1997, *Oxford Dictionary of the Christian Church*, 3rd edn, Oxford: Oxford University Press
SCM	Student Christian Movement
SPCK	Society for the Promotion of Christian Knowledge
SPG	Society for the Propagation of the Gospel in Foreign Parts (now USPG)
SVM	Student Volunteer Movement
WCC	World Council of Churches
WCE	David B. Barrett, George T. Kurian and Todd M. Johnson (eds), 2001, *World Christian Encyclopedia: A Comparative Survey of Churches and Religions in the Modern World*, 2nd edn, 2 vols, New York: Oxford University Press
WSCF	World Student Christian Fellowship
URC	United Reformed Church
YMCA	Young Men's Christian Association
YWCA	Young Women's Christian Association

1

Introduction

About this book

This book aims to offer a student-level introduction to the history of Christianity during what is generally termed the modern period, with an eye to its global development. I have chosen to take a long view of things – more than three and a half centuries – because the continuities between twentieth-century developments and what preceded them may easily be missed if one focuses only on the later period. It is not ground-breaking in the sense that it does not seek to advance new interpretations, but simply to tell the story as it appears from my vantage point: it is a survey rather than a work of original scholarship. My indebtedness to the secondary works listed will be obvious, even if it has not been possible to footnote every instance. I have not often discussed the interpretative controversies which surround most events of any significance in the history of the Christian religion; these are important, not least because of what they show us about those conducting the argument, but the focus of this book is primarily on introducing the history itself, rather than debates about the historiography. Some of the more important debates are footnoted.

The book covers a great deal of ground in a comparatively short space. It is a survey rather than a sustained argument for a particular interpretation, but the 'Questions for thought' at the end of each chapter are intended to stimulate the process of engagement with the topics covered, and to help you develop the skills of constructing historical arguments. I hope they may provide the raw material that you will turn into a coherent argument!

At the end of each chapter are suggestions for further reading and useful websites; these are also added for key figures at the point where they are first discussed. The suggestions are restricted to material available in English, because the primary use for this book will doubtless be where English is the language of teaching. However, many of the items listed or footnoted will lead readers to material in various languages, as well as to further material in English.

Notes are kept to a minimum, and have been used only for quotations, direct interaction with significant lines of argument, guidance as to useful sources or further discussions, and sometimes also for additional points of interest whose inclusion would disrupt the flow of the main text.

At a later point, the publishers and I intend to create a website to go with this book. This will provide further links (or extracts where the works in question are not yet available online) to primary sources, authoritative secondary discussions, and reliable and authoritative reference sites. It will also facilitate the updating of the bibliographies.

Key themes in modern church history

Every historian tries to reduce a chaos of dates, facts, actors, and interpretations to some kind of order so as to produce a coherent narrative. Underlying this is often a commitment to a particular 'master narrative' which both enables the historian to make sense of the evidence and affects the selection and balance of topics to be covered. In the present period, many historians see the dominant master narrative as one of secularization, while others major on the globalization of Christianity. Each of these may be worked out in somewhat different ways by individual writers. In addition, they will differ on the place accorded to theological, rather than strictly historical, developments; I have majored on the history but have felt it essential to include some discussion of the main theological developments, since these motivated some of the actors in the story and indeed provoked some of the twists and turns of its plot. This is not, however, a textbook on historical theology, of which there are plenty in existence; you may find it helpful to read one in parallel with this volume.

This book is still traditional enough to focus on the history of the churches rather than that of Christianity. There is a difference, in that it majors on the issues confronting the institutional bodies rather than offering across-the-board assessments of the impact of such external phenomena as urbanization and industrialization (though some discussion of these does appear), or discussion of how Christian concepts have been applied in the worlds of art and literature. If a justification is required for the approach adopted, it is simply that excellent introductions to the period already exist which take the other approach,[1] whereas I was unable to find suitable course texts to recommend, which adopted the approach found here. Accordingly, within each chronological division of the story I have adopted an approach which treats each major confessional family – Orthodox, Roman Catholic, and Protestant – separately. With the globalization of Christianity in the final period, that approach breaks down as large Pentecostal or indigenous traditions emerge which do not fit easily into such a scheme, and the confessional approach is there supplemented by thematic consideration of certain issues such as ecumenism and the churches' response to war.

It will be evident that equal space has not been accorded to each region of the world. Apart from the gaps in my own knowledge and the limitations inevitable in my personal perspective, all areas are not equally well provided for in terms of historical literature. Furthermore, whatever one's perspective, it may surely be acknowledged that some have been more significant than others in terms of global developments. The leading global role played by nineteenth-century Britain meant that developments in its churches (especially the English ones) were of particular significance for churches elsewhere, as were those in German scholarship of the period. After a slow start, British missionaries played a key role in the globalization of Christianity, and much that has happened since has followed the agenda set down by their activity, if only by way of reacting against aspects of it. While there are deficiencies in an approach which treats each nation's ecclesiastical history in isolation, the likely readership of this book has dictated that specific chapters are devoted to developments in Britain and (in the middle period) the United States. Nevertheless, the very unfamiliarity of the story of the churches in Korea, say, or what is now Iraq, makes it interesting to follow, and a change from many of the standard textbooks that were written in an era when the West was the preserve of the churches, and what we now call the Majority World was the preserve of the missions: real church history happened in the West, or at least had Western actors playing the leading roles. I hope that this book, like others that are beginning to appear, has taken a few steps away from that approach.

Several key themes will recur throughout the narrative:

- changing patterns of mission
- global expansion and a shift in the centre of gravity of the Christian population
- the relationship between religion and national identity
- church–state relations
- the churches' response to modernity
- the process of secularization
- the quest for a meaningful and relevant spirituality
- changing patterns of believing.

The questions will draw out various aspects of these, and you may find it helpful to keep an eye open for material bearing on them as you work through the book.

Global Christianity in 1648

Why have I chosen 1648 as the starting point for this book? It was in this year that the Peace of Westphalia was concluded, ending the Thirty Years' War. By its recognition that Europe was henceforward to be divide in its religious allegiance between several forms of Christianity, it marked a transition from the religious unity of medieval Western Europe to the pluralism of the modern era. In addition, the main lines of development of the Protestant Reformation had been marked out.

Where were Christians to be found, and of what types? Christianity had previously expanded throughout North Africa, and then as far east as China, before being forced to contract to Europe and the Eastern Mediterranean, with the addition of small enclaves in India and the Middle East. At this stage, therefore, it was primarily a European religion, and one which existed within the Christendom paradigm of relationships between church, state, and society.

Protestantism was very much a Northern European phenomenon. Orthodoxy was restricted almost entirely to Eastern Europe, the Middle East, Egypt, and Ethiopia (as well as an enclave on the west coast of India). It was Catholicism which had the widest distribution, having established a footing in South and North America, Central Africa, and the Far East, as well as its heartland in Southern and Central Europe. The modern era of Catholic mission was already well under way; only a few visionary Protestants had yet begun to look outwards; Orthodoxy had lost its earlier missionary impetus, preoccupied with the struggle for survival under Ottoman rule or (like many Protestant churches) limited in its vision by the responsibility of providing divine support for national interests. Serious encounter and engagement with other faiths was almost non-existent at this point, although it had been evident during the later medieval period in both Catholicism and Orthodoxy. The Christian world was thus very different from that of today.

Yet it was also recognizably like that of today: the religious boundaries of Europe have not changed very much, and the areas of Christian concentration elsewhere have endured. Furthermore, Christians then were wrestling with many of the same problems that face the churches now. There is, therefore, a reassuring degree of continuity about this story which makes it easier to follow. I hope that you will enjoy it, but also that the way it is presented here will stimulate plenty of serious thinking about the issues it raises. Enjoy your reading!

Note

1 E.g. Hugh Mcleod, 1997, *Religion and the People of Western Europe, 1789–1989*, Oxford: Oxford University Press.

PART 1　1648–1789

Timeline: World events, 1648–1789

1648   Peace of Westphalia
1663   Société des Missions Étrangères founded
1666–7   Old Believer schism begins in Russia
1675   Spener, *Pia Desideria*; *Helvetic Consensus*
1685   Edict of Nantes revoked
1696   Francke founds orphanage at Halle
1704   Chinese Rites controversy reaches its peak
1706   First Lutheran missionaries (to Tranquebar)
1713   Jansenism condemned
1721   Patriarchate of Moscow suppressed
1722   Herrnhut founded
1732   First Moravian missionaries (to West Indies)
1751   Diderot's *Encyclopédie* begins to appear
1756–63   Seven Years' War
1773   Jesuits suppressed
1782   The *Philokalia* published
1789   French Revolution begins

2

European Protestantism after 1648

The outlook for Christianity was not particularly propitious at the start of the period covered by this book. In this chapter we outline the condition of the European Protestant churches, and discuss some of the main internal and external developments which shaped their history during the next 140 years.

The aftermath of war

The Thirty Years' War (1618–48) had bankrupted nations and ravaged vast tracts of countryside. Yet at the end the religious landscape was not much changed. Most of Northern Europe was Protestant; southern countries were Catholic; and Eastern Europe was largely Orthodox, though parts of it were under Muslim rule. Little was to change until the end of the First World War, and even today the religious landscape in its Christian aspect is not greatly altered.

The agreement followed the lines laid down by the Peace of Augsburg (1555), which had put forth the principle of *cuius regio, eius religio*. This may be paraphrased as 'the religion of the people is to be that of their ruler'. But whereas Augsburg had recognized only Catholicism and Lutheranism as legitimate religious options, Westphalia acknowledged the growing political as well as religious significance of Calvinism, by including it (in the face of some Lutheran reluctance) as a third option in its provisions relating to German territory. Furthermore, except in most of the imperial territories (whose ruler, the Austrian Habsburg Emperor Ferdinand III, was staunchly Catholic) members of a religious minority had the right to practise their faith in private, so long as they obeyed the law. Protestant worship was to be permitted in Catholic territories where it had existed in 1624, and vice versa. The Holy Roman Empire was weakened, as its princes were granted the right to make their own alliances with foreign powers. The independence of Protestant Holland, which had been the cause of bitter conflict during the late sixteenth century, was formally recognized by the Spanish, and the independence of Switzerland was now given formal recognition. Although the pope condemned the treaty, his declining political importance ensured that this did not affect its practical workability. The treaty dealt a fatal blow to the idea that religious unity was a necessary prerequisite for a state's political stability, as it recognized that such unity was impossible to achieve.

The war had had a considerable impact on the worldview of many in Continental Europe, not so much because war itself was an unfamiliar phenomenon (it was not), but because much of the conflict during the previous century either was triggered by religious differences or else co-opted these in order to create ideologies which would explain and justify the use of force against those deemed to be enemies. Secularization, rationalist thought, and religious toleration and renewal all owed something to the exhaustion felt by many as the Peace of Westphalia was concluded.

Furthermore, events during the following decades showed that the treaty was unable to guarantee the security which Protestants had hoped for. In some Roman Catholic territories Protestants were effectively abandoned by its provisions and left to the mercies of local rulers, as in Salzburg, Poland, or Transylvania. This, coupled with a continuing trickle of princely conversions to Rome, helped to beget a sense of pessimism among Central European Protestants. However, Catholicism failed to capitalize fully on its earlier gains at Protestant expense, not least because the two leading Catholic powers, the Habsburgs and the Bourbons, were preoccupied with their own rivalry.

The state of the churches

Doctrinal developments

The process of 'confessionalization' continued, by which each communion defined itself with ever-increasing precision over against others. The advance of Calvinism in parts of Germany and Eastern Europe resulted in a measure of tension as Lutherans reacted to what they regarded as Calvinist errors. The sense of Protestant solidarity weakened in the face of division, and in such a climate there was little vision for reconciliation between Protestant communions, let alone between Protestantism and Catholicism. Such attempts as there were tended during the seventeenth century to focus on achieving a measure of doctrinal agreement, or else to be politically motivated and therefore to bypass theological issues. The most important exception was the German Lutheran Georg Calixtus (1586–1656), who sought to reconcile the different Christian traditions on the basis of their shared acceptance of the Apostles' Creed, and argued that differences in doctrine did not touch on matters essential to salvation; he was charged with 'syncretism' for his pains. It was, perhaps, inevitable

8

that in the contemporary climate his views should fail to take root among Lutherans at large. The German philosopher G.W. Leibniz (1646–1716) also sought to reconcile Prussian Protestants of differing outlooks and investigated the possibilities for reunion with the Catholics.

As part of the confessionalizing process, the doctrine of the verbal inspiration of Scripture was elaborated as a safeguard to the Reformation principle of *sola Scriptura*, the supreme authority of Scripture. In the words of the Lutheran theologian Johann Quenstedt (1617–88): 'The Holy Spirit did not simply inspire the meaning or sense of the words contained in Scripture, which the prophets and apostles then set forth, expressed and embellished with their own words by their own will. The Holy Spirit supplied, inspired, and dictated the very words and each and every utterance to the writers.'[1] Reformed thought moved in a similar direction. François Turretin (1623–87) was a professor of theology in Geneva, best known for his influential *Institutes of Elenctic Theology* (1679–85). This was typical in deploying medieval scholastic arguments to establish the role of reason as a handmaid in theology. Like Quenstedt, Turretin affirmed the inspiration of the vowel points of the Old Testament. He was one of the drafters of the *Helvetic Consensus* (1675), which served for fifty years as an authoritative doctrinal standard for Swiss Calvinism. It affirmed that 'the Hebrew Original of the Old Testament . . . is, not only in its consonants, but in its vowels – either the vowel points themselves, or at least the power of the points – not only in its matter, but in its words, inspired of God'.[2] Such an argument was directed not only at contemporary textual critics, whose efforts to emend the Hebrew on the basis of evidence from other versions or other Hebrew manuscripts were condemned, but also at Roman Catholic insistence on the Latin Vulgate as the normative text of the Old Testament, a text which had been shown to differ at many points from the Hebrew and Greek manuscripts.

The fate of Protestant minorities

Following the end of the Thirty Years' War, religious differences continued to be a thorn in the side of some European rulers. France is a case in point. Following the revocation of the Edict of Nantes[3] in 1685 by Louis XIV, who was concerned to build a united nation (understandably, given the impact of religious conflict on the country from 1562 to 1598), at least 200,000 Protestants (the Huguenots) fled the country. Many settled in England; others went to Switzerland, the Netherlands, Prussia, and North America. Those who remained faced constant Catholic pressure; some (known as Camisards) reacted by instigating an unsuccessful rebellion in 1702–03. In the mountainous area of southern France known as the Cevennes, ecstatic phenomena such as speaking in tongues and prophecy appeared among them, with children among those manifesting these powers, and some who fled to England became known as the 'French Prophets'. From being an influential and powerful feature of the French political and religious landscape, Protestants became a marginalized group, amounting to no more than 2 per cent of the population; only in 1802 did they gain the legal right to exist.[4]

Elsewhere twenty thousand Lutherans were expelled from Salzburg in 1731–2. Most found a home in Prussia, as did Huguenots, Mennonites, and Bohemian Brethren. Tolerance in Prussia was not only a fruit of economic prosperity, but a practical necessity given that the rulers were Reformed (i.e. Calvinist) but the state church remained Lutheran. By contrast, uniformity was the value espoused by the Catholic Austrians. In Poland, boundary changes resulted in non-Catholics being incorporated into other neighbouring states, leading to the creation of 'Catholic Poland'. Until this point, Roman Catholics had actually been a minority in the nation as a whole. Orthodox as well as Protestants were affected by this.

Among more radical Protestants, the Hutterites faced severe and continued persecution because of their attachment to community living, and in some areas they capitulated and abandoned the practice (for example Transylvania, 1690–1762). Gradually many moved eastwards to escape Habsburg persecution. From 1770 many Hutterites settled in Ukraine, where they were granted land by Catherine the Great. A larger number of Mennonites did likewise, and some of their descendants remain.

Church–state relations in the age of 'enlightened absolutism'

The eighteenth century saw the rapid decline in what might be called 'confessional politics'. Attempts were made to reconstruct the machinery of government on rational, rather than traditional, lines. Growing confidence in the ability of reason to discover everything about the world was paralleled by its adoption as the basis for the principles of government. Consequently the Church often came to be seen as a department of state, religion being regarded as a social utility (whether or not it was seen as divinely inspired): it kept records (especially at parish level), provided a structure for education and charity, and had a ready-made communications network in its pulpits, which could also be used to inculcate the virtue of loyalty to the 'powers that be' (Romans 13). Inevitably the Church found its power and influence restricted under the new order; its domination was a hallmark of the old, and could not survive in the Age of Reason. So in the eighteenth century German Lutheran pastors were seen as state functionaries. (A parallel development in Peter the Great's

Russia owed much to German models.) Not only so, but they served as links between the government and the populace.

Piety in the age of 'high orthodoxy'

It is not easy to determine how far church attendance was evidence of inward piety, and how far it was a matter of outward conformity; in states such as Lutheran Sweden, for example, attendance at church was compulsory by law. However, it is clear that there was an enormous market for sermons and devotional works during this period, created by a higher level of literacy than ever before, and the likelihood in many areas (though by no means all, especially at the lower levels of society) that churchgoers were better taught than previously and therefore more willing to read religious works.

However, among the peasantry, especially in rural areas, a mixture of Christianity and superstition continued to be widespread in all traditions. Whether this was a matter of hedging one's bets or simply the result of a lack of teaching or failure to reflect on its implications, it presented a formidable challenge to those who sought to Christianize these people. One particularly problematic manifestation of this was witchcraft. During the sixteenth and seventeenth centuries, many parts of Europe had seen numerous executions for this crime, especially in areas marked by religious conflict. However, with the advent of calmer political conditions and the growth of new modes of scientific and theological thought, witchcraft became less of an issue for the churches in most places. In Britain, for example, it ceased to be a crime after 1736.

It should not be thought that the confessionalizing concern for right doctrine had overshadowed all interest in the cultivation of personal spirituality. The seventeenth century saw a steady stream of devotional works and hymns in all branches of Protestantism, often drawing directly or indirectly on late medieval traditions of spiritual writing. This, rather than contemporary Protestant theology, was what sustained many in challenging times.

Magisterial Protestantism and mission

It was argued in the seventeenth century that the Great Commission to preach the gospel throughout the world (Matthew 28.18–20) had been fulfilled by the apostles. Luther's doctrine of vocation, which encouraged each person to see their work in the world as a calling from God, was used to discourage people from stepping out of their appointed sphere by offering themselves as missionaries; only the apostles had been given such a calling, it was argued. In 1722, therefore, the divinity faculty at Wittenberg, Luther's university, denounced advocates of mission as false prophets. Calvinist theologians argued that the failure of nations to respond to the apostles' mission indicated that they had not been predestined to receive salvation, and therefore should not be given a second chance; in any case, for many the conversion of the world was associated with the return of Christ and hence still in the future.

The German Catholic theologian Hans Küng argues that Protestant thinkers still thought in terms of the medieval concept of 'Christendom' and could not conceive of mission into countries where there was no Protestant government because they saw mission as involving church and state working together.[5] With the growth of Protestant colonial powers, notably England and Holland, this was to change, but it is noteworthy that early advocates of mission saw it as tied to state support, and even as the state's responsibility. On such a reading, colonization could sometimes be equated with the establishment of a theocracy.[6] However, it took the Pietist movement to give the missionary cause any real degree of impetus, as we shall see below.

Curiously enough, one of the early Protestant mission fields was Greenland. The Norwegian Lutheran Hans Egede went there in 1721, initially intending to make contact with any surviving remnants of medieval Scandinavian explorers; he found none, but commenced a work among the indigenous Inuit people which resulted in most of them converting to Christianity before the end of the century. Lutheran missionaries had also been active in the Danish colony of Tranquebar, in the south-east of the Indian subcontinent, from 1706.

As much as anything, it was the development of a new form of eschatology which cleared the way for an upsurge of interest in mission. The view in question was known as 'postmillennialism' from its belief that the return of Christ would take place after (Latin *post*) the millennium, a period (literally, a thousand years) of unparalleled blessing on earth, which would be marked by mass conversions among the Jews and subsequently among the Gentiles as the gospel spread throughout the inhabited earth. Its first main proponent was the Anglican Joseph Mede (1586–1638), and it was taken up with enthusiasm by the later seventeenth-century Puritans in the English-speaking world. Thus in North America Cotton Mather (1663–1728) argued that the worldwide proclamation of the gospel would usher in an eschatological outpouring of the Holy Spirit.

The first British mission agencies were the Society for the Promotion of Christian Knowledge (SPCK, 1698) and the Society for the Propagation of the Gospel in Foreign Parts (SPG, 1701). Both owed their origins to Thomas Bray (1656–1730), the Church of England Commissary for Maryland. The SPG made overseas mission a priority; at first this was seen primarily in terms of ministry to expatriates in North America and the West Indies, but missionaries were also encouraged to work among slaves and native Americans. Initially, the SPCK was concerned primarily with the provision of literature for chaplains' use.[7]

Reaction against confessionalization (i): Pietism[8]

According to the Methodist historian Ted Campbell, Pietism was one example of a phenomenon known as 'the religion of the heart' which is observable in all streams of Christianity, as well as in Hasidic Judaism, during the late seventeenth and eighteenth centuries.[9] What these movements had in common was the belief that the separation between God and human beings was to be overcome primarily in the realm of affective experience rather than those of doctrine, sacramental observance, morality, or ascetic discipline. Doctrinally, Pietism stressed Christ's work in, rather than for, the believer; in precise theological terms, the focus shifted from justification to regeneration, conversion and sanctification. The result of the stress on personal religious experience, and the consequent empowerment of groups who had little influence within existing church structures, was the formation of a number of new movements of varying degrees of sectarian outlook.

Origins

It was in Holland that Pietism first appeared, among Reformed Christians. There were traditionally strong links with British Puritanism: a number of radical Puritans (especially those who became known as Separatists and Baptists) had found asylum in the early seventeenth century, while Puritan theologians had been involved with the Synod of Dort (1618–19; this offered a landmark definition of the Calvinist understanding of salvation) and continued to exercise a measure of influence on the development of Dutch Calvinism. By the middle of the century Pietism was developing into a recognizable movement; links with Reformed churches in north-west Germany facilitated its spread eastwards. Among its distinctive features were the use of small groups in which members could discuss issues related to spiritual experience, and the avoidance of doctrinal controversy (during the early seventeenth century Holland, then under Spanish Habsburg rule, had lately been racked with bitter disagreement over the Arminian question, which had threatened to spill over into the political sphere because of the association of Arminianism with pro-Spanish sentiment[10]).

An influential if somewhat extreme representative of Reformed Pietism was Jean de Labadie (1610–74). His religious pilgrimage took him from being a member of the Jesuits to Jansenism (a Roman Catholic renewal movement stressing an Augustinian understanding of the necessity of divine grace), to the Reformed Church, and finally to found his own sect, which rejected outward sacraments and religious acts.

Among the Lutherans there was a continuing tradition which combined a commitment to theological orthodoxy with drawing upon the inspiration of the late medieval Rhineland mystics, who stressed the direct relationship of the believer with the indwelling Christ.[11] Johann Arndt (1555–1621) was the best-known example of this, and he has been seen as the father of Pietism. But it was Philip Spener (1635–1705), a Lutheran pastor in Frankfurt from 1666 to 1686, who was responsible for the emergence of Lutheran Pietism. Spener was influenced by Reformed and Puritan writers, notably Labadie (whom he had met as a student in Geneva), and in his thought Lutheran devotion and Reformed Pietism coalesced. In Spener's opinion, while Luther's teaching had endured, the faith which he had advocated had largely vanished: part of the problem was the contemporary stress on sound doctrine, but for Spener the other part was the prevalence of nominal Christianity within the Lutheran territorial church, a problem which Luther had foreseen. What makes Spener important is that he did not merely preach and write about the issues which were of concern to Pietists, but his eschatologically based certainty that the Church would in time be renewed led him to take steps to create structures in church life which could foster personal spiritual growth. In particular, he developed the practice of meeting regularly in small groups (*collegiae pietatis*) for prayer and the discussion of the Bible or some other spiritual work.[12] He set out his strategy in *Pia Desideria* ('Pious Desires'), published in 1675 as an introduction to one of Arndt's works. In it, he asserted (with appeals to Luther) that:

1 Infants born to Christian parents received forgiveness and new birth at baptism; this was official Lutheran teaching. However, most of the baptized had lost this grace, and needed to be converted. This was the problem with the contemporary Church.
2 The Church must be renewed through small groups meeting for Bible study and prayer. These would provide an additional means of instruction to supplement the sermons.
3 True Christianity should show itself in a changed life, and believers should care for, exhort, encourage, and teach one another, rather than leaving everything to the minister.
4 An overhaul of theological teaching was needed to make it more vocationally relevant. It should only be given by converted and holy men, and should promote holy living by the pastors-to-be.

Pietism achieved a quasi-established status in Prussia, where the different confessional allegiances of rulers and people inclined the authorities to look with favour on a movement which downplayed the importance of confessional distinctions. Under Friedrich Wilhelm I (1713–40) a close relationship was established between the Church and the army, which reinforced the status of Pietism. By contrast, it became a popular movement in nearby Silesia, whose Protestants faced the very real threat of assimilation by the Roman Catholic Church. Children took a leading role in this awakening, holding prayer meetings during 1707 in which they prayed for the politically sensitive objects of the return of Protestant church and school buildings; it was the closure of these by the authorities which had resulted in the burden of Protestant religious instruction falling on unofficial Pietist groups.

Development: radical and church-Pietists

Although early Pietist leaders sought the renewal of existing churches, there was inherent within their teaching a dynamic which impelled some towards separation from the churches in order to found new movements of their own, such as the Church of the Brethren, founded in north Germany in 1708. The movement thus divided into what became known as church-Pietists and radical Pietists. Among the latter, the German 'spiritualist' tradition[13] of Schwenckfeld, Arndt, and Boehme resurfaced. For such writers, two corollaries of the invisibility of the true Church were (i) that its members could be found within all communions, and (ii) that they might find themselves the subjects of persecution by the visible, institutional Church. The mystic Jakob Boehme (1575–1624) had spoken of the true Church of Abel as a hidden reality within the false Church of Cain (cf. Genesis 4), albeit persecuted and destroyed.[14] He believed that his books could hasten the destruction of the institutional churches. Influenced by Boehme, Gottfried Arnold (1666–1714), who had been converted through Spener's influence, wrote a *Dirge over Babylon* (1698) stressing the invisible nature of the true Church, foretelling the disappearance of the visible Church, and calling for efforts to hasten the process! Surprisingly, he later became a Lutheran pastor. Arnold's most important work was the *Non-Partisan History of Churches and Heretics* (1699–1700). This was distinguished by its attempt to focus on those mystical and dissenting groups which the mainstream Church had often marginalized as heretical. In them he discerned the succession of true believers, and they could be recognized because they were always persecuted by the institutional church.

Pietist spirituality

The stress on the need for practical outworking of Christianity as evidence of a regenerated heart meant that Pietists were great activists. Halle in particular became famous for the institutions founded there. After a Pietist conversion in 1687, August Hermann Francke (1663–1727) was forced out of his professorship at Leipzig, and took a post in the newly founded university at Halle (founded in part due to Spener's influence as court preacher at Dresden). He was best known for founding a large orphanage in 1696, for which he refused to make appeals for funds, believing that God was able to supply the institution's financial needs without resorting to such measures. Other institutions at Halle included a Bible institute (which accommodated 3,000 people in its enormous building), a drug factory and dispensary, and a publishing house. Enjoying royal support, Halle became the intellectual centre of Prussia with responsibility for training its clergy, which helps to explain the dominance of Pietism in the region. Francke made his own lengthy struggle to experience repentance and faith into a norm for others in his teaching, which was also marked by a strict code of ethical conduct.

A theme on which Pietist thought was to be immensely influential on the development of Western Protestantism was that of ecclesiology. Pietist thinkers sought to overleap the doctrinal walls separating various Protestant communions from one another by advocating a unity based on shared personal experience rather than shared doctrine. This paralleled the Pietist insistence that the concern for right doctrine had overlooked the vital importance of true piety and Christian morality. Rather than attempt to divide Christian doctrines into fundamental and non-fundamental, it seems as if some were now arguing that, in terms of precise verbal formulation at any rate, all could be seen as non-fundamental. A prime example of this was Count Nikolaus Ludwig von Zinzendorf (1700–60), godson of Spener and student under Francke.[15]

It was Zinzendorf's youthful desire to devote himself to religious work, and he would use his estate at Berthelsdorf, between Dresden and Prague, for such purposes. A group of Bohemian Brethren (descendants of the fifteenth-century Hussites) from the area known as Moravia took refuge with him in 1722, and founded a settlement known as Herrnhut ('Watched over by the Lord'), which became a refuge for all types of persecuted Protestant. In this way, a unique ecumenical laboratory came into existence; incidentally, it is said that Zinzendorf was the first to use the term 'ecumenical' with reference to the reunion of divided Christians. In 1727 the community, which had been divided between Lutherans led by Zinzendorf and a Reformed group of separatist inclinations, underwent a deep and transforming experience which welded together the different groups. Zinzendorf, who was always something of an autocrat, organized them into a body known as the *Unitas Fratrum* ('Unity of Brethren', rapidly known as the Moravians), which he insisted was not a new denomination but a movement for the reunion of Christians (by which he appears to have meant Protestants) which would cease to exist when its work was done.[16] It was a church within the Church, having no distinctive doctrines but serving as a focus for Christian unity by its cultivation of a shared experience of Christ. Members were, at this stage, encouraged to maintain their existing religious allegiance: each denomination was regarded as possessing something of value to the wider Christian community, and proselytism was discouraged. Zinzendorf's beliefs were attacked (but found orthodox) and then he was exiled from Saxony from 1736–47. While in exile, he was ordained as a Moravian bishop in 1737 on the advice of the Prussian King Friedrich Wilhelm I without renouncing his Lutheran allegiance.

Zinzendorf argued that divisions were usually over doctrinal concepts, which could in his view become a positive hindrance to faith; by contrast, believers were united by a shared experience of Christ. Unity, which was regarded as a given rather than a not-yet-realized ideal, could become a visible reality as they recognized this. His stress on experience paralleled the contemporary epistemological emphasis on experience as the most reliable source of knowledge.

In his thinking Zinzendorf drew on the medieval idea that the true Church was invisible, arguing that it became visible as believers overcame their disunity. For such thinkers the renewal of the Church began with the rebirth of individuals. His emphasis on deep personal experience of devotion to Christ shifted the balance from reason to feeling; initially, this led to some bizarre outworkings among the Moravians as they fell prey during the 'time of sifting' (1745–50) to an extravagant devotion to the wounds of Christ and an anti-intellectualism which gloried in the most childish self-designations. As they left this behind and reverted towards Protestant orthodoxy, they came to see their independent existence as a permanent phenomenon, and so the denomination is still active today. However, this came at the cost of the disappearance of the original ecumenical vision of an inter-confessional society.

The key theme in Pietist spirituality was, as we saw, the call for inner transformation through personal conversion to a living faith in Christ. However, from the 1730s a division became evident within the movement. Francke's son insisted, as his father had done, on the necessity of a lengthy pre-conversion agony of conviction of sin and repentance; by contrast, Zinzendorf (who had not undergone such an experience) alleged that such teaching only served to delay conversion for many seekers, and he stressed the joy and assurance which should characterize Christian spirituality. He advocated vivid preaching on the blood and wounds of the crucified Christ, with the objective of drawing hearers to conversion as they meditated upon these mysteries.

The third key theme to highlight is that of mission, which was rooted in the Pietist eschatological vision. In spite of their frustration with existing churches, many Pietists expected a time of millennial blessing, and in particular of unparalleled response to the proclamation of the Christian gospel throughout the world. This, coupled with their stress on personal conversion, helps to explain their zeal in the cause of overseas mission. However, mission was seen as a matter for individuals rather than for the Church as a whole; Pietist missionary agencies thus tended to lead a rather independent existence, something which continued to characterize Continental missionary agencies until the early twentieth century. The lack of a churchly outlook also affected their understanding of their objects: according to Zinzendorf, missionaries should merely establish provisional groups of believers, not churches.[17]

Under the provisions of the Treaty of Westphalia, Moravians had no right to remain in the Holy Roman Empire as a distinct denomination, a factor which helped to turn their vision outwards. The first Moravian missionaries arrived in the West Indies in 1732; thereafter others were sent to Greenland (1733), South Africa (1736), and elsewhere. Like most from this tradition, they were not highly educated or trained, and their impact derived far more from their thorough and consistent attempts to live out the message which they preached, even to the extent of selling themselves into slavery in the West Indies in order to be able to reach the African slaves. Another factor was their ability to distance themselves from national or colonizing interests, by virtue of the voluntary nature of Pietist missionary enterprise. Nevertheless, several interdenominational support structures were developed, especially at Halle, where there was a college for training missionaries to the Slavic peoples of Eastern Europe. Societies followed the founding of such institutions.

Pietist mission strategy focused on the need for all to be able to read the Bible in their own language; in essence, it represented an outworking of the Protestant Reformers' belief that 'faith comes by hearing' (Romans 10.17). Therefore education and literacy were key planks in Pietist missionary activity. Attitudes towards the host culture varied. In India, Bartholomeus Ziegenbalg's efforts to understand Hindu culture were misunderstood by Francke; by contrast, in the territories on the east of the Baltic such as Estonia and Livonia, Moravians and Pietists were responsible for the eradication of pre-Christian traditions from local culture and belief.

Pietism did not necessarily entail anti-intellectualism: J.A. Bengel (1687–1752), who has been regarded as the father of modern approaches to textual criticism of the Bible, was a pastor and professor at Tübingen, in the state of Württemberg, in south-western Germany. Pietism there was more open to academic study than the more pastorally led and establishment-orientated Prussian movement. Troubled by the emerging evidence of variant readings in manuscripts of the New Testament, Bengel produced a critical edition in 1734 and his famous *Gnomon Novi Testamenti* in 1742, a commentary which was to be highly influential on John Wesley. Among other principles Bengel formulated was that of preferring the more difficult reading where variant forms of a given text existed. He also began the practice of classifying New Testament manuscripts into 'families' which shared a certain likeness. Although a Pietist, he produced a critique of the kind of extravagant piety exemplified by Zinzendorf and the Moravians, another indication of the divergent streams within Pietism.

Pietist spirituality found enduring and popular expression in its hymnody, as have so many renewal movements. This continued an orthodox Lutheran tradition of devotional hymnody which could be traced back to Luther himself. Among the best-known German Pietist hymnwriters are: Paulus Gerhardt (1607–76), whose meditation, 'O sacred head! now wounded', epitomizes Pietist devotion to the crucified Christ; Joachim Neander (1650–80), whose hymns of adoration betray nothing of the alleged religious extravagance for which he lost his post as a school rector; and the devotional writer Gerhard Tersteegen (1697–1769), perhaps the most explicitly mystical of the Pietist hymnwriters who have been translated into English.[18] Pietist influence may also be discerned in the religious works of J.S. Bach (1685–1750), with their expressions of devotion to Christ and vivid evocations of his crucifixion. G.F. Handel (1685–1759), too, studied in Halle during its Pietist period.

Reaction against confessionalization (ii): Deism and the Enlightenment

The persistence and bitterness of doctrinal controversy during the mid-seventeenth century had done much to hasten the decline of the belief that any one set of doctrines could be absolutely right; this was reinforced by the increased contact with other faiths which ensued from the process of exploration and colonization. The following century was the heyday of Deism, a current of thought which affirmed the existence of a just and benevolent Creator whose universe was governed by rational laws, and minimized or eliminated any role for revelation and the supernatural in religion. Humanity was seen as capable of progress as it applied rational principles to the study of the physical universe, but as held back by the Church and the clergy, the traditional guardians of religious authority. Truth was to be arrived at by observation and rational reflection, not by submission to the pronouncements of the traditional authorities. If all religions were human constructions, then their value could be measured in terms of their usefulness to society rather than their theological accuracy.

From 1695 the relaxation of censorship in England allowed the publication of a stream of Deist writings. Thinkers such as Voltaire (1694–1778) disseminated their arguments and conclusions, which were more influential in France than they were in Britain. The result was the Enlightenment (the philosopher Immanuel Kant (1724–1804) coined the German term *Aufklärung*) was not an organized movement, but a widespread current of thought. It stressed the ability of reason to understand the world, and the need to arrive at our understanding on the basis of deduction from experience rather than the pronouncements of an authority such as the Church.

Key Deist ideas, many of which were taken up by the Enlightenment, may be summarized as follows:

1 Divine revelation was minimized, given a less significant role, or excluded altogether. Anything deemed not in harmony with rational principles was written off as superstition, which included much traditional Christian ritual and practice.

2 Opposition to superstition fuelled a polemic against 'priestcraft'. The clergy were condemned for encouraging people to remain in servile bondage to outgrown ways of thinking, as well as for their alleged monopoly on knowledge through their status as guardians of ultimate authority. (In Germany, however, the Enlightenment was much more a churchly entity, and manifested itself in internal theological reconstruction along Deist lines. A similar phenomenon was evident in mid-eighteenth-century Scotland, where many Enlightenment thinkers were ministers in the national church.)

3 By contrast, free enquiry, without the constraints of orthodox opinion, was upheld as a virtue. Enlightenment thinkers advocated intellectual freedom and its corollary, religious toleration. The British philosopher John Locke (1632–1704) argued for religious toleration on the basis that:

   – The state is not able to adjudicate between competing religious truth-claims.
   – Even if it could, attempts to enforce the right view by legal means would not produce the desired objective because religion is an inward matter.
   – The results of a politically imposed religious uniformity are worse than those of allowing religious diversity (note that he distinguished between religious and moral diversity).[19]

However, the influence of writings advocating toleration must not be overstated. Often, it was the mere fact of the survival of a religious minority in a hostile climate, along with its proven ability to contribute to the building up of a society exhausted by religious wars, which brought about a change in attitude.

4 The essence of religion was seen as morality (hence French thinkers upheld the necessity of religion for the masses). Morality was important to these thinkers because of their concern to restructure society on rational principles in order to facilitate human progress and promote human welfare. Deist religion was believed to be founded on universal principles which were seen as common to all religions. (This was the age when Northern European colonial expansion really got going, with the result that Protestant cultures began to encounter adherents of other faiths on a scale previously unknown.) Locke argued that the major religions agreed on moral issues, an interpretation which fitted well with the belief that the essence of religion was common to them all.

5 The new approach to revelation was coupled with a fairly consistent anti-supernaturalism: Enlightenment criticism of Christianity challenged supernatural phenomena such as miracles and divine revelation; miracles and prophecy had traditionally been employed as evidences for the truth of Christianity. This extended to historiography, since the supernatural could no longer be admitted as a factor in history in the way that it had been as recently as the seventeenth century. Events could be explained in terms of finite causes and effects, without recourse to God. Christian historians had, therefore, to rethink their conception of the way that God was deemed to be active in history. Paradoxically, the removal of mystery from Christian faith meant that people sought it elsewhere; this was the great age of esoteric groups such as the Freemasons (who in France were strongly anticlerical) and the Rosicrucians.[20]

The historical theologian Alister McGrath distinguishes three stages in the effect of Enlightenment thinking on Protestant theology; whether we see them as successive stages or contemporaneous, they represent the three main ways of adapting to the new outlook:[21]

1 The attempt to demonstrate the rational nature of Christian belief. Locke exemplified this in his use of rationalist assumptions and approaches to challenge rationalism. For Locke, reflection on experience, not the pronouncements of traditional authorities, formed the basis for human knowledge; he thus became the founder of a philosophical school known as Empiricism. Christianity is accepted because of its rational character (miracles he deemed not unreasonable), and the primary function of revelation is to confirm what can be known by the application of reason. The main message of the Bible is in harmony

with reason, and the most important thing about Jesus is his ethical teaching.

2 The assertion that Christian beliefs could be derived from reason alone, revelation not being seen as adding anything to this. Two further British thinkers will serve as examples. John Toland (1670–1722), in *Christianity not Mysterious* (1696) argued that the Bible should be interpreted as subordinate to, and in harmony with, reason. Revelation must be intelligible; he therefore opposed the clergy's claim that we must adore where we cannot understand, seeing this as an implicit assertion of control over the thoughts of their hearers. Anything unintelligible or mysterious or simply impossible must be rejected. Matthew Tindal (1655–1733) equated the Christian gospel with natural law in his *Christianity as old as the Creation, or the Gospel a Republication of the Religion of Nature* (1730) and portrayed Christianity as an ethical system.

3 The claim that reason has the right to sit in judgement on revelation. In France, this found public expression in the *Encyclopédie*, which began to appear in 1751. This multi-volume work, intended to cover the whole field of human knowledge, was edited by Denis Diderot and compiled by a group of writers who became known as the *Philosophes*.[22] Diderot, who had been intended for the Catholic priesthood, had become an atheist, and the work was strongly anticlerical and frequently sceptical of revealed religion. It was also marked by repeated calls for intellectual toleration. Growing opposition forced the publication of later volumes under a false imprint or outside the country, but it was probably the most influential work to come out of the Enlightenment for it helped shape the intellectual context of the French Revolution.

One area in which Deist and Enlightenment thinking had a profound impact on the churches was that of the authority of Scripture and the study of its texts. One example of the relationship between these two issues is the German scholar and playwright G.E. Lessing (1729–81), who put forward the idea that there was a source behind the Synoptic Gospels, thus implicitly challenging the idea that the Gospels in their final form were divinely inspired. Lessing also argued that the truth of Christianity was to be found in its ability to meet the universal needs of the human soul rather than its factual basis because particular or 'accidental' historical events can never be the foundation for universal or 'necessary' truths.

It is not possible here to do more than offer the briefest of sketches of the rise of biblical criticism. The historical-critical method of interpretation, in which the primary significance was assigned to the original context of the writings rather than their status as divinely inspired, or the needs of contemporary readers, began in the mid-seventeenth century; it was in origins largely a German phenomenon, and few English scholars made much use of it until the end of the eighteenth century. A major reason for this was that the earliest English biblical critics such as the Unitarian Joseph Priestley (1733–1804) were often theologically unorthodox and seemed to be co-opting the new methods in the service of a particular theological agenda (not that this was anything new in the history of hermeneutics, as the early Fathers did something similar in adopting a typological approach to the Old Testament). During the conservative backlash which followed the French Revolution, such men were also suspected of revolutionary sympathies.

So widespread were expressions of Deist and anticlerical views that some orthodox churchmen feared for the future of organized Christianity. A number of works therefore sought to respond to the new ideas. Ironically, as we saw in Locke's case, many churchmen were deeply affected by the very ideas they opposed. Even more ironically, Deism itself began to decline in popularity from the middle of the century. For example, the Scottish philosopher David Hume (1711–78) foreshadowed later thought in demonstrating the inadequacy of contemporary rationalism.

The influence of Deist ideas may also be discerned in the field of apologetics, where much stress was laid on 'evidences' from the physical world, the fulfilment of Old Testament prophecies in Christ, and the occurrence of miracles in connection with his ministry. The Anglican bishop Joseph Butler (1692–1752) is one example; he argued that our interpretations of both nature and revelation can never be established beyond question, but may be accepted on the grounds of their probability. In his *Analogy of Religion Natural and Revealed, to the Constitution and Course of Nature* (1736) he sought to meet objectors on their own ground, but whereas they argued for a contrast between natural and revealed religion, he discerned an analogy between them. Following the early church Father Origen (185–254), Butler asserted that if the same God was responsible for both nature and Scripture, we should expect to encounter the same difficulties in each. Arguments against Christianity could thus be applied equally to the physical universe. William Paley (1743–1805), in his works *A View of the Evidences of Christianity* (1794) and *Natural Theology* (1802), popularized the argument from design: as the existence of a watch implies the existence of a watchmaker, so the existence of an ordered and rationally comprehensible universe implies the existence of a divine creator.

It should be clear by this point that the traditional view of the Enlightenment as entirely anti-Christian needs to be modified since in most countries it was rooted in a reforming strain of Christianity which sought a measure of accommodation with contemporary thought. It is true that the French Enlightenment became more explicitly anti-Christian from the middle of the century, but in Germany it related more positively to the Protestant churches in particular, as they were seen as supporting progress (Catholicism had on occasion expressed itself publicly as opposed to it, as in the condemnation of Galileo). However, we shall see later that there was a reaction against Enlightenment rationalism in which the churches shared to the full – Romanticism.

Questions for thought

1 Why do you think the process of confessionalization continued in Europe during this period, and why was there also an opposite trend, towards a more minimalist approach to doctrine?

2 Why, in your opinion, did a more 'rational' approach to church–state relationships lead so often to the subjugation of the Church to the state?

3 How would you sum up the view of history which underlay thinking about mission during this period?

4 How would you account for the fact that the quest for a 'religion of the heart' took place in all branches of Christianity, and even beyond it? How convincing do you find Campbell's approach?

5 What evaluation would you offer of Arnold's approach to church history? Can you think of more recent parallels? What factors give rise to such approaches, and how could historians take those factors into account in their work?

6 What do you consider to have been the strengths and weaknesses of Pietist spirituality and practice? What evidence would you offer for your views, and how would you account for these strengths and weaknesses?

7 Roman Catholics were often excluded from eighteenth-century arguments for religious toleration. Why do you think this was?

Further reading

Gerald Bray, 1996, *Biblical Interpretation Past and Present*, Leicester: Apollos.

Colin Brown, 1990, *Christianity and Western Thought: A History of Philosophers, Ideas and Movements*, vol. 1: *From the Ancient World to the Age of Enlightenment*, Leicester: Apollos.

Stewart J. Brown and Timothy Tackett (eds), 2007, *Cambridge History of Christianity*, vol. 7: *Enlightenment, Reawakening and Revolution 1660–1815*, Cambridge: Cambridge University Press, parts 1–3.

Nicholas Hope, 1995, *German and Scandinavian Protestantism 1700–1918*, Oxford History of the Christian Church, Oxford: Oxford University Press, part 1.

John McManners, 1998, *Church and Society in Eighteenth-Century France*, Oxford History of the Christian Church, 2 vols, Oxford: Oxford University Press.

Dorinda Outram, 2005, *The Enlightenment*, 2nd edn, Cambridge: Cambridge University Press.

W.R. Ward, 1999, *Christianity under the Ancien Régime 1648–1789*, Cambridge: Cambridge University Press, chs 1, 4–8.

W.R. Ward, 1992, *The Protestant Evangelical Awakening*, Cambridge: Cambridge University Press, chs 1–6.

Notes

1 Johann Quenstedt, 1715 (first published 1685), *Theologia Didactico-Polemica*, ch. 4.2, q. 4, in Eric Lund (ed.), 2002, *Documents from the History of Lutheranism 1517–1750*, Minneapolis, MN: Fortress, p. 225.

2 *Helvetic Consensus* (1675), II, in John H. Leith (ed.), 1973, *Creeds of the Churches*, rev. edn, Atlanta, GA: John Knox, p. 310.

3 The Edict of Nantes was issued in 1598, and granted French Protestants toleration and the right to maintain their own military force. During the seventeenth century its provisions were gradually rescinded.

4 However, their loyalty during the Seven Years' War (1756–63) had helped to gain them an edict of toleration in 1787. This conflict had pitted Austria, France, Russia, and others against Britain, Prussia, and Hanover.

5 Hans Küng, cited in David Bosch, 1991, *Transforming Mission: Paradigm Shifts in Theology of Mission*, American Society of Missiology Series 16, Maryknoll, NY: Orbis, p. 246.

6 Bosch, *Transforming Mission*, p. 259.

7 For more on these societies, see Chapter 5.

8 On Pietism, see Carter Lindberg (ed.), 2005, *The Pietist Theologians: An Introduction to Theology in the Seventeenth and Eighteenth Centuries*, Oxford: Blackwell; F.E. Stoeffler, 1965, *The Rise of Evangelical Pietism*, Studies in the History of Religions 9, Leiden: E.J. Brill; *idem*, 1973, *German Pietism in the Eighteenth Century*, Studies in the History of Religions 24, Leiden: E.J. Brill.

9 Ted A. Campbell, 1994, *The Religion of the Heart*, Columbia, SC: University of South Carolina Press. My discussion of Pietism is considerably indebted to Campbell's work.

10 Jacobus Arminius (1560–1609) denied aspects of Calvinist teaching concerning salvation, asserting that Christ died for all and not merely for those elected to salvation, that an individual possessed free will to choose whether to turn to Christ, and that it was possible for a true believer to fall away from the faith and be lost.

11 They included such writers as Thomas à Kempis (1380–1471), author of the best-selling *Imitation of Christ*.

12 Luther had called for the formation of such groups as *ecclesiolae in ecclesia* ('churches within the church'), in which true believers could meet together.

13 In this context, 'spiritualism' refers to the tendency in the sixteenth-century Radical Reformation to exalt the 'inner word' spoken by the Holy Spirit to the

soul above the 'outer word' of Scripture and church teaching. Some spiritualists, like some earlier mystics and later Quakers, drew the conclusion that outward sacraments were therefore unnecessary, and in extreme cases all outward religious observances were abandoned.

14 Boehme's writings have proved an enduring source of interest to mystics. During the seventeenth century, for instance, his writings led to the foundation in London in 1694 of the Philadelphian Society, led by Jane Leade (1623–1704) and an Anglican cleric, John Pordage (1607–81). The society issued tracts offering a simplified exposition of Boehme's cosmology, which ensured the influence of his writings in Germany.

15 On Zinzendorf, see A.J. Lewis, 1962, *Zinzendorf: The Ecumenical Pioneer*, London: SCM Press.

16 On the Moravians, see Colin Podmore, 1998, *The Moravian Church in England, 1728–1760*, Oxford: Clarendon. A standard older history was J. E. Hutton, 1909, *A History of the Moravian Church*, enlarged edn, London: Moravian Publication Office, available online at: http://www.npmc.org/hutton.

17 Bosch, *Transforming Mission*, p. 254.

18 Tersteegen was extensively influenced by a parallel Catholic movement known as Quietism, on which see Chapter 3.

19 Alister E. McGrath, 1998, *Historical Theology: An Introduction to the History of Christian Thought*, Oxford: Blackwell, p. 215.

20 Secret societies which first appeared in eighteenth-century Europe and drawing on pamphlets published in seventeenth-century Germany expounding secret spiritual teachings. These groups were linked with Freemasonry. Rosicrucian ideas have been revived in the English-speaking world through more modern groups bearing the same designation.

21 McGrath, *Historical Theology*, pp. 221–2.

22 A forerunner was the French Protestant Pierre Bayle (1647–1706), whose *Historical and Critical Dictionary* began to appear in 1695. Bayle argued for religious toleration and his writings were marked by scepticism.

3

Roman Catholicism

During the eighteenth century the administrative reforms envisaged by the Council of Trent (1545–63) came to fruition: a higher degree of centralization of ecclesiastical authority, properly trained and professional clergy, active religious orders, and a higher quality of lay devotion. On the other hand, no further progress was being made in reconverting Europe to Rome, and in several countries the Church was losing its hold on the upper classes and intellectuals. The papacy was still failing to give the Church a sense of purpose, and the Church as a whole was on the back foot in dealing with new intellectual and theological challenges (as we shall see in connection with topics as diverse as Jansenism and 'Chinese rites'); it also found its political power under threat as national monarchies gained in strength and confidence. This chapter explores these themes, as well as analysing the results of Catholic missions beyond Europe, so painting the background to the outbreak of revolutionary feeling which rocked Europe from 1789.

The eighteenth-century papacy

The period from 1648 to 1789 saw a marked decline in the temporal influence of the papacy, continuing a process which had been going on since the fourteenth century. Increasingly, papal attempts to intervene in the political realm were simply ignored. While it has been argued that this period saw the transformation of the papacy into an absolute monarchy,[1] it does not appear to have been a very efficient one. Popes were usually elderly when appointed, and so most had little time to achieve very much; appointments to office in the papal bureaucracy often depended on an individual's connections rather than their merit.

If the papacy was not in a position to give a political lead, neither was it distinguished for giving a spiritual one. Most popes had a legal rather than a theological background, and none during this period were men of the stature of those who had overseen the sixteenth-century reforms. Zeal was not a quality in great demand generally during the eighteenth century, and this was reflected in the occupants of the papal throne. Significantly, few have since been canonized.

The major popes	
Innocent X (1644–55)	Opposed the use of Chinese in the liturgy, the Treaty of Westphalia, and Jansenism
Alexander VII (1655–67)	Allowed the liturgical use of Chinese
Clement X (1670–6)	Canonized a large number of saints, thus attempting to give direction to, and exercise central control over, devotion to such figures
Innocent XI (1676–89)	Condemned Gallicanism and Quietism
Innocent XII (1691–1700)	Concluded an agreement with Louis XIV which ended decades of tension
Clement XI (1700–21)	Forbade the use of Chinese in the liturgy; condemned Jansenism
Benedict XIV (1740–58)	Ended the ban on Copernican astronomy; began cataloguing the Vatican's manuscript holdings
Clement XIV (1769–74)	Suppressed the Jesuits

Perhaps the most remarkable indicator of the weakness of the papacy in the face of pressure from Catholic states was the suppression in 1773 of the religious order distinguished above all others for loyalty to the pope, the Jesuits. By 1749 they were one of the largest Catholic religious orders, with 22,600 members, and responsible for 669 colleges and 176 seminaries and schools. However, in an age when national rulers sought to restrict the Church's power and influence within their borders, an order owing such direct allegiance to Rome could not expect to remain unopposed. Jesuit bids for power and their propensity for political intrigue had proved their undoing, and they had already been expelled from Portugal (1759), France (1764), Spain (1767), and Naples (1768). In 1772 the pope was even warned that the strong Spanish church would become semi-independent along Gallican lines (see below) unless the Jesuits were suppressed. Clement XIV delayed action for four years but finally caved in. In doing so, Rome may have lost more than it gained: 'The Church had lost its most successful educators, its most effective missionaries and its most innovative thinkers. The papacy abandoned a body of men dedicated to its service.'[2] Yet the order did not cease to exist; ironically, given their leadership of sixteenth-century attempts to reconvert Protestant territories, they were given shelter in Protestant Prussia and Orthodox Russia, and would once again be granted papal approval in 1814.

However, the papacy was able to give a lead in one area of church life, in which the trend to increased centralization of authority was evident – that of canonization, the process by which saints achieved formal recognition. Whereas before Trent there had been a vast number of 'saints' whose cult was restricted to small areas and whose very existence was sometimes open to question, this period saw the recognition of men and women who could be portrayed as models for the contemporary Catholic; from 1588, canonization was the responsibility of one of the new Congregations (Vatican departments) founded in the wake of the Council of Trent, the Congregation of Rites. Individuals could be declared saints, and thus worthy of veneration by the faithful, for a variety of reasons: their contribution to theology, their spirituality, or their example in zealous mission or self-sacrificing pastoral care or philanthropy. Many of the new saints were popular workers of charity, whose cult effectively served to draw popular devotion, which was concerned with obtaining tangible benefits such as healing, into officially approved channels. What is more, such saints were models of loyal devotion to the Church, and their example could foster more 'churchly' expressions of popular devotion. Most were clergy or members of religious orders and were either Italian or Spanish – the Church's two Western heartlands.[3]

The Church in the Baroque era

The flamboyant Baroque style of the seventeenth and early eighteenth centuries was an expression of the increased confidence of the Church in the decades following the Council of Trent, and its desire to utilize all the senses in order to produce an impact on the faithful. Its best-known expression is in the architecture of many Catholic church buildings of the period, but the same mood was also evident in other aspects of the Church's life.

The Baroque mood was as evident in what was said from the pulpit as it was in its physical design. Some have seen the century 1650–1750 as the greatest era for oratorical preaching. France produced a succession of brilliant Catholic preachers whose output influenced the national church significantly, among them J.-B. Bossuet (1627–1704), who also engaged in controversial writings against Quietism (see below) and Protestantism, and the archbishop and mystic François Fénelon (1651–1715). This preaching, however, bore little relation to its liturgical setting as part of the Mass, and was marked by a tendency towards moralism rather than biblical exposition.

At a more populist level, in 1732 the moral theologian Alphonsus Liguori (1696–1787)[4] founded the Redemptorist order to engage in preaching among the poor. To fulfil this objective, he developed the idea of parish missions, in which teams of priests would visit parishes for a set period and engage in daily preaching on set topics. The aim was to encourage a renewal of baptismal commitment, and the preaching employed such devices as processions, visual aids, music, and services designed to create an emotional impact, reinforced by what might be described as 'brimstone and treacle' preaching, dangling hearers over the abyss while holding out the consolations available through Christ. Such missions bear comparison with Protestant revivalist techniques, although the two appear to have developed largely independently. However, the results were somewhat different: Catholic missions had more of a corporate aspect than Protestant revivalism (which focused on securing individual conversions), with large-scale attendance at confession and reconciliation between estranged family members. In rural areas they were often fruitful because they represented a welcome change from normal routine, and there was little if any competition for attention. By the late eighteenth century they became more catechetical and less theatrical, ironically at a time when the hunger for 'heart religion' had never been greater.

Church and state in the pre-revolutionary period

National Catholic communities saw their ties with the Vatican restricted as a way of minimizing foreign influence over the Church, and their power eroded by the growth of the modern apparatus of state. Even in Spain and Portugal the 1750s and 1760s saw fierce debate between church and state, with a restriction of the Church's power and privileges. However, the tension between church and state and between various conceptions of their relationship was most evident in France, which had the strongest Catholic national church, and it is primarily with reference to the French situation that we shall explore this tension.

Louis XIV, who reigned from 1643 to 1715, was determined to weld a divided nation into a unity. As part of this, he exerted increasing pressure on Protestantism from the 1660s, culminating with the revocation of the Edict of Nantes in 1685. Thereafter only Catholics could be French citizens. However, he was equally determined to maintain the French church's high degree of autonomy from Rome. This can be seen in the history of the Gallican movement, which provides an example of the tendency widespread throughout eighteenth-century Europe to treat the Church as a department of state. Gallicanism was a term applied initially to the French insistence on relative independence from Rome, which went hand-in-hand with a low view of papal authority. Its opposite was Ultramontanism (from the Latin *ultra montes*, 'beyond the mountains'), the view that the pope possessed universal authority not only in matters of doctrine and morals but also in the fields of liturgical order and church administration.

Most appointments to high office in the French church were the prerogative of the monarch. Roman legal authority was rejected, the civil courts being seen as competent to deal with church affairs where these touched matters of secular government. Agreements with Rome in 1438 and 1516 had codified this independence, and the French church had refused to accept the administrative dictates of the Council of Trent. Louis XIV had continued to claim the right to nominate to vacant bishoprics (and to draw the income from them), but the pope rejected the extension of his claim to episcopal revenues from territories which had newly been brought under French rule (notably Alsace), refused to institute the bishops appointed by Louis, and declared their acts to be invalid. In 1682 a declaration drawn up by Bossuet and approved by the French clergy asserted that the king was not subject to any other temporal power (in particular, to the pope). It upheld the decrees of the Council of Constance (1414–18), which had claimed that the pope was subject to the authority of a General Council of the Church, and insisted that the customary rights of the French church could not be altered, since the papacy itself acknowledged the permanent validity of laws established with its consent. The result was deadlock: the papacy refused to institute any bishops who had signed the articles contained in the declaration (resulting in about a quarter of French dioceses becoming vacant by 1688), and the excommunicated Louis was reluctant to back down. Although he retracted the offending articles by 1693, the spirit behind them continued vigorous.

A parallel movement in Germany was known as Febronianism, from the pseudonym 'Febronius' adopted by the auxiliary bishop of Trier, J.N. van Hontheim (1701–90). He had been asked by the three Archbishop Electors (so named because they had a vote in the election of the Holy Roman Emperor) to investigate the grievance of German Catholicism against Rome in 1742, and published his findings pseudonymously in 1763, in *On the State of the Church and the legitimate Power of the Roman Pontiff*. He asserted the primacy of a General Council over the papacy; as Luther had done in 1520 'Febronius' argued that secular princes should take up the task of reforming the Church, whose unity would be facilitated by its division into state-controlled national churches. The book was placed on the Index of Prohibited Writings in 1764, and his proposals ran into the ground because of papal refusal to accept the movement's contentions, as well as opposition from other German bishops.

Similar developments were also apparent in Austria under the Empress Maria Theresa (1740–80) and her son and successor Joseph II (1765–90). She had denied the authority of papal instructions except where given her express sanction, stopped religious persecution and the work of the Inquisition, and secured the expulsion of the Jesuits, as well as ending clerical tax exemption and taking control of seminary education.

As a convinced believer in religious toleration Joseph took things further, even allowing Protestants and Orthodox to hold state office. His policy towards the Church sought to bring it more firmly under state control, and his rationally based and thoroughgoing reform of all aspects of public life was extended to reform of church administration and the purging of monastic orders not deemed to be fulfilling socially useful functions. He introduced civil marriage and divorce, suppressed about six hundred religious houses, and nationalized church property, but was defeated in his attempts to reform popular devotional practices.

The boundaries between debate on church–state issues and calls for spiritual renewal were sometimes fluid, and movements could combine both. (A partial Protestant parallel is Prussian Pietism.) Such confusion of objectives is visible in the history of the Jansenist movement. In its origins, Jansenism represented a Catholic (and even anti-Protestant) response to Protestant challenges in the form of a reappropriation of the teaching of Augustine of Hippo on the topic of divine grace, with its strong stress on human sinfulness and need of divine assistance. The movement gained its name from Cornelius Jansen (1585–1638), who presided over a theological college at Louvain (now in Belgium) before becoming Bishop of Ypres. Jansen studied the relevant works thoroughly and the fruit of his researches appeared in the posthumously published *Augustinus*.

Coupled with the emphasis on the need for grace, Jansen expressed a strong hatred of sin and a consequent rigorist approach to ethics; the two led him to oppose with vigour the ethical direction given by the Jesuits. In an attempt to make the practice of the Christian life accessible to all, they had adopted an approach known as probabilism, in which an individual making an ethical decision was free to choose any possible course of action, not necessarily that which was safest or most likely to be right, so long as it was at all probable. Confessors might therefore grant absolution if there were good reason to do so, even if the reasons against doing so appeared stronger. Furthermore, their emphasis on the externals of Christian practice, such as reception of the sacraments, risked neglecting the need to cultivate a proper attitude of heart. Jansen insisted on the need to receive the sacraments in a right spirit, with contrition seen as a prerequisite for priestly absolution at confession (the mainstream view at the time was that 'attrition', a desire for forgiveness motivated by fear rather than love, was sufficient). The operation of sacramental grace was not automatic, but dependent on the right inward attitude (hence it can be seen as another form of the 'religion of the heart'). He also asserted (as Augustine had done) that grace was give only to those to whom God willed to give it, and that its operation was irresistible (that is, bound to secure its intended effect).

The movement rapidly made headway in northern France and its centre became the convent of Port-Royal, outside Paris. This came to be regarded as a model monastic community. Many serious-minded Catholics were drawn to it, among them the mathematician and philosopher Blaise Pascal (1623–62), whose sister was a nun there. He experienced a personal conversion in 1654, which he described as meeting with the 'God of Abraham, Isaac and Jacob' rather than the 'God of the philosophers'. For the rest of his life, he kept a piece of paper inside his coat bearing this description of his experience. His *Provincial Letters* wittily and sharply exposed what he saw as the failings of Jesuit moral theology.

It was inevitable that the movement should come under suspicion, especially because its key theological emphases echoed some of those to be heard from Protestant pulpits. In 1653, five propositions said to have been taken from Jansen's writings were condemned by Rome, as a result of Jesuit activity. These expressed Augustinian views of grace and human inability, and Rome was anxious to avoid a repetition of the fierce controversy about grace which had plagued the post-Tridentine Church until its settlement in 1607. Jansenist apologists, while affirming the pope's right to condemn such propositions, often argued that the propositions could not actually be found in Jansen's works. They worked with a restricted understanding of papal authority which included matters of doctrine and morals but excluded matters of fact, such as whether a particular writer taught a particular doctrine. However, Rome's response was that the propositions had been in Jansen's work, and that they had been condemned in the sense in which Jansen had understood them.

Ultimately the movement succumbed to Jesuit pressure, coming under formal papal condemnation in the bull *Unigenitus*, which was issued in 1713. This was directed at the *New Testament with Moral Reflections* published by Pasquier Quesnel in 1694. Church leaders in France and the Low Countries appealed in vain to the pope to convene a General Council to settle the issue. The French bishops were forced into line by Louis XIV, but after the Dutch state forbade a vicar apostolic to officiate within its borders, a Jansenist archbishop of Utrecht was consecrated in 1723 and the movement began its separate existence. It continues today as part of the Old Catholic Church.

Jansenism was damaged by the appearance among some of its adherents of ecstatic phenomena such as speaking in tongues and claims to be able to work miracles, the extremism owing something to persecution (as with the near-contemporary French Prophets in the south of the country). The miracles were centred on the grave of a Jansenist in a Paris cemetery, and in 1732 the cemetery was closed in order to put a stop to these activities, which to many had appeared to be tokens of divine approval of a movement condemned by the papacy.

In spite of this (and the destruction of Port-Royal in 1707), the movement continued to excite controversy, centring on the bull of 1713 which had condemned it. It also changed character, shedding its earlier ultramontane outlook and becoming more of a political pressure group opposed to absolutism. Like Jansenism, Gallican thinking was opposed to Jesuit attempts to bring the Catholic Church in each country directly under Roman control. Jansenist and Gallican concerns brought the two streams closer together (though Louis was keen to extinguish the movement because it threatened his cherished ideal of religious uniformity). Both were thus against the Jesuits, the former because of their allegiance to Rome and the latter because of the alleged laxity of their ethical direction. The prolonged vacillation of Louis XV concerning what action to take ensured that battle continued to rage until 1757, when all discussion of the bull was formally forbidden. Thereafter, it withered away as a visible phenomenon, but it may have prepared the way for the French Revolution.[5]

Hierarchy and clergy

During this period two contrasting developments are evident: on one hand the hierarchy became increasingly out of touch with the people in France, and to some extent elsewhere, and on the other the clergy became better trained and more diligent in performing their duties.

Episcopal appointments were a part of a wider network of patronage which worked through personal connections and kinship ties and from which appointments were made to political as well as ecclesiastical office. (The two realms coalesced in the German prince-bishops, who combined ecclesiastical and political rule, and the last of whom survived until 1803.) Not surprisingly, this resulted in the domination of the higher echelons of the clerical ladder by younger sons of the nobility (this was as evident in Protestantism as it was in Catholicism outside Italy). It was therefore rare in most countries for an appointment to be made on the basis of merit, although some turned out to be highly meritorious once appointed. Few Catholic bishops had been parish priests, most of the latter coming from the educated lower middle classes. There was thus a great gulf fixed between the hierarchy and the body of parish clergy. The laxity of many higher clergy helped make many among the French aristocracy sympathetic to notions of democracy, which as advocated by the *Philosophes* went hand-in-hand with anticlericalism. It was this class which showed the first symptoms of decline in religious observance.

While the Church enjoyed official favour and immunity from taxation, it aroused resentment in France because it was less than efficient in fulfilling its responsibilities for charity and education. Many of the 130 French bishops lived in princely style, paying little attention to their diocesan responsibilities. During the eighteenth century, there had been a change in the character of the nation's episcopate, from scholarly preachers to aristocratic courtiers, increasingly out of touch with their flocks and with their clergy. All this, coupled with the Church's vast wealth (and the state's comparative poverty), fuelled rising discontent which was to have fateful consequences.

By contrast with the hierarchy, parish clergy appeared admirable: they lived in the real world rather than spending their energies in theological hair-splitting, and their usefulness as an agent of social influence (or control) was as easy for politicians to see as their active involvement in works of charity was for the laity; much good work was done in the educational field in France, with almost all the teachers being drawn from the ranks of the clergy and the religious orders. The moral abuses about which so many pre-Reformation writers had complained were gradually being overcome (although in southern Italy, for example, the practice of clergy taking a concubine persisted until the middle of the eighteenth century). Furthermore, by the end of this period most Catholic dioceses had their own seminary, as prescribed by the Council of Trent, and the clergy were better educated as a body and had undergone a thorough spiritual formation to mould them into serious and diligent servants of the Church. Incidentally, seminary provision for Protestants was patchy during the eighteenth century: German Lutherans and some Reformed churches enjoyed it, as did many English Dissenters, but Anglicans were notable for the lack of training provision and the lax procedures governing ordination and appointment to office.

Catholic devotion

As part of the drive for rational government and enlightened religious practice, a number of Catholic nations sought to channel, reform, or restrict monasticism. While the result tended to be the closure of many monastic houses deemed to be moribund or performing no useful social function such as education or care of the sick, Poland and Lithuania saw around two hundred new establishments founded during the eighteenth century, and some major new religious orders were also founded in Western Europe during this period: the Christian Brothers (1680), founded in France by Jean Baptiste de la Salle to educate poor children (since 1690, they have been an exclusively lay order); the Passionists (1720), a preaching order founded in Italy to promote personal holiness and counter superstition through evangelizing the poor; and the Redemptorists (1732), mentioned above.

These played a crucial role in Christianizing the countryside. In France especially, a number of religious orders conducted missions in rural areas, so that the eighteenth century has been described as 'the great age of missions into rural Europe'.[6] The result was that French Catholicism in particular became a rural rather than an urban religion, a development which fuelled a Rome-centred approach which contrasted with the Gallican tendency to minimize the significance of Rome for Catholic thought and polity.[7] There was also an increase in the number of lay organizations such as brotherhoods, confraternities, and 'third orders'.

At what we might call the 'middle-class' level, between the aristocracy and the peasantry, many Catholics were serious, Bible-reading (Benedict XIV had authorized the use of officially approved vernacular translations in 1757), prayerful, diligent in good works, and frequent communicants. Such people supported enthusiastically the new or newly approved devotional rites which gradually made headway at the popular level. By 1800 the Rosary was firmly established; the Stations of the Cross became widespread after receiving approval for parish use from Benedict XIV; and the Forty Hours' devotion before the reserved sacrament (first introduced in sixteenth-century Italy) had become an accepted feature of church life.

Affective devotion also received expression in the development of the cult of the Sacred Heart of Jesus, which received its own feast day in 1765 (though this permission initially applied to Poland and did not become universal until 1856). This form of devotion had its roots in the medieval Western stress on the suffering and wounds of Christ, and regarded the heart as symbolizing the love of God in becoming incarnate to redeem sinners. It was given a theological basis and liturgical expression by Jean Eudes (1601–80), but owed its spread to Margaret Mary Alacoque (1647–90), who claimed in 1675 to have seen a vision of Christ commanding her to take the message of this form of devotion to the world.

In spite of these channels for affective devotion, pre-Christian rituals continued to survive in many parts of Europe; the more recent developments in encouraging devotion to centrally approved saints (rather than local figures) made little headway unless they could be linked to the provision of some tangible benefit such as physical healing. Any attempt to reduce the number of officially approved feast days (and hence the number of holidays) by abolishing local observances was liable to meet with resentment. However, in the field of morality the Church was thought to have been somewhat more successful, with its crackdown on sins such as drunkenness and sexual immorality.

More controversial in the way in which it stressed personal religious experience was Quietism. This movement of thought arose in seventeenth-century Spain, and drew much of its inspiration from earlier Carmelite mystics such as St Teresa of Avila (1515–82) and St John of the Cross (1542–91). At its heart lay the claim that in the highest states of religious consciousness, human effort was a hindrance to the soul in its quest for union with God, and passivity was required (hence the name). It was necessary to abandon oneself to God, laying aside all concern for personal salvation. To do so, Quietists advocated the practice of a passive form of prayer, in which any active expression of spiritual feeling was rejected in order simply to hold oneself in the presence of God. The corollary of this was that outward acts of piety and charity were at best superfluous and at worst a hindrance to union with God. More controversially, Quietists were also accused of undermining Christian moral teaching by claiming that the soul which had reached a state of union with God could not sin, because for an act to be sinful it required the exercise of the will. It was perhaps these outworkings which caused most concern; the teaching itself has parallels in the earlier Christian mystical tradition, especially in the Eastern stress on apophaticism (the belief that we can only speak about God in negatives, because no human concepts can be applied to him, since God is unknowable in his essence).

Quietist teaching was condemned by Innocent XI in 1687, but before this the Spanish priest Miguel de Molinos (1628–96) had been imprisoned for such ideas, even though he had repudiated them. However, some of his followers ceased to pray vocally or to take the sacrament, and 'took disregard of temptation to immoral lengths'.[8] Others associated with the movement included Madame Guyon (1648–1717) and Archbishop François Fénelon (1651–1715). Through edited versions of their writings, it would influence John Wesley and certain currents of evangelical Protestantism.

Catholic mission

For Catholics, what constituted a missionary territory was the absence of a local clerical hierarchy. Underlying this was the belief that mission was about making grace available through the Church's ministrations. Since Catholic sacramental theology was predicated on the Church as a sacral and hierarchical institution, mission must proceed by means of formal authorization to commence work in a particular area. Such a paradigm survived until the Second Vatican Council (1962–5).

This 'top-down' approach to mission fitted well with the widespread tendency to link mission and colonization (although the Jesuits form a notable exception to this). It is customary to condemn such an approach, but the missiologist David Bosch makes the point that the colonization process may be seen as an expression of genuine Christian concern for the areas being colonized: Christians responded to new challenges in the only way which made sense to them, as they had been doing in the evangelization of Europe for at least a millennium.[9]

Reflecting the changing political scene in which new powers ended the global dominance of the Spanish and Portuguese, France replaced Spain and Portugal as the main source of missionaries. In 1663, the Société des

Missions Étrangères was founded in Paris as a seminary to train missionary priests. During the eighteenth century, French colonial expansion ran up against British ambitions in the West Indies and North America, although French missionaries succeeded in establishing an enduring Catholic presence in areas such as Quebec.

In 1622 Pope Gregory XV had founded the Sacred Congregation for the Propagation of the Faith to oversee Catholic missions, often known from its Latin title as *Propaganda*. The intent was that it should replace the 'patronage' (Spanish *Patronato* / Portuguese *Padroado*) system, under which at the end of the fifteenth century responsibility for mission to the non-Christian world had been divided between Spain and Portugal, then the dominant powers. Although they had been assigned responsibility for establishing dioceses and appointing bishops and clergy, there had been no consistent attempt to fulfil their obligations. In the climate of earnestness which followed the Council of Trent, *Propaganda* was to change all this, finding and training recruits, and providing monetary and literary resources for mission.

A key element of its strategy was the appointment of vicars apostolic. These were clergy who were authorized to perform episcopal functions in missionary areas as representatives of the pope, responsible directly to *Propaganda* and thus free from any political loyalties or local rivalries which might conflict with the internationalist and centralizing outlook of the Church. They were given the titles of sees *in partibus infidelium*, that is, in areas now lacking a Christian presence, such as much of Asia Minor. Since they were not strictly bishops, it was possible to get round the patronage system's assigning the right of episcopal appointment to Spain and Portugal.

At this point, it is worth making a brief survey of Catholic missions. During the eighteenth century the centres of gravity for Catholicism in Asia were South Vietnam and the Philippines; strong communities were also present in India (including the 'Thomas Christians', an ancient Eastern communion which was in communion with Rome from 1599 until a large portion became independent again in 1653), Ceylon, and China.

A pioneer in India had been the Jesuit Roberto de Nobili (1577–1656), who adopted the dress of a Hindu holy man and broke off visible connection with the Church in order to reach the Brahmins. Meeting with considerable success, he ensured that other members of his order would work among the lower castes, and by the end of the seventeenth century there were up to 200,000 converts. Although the pope condemned observance of the caste system and local liturgical variations in 1744, Indian Catholicism continued to grow, with a million converts by 1800.

In seventeenth-century Vietnam, the use of a group of catechists to spread the faith was pioneered by Alexandre de Rhodes (1591–1660) as the only priest in a hostile setting. He worked undercover between 1624 and his final expulsion in 1645, after which he became an advocate in Europe for the Vietnamese church. Basing his approach on an existing Buddhist institution, he established the *Domus Dei* ('House of God'), a group of men trained in medicine as well as catechesis and committed to a rule of life which included celibacy and communal living. The result was that by 1650 Rhodes claimed 300,000 converts and besought Rome to provide a hierarchy to lead the young church. Although there were very few priests to begin with, lay leadership enabled the community to survive severe opposition in which tens of thousands were martyred.

Under Spanish rule, the Philippines saw the conversion of most of the population to Catholicism by the end of the eighteenth century. Although the depth of such conversion may be questioned in view of the extent to which non-Christian religious practices continued, it was arguably the 'fit' of Catholicism with existing beliefs which ensured a ready acceptance for the new faith.[10] This proved something of a mixed blessing, as Christianity was both easily understandable and easily misunderstandable. Furthermore, the 600,000 indigenous converts by 1700 were cared for by four hundred Spanish priests, indicative of Spanish reluctance to encourage vocations to the priesthood among the peoples whom they colonized (the same reluctance was evident in Latin America).

Korea saw a Christian presence established from 1784; it was Roman, rather than Russian Orthodox, as might have been expected, and was the result of local lay initiative rather than official strategy: lay people replicated in Korea the rites which the first convert had observed Christians celebrating in Beijing. Inevitably, this meant that the new Christian community lacked a firm theological grounding, a deficiency which was to cause problems later on.

The country which was to cause most problems for the Vatican, however, and to show up its inability to respond to new challenges effectively, was China. Part of the problem was the mixed messages sent out from Rome: in effect, one pope's policy might be reversed by his successor. The Confucian practice of ancestor worship was condemned by the Holy Office in 1645, yet in 1659 the Jesuit approach to mission, which stressed the need for a sound and sympathetic understanding of the host culture and a sensitive translation of the gospel into understandable terms and concepts, received official approval in the form of a set of instructions issued by *Propaganda* to its vicars apostolic. This was noteworthy because most Catholic missionaries apart from the Jesuits took the line that converts should make a complete break with their previous culture.

The first ordination in China of Chinese priests by a Chinese bishop took place as early as 1688, but this promising development was followed by disaster resulting from controversy between the Jesuits, who had become very influential at court as the 'scholar-Christians' through their dissemination of Western astronomical and mathematical knowledge, and other more recently arrived orders such as the Franciscans and Dominicans. The stricter orders feared that the Jesuits were guilty of syncretism in their readiness to use concepts drawn from local religious belief as vehicles for the gospel, in their presentation of Christianity as something essentially in line with Confucian ethics (a presentation in which distinctive Christian beliefs and practices might be de-emphasized during the initial stages, as in the practice of Matteo Ricci (1552–1610), who did much to shape the Jesuit approach to mission in China), and in their willingness to countenance the continued observance of such traditional rites as veneration of the ancestors. The Jesuits accused other orders of alienating potential converts by their strictness and lack of understanding of the local culture. A case in point was the Jesuit use of terms for 'God' drawn from Confucian thought, which was technically non-theistic. Familiarity with Chinese civilization, as a result of their policy of careful study of the local culture, had led Jesuits to a more positive estimation of non-Christian religions as having retained elements of a primitive revelation of God which were evident in certain key terms and concepts. These terms were used in translating the Catholic liturgy into Chinese. Debate was complicated by the fact that both sides could cite evidence supporting their approach: whereas the Jesuits formulated their positive attitude toward indigenous religion on the basis of what they encountered at court, the other orders drew their more negative conclusions on the basis of their experience of popular superstition. Furthermore, many members of the stricter orders were Spaniards, who were hardly likely to welcome the new order which had replaced the patronage system or to sympathize with the Jesuits who were its most visible expression.

The controversy dragged on for decades as each side appealed to Rome for vindication. Jansenist opposition to the Jesuits (which included such matters as their attitude to non-Christian religions) resulted in the Sorbonne's condemnation of Chinese liturgical rites. In 1693, one of the vicars apostolic for China forbade the Jesuit use of traditional terms for God and the observance of traditional rites such as offering incense to the ancestors. In 1704 Rome upheld this ban; further condemnations followed during the period to 1744 (Vietnam was also affected by these rulings).

The results were devastating. Concluding (on the basis of Rome's attitude towards Chinese rites, its refusal to allow Christians to participate in the rites which bound society together, and its failure to respond to an imperial appeal for reconsideration, as well as the allegiance of the Jesuits to a foreign superior) that Christianity was a deviant ideology, evangelism was forbidden by imperial edict, almost all Catholic missionaries were expelled because they would not agree to be bound by Ricci's approach, and many Christians suffered persecution.

Liturgically, the result was that Roman liturgical practice was to become the norm for missions, including the use of Latin in the Mass. This was consistent with the liturgical standardization which had resulted from the Council of Trent, but it placed a major obstacle in the way of mission and especially the attempt to grow an indigenous church.

In South America Jesuit mission strategy again fell foul of Iberian interests. Jesuit *reductions* or villages were set up in Paraguay from 1650 to 1720 to provide a haven for Indian converts. At their peak about sixty of these communities were home to 100,000 people. Worship was in the vernacular, and incorporated local customs such as processions and dancing. Unfortunately, a legacy of this approach to mission was a culture of dependence on outside leadership, as indigenous Christians were slow to take on responsibility for church affairs. These communities were destroyed during the 1750s, because they had got in the way of Spanish and Portuguese colonial concerns.

Since Spain and Portugal had between them colonized the whole of Latin America, they continued to control ecclesiastical appointments; there was thus a close link between the Church and the colonial powers. Vast numbers of missionary priests served on the continent but the conversions achieved were often superficial; under a Catholic veneer most people continued in their pre-Christian beliefs and practices, although these were often given a Christian interpretation. Indigenization in terms of leadership, however, was another matter: the missions refused to train and appoint clergy from the local ethnic groups.

Further north, Catholic missionary orders were also active in what is now the south-western United States. Canada saw a solid base established, mainly through colonization, although some attempts were made to reach indigenous tribes. French Jesuits had explored the Great Lakes in the mid-seventeenth century. In 1674 Quebec had been made a diocese and the establishment of a local hierarchy meant that, technically at least, it was no longer a mission territory.

The other main area of Catholic mission at this time was western sub-Saharan Africa, which had seen episcopal sees established during the sixteenth century. Work in what is now Angola and the Congo had resulted in over half a million converts by 1700. However, the depredations of the slave trade, for which there was sustained competition between European powers, militated against the ability of the fledgling communities to become established.

The general policy of *Propaganda* was to recruit indigenous clergy (apart from anything else, they were less conspicuous during times of persecution) and to respect local customs wherever possible. However, we have seen that progress on the first was slow, and in practice the second was often not observed. Nevertheless, by 1789 there may have been as many as sixty dioceses outside Europe, strung out from Mexico to East Asia, and mostly in the tropical and sub-tropical regions. But the baton was passing to the Protestant missions, as Catholic colonial powers grew weaker, travel by French missionaries grew more difficult in the face of English maritime dominance, and the suppression of the Jesuits deprived the Church of its key missionary force. Catholic mission would, however, experience a dramatic resurgence in the second half of the nineteenth century.

Questions for thought

1 What light, historically speaking, is shed on the eighteenth-century papacy by regarding it as an absolute monarchy?

2 Compare and contrast the spirituality of Jansenism and Pietism. Are there any similarities in what each was reacting against?

3 Why was it so important for the Catholic Church to centralize and standardize many aspects of its life during this period?

4 Imagine that you were a Catholic missionary involved in the Chinese Rites controversy. Which side would you have taken, and why?

Further reading

Nigel Aston, 2002, *Christianity and Revolutionary Europe c.1750–1830*, Cambridge: Cambridge University Press, part 1.

Nicholas Atkin and Frank Tallett, 2003, *Priests, Prelates and People: A History of European Catholicism since 1750*, Oxford: Oxford University Press, ch. 1.

W.J. Callahan and D. Higgs (eds), 1979, *Church and Society in Catholic Europe of the Eighteenth Century*, Cambridge: Cambridge University Press.

Jean Delumeau, 1977, *Catholicism between Luther and Voltaire*, London: Burns & Oates.

J. Derek Holmes and Bernard Bickers, 2002, *A Short History of the Catholic Church*, with a postscript by Peter Hebblethwaite and final chapter by Peter Doyle, London: Burns & Oates, ch. 5.

R. Po-Chia Hsia, 1998, *The World of Catholic Renewal, 1540–1770*, Cambridge: Cambridge University Press.

Richard P. McBrien (ed.), 1995, *The HarperCollins Encyclopedia of Catholicism*, New York: HarperCollins.

John McManners, 1998, *Church and Society in Eighteenth-Century France*, 2 vols, Oxford: Oxford University Press.

Stephen Neill (revised by Owen Chadwick), 1986, *A History of Christian Missions*, The Pelican History of the Church, 6, Harmondsworth: Pelican, ch. 6.

W.R. Ward, *Christianity under the Ancien Régime 1648–1789*, chs 2–3.

Notes

1 Hsia, *Catholic Renewal*, p. 92.

2 Atkin and Tallett, *Priests, Prelates and People*, p. 35.

3 For an analysis of canonizations during the period 1540–1770, see Hsia, *Catholic Renewal*, pp. 122ff.

4 Liguori's *Moral Theology* remained a standard seminary textbook throughout the nineteenth century, and his devotional work, *The Glories of Mary*, was translated into eighty languages. In 1871 he was proclaimed a 'Doctor of the Church', i.e. a teacher whose contribution was deemed of exceptional significance.

5 Aston, *Christianity and Revolutionary Europe*, p. 168.

6 Aston, *Christianity and Revolutionary Europe*, p. 3.

7 This argument is developed by Ward, *Christianity*, p. 68, following the French historian Louis Châtellier.

8 *ODCC*, art. 'Molinos'.

9 David Bosch, 1991, *Transforming Mission: Paradigm Shifts in Theology of Mission*, American Society of Missiology Series 16, Maryknoll, NY: Orbis, pp. 229–30, 237.

10 Scott W. Sunquist *et al.* (eds), 2001, *Dictionary of Asian Christianity*, Grand Rapids, MI: Eerdmans, art. 'Philippines'.

4

The 'Babylonian Captivity' of the Eastern Churches

The year 1648 is a somewhat arbitrary choice for a point at which to survey the state of the Eastern churches, but at least it allows us to make a comparison with Western Europe as it recovered from the Thirty Years' War. What we see is a communion almost entirely under Muslim rule and therefore hindered from developing fully its theological and liturgical life; even the chief exception to this, the Russian church, was to experience its own form of captivity from the late seventeenth century, during the reigns of Peter and Catherine. This period also saw a great deal of effort expended by Roman missionaries and hierarchs in the quest to bring the Orthodox under papal allegiance. ('Babylonian Captivity' is sometimes used as a description of the enforced subservience of Orthodoxy to other powers, religious and political, during this period.) In all this, national sentiment complicated things severely, leading hierarchs to seek union with Rome or to reject it as a way of bolstering ethnic identity.

The result is that, to those accustomed to thinking of Eastern Christianity as monolithic or united by contrast with the fragmented state of Western Protestantism, the Eastern scene was (and remains) surprisingly complicated, as Table 4.1 indicates. There were (and are) Eastern Orthodox (those who accepted the decrees of the Seven Ecumenical Councils); Oriental Orthodox (often now known as 'pre-Chalcedonian' churches because they did not accept the decrees of the Council of Chalcedon in 451, nor those of the councils which followed it); Eastern-rite Catholics (who used the Orthodox liturgy and were allowed to retain a married priesthood and observe other traditional customs so long as they submitted to Rome); Latin-rite Catholics (as in the West); the Church of the East (which has existed apart from the main Eastern Christian traditions because of its perceived Nestorian theology); and an array of dissident groups (especially in Russia). In Poland, the Baltic countries, Hungary, and Romania there were also sizeable Protestant communities, and from the reign of Catherine the Great (1762–96) Anabaptist groups settled in Ukraine and Southern Russia.

Table 4.1: Roots of the main eighteenth-century Orthodox jurisdictions.

ROME			
CONSTANTINOPLE[1]	Italo-Albanians[2]		
	1346 ^Serbia[3]	1698 Eastern-rite Catholics in Transylvania	
	#1448 ^1589 MOSCOW[4]	*1596 Greek Catholics[5]	1646 Ruthenian Catholics
		1670s Old Believers	Popovtsy
			Bespopovtsy
ALEXANDRIA	*451 Coptic Orthodox Church	1741 Coptic Catholic Church	
ANTIOCH	*431 Church of the East[6]	1553 Chaldean Catholic Church	
		1599–1653 Syro-Malabar (India, East Syrian rite) to Rome	
	*451 Syrian Orthodox Church[7]	1662 Syrian Catholic Church	
		Indians under Syrian Orthodox Church from 1653	late 18th c. Malabar Independent Syrian Church
	*after 451 Armenian Apostolic Church	between 1635 and 1740 Armenian Catholics	
	^5th c. Cyprus		
	^c.500 Georgia		
	1182 Antiochian Syrian Maronite Church		
	1724 Melkite Catholic Church		
JERUSALEM	#1575 Sinai		

NB: The Ecumenical Patriarchate claims the exclusive right to recognize Orthodox jurisdictions as autocephalous; dates refer to such recognition unless otherwise stated.[8]

PATRIARCHATES are in upper-case.

Eastern-rite Catholic (also known as Uniat) bodies are underlined.[9]

Key
* originated through schism
# granted autonomy
^ granted autocephaly

Notes
1 Also known as the Ecumenical Patriarchate.
2 Also known as Italo-Greeks.
3 No patriarchate 1459–1557, 1766–1920.
4 Patriarchate abolished 1721–1917.

continued

45

5 Union of Brest-Litovsk; from Polish Ukraine.
6 Also known as Nestorian, East Syrian, or Persian.
7 Also known as Jacobite, West Syrian, or Monophysite.
8 Many dates in this table are taken from the online version of Ronald G. Roberson, *The Eastern Christian Churches: A Brief Survey*, 6th edn, at http://www.cnewa.org/generalpg-verus.aspx?PageID=182, accessed 26 June 2005.
9 Greek or Eastern-rite Catholics of all types are also known as Byzantine Catholics because their Liturgy follows the Byzantine rite.

East and West

Reaction to Uniatism as a Roman Catholic missionary strategy

Eastern-rite Catholics (communities who were allowed to use a basically Orthodox liturgy but who acknowledged the pope as their supreme head), often to their annoyance known as 'Uniats', were seen by Rome as manifesting the universality of the Roman communion and as a bridge to union between East and West. However, rulers varied widely in their attitudes to such communities. They were often persecuted by the tsars in Russia, Catherine the Great seeing their existence as a threat to her sovereignty; she supported Orthodox proselytism among them, and from 1773 parts of Poland saw forcible conversions at the hands of the Cossacks. By contrast, Maria Theresa, as might be expected from a Catholic, protected their independent status.

A particularly complex situation, demonstrating many of the factors at work in the Uniat impulse, was that obtaining in Transylvania, now Northern Romania. Here Orthodoxy found itself challenged first by Calvinist Protestantism (favoured by the Hungarians) and then by Catholicism. A Uniat church came into existence in 1698, following the replacement of Ottoman rule by that of the Habsburgs in 1687. This was the fruit of the Habsburg desire to secure religious unity; Jesuit attempts to convert the substantial Protestant community having proved ineffective, they had turned to the majority Orthodox population (which was ethnically Romanian, whereas the Protestants tended to be German or Hungarian). By contrast with the situation in the Ottoman Empire as a whole, Orthodoxy was not one of the three officially recognized forms of Christianity in Ottoman-ruled Transylvania (Catholicism, Lutheranism, and Calvinism), each of which was seen as the preserve of a particular ethnic group. The Orthodox Romanian population continued to be looked down on, and was deemed by the Jesuits to have little grasp of theology; thus it was thought that their submission to Rome could easily be secured if they were allowed to keep their liturgy and religious practices.

Uniatism also resulted in a hardening of Orthodox attitudes; whereas during the seventeenth century Orthodox bishops in some areas had often invited Jesuits to preach and initiate educational work, and Orthodox continued to share communion with Roman Catholics, such co-operation (which occurred in spite of the estrangement between Rome and Eastern Orthodoxy which had been formalized in 1054) came to a virtual end during the eighteenth century. Whereas Rome had regarded Orthodox as erring members of the universal Church, it now began to adopt a more hard-line attitude, regarding them as outside the Church and needing to be brought into it by conversion. After the pope had prohibited common worship in 1729, in 1755 the Patriarchs of Constantinople, Alexandria, and Jerusalem declared Roman Catholic and Armenian baptisms to be invalid (thus necessitating rebaptism of converts), not because they had been performed by heterodox clergy but because the rite was deemed uncanonical since triple immersion was not used. The new climate was epitomized by a schism in Antioch during 1724 which resulted in the creation of another patriarchate, loyal to Rome. Over time, there have been no fewer than six patriarchates of Antioch, five of which coexisted for much of the eighteenth century: Greek Orthodox, Syrian Orthodox (that is, Oriental Orthodox, formerly called Monophysite), Greek Catholic (that is, observing the Byzantine rite but acknowledging the authority of the papacy; also known as Melkite), Syrian Catholic, and Maronite; there had also been an earlier Latin patriarchate.[1]

Western theological influence

Theological education in much of the Orthodox world came to be conducted in Latin (deemed essential for those wishing to be considered as educated), using Western models and texts. A clear distinction should be drawn, however, between Romanizing theological tendencies and the question of reunion with Rome. Peter Mogila (1596–1647), Orthodox Metropolitan of Kiev and one of the foremost exponents of the former, was a vocal opponent of anything which savoured of the latter. He adapted the Jesuit pattern of seminary training for Orthodox use; in addition, some of the many Uniat clergy who were able to study in Catholic institutions later reverted to Orthodoxy, bringing Latinizing influences with them. The influence of Latin theology can also be discerned in confessional statements of the period, such as that put out by Mogila himself in 1640[2] or that issued by authority of the Patriarch of Jerusalem, Dositheus, in 1672; and while their value in their time and context has been recognized, they have not continued to be acknowledged as definitive Orthodox doctrinal statements.[3]

As for Protestant influences, Pietism spread eastwards through colonies

of German and Swedish merchants; translations of Pietist writings produced at Halle were significant in opening up some Orthodox writers to
Pietist ideas. For example, St Tikhon Zadonsky (1724–83) was a bishop
who in 1767 retired to a monastery to devote himself to prayer, correspondence, and receiving those who flocked to him for counsel. Tikhon
considered Arndt's *True Christianity* (which had been translated into
Russian) one of his favourite works (another was a devotional work of
1695 by the Anglican bishop Joseph Hall), and Tikhon's veneration of
the passion of Christ has been paralleled with Zinzendorf's devotion to
Christ's Five Wounds.[4]

Russia

Guardian of Orthodoxy

The notion of Moscow as the 'Third Rome' has been seen as expressing the
subordination of church to state, arising as part of the sixteenth-century
move across Europe to create strong centralized monarchies.[5] However,
it must also be understood from a theological perspective: the assertion
that there would be no fourth Rome was an implicit claim that the end
of all things was near. Furthermore, it represented an assumption of
authority on the part of the Russian church: Constantinople had forfeited
its right to be called 'the second Rome' because of its compromise with
the Latins in 1438–9 at the Council of Florence-Ferrara (a compromise
which had been categorically rejected by the city's Orthodox populace).
It could therefore no longer give a lead to Orthodox Christians. Yet even
Moscow was to find itself racked by schism and written off as apostate
by a breakaway group, the Old Believers.

The 'Old Believer' schism

One factor giving rise to the schism was not theological but political:
a Cossack-led rebellion in Ukraine had resulted in an inconclusive war
between Russia and Poland from 1654 to 1667, and to the incorporation
of Ukraine into Russian territory once more, thus bringing a Westernized
population under Russian rule and a Uniat church back under Orthodox
jurisdiction (now under Moscow rather than Constantinople, because
Ukraine was deemed to form part of Russian 'canonical territory' (i.e.
that area deemed to belong to the jurisdiction of the Russian hierarchy
and which was therefore off-limits to other jurisdictions). Realization of
their own inferiority as a nation led Russians to seek reforms in various
areas, including that of church life.[6] At the same time, a reforming party
was gaining ground among the clergy: a group known as the 'Zealots of

Piety' introduced new standards of dedication to ministry and preaching, challenging openly what they saw as injustice or superstition. Underlying this was a belief in Russia's unique mission to the world, a mission which they saw as requiring the purification of the people in order to fulfil it. Nevertheless, most people saw spiritual authority as residing chiefly not in the clergy but in the monks and holy men who withdrew from society to live on the margins of human habitation in the forests. It seems that this duality made it possible for division to secure a widespread following.

The reform-minded Nikon became patriarch in 1652 and began his reforms the following year. He considered agreement on ritual necessary if the Russian church were to be able to accept fully non-Muscovite Orthodoxy. This was vital if relationships of mutual trust were to be built in order that Russia, as the only remaining Orthodox power, could provide military assistance to those churches suffering from oppressive rule (whose take on the situation was somewhat different: the Greeks in particular looked down on divergent Russian customs and inadequate liturgical translations). Russia's cultural isolation meant that its church had retained the rituals delivered at the time when the nation's conversion began in the tenth century, whereas the usages of other Orthodox churches had continued to evolve during the intervening centuries. All were therefore shocked by his attempt to introduce Greek usages, which he considered more correct, such as making the sign of the cross with two fingers instead of three, but curiously it was the reforming clergy who were most strongly opposed. The symbolic value attached to ritual actions in the liturgy meant that such changes were believed to affect the substance of the faith being confessed as much as might a change in the wording of the creed itself. It was claimed that the Greeks were the ones who had betrayed Orthodoxy by making their submission to Rome at the Council of Florence-Ferrara, whereas Russia was believed to have been divinely called to serve as the 'Third Rome'. Greek clergy moving to Russia were required to undergo a period of orientation in a Russian monastery before ministering, and Greek merchants were not allowed to take communion for fear that they might not be Orthodox. The Russians therefore had no wish to introduce Greek usages. With state assistance, Nikon persecuted his opponents, who were led by Archpriest Avvakum (c.1620–82). Nikon claimed that the patriarch was above the tsar, and had the right to exercise temporal power (on the basis of the *Donation of Constantine*, discredited in the West since 1440 as a forgery).

It may be argued that his reforms were rooted in a sense of responsibility to non-Muscovite Orthodox, a concern which the Moscow Patriarchate did not always show in its dealings with subject churches, or that he saw them as an essential prerequisite for extending the Russian church's sphere of influence and winning over potentially suspicious Orthodox jurisdictions. But when in 1658 Nikon intimated his wish to resign, possibly as a means to secure royal support, his move backfired; the tsar accepted his wish, assuring him of his continuing friendship, and Nikon retired to a monastery – although without formally resigning. (Doubtless Nikon's insistence that the Church was pre-eminent over the state was a factor in this; it did not square with the traditional Byzantine notion of 'symphony' between the two.) The resulting vacuum in the patriarchate was only ended in 1666–7, when a council of the Russian church, called by the tsar, accepted Nikon's reforms and condemned his opponents (as well as implicitly condemning the 'Third Rome' ideology and the decrees of a 1551 council which had set up Russian practice as the model for Orthodoxy everywhere) but deposed him.

The result was a devastating schism, involving at least a third of Russian Orthodox. The breakaway group took the name of 'Old Believers' (*raskolniki*) because of their adherence to traditional ritual practice. Many monastics joined them from the start, and further accessions of monastics and others occurred during the reign of Peter the Great in protest at his reforms, since the Church's failure to resist these changes appeared to them an indication of its spiritual bankruptcy.

Like Nikon, the Old Believers accepted the idea of Russia's unique divine mission as the guardian of Orthodoxy and 'Third Rome', but stood his arguments on their head by asserting that the Church had in fact apostatized from its calling. That being so, they anticipated the appearance of the Antichrist and the imminent end, since no fourth Rome could be expected. The fact that the rest of the Orthodox world followed the Greek customs in question was beside the point; Avvakum was the movement's Athanasius, standing against the whole world for what he believed to be the true way of worship.

In turn, the Old Believers divided into two. The minority group were the *popovtsy*, who maintained priestly ministrations, usually by occasional ordinations at the hands of sympathetic bishops or by priestly conversions. From the mid-nineteenth century they were able to revive a full sacramental life after securing the allegiance of a bishop and thus being able to conduct ordinations. The majority were the *bespopovtsy* or 'priestless ones', who believed that since there was no longer a true Church on earth, there could therefore be no true priests either. Since they believed that only priests could celebrate the sacraments, they were forced to adopt a spiritualizing explanation of these to explain how they could enjoy the benefits of the sacraments without physically celebrating them, or else to deny themselves the benefit of certain sacraments. Thus they divided over marriage, which some felt required priestly blessing, in the absence of which celibacy was the only option open to them. Such was their apocalypticism that initially they committed mass suicide by gathering in churches and setting fire to them, although later they took the path of exile instead, withdrawing into the forests from anti-

Christian society and rule. (It is ironic that two groups who wished to withdraw from the world, the Old Believers and the monastics, in fact played significant roles in opening up new tracts of territory for Russian exploitation and rule.) When some migrated to the West, they found they had much in common with some streams of Protestantism.

While the Old Believer spectrum came to include a wide range of views, from those who rejected outward religious observances to those who laid great stress on such things, all groups were united in their backward-looking vision and their disapproval of the contemporary Church and state. Such a perspective presented a sharp contrast to the forward-looking and rationally based outlook of the Enlightenment, which was to influence Russian society just as it did that of Western Europe.

The emergence of non-Orthodox dissent

Further schisms continued to affect the Russian church (it suffered far more from these than did other Orthodox jurisdictions), the various groups appearing during the late seventeenth and eighteenth centuries sometimes being lumped together as 'Spiritual Christians' and often being indistinguishable from the *bespopovtsy*, especially in Ukraine, where many such groups emerged. This was a region which had experienced considerable political change and which was the main battle-ground between Eastern and Western forms of Christianity during this period. Campbell points out that many of the schismatics adopted illuminist or 'spiritualist' views, claiming to have direct communication with God which bypassed the institutional Church.[7]

The *Khlysty* or 'People of God' appeared from the 1690s, and were an ascetic, spiritualist, and ecstatic group, led by 'Christs' in whom a spark of the divine resided (they believed that Christ was not uniquely the Son of God). From this group emerged in the late eighteenth century the *Skoptsy* ('Castrators', so named from their belief that male adherents should be castrated).

The *Doukhobors* or 'Spirit Wrestlers', who began in Ukraine about 1740, had many parallels with the Quakers; they made the 'inner word' of the Spirit to the soul the supreme religious authority and rejected external rites and sacraments. For them, all human beings have within them a spark of the divine, and Christ was just one of a succession of inspired spiritual leaders (they also called their leaders 'Christs'). This pacifist group was forced to migrate at various points in its history, and came to Western attention in the late 1940s when members who had emigrated to Canada from 1897 set fire to their properties and stripped off their clothes in public as an anarchist protest at state requirements regarding education and registration of births, marriages, and deaths.

The *Molokans* ('milk drinkers', also known as 'Spiritual Christians') emerged in Ukraine late in the eighteenth century. They too rejected outward baptism, but maintained the authority of the Scriptures, even to the extent of observing biblical dietary regulations.

Peter the Great's enforced Westernization

Ever since Moscow gained its independence from the Mongols in the fifteenth century, there had been a constantly see-sawing relationship between church and state.

It was to avoid a repetition of anything like the Old Believer schism that Peter (who ruled from 1682 to 1725) subordinated the Church to the state, suspending the patriarchate from 1700 and abolishing it in 1721. Its replacement, the Holy Synod, was headed by a lay procurator who was also responsible for non-Orthodox Christians and non-Christian faiths, and modelled on the Lutheran consistory; much of the inspiration for Peter's reforms had come from Leibniz. Peter had ensured that bishops appointed were from his supporters and so he was able to pack the Synod with bishops and other ecclesiastical dignitaries of his choice. The Church thus became more or less a department of state, and the clergy civil servants.

Walters points out that Peter also put church leadership in the hands of clergy from Ukraine, who would have been most influenced by Western trends of thinking.[8] The metropolitanate of Kiev came under the patriarchate of Moscow from 1685 in the wake of Russian political expansion into Ukraine; this introduced a current of thought which had been shaped by the Westernized theological ethos favoured by Mogila.

Peter the Great's innovations deepened the divide between the monastics (from whom the hierarchy was drawn) and the married parish clergy; the former were well educated and on occasion benefited from state support, while the latter were uneducated and often extremely poor. Both, in different ways, were made servants of the state, the former by virtue of their entanglement in political affairs, and the latter because they were expected to report to the authorities any local manifestations of discontent. Parallel to this was the gulf opened up by the reforms of Peter and his Germanic successors between the upper classes and the peasantry; apart from any economic aspect this was because the upper classes became Westernized in outlook (the court having moved to St Petersburg in an attempt to break the dominance in Moscow of the Byzantine cultural tradition) while the rest remained Russian. In Zernov's words, Peter 'enslaved the peasants and paralysed the Church'.[9] It was even put about that he was the Antichrist.

Nonetheless, Russia continued to see itself as protector of Orthodoxy, an assertion of role which could not have been congenial to Greeks and others, and which was to cause problems in the nineteenth century.

Catherine the Great and Enlightenment thought

Peter and Catherine shared the anti-monastic sentiments of Western rulers influenced by Enlightenment thinking, and closed many monasteries. As a German Deist, Catherine the Great continued Peter's drive for enlightened government and church reform along Western lines; during her reign (1762–96) almost three-quarters of surviving monasteries were closed. Repression drove many monastics to the fringes, northwards to the forests or beyond the boundaries of the Empire to Mount Athos or to Romanian monasteries. However, enlightenment did not extend as far as the training of most parish clergy. There were seminaries, but few parish clergy were among the students. In the first few years of Catherine's reign, the Church was also brought into a position of economic dependence on the state by being deprived of much of its land holdings and the two million serfs who worked them.

Political expansion and Orthodox mission

Frequently there was a close link with imperial expansion, perhaps closer than anything associated with Western powers; the government saw mission as a means of Russifying the Siberian tribes. Orthodox mission practice during this period tended to be far below the ideals set during earlier centuries. Inducements might be offered to potential converts and teaching was often weak. Many converts, therefore, were merely nominal and could as easily revert to their previous allegiance. Nevertheless, a number of Siberian tribes saw missionaries translate parts of the Bible and the liturgy into their own languages, and the ideal of an indigenous church was not wholly lost sight of. Mission reached as far east as Alaska (under Russian rule until 1867), where conversions began to occur among various Inuit tribes from 1747.

Elsewhere Nestorian mission had reached China many centuries earlier, and travellers such as Marco Polo testified that the Church of the East had maintained a presence there until the fourteenth century. Orthodoxy did not arrive until 1683, when some Russians were captured by Chinese forces; Russian missionaries were regarded as civil servants until 1737, and did little work during this period beyond the confines of the Russian embassy in Beijing.

Christianity under Ottoman rule

The impact of oppression

For much of the time, the Ottoman Empire was a peaceful society in which Christianity was tolerated, but when persecution did occur it could be fierce. The death penalty was imposed on those who converted from Islam to Christianity, and those were deemed to have insulted the Prophet (as opposed to merely expressing disagreement with his teaching). Those who were put to death for such reasons have been recognized by Orthodoxy as 'New Martyrs' (the old ones being those who died during the persecutions of the early centuries).[10]

The decline of theology under Islam was in part the consequence of oppression (though the extent of this during the seventeenth century should not be overstated), but perhaps there was also a sense that no more work remained to be done because the Fathers and the Ecumenical Councils had provided all that was needed. The low level of theological education, however, did not help matters. Clergy who wished to study in any depth had to go to Western institutions, and frequently either converted to Catholicism or else returned as bearers of Western ideas (such as the concept of transubstantiation as an explanation of the nature of the real presence of Christ in the Eucharist, something which Orthodox have traditionally preferred to leave undefined as a mystery). The result was a Westernization of Orthodox theology which lasted until the nineteenth century. Even in countries which were not under Ottoman rule, Latin became widespread as the language of theological education and Latin models were adopted, as we have seen.

Among those who were not influenced by the West, however, enforced introversion bred conservatism; theological education might not be a possibility, but the liturgy could still be celebrated each week, and (as was to happen under Communism) this became the bearer of the community's faith. At its best this enabled members to stand firm in their faith under persecution; at its worst it degenerated into a barely understood set of superstitious rituals.

South-East Europe and Turkey

Gradually other Orthodox jurisdictions were brought under the Ecumenical Patriarchate, partly because of an Ottoman policy of Hellenization (for which the Phanariots, the powerful Greek merchant families in Constantinople, were largely responsible) and partly because the Ottomans treated Christians as a *millet*, a subject people whose leaders and bureaucracies were responsible for civil as well as religious matters, 'a nation defined by religion, not geography'.[11] (Muslim thought did not differentiate between the spheres of religion and politics.) In 1766 it was the turn of the Serbs and in 1767 the Bulgarians. Under the *millet* system the Ecumenical Patriarch represented all Chalcedonian churches, while the Armenian Patriarch represented all others from 1461 until they began to be granted *millet* status on their own account from the 1830s, as did Catholics and Protestants.

The Phanariots saw to it that the Ecumenical Patriarchate focused on Greek concerns, thus fuelling a resentment which still on occasion colours relationships with other Orthodox jurisdictions in the region. From the eighteenth century Western conceptions of nationalism began to influence Eastern thought. As well as political independence, there was a desire for national churches. The result of this and the *millet* system was that Orthodoxy and nationalism became synonymous in the minds of most, especially the Greeks, both because of the nature of the administrative arrangements and because of the way in which the Church was often the sole vehicle for expressing nationalist sentiment.

The strategy of Uniatism has bequeathed a complicated legacy to modern ecumenists (and politicians). Roman missionaries worked to secure conversions at the individual as well as the corporate level. In time, all areas of the Ottoman Empire saw the establishment of Uniat as well as Oriental Orthodox churches, complicated by the presence in most countries of Western-rite Catholics. A number of the Eastern-rite churches established during this period had in their origins an element of resentment at the power over them given to Constantinople and a belief that their distinct ethnic identity could better be preserved in this way than by remaining under a Patriarchate increasingly preoccupied with Greek concerns.

One problem which hindered the churches, perhaps more than the Muslim religious allegiance of the Ottoman rulers, was that of corruption. The sultans required a large payment from each new patriarch before issuing a document which allowed them to assume office. It was, therefore, in the sultans' financial interests to ensure that this happened as frequently as possible; patriarchs were appointed and deposed (or assassinated) with depressing regularity, making the office an insecure one and subject to constant intrigue in which Jesuits and agents of Western powers were on occasion involved. Deposed ex-patriarchs were also looking for opportunities to regain the throne. Furthermore, the patriarchs had to recoup their outlay, which they did by levying taxes on their bishops, who taxed their clergy, who in turn taxed the laity. More generally, Christians (who were looked down on as second-class citizens) were heavily taxed and their eldest sons frequently seized for training as civil servants or soldiers, which involved forcible conversion to Islam.

Greece

While there was little of note to report as far as the Church's external life during this period is concerned, it did see the production of one of the most influential spiritual works ever to have appeared in Eastern Christianity. The *Philokalia*, first published in 1782, was a collection of writings on prayer and the spiritual life drawn from 36 Eastern authors between the fourth and fifteenth centuries and following the Hesychast tradition of spirituality. The editors, St Macarius of Corinth (1731–1805) and St Nikodemos of the Holy Mountain (1748–1809), were among the leaders of a traditionalist movement, the Kollyvades, which began on Mount Athos, a rocky promontory off the coast of Greece which had for centuries been home to an international collection of monastic communities and which was regarded as uniquely holy. For these men, Greek renewal would come not through the adoption of Western Enlightenment ideas but through a rediscovery of Orthodox roots. To this end they began a programme of publication which included patristic writings, lives of the saints, and liturgical texts. Curiously, it was also St Nikodemos who edited Greek editions of two Roman Catholic works, Ignatius Loyola's *Spiritual Exercises*, and Lorenzo Scupoli's *Spiritual Combat*.

While many of the writings comprising the *Philokalia* had originally been intended for monks, the compilation became extremely popular among devout laity. In 1793 it was translated into Slavonic by St Paisius Velichkovsky (1722–94), a Russian monk who had lived on Mount Athos and later in Romania. Through his followers, it became known in Russia, where it would have a profound influence on nineteenth-century Orthodox spirituality, as we shall see. Above all else, such works were seen as enabling Orthodox to rediscover the riches of their own spiritual tradition and so free themselves from captivity to Western modes of thought.

Questions for thought

1 Why was Orthodoxy susceptible to Western theological influence at the same time as it was suspicious of Western ecclesiastical expansionism?

2 How far is it justified to see the Old Believers as a reaction against imperial attempts at centralization?

3 From an ecclesiastical standpoint, what arguments could be offered in favour of the reforms attempted under Peter and Catherine?

4 Why was the Orthodox liturgy able to function as the bearer of the faith of the people under Ottoman rule?

5 Compare and contrast the position of the Russian church and the Ecumenical Patriarchate in their relations with the state.

Further reading

Michael Angold (ed.), 2006, *Cambridge History of Christianity*, vol. 5: *Eastern Christianity*, Cambridge: Cambridge University Press, chs 8, 15–16, 20.

Aziz S. Atiya, 1968, *A History of Eastern Christianity*, London: Methuen (deals with the non-Chalcedonian churches).

Wil van den Bercken, 1999, *Holy Russia and Christian Europe*, London: SCM Press, chs 5–6.

Ted A. Campbell, 1994, *The Religion of the Heart*, Columbia, SC: University of South Carolina Press, ch. 6.

G. P. Fedotov (ed.), 1950, *A Treasury of Russian Spirituality*, New York: Harper & Row.

Ken Parry *et al.* (eds), 1999, *The Blackwell Dictionary of Eastern Christianity*, Oxford: Blackwell.

Steven Runciman, 1968, *The Great Church in Captivity*, Cambridge: Cambridge University Press (on the Patriarchate of Constantinople from 1453 to 1821).

Alexander Schmemann, 1963, *The Historical Road of Eastern Orthodoxy*, London: Harvill, chs 5–6.

Philip Walters, 1999, 'Eastern Europe since the fifteenth century', in Adrian Hastings (ed.), *A World History of Christianity*, London: Cassell.

Timothy [Kallistos] Ware, 1997, *The Orthodox Church*, rev. edn, Harmondsworth: Penguin, chs 5–6.

Nicolas Zernov, 1961, *Eastern Christendom: A Study of the Origin and Development of the Eastern Orthodox Church*, London: Weidenfeld & Nicolson, ch. 5.

Nicolas Zernov, 1964, *The Russians and their Church*, London: SPCK, chs 10–11, 13–15.

Notes

1 Similarly, in Alexandria there are the Coptic Patriarch, the Greek Patriarch, a Coptic Catholic Patriarch, and until the twentieth century a Latin Patriarch (though this was a titular office and did not denote a hierarchy actually based in the city).

2 The attentions of a Greek theologian were deemed necessary before its acceptance in toned-down form at a synod in Iaşi (modern Romania) in 1642.

3 For these and other creeds and confessions of faith, see two comprehensive collections of such documents: Jaroslav Pelikan and Valerie Hotchkiss (eds), 2003, *Creeds and Confessions of the Christian Tradition*, 4 vols, New Haven and London: Yale University Press; Philip Schaff (ed.), 1998 (reprint of 1931 edn), *The Creeds of Christendom*, 6th edn, 3 vols, Grand Rapids, MI: Baker. A handy compilation of the most important is John H. Leith (ed.), 1973, *Creeds of the Churches: A Reader in Christian Doctrine from the Bible to the Present*, Atlanta, GA: John Knox.

4 Fedotov, *Treasury*, p. 183.

5 Walters, 'Eastern Europe', p. 292.

6 Zernov, *Russians*, p. 92.

7 Campbell, *Religion*, p. 134.

8 Walters, 'Eastern Europe', p. 297.

9 Zernov, *Russians*, p. 120.

10 Those who died for their faith under Communism have also been recognized as 'New Martyrs'.

11 Parry *et al.*, *Blackwell Dictionary of Eastern Christianity*, p. xviii.

5

The Churches in Britain, Ireland, and North America, 1688–1789

It was during this period that England experienced a dramatic shift in its religious identity: whereas in 1688 the established church commanded the allegiance, at least in nominal terms, of the great majority of the population, a century later the landscape was far different. Dissent and Catholicism had both come out into the open and grown (the former more than the latter); non-Trinitarian Protestantism had also appeared and claimed the allegiance of many formerly Trinitarian congregations; and open irreligion had also grown.

In the light of these trends, the tendency has been to utter blanket condemnations of the eighteenth-century churches, and especially of the established churches of England and Scotland. Such a negative view owes something to the way in which renewal movements have often exaggerated the darkness of the situation into which they saw themselves as bringing light – the movement in question in this case being Evangelicalism. (Rupp is right to remind us that this movement did not spring out of nothing, but possessed roots in recent church history, and that it built on a renewal which had already begun.[1]) More recently, however, scholars have insisted on the need to understand the churches in context, in order to see what they were trying to achieve. There has also been a revival of interest in such topics as eighteenth-century Anglican spirituality, which has shown that the clergy were by no means all as ignorant, unspiritual, negligent, or time-serving as John Wesley or (more often) his intellectual successors claimed.[2]

All the same, the period was seen by contemporaries as an age of decline. The lapsing of the Licensing Act in 1695 left publishers free to print anti-clerical literature, which soon appeared in worryingly large quantities. For an increasing number the Church's chief enemy was no longer Rome but unbelief. The moral climate may perhaps be gauged more accurately from the nature of much contemporary drama and literature than from the complaints of concerned churchmen. As society sought to throw off the Puritan yoke, it went to the other extreme.

Timeline: Events in Britain, Ireland, and North America, 1689–1789

1689	Toleration Act
1690	The Church of Scotland finally established as Presbyterian
1698	SPCK founded
1701	SPG founded
1707	Union of England and Scotland (they had been ruled by the same monarchs since 1603). Watts publishes his *Hymns and Spiritual Songs*
1712	Scottish Episcopal Church granted official toleration; patronage re-established in Scottish Presbyterianism
1715	Jacobite rebellion in Scotland
1719	Salters Hall debate regarding subscription to creeds; Presbyterians granted toleration in Ireland
1726	The American 'Great Awakening' begins
1733	Secession from the Church of Scotland over patronage
1735	Evangelical revival begins in Wales
1736	Joseph Butler, *Analogy of Religion*
1738	John and Charles Wesley experience evangelical conversion
1743	Reformed Presbyterian Church takes Covenanters out of Church of Scotland
1744	First Methodist Conference
1745–6	Another Jacobite uprising in Scotland
1761	Relief Church founded in Scotland
1770	New Connexion of General Baptists founded
1775–83	War of American Independence
1778	Catholic Relief Act
1780	Gordon riots; Robert Raikes commences a Sunday school in Gloucester; John Wesley, *Collection of Hymns for the Use of the People called Methodists*
1781	Countess of Huntingdon's Connexion becomes a Dissenting denomination
1784	First Methodist ordinations
1787	New Jerusalem Church founded

England and Wales

The legacy of James II's brief reign (1685–8) included a revival of popular anti-Catholicism in reaction to his own Catholic allegiance, the other side of the coin being the association of Protestantism with political liberty. Thus the 'Glorious Revolution' of 1688, which saw James flee the country and William III take the throne (Parliament had declared it vacant and offered it to the Dutchman William of Orange and his wife, James's daughter Mary), came to be celebrated as a divine deliverance, perhaps all the more because William landed in England on 5 November, the same day that the Gunpowder Plot had been foiled in 1605.

The Church of England, the bishops, and the state

Whereas the Council of Trent had sent Roman Catholic bishops back to their dioceses to concentrate on such tasks as fostering the practice of preaching, overseeing the clergy, and administrative reform, Anglican bishops of the early eighteenth century were noted for their absence from their dioceses. As members of the House of Lords, they were expected to spend at least seven months in London, and many remained there or in their country retreats for the rest of the year as well. When they did visit their dioceses, lack of time meant that they were obliged to conduct mass confirmations (often involving hundreds of candidates) and hasty ordinations. As well as non-residence, pluralism was rife among the episcopate, in part because the revenues of many sees were not sufficient to support them in the style which was expected by the society of which they were a part. It therefore became common for them to hold other offices, such as deanships or wealthy livings, in conjunction with their episcopal role.

Membership of the Lords meant that bishops were often heavily involved in government affairs, and successive governments were not immune to the temptation to appoint as bishops men who would be supportive of official policies and serviceable in their outworking (or as a reward for political services already rendered), nor to the widespread European trend to treat an established church as something akin to a department of state. Increasingly, it was ministers rather than the monarch, the nominal head of the church, who made the appointments. Nevertheless, a minority of bishops were distinguished for their pastoral approach and diligent attention to duty, most notable among them being Thomas Wilson (1663–1755), who was appointed Bishop of Sodor and Man in 1697 and remained in office until his death – a record for an Anglican bishop and a marked contrast to the usual pattern of seeking promotion to a more lucrative diocese.

Like bishop, like priest: pluralism was widespread among parish clergy, again at least in part because of economic necessity. Since it was usually impossible for them to fulfil their Sunday duties in all their livings, they relied on curates, who could be paid a pittance, to fill the gap. In part, this was a consequence of an over-supply in the clerical market. It was all too easy to obtain ordination (so long as the bishop could be tracked down), and a proportion of clergy were notorious for their lack of attention to duty (and worse). Most were poor, but there was also a minority who were able to live well, thanks to holding several lucrative benefices in plurality. Few were regarded as distinguished exponents of the art of pastoral care, but it must be said that many did their duty according to their lights.

This was the era when a two-party system emerged in English politics: the Tories, who upheld the divine right theory of monarchy and were strongly pro-Anglican, and the Whigs, who held a higher view of the role of Parliament in government and were considerably more open to religious toleration of Protestant Dissenters. It was paralleled by the development as distinct groupings of two parties in the Church of England, the high churchmen and the Latitudinarians. The high church outlook drew extensively on the tradition of spirituality established by the seventeenth-century Caroline divines such as Andrewes, Laud, and Taylor. The stimulus was, to a considerable extent, political: as a Dutch Calvinist and advocate of a measure of religious tolerance, William had no real sympathy for the high church outlook, whereas high churchmen believed that the Church could recapture its former dominant position by political action. Reacting against moves away from a narrowly confessional society, they therefore raised the cry of 'the Church in danger'. Since it was the Whigs who were the cause of concern, high churchmen tended to gravitate towards Toryism in politics. By contrast Latitudinarians (of whom more below) preferred the Whigs.

Not surprisingly, it was high churchmen who were largely responsible for the Church of England's slowness in adapting to the changing religious landscape, as much for political reasons as theological ones. In 1709 the high churchman Henry Sacheverell (1674–1724) notoriously described Dissenters as 'miscreants begat in rebellion, born in sedition, and nursed in faction'.[3] He was by no means alone in so thinking, as his considerable popularity showed. Nevertheless, high churchmanship soon came to be recognized as having a sacramental as well as a political dimension. The movement accordingly developed two wings: the 'two bottle orthodox' who gave it a reputation for worldliness and lack of spiritual vitality and the ascetic high churchmen who cultivated a deep spirituality in the Caroline tradition.

Events of 1688 had placed high Anglicans in an intolerable position. In Norman Sykes's words, 'at the Revolution the clergy were faced with the difficult dilemma of acquiescence in the destruction of Anglicanism by the

Popish ruler *divino jure*, or recantation of their theories of indefeasible hereditary right'.[4] From now on, it was an Act of Parliament rather than divine right which legitimized a monarch's rule. Anglicans had to decide whether to continue to acknowledge James II as the lawful occupant of the throne (even though he was a Roman Catholic) on the ground that they were bound by the oath of allegiance which they had sworn to him, or to swear allegiance to William III and in so doing effectively abjure their belief that the sovereign ruled by divine right. Many considered themselves bound by their oath to James, and the result of their refusal to swear allegiance to William was that they were deprived of their livings. They became known as the Non-Jurors, and among them were nine bishops and about four hundred clergy, including some of Anglicanism's best-known devotional writers. Even Archbishop Sancroft of Canterbury lost his position. Clergy and lay people who believed the deprived bishops still to be the lawful occupants of their offices followed them out of the Church of England.

Their rigidity made it impossible that the Non-Jurors would produce any significant creative theology, but they did contribute a great deal in the areas of liturgical scholarship (in particular, the quest to reconstruct the supposed primitive liturgy) and pastoral care and catechesis. Their movement did not die out until the beginning of the nineteenth century. Before that, they divided over several issues, among them the legitimacy of worshipping in their local parish church rather than remaining apart, aspects of communion ritual, and whether they had any grounds to remain in schism after the death of the last deprived bishop.

Perhaps the most widely read Non-Juror was the mystic William Law (1686–1761). His fame rested on two works, *Christian Perfection* (1726) and *A Serious Call to a Devout and Holy Life* (1728). Another was Thomas Ken (1637–1710), who had been Bishop of Winchester and whose hymns 'Awake, my soul, and with the sun' and 'Glory to thee, my God, this night' have remained in use throughout the English-speaking world.

At the opposite end of the spectrum from the Non-Jurors were the Latitudinarians, so called because of their willingness to tolerate greater latitude of opinion in theological matters than high churchmen or Puritans. For them, the Bible was to be interpreted according to the dictates of reason (rather than those of experience, which so often risked becoming 'enthusiasm', or of infallible ecclesiastical authorities), and the number of essential doctrines was minimized. Religion was as much about living a prudent and moral life in this world as it was about preparation for the next. Indeed, the former came to be seen as the preparation for the latter, and preaching tended to major on morality to the near-exclusion of more overtly doctrinal themes.

The most famous exponent of Latitudinarianism was John Tillotson

(1630–94). From a Puritan background, Tillotson's views had broadened out somewhat by the time he was appointed Archbishop of Canterbury in 1691, one of several Latitudinarians who filled vacancies left by the Non-Jurors. His significance lies in the fact that he has been regarded as the greatest of the Latitudinarian preachers. The burden of many of his sermons was practical morality, but it should be said in his defence that this was an age when churchmen of all shades perceived a catastrophic moral decline which threatened the foundations of society. Tillotson's sermons were frequently reprinted, and many parish clergy took to reading them from the pulpit instead of composing their own. In addition, their rational and almost dispassionate tone would have been welcomed by many who had tired of the fever-pitch of religious enthusiasm which marked the later Puritan period; it was a mode of communication which fitted in well with the temper of an enlightened age, and Dissenters as well as Scottish Presbyterians adopted it too. Puritan theology, therefore, suffered an eclipse in Anglican circles which lasted until the Evangelicals began to appear in numbers from the 1730s.

The events of 1688 had resulted in a widespread Erastianism, paralleling that evident elsewhere in Europe. Benjamin Hoadly (1676–1761), bishop of four successive dioceses, provoked what became known as the 'Bangorian controversy' (he was Bishop of Bangor at the time) by his defence of Erastianism and his inability to see any divine aspect to the constitution of the Church: for him, it was nothing more than a society of faithful men, which had no need of creeds, orders, or discipline to secure or shape its existence. His sermon before the king on John 18.36 ('My kingdom is not of this world') in 1717 was condemned as subversive of all external church government and discipline, but Hoadly claimed that he was referring to the invisible Church; he was rejecting authoritarian claims (such as were made by the Non-Jurors) to absolute obedience, and opposing the use of force rather than persuasion in religious matters. It is a reflection of the temper of the age that most of the response to him likewise rose no higher than viewing the Church as a necessary part of the socio-political establishment.

During this period we see the emergence of a range of voluntary bodies working alongside the Church in order to promote its objects of spiritual growth and social order. A number of small groups appeared, similar in organization and purpose to those deployed by the Pietists, although working with a somewhat different theology. The earliest societies appealed to literate workers dissatisfied with their spiritual condition; perhaps one reason for this was the power of self-determination which involvement in such groups gave them. Practical philanthropy found an outlet through these groups, as in the 'Holy Club' of which John Wesley was a member in 1730s Oxford, whose activities included visiting prisoners and the sick, as well as meeting to read the Greek New Testament and devotional works. Their progenitor in England was a German, Anthony Horneck, minister of the Anglican Savoy Chapel in London from 1671. Devoted to the study of the early Fathers, he nevertheless secured a hearing among the poor.

At the national level, the Society for the Reformation of Manners was founded in 1691, the Society for the Promotion of Christian Knowledge (SPCK) in 1698, and the Society for the Propagation of the Gospel in Foreign Parts (SPG) in 1701.[5] The SPCK focused on publishing, with the aim of 'promoting Religion and Learning in any part of His Majesty's Plantations abroad, and to provide Catechetical Libraries and free Schools in the parishes at home'.[6] However, it also developed a missionary thrust and benefited in both aspects of its work from close links with Halle Pietism.

One of the chief activities of the religious societies was, as the charter of the SPCK indicates, the establishment of charity schools. These were intended to educate the children of the poor, but not in such a way as to make them liable to challenge the social order: poverty was seen as a threat to the stability of society, and it seems to have been on that ground rather than any humanitarian one that many early schools were set up. Their main task was the teaching of reading; writing and arithmetic were less important, perhaps because the pupils were seen as occupying the station of passive receptors in society rather than being allowed a share in opinion-forming.

By 1750, the SPG had established over 1,500 such schools in England alone. Even this, however, was eclipsed by the achievements of the dyspeptic Griffith Jones (1684–1761), from 1716 rector of Llandowror in West Wales. He devised a system of 'circulating schools', by means of which adults as well as children were taught through short (up to three-month) courses, mostly during the winter, when agricultural work was slack. Jones's success was due in part to the fact that the schools were conducted in Welsh (except in English-speaking Pembrokeshire). One of his arguments for doing so was that English was an immoral language and ill-suited as a vehicle for the gospel, an understandable verdict in the light of the character of Restoration drama, for instance. By his death 3,325 such schools had been conducted, and upwards of 150,000 people (of a total population of 4–500,000) had learned to read. This provided a huge audience for evangelistic literature, and the relaxation in 1695 of printing restrictions had allowed presses to be set up outside London, thus facilitating the production of Welsh-language material.

From the middle of the century charity schools began to disappear, to be replaced from 1769 by Sunday schools. (It would be interesting to explore the extent to which this was related to the rise of the Industrial Revolution, which brought in its train a rapid urbanization and consequent social instability in many areas, challenging the prevailing culture of deference in which the charity schools were rooted.) Robert Raikes of Gloucester, traditionally seen as the founder of Sunday schools, ran them from 8 a.m. until 8 p.m., with breaks for church attendance.[7]

'Old Dissent'

This is the name given to those denominations whose origins pre-date the 'Evangelical Awakening' of the 1730s. It is normally seen as comprising Baptists, Independents, Presbyterians, Quakers, and Unitarians (though the last did not become a separate denomination until the nineteenth century); the first three co-operated in relating to government through the Protestant Dissenting Deputies, founded in 1732.

Repression had not worked, and was now regarded as irrational, even fanatical; toleration was therefore the 'in' approach. The 1689 Toleration Act represented an attempt to win back moderate Dissenters to the Establishment, or at least to unite Protestants in resisting any attempts by James II to regain his throne; it was followed by the suspension and ultimate repeal of much of the penal legislation passed under Charles II.[8] Dissenters were now allowed to worship in premises registered for the purpose, so long as they took the oaths of Supremacy and Allegiance, made a declaration against transubstantiation, and their ministers affirmed all the Thirty-Nine Articles except those dealing with questions of church government. (Quakers were able to avoid swearing the oaths and to make a general declaration of belief rather than subscribing to the Thirty-Nine Articles.) However, the result was the opposite of what was intended – an explosion of chapel-building as congregations came out of hiding and began to worship openly. This was partly because Parliament had rejected a Comprehension Act which was intended to complement the Toleration Act, setting out the requirements for Dissenters who wished to conform to the Church of England, and so the Toleration Act had to be applied to a much larger community than had been intended. By 1718 there were about two thousand congregations in existence, and many more licences had been taken out for Dissenting worship.

Occasional conformity (that is, reception of communion in the Church of England) appears to have been quite widespread early in the eighteenth century, especially among Presbyterians, who had not entirely forgotten their aspirations to become England's national church during the Civil War period. For some it would simply have been a means to the end of holding public office; but for others it represented a testimony to their acceptance of the Church of England as a reformed community. For a steady trickle, however, conformity to the Church of England became a permanent thing as they moved from Dissent to the Establishment. From

1710 to 1714 a Tory government sought to put an end to the practice of occasional conformity, but the Whig dominance of government from 1714–60 allowed Dissenters a long political breathing space (apart from the Quakers, whose refusal to bear arms or pay tithes caused them to be regarded with suspicion).

Instances continued to occur of mob violence directed at Dissenting meeting-houses (as, for example, in May–June 1715, when over forty were damaged, almost all of them Presbyterian[9]). For the most part, however, Dissenters were allowed to continue their existence as 'the quiet in the land' and the laws against them were not consistently enforced. In spite of the number of chapels being built the actual size of the Dissenting community began to shrink, as English Dissenters suffered something of a loss of momentum. On one hand they no longer had to struggle to survive, as systematic persecution had become a thing of the past; on the other hand they had lost something of their initial vision to see the whole of society won to their views, having settled for what, in modern terms, might be described as a mentality of maintenance rather than mission. For those who were happy to accept that they were second-class citizens, still subject to certain legal disabilities, accommodation to society and the world soon followed. This, as much as their separatist outlook or the prevalence of high Calvinism and rationalism, made Dissenters slow to accept responsibility for those outside their congregations; certainly ecclesiological separatism had not hindered them from engaging in vigorous evangelism during the Civil War period.

Dissenting worship gave pride of place to preaching, as Puritan worship had before it. Meeting-houses were designed to focus on the pulpit and to ensure maximum audibility and visibility for the preacher by the use of devices such as galleries round three sides of the building and the use of plain glass in the windows (Anglican church-building during this period followed similar lines). This was the Enlightenment in architectural form.

In the field of hymnody Dissenters led the way; not for at least a century would Anglicans catch up with them. The Reformed tradition had tended to see the Psalms (and other portions of Scripture) as the only suitable hymnody for the Church, since they were divinely inspired. To be sung congregationally they had to be put into metrical form as Dissenters rejected the Anglican practice of chanting (in any case, the latter excluded the congregation and was carried on by the parson and his clerk). A succession of English-language metrical psalters had appeared from the 1560s, but few of their versions were of any great poetic merit. A few Dissenters, such as the Particular Baptist[10] Benjamin Keach (1640–1704), pioneered the use of hymns as responses to the sermon, but it was a young Independent named Isaac Watts (1674–1748) who took metrical psalmody and hymnody out of obscurity by producing versions of sufficient merit to remain in use, some until today. In 1707 he published his first collection, *Hymns and Spiritual Songs*. Several others followed, including his *Psalms of David imitated in the language of the New Testament* (1719): as in the early centuries of the Church, treating the Old Testament as pointing forward to Christ was seen as the only way of legitimizing its continued use by Christians. Watts's versions were a great success and his collections became the staple diet of Independents, Particular Baptists, and Presbyterians until the mid-nineteenth century.

While Dissenting hymnody ranged over the full compass of Christian theology, some of its most striking content concerned the doctrine of the Church, portraying it as a body of believers called out from the world by God. Belief in this 'gathered church' entailed the practice of church discipline, the objective of which was primarily to maintain the purity of the congregation, and secondarily to reclaim the offender. Discipline could involve a private or public rebuke from the minister, or (more seriously) suspension from membership and from the privilege of participating in the Lord's Supper, either for a set period or permanently. Offences calling for discipline included a wide range of misconduct: drunkenness, sexual immorality, marrying a non-believer, advocating erroneous doctrine, and causing dissension within the congregation. Whereas discipline in the Church of England lessened in both severity and frequency during this century, it remained a significant feature of dissenting life. Dissenters took sin as seriously as other aspects of their faith.

The contemporary trend towards a measure of doctrinal indifference did not leave Dissent untouched. Since Dissenters were excluded from Oxford and Cambridge by the requirement to subscribe to the Thirty-Nine Articles, they began to set up alternative institutions, the academies, to train future ministers and also to educate the sons of members. At their best, these institutions were able to offer an education more rigorous than that which the universities were providing, and several future Anglican leaders were trained in them (such as Bishop Butler). Later in the eighteenth century the academies gradually disappeared. Baptists and Independents were setting up their own colleges in the wake of the Evangelical Revival, and Presbyterians (now largely Unitarian in belief) saw fewer ministerial candidates coming forward.

But before that, these institutions had helped to introduce new theological currents into Dissenting life, with divisive results. They encouraged an adventurous questioning and frequently also a refusal to be bound by denominational confessions of faith. In particular, the new emphasis on the role of reason in theology led to controversy regarding the doctrine of the Trinity. Socinian views[11] had first appeared in England during the turbulent 1640s, propagated by John Biddle (1615–62), who has therefore been acclaimed as the father of English Unitarianism. In the eighteenth century, however, it was an Arian approach which was more influential: this acknowledged Christ as pre-existent and as divine in some sense and therefore to be worshipped, although not equal with the Father, as well as retaining the idea of Christ's death as atoning for sin. (Socinians tended to deny these things.)

Strictly speaking, non-Trinitarians were excluded from the provisions of the Toleration Act, but in practice little action was taken against them. Debate on the issue affected Anglicans as well as Dissenters: in 1712, the clergyman Samuel Clarke (1675–1729) published *The Scripture Doctrine of the Trinity*, which argued that only God the Father could properly be called God, since the Son and the Spirit derived their existence from him and so were neither co-equal nor co-eternal with him. While the orthodox theologian Daniel Waterland (1683–1740) issued a series of responses to such views, Dissent was to be deeply divided by them.

In 1719 a debate took place at Salters' Hall, London, regarding the matter of subscription to confessions of faith. It was convened in response to a request from ministers in Devon and Cornwall, and involved Presbyterians, Independents, and Baptists. While orthodox Trinitarians were found on both sides, the result of the debate was that by the end of the century, the great majority of English Presbyterian congregations, along with most General Baptists, became Unitarian. In Ulster, parallel developments led to the formation of a 'Non-Subscribing' presbytery (that is, not subscribing to the *Westminster Confession*, the standard Presbyterian confession of faith) in Antrim in 1726.

The issue did not go away entirely: the 'Feathers Tavern Petition' of 1771 called for Anglican clerical subscription to the Thirty-Nine Articles to be replaced by a general acknowledgement of the Bible as the source of revealed truth. This was rejected by Parliament, resulting in 1773 in the secession of Theophilus Lindsey, who set up his own Unitarian congregation, meeting in Essex Chapel, just off the Strand in London.

At this point, we need to survey the state of the main Dissenting denominations. Estimates of their strength for England during the period 1715–18 are given in Table 5.1.

Table 5.1: Dissenting denominations, 1715–18.

	Congregations	Adherents (000s)
Presbyterian	637	179
Independent	203	60
General Baptist	122	19
Particular Baptist	206	40
Seventh-Day Baptist	5	0
Quaker	672	40
Total	1845	339

Of the total population of England, about 6.2 per cent belonged to a Dissenting congregation; the proportion for Wales appears to have been slightly lower, at 5.74 per cent.[12]

General Baptists were riven by controversy during the first half of this period before sinking into a quiet decline during the second half. Apart from bitter disputes in the 1690s over the legitimacy of singing in gatherings for worship (opponents feared encouraging the unconverted to sing a lie by taking onto their lips words intended for believers, and also argued that the use of pre-composed words limited the Spirit just as much as the use of pre-composed liturgical prayers), debates about Christology and the doctrine of the Trinity caused major problems for the denomination after the Toleration Act allowed it to resume a more public existence. It was Matthew Caffyn (1628–1715), a farmer and pastor from Horsham who also served the Kent and Sussex churches as a Messenger (itinerant church-planter and representative in the denomination's assembly), who lit the fuse. It was alleged that he denied that Christ had the same nature as the Father, but also that he denied that Christ's humanity was the same as ours.[13] While many, especially from the inland churches whose origins owed more to Lollardy than to Anabaptism, rejected Caffyn's views as heresy, the denomination divided from 1704 to 1731, and when it reunited no move was made to exclude such views. Coupled with reluctance on the part of some General Baptists to grant any authority to creeds and confessions or to use theological terms not found in Scripture, the way was open for a biblicist Unitarianism (different in ethos to the more philosophically orientated Unitarianism which became widespread during the nineteenth century) to take root among them. This was facilitated by the loss of the movement's early leaders and the low estimation which it placed upon theological training (which meant that ministers were not aware of the Christian theological tradition).

Particular Baptists also tended to lose their evangelistic impetus. In this case, however, the cause was not Arianism or Socinianism but high Calvinism. This was a version of Reformed theology which laid such stress on the divine decrees of election to salvation or damnation that it left little room for a parallel insistence on human responsibility. Thus high Calvinists tended to disapprove of exhorting sinners to turn to Christ and denied that it was the duty of each individual to repent and believe ('the Modern Question' as the issue was called). Key leaders were three London pastors, John Skepp (d. 1721), John Brine (1703–65), and John Gill (1697–1771), although their ideas had mostly been derived from non-Baptist sources. The result was to reinforce Particular Baptist preoccupation with internal affairs at a time when Methodism and other forms of Evangelicalism were coming upon the scene, and so to lessen the benefit which the denomination reaped from the awakenings. However, away from London the effect was less marked; especially after the middle of the century, a succession of outward-looking and activist ministers were trained by the academy at Bristol, who engaged in vigorous church-planting in various parts of England.

In spite of the failure of the 'happy union' between Presbyterians and Independents (1691–4) in London, there came to be relatively little visible difference between the two polities: the elaborate structure of presbyteries and synods which evolved north of the border was lacking in England. All the same, it took a while for some English Presbyterians to leave behind the idea that they represented an alternative national church and to adopt the more sectarian mentality which characterized the Independents and the Baptists, who both stressed the idea of the Church as a gathered community. Evidence of this is that Presbyterians, unlike Independents and Baptists, did not require a profession of faith from those wishing to join them, and that they made less use than the others of the mechanism of church discipline to reclaim erring members. Their very breadth of outlook may have rendered them more susceptible to doctrinal change: as with the General Baptists, many Presbyterian congregations (and some Independents) became Unitarian during the course of the century. Unitarians were untouched by Evangelicalism, and experienced a fairly consistent decline through the century.

As for the Quakers, the bizarre exhibitions of early days were gone, individual inspiration giving way in large measure to a stress on conforming to the behavioural norms of the group. Quakers became known for their distinctive forms of dress as well as their refusal to use the polite 'you' in speech, preferring the more familiar 'thee' for all, rich and poor alike. They also established a reputation in various commercial fields, notably banking (the Lloyds and the Barclays). Unlike more established Dissenting denominations, Quakers allowed women to contribute audibly during their meetings for worship although even they stopped short of granting equality to women in the conduct of the business of the congregation.

A few new sects appeared during this period but gained little apart from notoriety. The best-known new group, however (apart from the Methodists, whom we shall look at in the next chapter), was the New Jerusalem Church of the Swedish scientist and mystic Emmanuel Swedenborg (1688–1772), which exists today as the 'New Church'. This was founded as a separate body in London in 1787, although Swedenborg had originally intended that his followers remain in their existing churches. His leading idea was that the physical universe is structured on spiritual principles (his philosophical system has been compared to Neoplatonism) and from the 1740s he began to experience visions and a sense of divine commission to spread his teachings. Perhaps the most famous exponent of some of these ideas was the poet and artist William Blake (1757–1827); they also influenced Romantic thinkers and nineteenth-century Spiritualists.

The Roman Catholic community

There were parallels between Catholics and Dissenters in their position as outsiders (Charles II and James II had tried to capitalize on this in the late seventeenth century, by granting concessions to Dissent which would also have benefited the Catholic community). However, while Dissenters experienced a relaxation of official pressure, the screw continued to be tightened on the Catholic community (although application of penal legislation was patchy and dependent in part on the extent to which Catholics were seen as fitting into the local scene). In 1692, they became subject to a double land tax, and in 1695 they were excluded from much of the legal profession. Papal support for the exiled house of Stuart, which did not end until 1765 with the death of James III, ensured that Catholics were linked with Jacobitism and therefore regarded as a potential threat to the stability of the British throne. That the Catholic community was able to continue its existence relatively untroubled was due in considerable measure to the eighteenth century's espousal of the virtue of toleration and the distaste felt by many for the penal laws, which relied largely on paying informers for their operation. (Informers ceased to be used after 1781.) At the local level, therefore, Catholic landowners were able to fit into the social network; to their neighbours they were usually English first and Catholic second. The Gordon Riots of 1780, which represented an outburst of opposition to the 1778 Relief Act removing some of the disabilities under which Catholics laboured, left about three hundred dead in London, but even this failed to cause more than a temporary halt to Catholic progress.

In 1700 there were perhaps 60–70,000 Roman Catholics in England, many concentrated in the north-west, where the Reformation had made only partial headway. The community continued to grow slowly, especially among the urban middle classes, and there was a steady trickle of conversions to Catholicism. By 1767 an estimated 40 per cent of English Catholics, whose numbers were now approaching 80,000, were to be found in Lancashire, with other sizeable communities in Yorkshire, Durham, Northumberland, the West Midlands, London, Sussex, and Hampshire.

Gradually the centre of gravity shifted from the country gentry to the urban middle classes. There were several reasons for this. Among them were the fact that a number of gentry families either died out or converted to Protestantism, and the growth of toleration, which lessened the need for safe houses and made it possible for Catholics to practise their faith more openly. A number of chapels attached to foreign embassies in London led the way, since their services were open to all who wished to attend. From 1791, a further Relief Act allowed Catholics to worship in registered buildings (though these were not allowed to be topped by a spire).

A key leader during this period was Richard Challoner (1691–1781).[14] He taught at the English Seminary in Douai before being consecrated a bishop in 1739. In 1758 he was assigned to the London District (one of four into which England was divided) as Vicar Apostolic. His devotional work, *The Garden of the Soul,* nourished the restrained spirituality of English Catholics for over a century.

Scotland

The final establishment of Presbyterianism

With the Act of Union (1707), the Church and the legal system became the bearers of Scottish national identity. However, it was only in 1690 that Presbyterianism had finally been established as the lawful form of church government in Scotland, and many clergy of Episcopalian sympathies remained in country parishes. In practical terms, large parts of the Highlands remained to be conquered for the Presbyterian cause. This was mostly accomplished from the 1730s, to the extent that Highland Presbyterianism has since become known as the bearer of what originated as Lowland religious traditions. Initially, the attempts of the Scottish Society for the Promotion of Christian Knowledge, which was seen as pro-English, to win over Gaelic-speaking Highlanders were rejected as an intrusion. Some Presbyterian ministers received rough justice from the communities to which they were sent, one being stripped naked and tied to a tree in the height of the midge season! However, from the 1730s the Reformed faith made rapid headway, thanks in part to 'The Men', lay elders who assisted the minister in pastoral care and instruction, and who assumed an important role as (among other things) arbiters of who should be admitted to communion. They were key agents in the transmission of Evangelicalism throughout much of the Highlands, which was what finally secured the area for the Kirk. The result was that the scholastic Calvinism of the *Westminster Confession* became an integral part of popular religious culture and shaped the experiential expression of faith, whereas in much of Europe movements of affective devotion amounted to reactions against confessionalism.

All the same, the stranglehold of Moderatism (the theological outlook of those influenced by Enlightenment thought, which was akin to English Latitudinarianism) on the Kirk's higher reaches was not matched by widespread allegiance at parish level. Many ministers were Evangelicals and many congregations were unsympathetic to Moderate views. The problem was that the Moderates, as the party of culture in Presbyterian ministry (during the eighteenth century Scotland was at the heart of the European Enlightenment network), were too entangled with the aristocracy and gentry who made up the bulk of the patrons of parish livings to be able to get at all close to the majority of their flock, and too concerned to play their part in the international cultural network to be able to preach in a way which the common people could hear gladly. While the Moderates did not question the *Westminster Confession* (at least, not directly and in public), neither did they preach on the understanding of salvation which it set forth; their preaching tended towards the kind of moralism which was seen as supporting the established social order, and those who wanted food for their souls often found themselves forced to resort to other expedients.

Inevitably tensions between Moderate and Evangelical led to schism. Thomas Carlyle's dictum that 'all Dissent in Scotland is merely a stricter adherence to the National Kirk in all points'[15] is no longer true, but it certainly was the case until the end of the eighteenth century, as groups seceded in protest at what they saw as the Kirk's failure to maintain its original principles.

An evangelical secession from the Church of Scotland took place in 1733, led by Ralph and Ebenezer Erskine. Although the trigger was the issue of patronage (who had the right to appoint a new minister to a parish),[16] the impetus to secession had built up over preceding years as a result of a debate about the nature of the gospel. The Erskines and their sympathizers were aggrieved that the General Assembly (the Church of Scotland's chief governing body) had dealt leniently in 1717 with George Simson, an incoming divinity professor at Glasgow University who had been accused of heresy, whereas it had been much harsher in its treatment of the 'Marrow Men', a group of proto-Evangelicals led by Thomas Boston of Ettrick (1676–1732), who subscribed to the revision of Calvinist doctrine expounded in *The Marrow of Modern Divinity* (reprinted in 1720). To some extent, there were similarities with the controversy over high Calvinist views which beset English Particular Baptists and Independents, but in Scotland confessional Calvinists united with the Moderates to oppose such teaching on the grounds of alleged antinomianism.

Adherents of the Covenanting tradition, which was rooted in the seventeenth-century struggles against the imposition of episcopacy on the Scottish church, found it hard to accept the changed realities of church–state relations which ensued from the Glorious Revolution and the Act of Union. For them, the state should be covenanted to uphold Christ's Reformed religion. In 1743, therefore, the Reformed Presbyterian Church was constituted, embracing those who since 1690 had withdrawn from the Church of Scotland.

Several further schisms followed within a short space of time. When the 1745 rebellion in support of James II's grandson Charles Edward Stuart necessitated the formation of bodies of men for purposes of local defence, an oath of allegiance was imposed on burgesses, requiring them to acknowledge and uphold the established religion of the country (that is, Presbyterianism, in contrast to the Episcopalianism or Catholicism of the Jacobites). The result was a schism in 1747 within the Secession Church between those who were prepared to swear the oath (Burghers) and those who were not (Anti-Burghers), as the latter excommunicated the former.

Another secession provoked by patronage issues followed in 1761 when Thomas Gillespie led a group which became known as the Relief Church. By 1766 Presbyterian Dissenters had an estimated 120 places of worship, with as many as 100,000 attenders.

The Scottish Episcopal Church

Episcopalianism in Scotland found itself marginalized in the wake of the 'Glorious Revolution'. The bishops could not swear allegiance to William III because they held themselves bound by their oath to James II; like the English Non-Jurors, they were deprived of their incomes and retired from public work. On the other hand, the Presbyterianism of the Church of Scotland was definitively acknowledged by the civil authorities, thus ending over a century of see-sawing between the two systems of church government. (The Episcopal Church was, however, granted official toleration in an act of 1712.) Episcopalians at this stage were concentrated in the Highlands and the north-east. Many were ejected from Church of Scotland livings and developed a marked sympathy for the Jacobite cause, which was to cause the Episcopal Church problems throughout the eighteenth century. Nevertheless, it did not moulder, and in 1764 there appeared a fine eucharistic liturgy which has exercised a considerable influence on its successors down to the present. Formally organized in 1766, the Episcopal Church made its peace with George III in 1792.

Ireland

Although James II had mounted military action in Ireland as part of his campaign to recover the English throne, he was finally driven out in 1691. But Stuart hopes, papal support, and Protestant memories of the massacres they had suffered in 1641 combined to make repressive parliamentary legislation inevitable. In 1691 the imposition of oaths abjuring transubstantiation and the power of popes to depose temporal rulers effectively excluded Roman Catholics from becoming Irish MPs; in 1695 they were disarmed; in 1703 primogeniture was outlawed for Catholic families and they were banned from purchasing or taking long leases on land, thus contributing to a decline in the proportion of Irish land held by Catholics from 22 per cent in 1689 to 5 per cent by the late 1770s. Finally, in 1728 they lost the right to vote. Between 1703 and 1789 an estimated 5,500 Catholics converted to the established church in order to avoid suffering discrimination, although many continued to practise their former faith at home. However, as in England, the legislation was not consistently enforced. In spite of these measures, the Protestant population actually declined during the eighteenth century. For some, emigration proved an attractive proposition; others were lost to Protestantism through inter-marriage with Roman Catholics, or because the Church of Ireland clergy lacked the pastoral diligence of the Catholic priesthood.

The Church of Ireland saw itself as catering to the 'New English', those who had settled there from the sixteenth century and who owned the broadly Protestant and culturally refined values of eighteenth-century London. It was strongest in the north and around Dublin, and suffered many of the same problems as the contemporary Church of England.

During the early eighteenth century the greatest challenge facing it was Presbyterianism. This was concentrated in Ulster, and the nucleus of the Presbyterian population was formed by descendants of Scottish settlers who had been granted land in Ireland by James VI/I. Many held views which would later be denominated evangelical, and the 'commun-ion seasons' had seen local religious awakenings from 1625 onwards, although we have also noted that controversy over creedal subscription occurred in Ireland. Presbyterians, while tardily and reluctantly granted toleration in 1719, were effectively barred from holding public office until 1780 by the imposition of the requirement to receive communion in the Church of Ireland, a test directed in the first instance against Roman Catholics.

Christianity in the New World

Between 1660 and 1760 the number of colonial settlers in North America increased from 25,000 to almost 1.6 million. Even at this early stage the plurality of denominations, ethnic origins, and religious outlooks is the most striking feature of North American Protestantism. Among those emigrating to the New World for religious reasons there were Lutherans from Salzburg, Baptists from North Germany (the Church of the Brethren, which had been founded in 1708), Schwenckfelders (a group owing their origins to the radical reformer Caspar Schwenckfeld (1490–1561)) from Silesia and Prussia, Moravians from Central Europe, Calvinists and Mennonites from South Germany and Holland, Huguenots from France, Dissenters of all types from Britain, and Presbyterians from Scotland and

Ulster. Some of these groups had already been influenced by Pietism, while others fell under such influences after arriving.

It is also important to note the established status of different forms of Protestantism in different regions. Congregationalism in Massachusetts enjoyed such a status until 1833. At first sight it may seem strange that Congregationalists, who believed in the ideal of the 'gathered church' (that is, one composed of believers gathered together by God out of the world), should be found practising the establishment of Christianity. However, many Congregationalists had retained something of the idea of establishment which Anglicanism had bequeathed to their first generation via the Puritan movement, and which found brief expression in the period of the English Civil War.

Elsewhere Roman Catholicism was briefly established in Maryland around the mid-seventeenth century, and by the 1690s the Church of England had become the established church in Virginia, North and South Carolina, Georgia, Maryland, and parts of New York. But it could not replicate the close supervision of community life which it sought to exercise in England. For one thing, parishes were vast, sometimes hundreds of square miles; for another, the British Parliament refused to allow the consecration of bishops for the colonies for political reasons. Thus there was a shortage of clergy (allowing the laity to play a more prominent role in church government). Some of the clergy who did minister in the Church had been failures back home for various reasons, and their misconduct helped to lower the estimation in which Anglican clergy as a body were held.

By contrast religious tolerance received its fullest expression in the state of Pennsylvania. This owed its origins to the British Quaker William Penn (1644–1718): in 1681 he was given a large tract of land by Charles II in settlement of a debt owed to his father. Here he set up a new social order, which he promoted vigorously in Europe. The result was the accession of a number of Protestant minorities of various types. By contrast with other American colonies, none was numerically large enough to dominate religious life, and so they had to learn to live together, not merely as a practical necessity but because this was something which Penn in any case advocated in principle.

As far as the Native American population was concerned, there was relatively little missionary vision among the colonists; the Puritans, for example, equated the indigenous population to the biblical Canaanites, to be dispossessed by themselves as the new Israel. However, there were exceptions and modifications to this approach. John Eliot (1604–90), a Puritan refugee from England, became known as the 'apostle to the Indians' because of his pioneering work among Native Americans in Massachusetts. His strategy involved the gathering of converts into 'praying towns' from 1651, which he found to be the only effective way of making and keeping converts; these were intended as imitations of Puritan settlements. Several thousand converts had been so gathered by 1675 but war between whites and Native Americans virtually decimated them. Eliot co-edited the *Bay Psalm Book* (1640), the first book to be printed in North America, and his translation of the Bible into Algonquian (1663) was the first translation into a Native American language. His activity led to the founding of the first English mission society, the Society for the Propagation of the Gospel in New England (1649), which was based in London but whose funds were applied to work across the Atlantic. The Presbyterian David Brainerd (1718–47), whose published diary would influence the English missionary pioneers William Carey and Henry Martyn, was supported by the Scottish Society for the Promotion of Christian Knowledge and worked among Native Americans in the Middle Colonies (those between New England and the South). His influence sprang from the fact that his missionary diary was edited into 'a heroic memoir and inspirational guidebook'[17] by his fiancée's father, the theologian Jonathan Edwards (of whom more in the next chapter). However, few Protestant missionaries achieved much success, and their influence lay more in their status as heroic examples for later generations of American Evangelicals. More successful were the Catholic missions in Canada, in which French missionaries (including Jesuits, who had a developed tradition of engagement with indigenous cultures) took a leading role.

Somewhat less concern appears to have been shown for the slave community; some plantation owners sought to prevent the preaching of Christianity among their slaves because of fears that it would encourage insubordination; some allowed it in the belief that it would inculcate the virtues of hard work and submission to authority; but few at this stage questioned its legitimacy as an institution until after the American Revolution, when the inconsistency of protesting against British tyranny and continuing to allow what amounted to tyranny over the slave population was gradually realized. One Christian leader who did protest was the Quaker John Woolman (1720–72); he not only argued against slavery (and against war) but insisted on paying slaves for any service he received from them and ultimately boycotted any food products known to have been produced by slave labour, such as sugar. Only slowly did black slaves turn to Christianity, not least because the slave-holding system had created an antagonism to Christianity which reinforced their allegiance to African religious traditions, but the first black-led churches were founded from the 1770s after the Great Awakening which began in 1734 had stimulated a concern to evangelize the slave population. By 1793, Christianity was strong enough among the black population of Nova Scotia in Canada (former slaves who had fought for the British during the War of Independence and been granted rather inhospitable tracts of land in return) for a group of Baptists to share in founding the West African state of Sierra Leone.

The Revolution of 1776 cannot be discussed in detail here, but it is important to consider it in relation to the churches. The importance of religion was acknowledged in all 13 founding states, so this could not be denied at a national level; but neither was it possible to establish one form of Protestant religion to the exclusion of others. So, as Noll has pointed out, the issue was ducked when the First Amendment was passed in 1791, which laid down that Congress would make no laws establishing or prohibiting a particular form of religion. In that way the buck could be passed to the state legislative bodies. But the national legislators were not thereby countenancing a secular society so much as regarding those principles held in common by all Protestants as axiomatic and not in need of restatement.[18] Denominationally speaking, as a very general rule, the closer a denomination was to the English establishment, the more likely it was to oppose American independence (although it should be noted that American Methodists were considerably less establishment-orientated than British ones).

Some writers have sought to argue that the United States was founded as a Christian country; underlying this is usually the desire to see it governed according to a particular understanding of Christianity associated with the 'religious Right'. It is certainly true that some seventeenth-century settlements were founded for religious reasons, especially in New England (Puritan), Pennsylvania (Quaker, upholding religious freedom), and Maryland (Roman Catholic). The Puritans saw their settlements in America as 'a city set on a hill', as famously expressed by John Winthrop in 1630. We have seen that many religious refugees from various parts of Europe also settled in North America, bringing with them their ancestral faith and so adding to the denominational mix. However, the majority of settlements, while acknowledging the role of religion, were founded for other reasons, especially economic ones. While the struggle for independence may have derived strength from the tendency to see it in cosmic terms derived from the Puritan belief in America's special vocation, it is probably more accurate to see the Declaration of Independence as offering formal sanction to what has often been called 'civil religion', a concept which has become broad enough to include the Jewish community, and Roman Catholics too, in so far as their loyalty to the American way could be demonstrated (and we shall see that this was not always the case). Thomas Jefferson (1743–1826), for example, did not believe in the divinity of Christ and rejected the supernatural elements of Christianity; for him, it was the ethical dimension which was of abiding (and practical) relevance. The public religious outlook of the Founding Fathers was closer to Deism than to anything else, although a number of them were in private devout and orthodox Christians. It drew on a range of classical as well as Christian sources for its inspiration, and aimed to establish the state on secular principles which would be acceptable (and self-evidently reasonable) to all. The corollary was the separation of church and state.

Anticlericalism was not a feature of the American Revolution in the way that it was to be in France, even though both movements were heavily indebted to the Enlightenment tradition with its criticisms of 'priestcraft' and the dominance of the churches in public life and intellectual discourse. A key reason for this was that the form of Enlightenment thought which became popular in North America was heavily Christianized, having been mediated through a group of eighteenth-century Scottish philosophers known as the 'Common Sense' school. Its main argument was that an accurate knowledge of the external world was possible for anyone who made responsible use of their senses; similarly, basic moral principles could be known be means of an innate moral sense.[19] Its confidence in the power of rational argument was to leave a deep mark on North American Evangelicalism which has persisted until today.

In Canada, Roman Catholics were granted freedom of religious worship and the right of political participation from 1774, a concession to the French population of Quebec which went beyond anything hitherto granted in Britain and Ireland. It is also noticeable that although the British had only taken over Quebec in 1763, it got a Catholic bishop as early as 1766, whereas the Americans had to wait until 1784 for an Anglican one (and then it was through the offices of the Scottish Episcopal Church rather than the Church of England; the first colonial Church of England bishop was consecrated in 1786 for Canada).[20] Not surprisingly, Catholics as well as Protestants tended to favour the British during the War of Independence. Protestant ranks were greatly augmented by Loyalists who had left the 13 colonies which became the United States. Thus Canada did not separate church and state but sought to recognize the pluralism which existed within its bounds by securing the rights of religious minorities.

Certain recurrent themes can be discerned in the material we have covered, most notably the shift from religious uniformity to a measure of pluralism, and the impact of Enlightenment thought both in theology and in state attitudes towards the churches. Another important theme is covered in the next chapter: the development and pervasive influence of Evangelicalism.

Questions for thought

1 How fair do you think it was to write off the eighteenth-century Church of England? What would your assessment of it be, and what evidence would you offer to support your argument?

2 Was early eighteenth-century Dissent more or less effective than the Church of England at ministering to the people?

3 What similarities do you notice between theological developments in Britain and those in the rest of Europe during the first half of the eighteenth century? Why do you think Catholicism in Britain was virtually unaffected by these changes?

4 Why do you think that most secessions from the Church of Scotland remained recognizably Presbyterian, whereas secessions from the Church of England during the seventeenth and eighteenth centuries did not usually remain recognizably Anglican?

5 In what ways did the early appearance of a plurality of Christian traditions shape the public role of religion in North America?

6 What comparisons do you notice between the effect of the Enlightenment in Britain and that in North America?

Further reading

John Bossy, 1975, *The English Catholic Community 1570–1850*, London: Darton, Longman & Todd, part 2.

Callum G. Brown, 1997, *Religion and Society in Scotland since 1707*, Edinburgh: Edinburgh University Press, chs 1–4.

Horton Davies, 1961, *Worship and Theology in England: From Watts and Wesley to Maurice, 1690–1850*, Princeton, NJ: Princeton University Press, parts 1–2.

Andrew L. Drummond and James Bulloch, 1973, *The Scottish Church 1688–1843: The Age of the Moderates*, Edinburgh: St Andrew Press, chs 1–5.

William Gibson, 1998, *Religion and Society in England and Wales 1689–1800*, London and Washington: Leicester University Press (extensive collection of primary source extracts).

Sheridan Gilley and W. J. Sheils (eds), 1994, *A History of Religion in Britain*, Oxford: Blackwell, chs 9–12.

Robert T. Handy, 1976, *A History of the Churches in the United States and Canada*, Oxford History of the Christian Church, Oxford: Clarendon, chs 2–5.

Kenneth Hylson-Smith, 1997, *The Churches in England from Elizabeth I to Elizabeth II*, vol. 2: *1689–1833*, London: SCM Press, parts 1–2.

Mark A. Noll, 1992, *A History of Christianity in the United States and Canada*, London: SPCK, part 2.

Edward Norman, 1986, *Roman Catholicism in England: From the Elizabethan Settlement to the Second Vatican Council*, Oxford: Oxford University Press, ch. 2.

Gordon Rupp, 1986, *Religion in England 1688–1791*, Oxford History of the Christian Church, Oxford: Clarendon.

Alan P. F. Sell (ed.), 2006, *Protestant Nonconformist Texts*, vol. 2: *The Eighteenth Century*, Aldershot: Ashgate.

Michael Watts, 1978, *The Dissenters: From the Reformation to the French Revolution*, Oxford: Clarendon, parts 4–5.

Notes

1 Rupp, *Religion in England*, p. 290.

2 For an accessible overview of the issues, see Hylson-Smith, *Churches in England II*, ch. 3.

3 H. Sacheverell, 1709, *The Perils of False Brethren in Church and State*, p. 36, quoted by Watts, *Dissenters*, p. 263. A hundred thousand copies of Sacheverell's sermon were printed, and the storm which it provoked led to his being impeached.

4 Norman Sykes, 1930, *Church and State in England in the Eighteenth Century*, London: Historical Association, p. 2.

5 For the origins, objectives, and early history of the SPG (now USPG), see its website at: http://www.uspg.org.uk/our_work/about_history.php; and for the SPCK, see: http://www.spck.org.uk/about_spck/history.php.

6 J. McLeod Campbell, 1946, *Christian History in the Making*, p. 35; quoted by J.R.H. Moorman, 1973, *A History of the Church in England*, 3rd edn, London: Adam & Charles Black, p. 267. Bray founded over eighty parish libaries before his death.

7 On Sunday schools, see Philip B. Cliff, 1986, *The Rise and Development of the Sunday School Movement in England 1780–1980*, Redhill: National Christian Education Council; T.W. Laqueur, *Religion and Respectability: Sunday Schools and Working Class Culture 1780–1850*, New Haven, CT: Yale University Press, 1976.

8 The Irish Parliament did not pass a Toleration Act until 1719.

9 Given the context of Jacobite rebellion, it is understandable that Dissenters should have tended to Whig sympathies, and this was reinforced by their belief that loyalty to the Hanoverian dynasty (which held the throne from 1714) was the best guarantee of continued toleration. The Stuarts, in the eyes of Dissenters, could not be trusted, and they were seen as allied to high churchmanship or (worse still) popery.

10 The main groups of Baptists in England were Particular Baptists (who believed in particular redemption, the doctrine that Christ died for the elect alone), General Baptists (who believed that Christ died for all), and the much smaller Seventh-Day Baptists (who worshipped on Saturday rather than Sunday).

11 So named from their first exponents, Lelio (1525–62) and his nephew Fausto Sozzini (1539–1604); the latter laid the theological foundations for the Minor Reformed Church, a Polish Unitarian body.

12 Watts, *Dissenters*, pp. 269–70. Watts bases his calculations in part on a list of Dissenting congregations compiled by a Dr Evans in 1715–18, which he regards as fairly comprehensive, especially in its listing of Independents and Presbyterians.

13 Caffyn's view of the humanity of Christ owed much to a sixteenth-century radical, Melchior Hoffman (1495–1543), whose views influenced Dutch Mennonites. Hoffmanite Christology appeared in Kent as early as 1550 when a

Lollard turned Anabaptist, Joan Boucher, was tried for heresy. Some of the first General Baptists, led by John Smyth, developed links with the Mennonites in Amsterdam at the beginning of the seventeenth century, although another group led by Thomas Helwys (1550–1616) withdrew and returned to England in 1611, partly because they rejected Hoffmanite Christology.

14 On Challoner, see Eamon Duffy (ed.), 1981, *Challoner and His Church: A Catholic Bishop in Georgian England*, London: Darton, Longman & Todd.

15 T. Carlyle, 1932, *Reminiscences*, ed. C.E. Norton, London: J.M. Dent, p. 176.

16 This issue was a running sore on Scottish Presbyterianism from 1712, when lay patrons had their prerogatives restored to them, until its abolition in 1874; we shall see later that it caused a major schism in 1843, and countless acrimonious debates at every level of church life.

17 Daniel G. Reid (ed.), 1990, *Dictionary of Christianity in America*, Downers Grove, IL: InterVarsity, art. 'Brainerd, David'.

18 Noll, *History*, p. 145.

19 On Scottish 'Common Sense' philosophy, see Harriet A. Harris, 1998, *Fundamentalism and Evangelicals*, Oxford: Clarendon.

20 The Episcopal Church in the United States became independent in 1789.

6

The Rise of Evangelicalism

Although Evangelicalism has often failed to attract much serious theological attention from the churches at large, from a historical perspective its numerical significance and worldwide distribution amply justify the devoting of a chapter to it. Indeed, it is increasingly recognized in ecumenical circles that Evangelicalism (along with Pentecostalism, whose origins are evangelical) is now one of the major expressions of the Christian faith. However, it has displayed a protean tendency to adapt itself according to the prevailing cultural and social climate, and it is vital to avoid reading back our own notions of the movement into accounts of its origins or extrapolating our own experience globally. This chapter therefore offers an account of Evangelicalism's origins; its development will be taken up at various subsequent points.

What was Evangelicalism?

To answer that question, we can take a brief tour of some of the main historiographical interpretations of the movement. (If you wish to cut to the historical chase, you may prefer to return to this section after working through the rest of the chapter.)

Early in the twentieth century the French historian Elie Halévy argued that it was the Evangelical Revival which staved off the threat of a revolution in England like that in France, by creating a body of working-class opinion which was politically and socially conservative and passive regarding calls for social change.[1] Such a view was understandably congenial to Methodists, who themselves had claimed such a thing. But his thesis has been widely discredited as claiming too much for Evangelicalism at the expense of other social or political factors. More recently E.P. Thompson has argued that Methodism offered a kind of psychological release of frustration which enabled them to cope with their 'enslavement' in the new capitalist system of factory production and thus took the pressure from any potential upsurge of revolutionary discontent.[2] John Wesley certainly retained his high church emphases on divine right monarchy and submission to lawful authority, and many Methodists went out of their way to stress their loyalty to king and country in order to demonstrate their right to be treated as respectable citizens. However, they were on occasion suspected not of Jacobinism (sympathy with the principles of the French Revolution) but of Jacobitism, a viewpoint which was not uncommon in the network of high churchmen among whom Wesley's father had moved.

Traditionally Evangelicalism regarded itself simply as a continuation of the religion of the Protestant Reformers, Puritans, and Pietists. This has been interpreted so as to place eighteenth-century Evangelicals in opposition to Enlightenment thought. However, recent scholarship has challenged this in various ways, implicitly or explicitly, and four recent interpretations of Evangelicalism deserve to be noted (those by – in chronological order – Bebbington, Campbell, Ward, and Walls).

Most influential among Evangelicals themselves, at least in English-speaking scholarship, has been the interpretation put forward by David Bebbington in his *Evangelicalism in Modern Britain* (first published in 1989); he argues that the movement should be seen as essentially an eighteenth-century phenomenon, a modification of the Puritan tradition under Enlightenment influence which resulted in a pan-denominational movement whose hallmarks (evident at all times and in all places) were:

- *Bibliocentrism*: an affirmation of the Bible as the supreme authority in matters of Christian faith and practice, and also a claim that Evangelicalism restored the Bible to centre stage in Christian proclamation, in contrast to much mainstream church life.
- *Crucicentrism*: the focus on the Cross in evangelical proclamation is well known; it derived from the belief that it was primarily through the atonement rather than the incarnation that sinful human beings were saved. The atonement was understood by the great majority of Evangelicals as being substitutionary: Christ died as the substitute for sinful humanity, bearing the punishment of death and separation from God which was their due.
- *Conversionism*: the belief that each individual needed to be converted and the devotion of vast amounts of effort and resources to present that challenge to as many as possible. Conversion was a divine work in that it represented the Holy Spirit's operation within the heart to beget spiritual life. This was often called the 'New Birth' and distinguished from the human part in conversion, which was to repent of sin and exercise faith in Jesus Christ as the one who by his death and resurrection had opened up a way for sinful human beings to be saved.
- *Activism*: the belief that the proper response of gratitude for salvation is a life full of good works done for God's glory, and in particular works connected with the spread of the gospel to others, both at home and abroad. Closely connected with this was a predilection for

pragmatism: the overriding need to save souls made most Evangelicals impatient with too great a degree of attention to principles of church order.

According to Bebbington, what marked Evangelicalism out as distinct was its stress on assurance of salvation as instantly attainable and as normative Christian experience. Evangelicalism represented an application of Locke's assertion that all knowledge was based on sense-experience. Bebbington's definition has been widely accepted, although its applicability beyond the English-speaking world has been questioned, as has the extent to which his four hallmarks are actually distinctive of Evangelicalism as opposed to other expressions of Christian faith; his stress on the discontinuities between it and Puritanism has also been challenged.

Ted Campbell has portrayed Evangelicalism as an example of the seventeenth- and eighteenth-century quest for a 'religion of the heart', a quest which was also manifest in movements as diverse as Jansenism and Hasidic Judaism.[3] It is salutary to have attention drawn to the way in which members of various movements were drawing on the thought of others and were sometimes aware of the parallels between them and other groups, and his interpretation is illuminating in its demonstration that a range of religious traditions were responding to contemporary cultural trends, although there is a risk that his argument could be taken to embrace virtually all expressions of Christian faith and spirituality during this period, not excepting confessional orthodoxy; the broader such generalizations become, the less use they are in explaining the origins and impetus behind any one movement.

W.R. Ward has developed the thesis that 'Almost everywhere the revival began in resistance to a real or perceived threat of assimilation by the state in its modern shape.'[4] Its first occurrence was among Protestant minorities in lands ruled by the Catholic Habsburg family and it gradually moved westwards. His work, like that of Campbell, is invaluable for its location of Evangelicalism in the context of wider European cultural and religious trends, a context to which English-speaking writers have frequently failed to do justice. However, it is sometimes a little difficult to see how every instance of evangelical awakening can be fitted into this scheme, especially if we extend our perspective down to the present day, although it is true that there was a widespread belief in mid-eighteenth-century Europe that further religious conflict was imminent. There was also a widespread sense that the Reformation had ground to a halt; since 1600 Rome had been regaining lost ground, in the face of the provisions of Westphalia. Fear of Roman intentions, of further conflict between Protestant and Catholic forces, and of the assimilation of Protestant minorities by Catholic states, remained a potent factor in shaping eighteenth-century political outlooks. One factor stimulating receptivity to Methodist preaching about justification by faith was that this was perceived as an antidote to Romanism.[5]

Andrew Walls has seen Evangelicalism as essentially a response to the problem of maintaining a vital faith in the context of Christendom, where nominal religion has tended to swamp it. It is, he claims, 'a religion of protest against a Christian society that is not Christian enough'.[6] Surprisingly, given his interests in mission and in the development of churches in the Majority World, he does not discuss the extent to which such an interpretation can be applied to Evangelicalism in areas where it represents the first or the dominant expression of Christianity. Nevertheless, as an explanation of the movement in its eighteenth-century British manifestation, it is of great value, and it challenges contemporary Evangelicals to consider the implications of the decline (or perhaps the demise) of Christendom for their own sense of identity.

The most recent account of Evangelical origins, by Mark Noll, sees Evangelicals as having three main roots: in the international Calvinist network, to which Puritanism had been central; in Pietism, which had already interacted extensively with Puritanism; and in the high Anglican spiritual tradition. To my mind this approach does most justice to the movement, and we may perhaps argue that it is the conjunction of these three streams which made Evangelicalism distinctive. Noll offers the following summary definition:

> evangelicalism grew out of earlier forms of heart-felt British Protestantism and was stimulated by contact with heart-felt continental pietism. It was grounded religiously in the innovative preaching of justifying faith. It was promoted and maintained by the effective exertions of capable spiritual leaders. It offered a compelling picture of direct fellowship with God for believers as individuals and in groups. It represented a shift in religiosity away from the inherited established churches toward spiritual communities constructed by believers themselves. It featured a form of conversion as much focused on personal experience, as much convinced of the plasticity of human nature and as much preoccupied with claims of certainty as any manifestation of the Enlightenment. And because its spirituality was adjusted to an opening world of commerce, communications and empire, that spirituality effectively resolved the psychological dilemmas created by this opening world.[7]

In concluding this brief survey, we should not overlook the need to understand how participants themselves, and other contemporary onlookers, viewed the movement. For the former, it was often something life-transforming, a felt encounter with God in Christ. Their self-understanding was frequently shaped by the movement's hymns, and those of Charles Wesley in particular stressed the joy which resulted from pardon for sin and release from its power. Onlookers varied in their reactions: some dismissed the evangelical message as 'enthusiasm' or condemned its socially levelling tendencies (like the noble lady who objected to George Whitefield's implication that her heart was no different from that of a common sinner at the bottom of the social scale). Others tried to be more objective, recognizing the good that was done by evangelical preaching yet not approving everything in it or its practitioners. A historically sensitive account will seek to empathize with contemporary participants and observers before offering its own interpretative judgements.

The rise of Evangelicalism

All too often, the impression is given that the eighteenth-century awakening began in England. The simple fact is that it did not. Quite apart from the matter of Continental influences from Pietism and Moravianism, Evangelicalism was already active in Scotland, Ireland, Wales, and North America by 1735, the year of George Whitefield's conversion (John and Charles Wesley did not undergo their life-changing experiences until 1738).

Wales

Although the Bible had been translated into Welsh in 1588 and had been highly successful in linguistic as well as religious terms, helping to ensure the survival of the language, and it had long been recognized that Anglicanism could only hope to make headway if Welsh was adopted as the language of worship, the Church was still seen as an Anglicizing force. This was not helped by the absence of native Welsh-speakers from the episcopal bench (or indeed by the absence of bishops in London). We have already noted in Chapter 5 the achievements of Griffith Jones and the circulating schools which prepared the way for Evangelicalism, and revival came first in the 1730s to parts of the western diocese of St Davids, where there had been discontent with the Church for several decades; Ward has suggested that it represents a reaction against assimilation by the English.[8]

The most prominent agent in the spread of Evangelicalism in Wales was Daniel Rowland (1711–90), curate of Llangeitho, near Lampeter. At first Rowland, who had been brought to personal faith by Griffith Jones, so emphasized the terrors of the Law of God in his preaching that an older Dissenting minister advised him in 1737 to desist lest he drive his hearers mad. He softened his approach and saw much fruit. Parish responsibilities did not hinder Rowland from itinerating with great success and (as with Methodism in England) converts were organized into societies to promote their spiritual growth.

Alongside Rowland worked the Anglican Howell Harris (1714–73), who had been a schoolmaster working for Griffith Jones. Converted in 1735, Harris immediately began an itinerant exhorting and preaching ministry arising from his concern to see others brought to faith in Christ, becoming one of the first lay and open-air preachers of the revival in Wales. He formed his converts into societies, and by 1750 there were 433 'Calvinistic Methodist' societies in Wales (as well as 29 in England). Harris and Rowland co-operated from 1737 until 1750 when a division took place, partly due to Harris's espousal of unorthodox theological views which came close to Patripassianism (the belief that the Father suffered on the cross as the Son). Reconciliation in 1762 was followed by another outbreak of revival but by now Calvinistic Methodism, like English Methodism, was heading for a break with the establishment. Indeed, Rowland was himself ejected from his curacy in 1763 and thereafter preached in a new chapel built specially for him. He frequently served as a trustee for the new chapels being built, thus ensuring that they remained faithful to evangelical theology.

Evangelical faith was given memorably poetic expression in the hymns of William Williams of Pantycelyn (1717–91),[9] who assisted Rowland from 1743, and of Ann Griffiths (1776–1805), which helped to shape the faith and experience of a sizeable proportion of the population. Welsh Evangelicals drew upon the writings of the Puritans but also those of their contemporaries Jonathan Edwards in America (see below) and the Scots Ebenezer and Ralph Erskine. They contributed to the transformation of Dissent from a faith which as late as the middle of the eighteenth century claimed the allegiance of less than 5 per cent of the population, to one which showed every sign of becoming the majority expression of Welsh Christianity.

Scotland and Ireland

Communion seasons were favoured occasions for revival phenomena in Scotland.[10] Large crowds would gather from surrounding parishes for a series of meetings following a set pattern of penitence, preparation, and thanksgiving. These extended from the Thursday or Saturday before the Communion Sabbath (as Protestant Scots called Sunday) to the following Monday, and since no church could contain them the practice of open-air or 'field' preaching was adopted, one which had roots in the mass Covenanter gatherings in out-of-the-way locations during times of persecution.[11] As in Scotland, communion seasons were the focus for religious excitement among the Ulster Presbyterian population, who were Scots immigrants resettled by James VI/I. Evangelical views were already being aired from many Scottish and Ulster pulpits and had even contributed to a schism from the Church of Scotland in 1733, as we noted in Chapter 5, but it was around 1740 that the movement really took off. Revival broke out at a communion season at Cambuslang in 1742, which had attracted an estimated 30,000 hearers, of whom 3,000 were communicants. From there it spread to a number of neighbouring parishes. Although it developed in its own way, it was sparked off by news of revival in New England, and the fire was fed by a visit from George Whitefield.

England

Arguably the most important Protestant figure of the century in England was John Wesley (1703–91).[12] Although both his grandfathers had been ejected from the Church of England in 1662 for their nonconforming views, Wesley's parents had converted to Anglicanism and he himself was something of a high churchman throughout his life. Early high churchmen were influenced by Arminian thinking, and this is evident in Wesley.

At Oxford, Wesley co-founded the 'Holy Club' and came under the influence of mystical teaching, especially as mediated by William Law. In 1725 he underwent what he seems to have regarded as his conversion, a decision to dedicate himself entirely to God based on reading Thomas à Kempis's *Imitation of Christ* and the seventeenth-century Anglican Jeremy Taylor's works on *Holy Living and Holy Dying*. His appointment to a fellowship at Lincoln College was the grounds for his ordination as priest in 1728, and he associated with a Non-Juring group from 1733, but in 1736–7 he worked in the colony of Georgia under the auspices of the SPG, seeking to pastor the expatriates and evangelize the indigenous population. However, his strict approach to religious discipline, as well as some high-profile personality clashes, led him to tender his resignation and return to England under a cloud: he had gone to Georgia to convert the natives, but who, he wondered, would convert him? The story of John Wesley's evangelical conversion has often been retold, but it is best to let him give it in his own words.

In the evening I went very unwillingly to a society . . . where someone was reading Luther's preface to the Epistle to the Romans. About a quarter to nine, while he was describing the change which God works in the heart through faith in Christ, I felt my heart strangely warmed. I felt I did trust in Christ, Christ alone, for salvation. And an assurance was given me that He had taken away *my* sins, even *mine*, and saved *me* from the law of sin and death.[13]

Wesley later described this as the moment when he exchanged the faith of a servant for the faith of a son,[14] and it was this confident assurance of sonship which came to characterize Methodist spirituality. (Incidentally, in this they followed the Moravian belief in sudden conversion as the norm.) But notice that in his case, as in others, it was Luther's Preface to Romans which sparked the change.

As he worked out the implications of what had happened to him, it has been argued that he was influenced by current philosophical thinking about experience as a source of knowledge. Locke had taught that human knowledge is based on experience and reflection, and it is claimed that Locke's thinking helped to shape evangelical thinking about religious experience. Methodists have certainly looked to experience, alongside Scripture, tradition, and reason, as an authority, but it should be noted that an emphasis on experience is also prominent in mid-seventeenth-century Puritanism.

In spite of the influence of Moravian thought and example on John Wesley, he shortly fell out with their English representatives. Almost immediately after his conversion, he had visited Halle and Herrnhut, though the Moravians rejected him as *homo perturbatus*, 'an unsettled or disturbed man'. From 1740 the London societies divided over the Moravian teaching of 'stillness' (rather similar to Quietism); Wesley, who believed that a diligent use of the 'means of grace' (which included prayer, Bible reading, attendance at worship, and receiving communion) could help to bring individuals to an assured faith, rejected this and withdrew with his followers. Many early Moravian hearers in London had previously belonged to one or other of the religious societies (as had the Wesleys and Whitefield), and it seems that they may have been ripe for a message which offered a certainty of salvation which the societies (and contemporary Anglican teaching on justification, which stressed the preparatory role of good works) could not give because their standards of life and spiritual discipline were so difficult to achieve and displayed a tendency to turn into legalism.

The second prominent evangelical preacher was George Whitefield (1714–70).[15] The son of an innkeeper, Whitefield's preaching was marked by the dramatic, even histrionic, talent which had early made him consider a career on the stage. Converted in 1735, he became an Anglican clergyman. His superb voice not only allowed him to make himself heard by vast audiences outdoors but also held their attention because of the quality of his delivery. By contrast with the contemporary appeal to the mind, Whitefield appealed to the affections because he saw them as key to securing the response of the whole person. Once he got into his stride, he is said to have preached often for a total of forty hours a week, and he travelled all over Britain to do so.

It was Whitefield who pioneered the use of open-air preaching in eighteenth-century England (it had begun slightly earlier in Wales). Initially forced to do so because churches were barred to him, he soon recognized that he could reach far larger audiences in this way, and so, 'since the self-righteous men of this generation count themselves unworthy, I go out into the highways and hedges, and compel harlots, publicans, and sinners to come in, that my Master's house may be filled'.[16] In 1739 he persuaded a reluctant John Wesley to do so. Given his high church concern for good order, Wesley required compelling reasons, which were to be found in the masses who did not attend worship and the refusal of many clergy to open their pulpits to him. If Wesley was a high churchman, he was even more an evangelist, and the rest of his ministry shows him ready to adopt pragmatic structures and solutions and to countenance exceptional measures, all in the cause of spreading the gospel. Such pragmatism has remained a central feature of Evangelicalism in its organizational life.

It was not long before the Wesleys and Whitefield parted company over their differing understandings of salvation: the Wesleys were Arminians, while Whitefield was a Calvinist (though he claimed on one occasion never to have read Calvin). In 1740 John Wesley preached a sermon on 'Free Grace' responding to a published sermon by the high Calvinist John Gill. In so doing he ignited a controversy which was to divide Evangelicalism, as Whitefield felt it necessary to make a public response. Wesley retained a warm affection for Whitefield, spoke at his memorial service, and refused to allow anyone to speak against him (although his funeral oration provoked a fresh outbreak of controversy because Wesley claimed that he and Whitefield preached essentially the same doctrines, omitting all reference to the latter's Calvinistic views). However, some of their followers on both sides were less gracious. The Calvinist clergyman Augustus Toplady (1740–78) of Broadhembury, Devon, clashed with John Wesley on this issue in verse and prose, and Charles Wesley wrote some trenchant critiques of Calvinist soteriology in the form of hymns; both men used intemperate language. The later stages of the controversy were fuelled by the fact that Evangelicalism was now becoming more widespread and attracting more 'respectable' people, with a consequent risk of lukewarmness or dilution; furthermore, those on the Arminian side were concerned at what they saw as a growth in antinomian careless-ness which they felt was encouraged by Calvinist doctrines of the eternal security of the believer.

Whitefield was less concerned than Wesley to create a national net-work of his converts, although others conserved his influence by doing so in Wales. But English Calvinistic Methodists tended to be associ-ated with Selina Hastings, Countess of Huntingdon (1707–91), and her

Connexion. She founded a number of chapels to which she appointed ministers of Calvinistic evangelical views to officiate, nominally as her chaplains; Whitefield was appointed in 1748 and became chief among them. She took advantage of the provisions of the Conventicle Act, which allowed worship to be conducted in private chapels so long as their doors were not open for the public to enter. In 1779 a test case was brought in relation to Spa Fields Chapel in Clerkenwell; it led to a court ruling which denied her the right to appoint as many clergy as she wished as chaplains. Thereafter she had to register her chapels as Dissenting places of worship, and her Connexion developed into a separate denomination, with the loss of many former chaplains in the process. Frequently using Prayer Book services for its worship, it became known for its presence in English watering-places such as Bath and Brighton. The Countess set up the first evangelical seminary in 1768 at Trevecca, near Brecon.

Wesleyan Methodism needs to be distinguished from other forms of Dissent because of its unique relationship with the Church of England. Throughout his lifetime John Wesley gloried in his Anglican allegiance and sought to encourage Methodists to become regular worshippers at their local Anglican church; to that end, he discouraged the holding of Methodist services at times which would clash with Anglican services. Whenever he arrived in a parish, it was his custom to ask permission to preach from the local Anglican clergyman. (He justified his itinerancy on the basis that he had been ordained not to a parish but to a fellow-ship of an Oxford college, which allowed him to preach anywhere in England.) However, his actions contributed greatly to the movement's eventual separation from the establishment. In particular, we shall notice two examples: his willingness to ordain and his establishment of quasi-denominational structures.[17]

In 1740 his mother Susanna had warned him not to reject the work of God going on through lay preachers, whose ministrations he had been reluctant to accept. She also influenced him by her example: when her husband was away it was her practice to conduct meetings in her kitchen for the flock, which seem to have been better received than her husband's church services. From the 1760s, therefore, John Wesley showed himself ready to approve women as preachers; apart from the pragmatic justifica-tion of the blessing attending their ministry, he argued that exceptional times called for exceptional methods (an argument which also justified itinerancy, open-air preaching, and the use of lay preachers), and that since women did not preach in church buildings, they did not contravene the Pauline injunctions to female silence in church. Lay preachers exer-cised a prophetic ministry, as opposed to the pastoral and priestly one exercised by clergy. His buildings were not churches but chapels, and his congregations were known as societies.

The development of quasi-denominational structures came about as the fruit of Methodism's success in going to where people were.[18] As with the use of women as preachers, the justification was usually pragmatic: since his organization was not a church, it was not covered by the ecclesiology forming part of John Wesley's high churchmanship. Wesley considered that the great advantage of Methodist societies (roughly equivalent to congregations of other denominations, though intended initially as a supplement to attendance at the Church of England), the first of which he founded in 1739, was that they did not require a profession of conversion from those who joined them, merely a desire to 'flee from the wrath to come'; neither did they require subscription by members to a doctrinal basis, although this was expected of preachers. They were 'a company of men having the form and seeking the power of godliness, united in order to pray together, to receive the word of exhortation, and to watch over one another in love, that they may help each other to work out their salvation'.[19] Of course, in a small-group setting leaders were able to help many to the point of conversion. However, while membership was open to all, there were strict expectations regarding conduct of meetings and the lifestyle expected of members.

In 1742 John Wesley began class meetings (small groups within each society), initially as a way of paying off the debt incurred in building the New Room in Bristol and taking over and converting the Foundery in London's City Road: the idea was that individuals would meet in groups of twelve and a leader would collect a penny a week from each of them. Wesley saw that they could serve a key role as part of a structured system of pastoral care. Women as well as men could serve as class leaders, and it was necessary to belong to a class in order to be part of the local Methodist society. For a short period there were also 'bands' for those claiming to have been converted, as well as groups for returning backsliders and other special needs. Such groups provided opportunities for each member to relate their spiritual experiences, good and bad.

The first annual Methodist Conference occurred in 1744. Clergy and travelling preachers made up the membership of Conference, and almost until he died John Wesley took a leading role in its deliberations. For instance, after his firm refusal at the 1760 Conference to ordain lay preachers it was two decades before the question resurfaced. From 1746, Methodist societies began to be organized into circuits, to which ministers and itinerant preachers were appointed. Following the judicial ruling concerning the Countess of Huntingdon's chapels, Methodists took steps to regularize their position. It was in 1784 that it was given legal form, in a deed of declaration naming a hundred preachers as the legal conference.

There was a tension in Methodism, as in the wider evangelical movement, between attachment to the Church of England and the demands brought about by their new experience. Some believed that they should remain in the Church of England, but others placed more emphasis on the fellowship of believers and wished to be free of what they saw as restrictions on the preaching of the gospel. We saw that such a tension was also evident in Pietism. From the 1750s there were also calls by preachers to be allowed to administer the sacraments and thus develop an independent identity and existence. (At this stage sacraments in Methodist chapels were celebrated by Anglican clergy who belonged to the movement.) What Wesley saw as binding him to the Church of England was his regular participation in his services and sacraments rather than any sense of the canonical obedience due to its bishops, but many of his followers did not have this experience and so did not share his sense of loyalty to the establishment. Often they had been brought up within Methodism or had experienced clerical hostility; the Prayer Book had not shaped their spirituality in the way that it had the first generation of Methodist leaders, that role having been played by Charles Wesley's hymns instead.

A crux issue for Methodism's relationship with the Church of England was ordination. John Wesley considered that bishops were not a higher order of clergy than presbyters (priests), a view which had some precedent in sixteenth-century Anglican ecclesiology (although Wesley's sources were drawn from the later seventeenth century). He therefore concluded that in certain circumstances the latter had as much right to ordain as the former. In 1784 he was finally forced to put his convictions into practice, the bishops having turned a deaf ear to his pleas that they should ordain men to care for Methodists in America, who were being starved of the sacraments because of the lack of clergy, a lack which had its roots in the longstanding refusal of the Church of England (or the British government) to countenance ordaining a bishop to care for its American congregations.[20] He ordained Thomas Coke (1747–1814) as a superintendent of the work in America; Coke in turn ordained Francis Asbury (1745–1816) as a second superintendent. Charles Wesley profoundly disapproved of such a move, seeing it as tending to separation.[21]

In 1787 Methodist chapels were first licensed under the Toleration Act, and in 1795 the Conference granted local societies the right to decide whether or not to hold their own communion services, a development for which there had been calls over four decades. This may be taken as marking the formal withdrawal of Methodists from the Church of England. Nevertheless, official separation was a long time coming in some areas: in Wales, it occurred in 1811, in Ireland it was 1818 (although a small group remained in the Church of Ireland until after disestablishment in 1871), and in the Isle of Man it was as late as 1836.

The Methodist message was given expression by the hymns of Charles Wesley (1707–88), among others; he wrote at least 6,500 and they enabled Methodists to give expression to all aspects of their faith.

In addition, John Wesley produced a steady stream of writings, among them his *Notes on the New Testament* to assist lay preachers, *Forty-Four Sermons* as a compendium of Methodist doctrine, and a succession of hymnbooks culminating in that of 1780 which he intended to serve as 'a little body of experimental and practical divinity', arranging it according to his taxonomy of spiritual experience. His *Journal* is reminiscent of St Luke in the Acts of the Apostles in its positive portrayal of the authorities (in Wesley's case, the Anglican hierarchy). He also edited a multivolume *Christian Library* containing works from a range of writers on the spiritual life, Eastern and Western, Catholic and Protestant.

Throughout his life John Wesley continued to press his doctrine of Christian Perfection, considering that Methodism had been raised up in order to make known the message of 'Scriptural holiness'. He aimed to encourage his hearers to pursue holiness. His understanding was rooted in the late seventeenth-century high Anglican spiritual tradition. For Wesley entire sanctification was an instantaneous event, like justification, although there was often much preparation for it beforehand and outworking of it afterwards. By it sin was expelled from the heart of the believer, and perfect love took control so that believers enjoyed unbroken fellowship with Christ. Since a believer could fall away, this experience could be repeated. But what did he mean by 'perfection'? Wesley distinguished between two kinds of sin: 'Sin properly so-called', voluntary transgression of a known law; and 'Sin improperly so-called', involuntary transgression of God's law, perhaps because of ignorance. He believed that it was possible to avoid the first but not the second. However, he admitted that he had not achieved such a state himself, nor did he know of many who had. Since few of his preachers followed him in this teaching, its importance should not be overstressed, although scholars view it as an important factor in the rise of modern Holiness and Pentecostal movements.

More women than men became Methodists, though it is unclear whether this is due to factors relating to Methodism or whether it reflects a general trend among men to leave organized religion to the womenfolk. By the time of Wesley's death in 1791, 72,000 people belonged to Methodist societies in Britain, with another 60,000 in North America. (It is not always remembered that Methodism also made considerable headway in Ireland; John Wesley made 21 preaching tours there from 1747 onwards.) By now the movement was developing in two streams, one each side of the Atlantic. This was inevitable given the political situation, and John Wesley's high Tory opposition to what he saw as rebellion on the part of the colonies did nothing to help matters. Each stream would in time produce a range of movements sharing a recognizable family likeness, Wesleyan, Holiness, and Pentecostal.

Whereas Old Dissent had appealed chiefly to those who were economically independent (and hence free from an employer's dictates regarding where they should worship), Methodism appears to have attracted many from lower social orders. However, John Wesley complained that as they developed habits of hard work and thrift and so became more prosperous, they gained for themselves 'riches with hell-fire'. For several generations, therefore, Methodist schisms attempted to begin their outreach at the lower levels of society, filling the gap left by the rise in wealth and social status of previous generations of converts.

Evangelicalism and the churches

It is important to note that the eighteenth-century evangelical awakening was pluriform from the beginning, and no one strand should be regarded as 'normative' at the expense of the others. As well as the Moravians, the Wesleyans and the Calvinists, a distinctly Anglican evangelical party emerged by the 1750s, which looked to the Puritans for much of its inspiration. Anglican Evangelicals may be distinguished from the Wesleys and Whitefield (who were also Anglican clergy) by virtue of their origins, which were largely independent of the earlier movement, and their objectives, which were concerned with renewal at the parochial level. Although John Wesley sought co-operation with them at various points during his ministry, response was rarely very positive.

An early example of their approach was Samuel Walker (1714–61), curate of Truro. Converted in 1749, he was described by John Wesley as the only Evangelical working within the parish system – an exaggeration, but it pointed to Walker's *modus operandi*. Disapproving of lay preachers and of itinerancy, he sought parish renewal by founding religious societies for members of his flock, although he controlled them. Wesley was not overly sympathetic to the Anglican Evangelicals' approach, especially when his designated successor John Fletcher (1729–85) buried himself in a parish at Madeley, Shropshire, instead of itinerating.

Other noteworthy figures included:

- William Romaine (1714–95), a scholarly cleric who for some years headed the only evangelical parish in London, St Andrew by the Wardrobe (in the City), to which he was appointed in 1766.
- John Newton (1725–1807), a former slave-trader, who ministered at Olney, Buckinghamshire, from 1764 to 1779, where he worked with the local Independents, who included the poet William Cowper (1731–1800): Newton and Cowper produced the *Olney Hymns* (1779), which expressed and shaped the spirituality of Anglican Evangelicalism in the same way that Charles Wesley's hymns did for Methodism. Thereafter, he moved to London, where he was able to influence the rising generation of clergy.

- Thomas Adam (1701–84) of Wintringham near Scunthorpe, whose influence was mainly on his fellow clergy.
- James Hervey (1714–58) of Weston Favell near Northampton, whose writing ability enabled him to reach the higher classes.
- Henry Venn (1725–97), who ministered at Huddersfield and then Yelling, near Cambridge. Venn belonged to a famous clerical dynasty whose later generations we shall encounter in due course.

Some were prepared to engage in a measure of itinerancy, such as William Grimshaw (1708–63) of Haworth, Yorkshire, who (unusually) was prepared to co-operate with local Methodists. The most notable example of what were sometimes known as the 'half-regulars' was John Berridge (1716–93) of Everton near Cambridge: although committed to the renewal of his parish, he appointed lay preachers, preached in the open air himself, and itinerated in other parishes.

More clerical in cast than the two Methodist streams, Anglican Evangelicalism tended to prize strict churchmanship, not least because it enabled them to demonstrate to critics their claim to be the true successors of the sixteenth-century Reformers and seventeenth-century Puritans. Few of them placed much emphasis on theological study, thus exemplifying a recurrent evangelical weakness – the tendency to focus on evangelism at the expense of theology. (In their defence, it may perhaps be said that the period was not, in any case, a bright one for theological development anywhere in Europe.) Thus their ecclesiology was essentially pragmatic: the Church of England was, as their successors sometimes described it, 'a good boat to fish from'.

Anglican Evangelicals were widely dispersed throughout England and only gradually did a network develop which facilitated their taking joint action in such matters as patronage and the financing of ministerial training. A major problem confronting them was that of ensuring continuity of doctrine: how could they ensure that their successors in a particular pulpit would preach the same gospel? To that end several societies were set up in order to purchase the rights of presentation to key livings. For example, there were Simeon's Trustees, and also the Church Pastoral-Aid Society. Such bodies also ensured that Evangelicals, who often struggled to obtain a living because most bishops and patrons disapproved of their 'enthusiasm', would be able to do so. In addition, agencies such as the Elland Society were founded to provide financial sponsorship for promising Evangelicals to prepare for the ministry and to enable ministers to meet together and discuss their work and doctrine.

While not rejecting the doctrine of assurance of salvation, Anglican Evangelicals looked for holiness of life rather than a sense of confidence as evidence that they had been converted. The biblical commentator

Thomas Scott (1747–1821), who had formerly held what amounted to Unitarian views, spoke of growth being the only evidence of life.

As for Old Dissent, different denominations were affected in different ways, some proving better soil for Evangelicalism than others. The Northampton Independent minister and hymnwriter Philip Doddridge (1702–51) exercised some influence over the development of Evangelicalism among Dissenters; he was neither a high Calvinist nor a Unitarian rationalist, and Dissenters who accepted the revival tended to follow a similar line.[22] Independents were to the fore in this, the high Calvinism of many Particular Baptists (added to the widespread Dissenting distaste for the Wesleys' Arminianism) inhibiting them at first. Few Quakers were affected until later on, although by the early nineteenth century there grew to be a sizeable evangelical stream among Friends.

In 1745, the General Baptist Assembly had condemned Methodism as unscriptural. However, Methodism was to be the inspiration for a renewal movement led by Dan Taylor, a Yorkshire convert of George Whitefield. Leaving Methodism because he disapproved of John Wesley's authoritarian leadership, he formed his own congregation, later adopting the practice of believer's baptism. In 1770 the New Connexion of General Baptists was formed from a union of a group of churches in the East Midlands planted by David Taylor, a servant of the Countess of Huntingdon, and Dan Taylor's Methodist-influenced churches in Yorkshire, along with a few General Baptist churches which had remained evangelical. In 1813 the New Connexion severed its remaining links with the old General Baptist Assembly, which thus became effectively Unitarian in outlook.[23]

Where English Presbyterians were affected by evangelical views (or simply where they wished to remain Trinitarian in theology and worship) there were often schisms, as groups and even entire congregations went over to Independency; such a move was relatively easy because of the similarity of polity between the two denominations. Other individuals migrated to sit under evangelical ministers in the Church of England. Presbyterianism north of the Scottish border was rather more influenced by Evangelicalism. As in North America, a key role was played by George Whitefield. Between 1741 and 1768 he visited Scotland no less than 14 times; yet even this was eclipsed by John Wesley, who between 1751 and 1790 paid 22 visits (against Whitefield's advice!). However, Methodism largely failed to take root north of the border, because of Wesley's Anglican allegiance and Arminian sympathies. It was Calvinist Evangelicalism (or perhaps more accurately evangelical Calvinism) which was to be the dominant expression of the new spirituality, especially in the Scottish Highlands. Revival in the Highlands burned more slowly than elsewhere, and for much longer, extending over many decades. It was marked by an absence of the physical phenomena such as prostrations and trances which attended the awakening elsewhere in Britain and America, a fact which may not be unrelated to its solid grounding in the piety of the *Westminster Confession* and associated Catechisms.

Evangelicalism proved able to adapt itself to almost all Protestant and Trinitarian forms of Christianity, because of its emphasis on individual renewal. However, its strength was also to be its greatest weakness, in that Evangelicalism often adopted a relatively low doctrine of the Church, which made it easier for Evangelicals to divide and set up parallel, even competing, agencies for outreach. Thus in England and Wales there were Anglican Evangelicals, Methodists (of two types), and Dissenting Evangelicals. (They would be joined in the nineteenth century by explicitly anti-establishment Evangelicals, many of whom seceded from the Church of England.) Furthermore, it has been claimed that 'Preoccupation with the inner experience of each soul deflected attention from the political, economic, and intellectual implications of the Gospel.'[24] For much of the eighteenth century this was true, but we shall see that during the half-century following the French Revolution things would be very different.

The 'Great Awakening': early North American Evangelicalism

The evangelical revival in North America during the 1730s and 1740s came to be known as the Great Awakening, its earliest manifestations being the Pietist influences among European immigrants. T.J. Frelinghuysen (1692–1747), a Dutch Reformed minister who had been influenced by Pietism in Germany and Holland, was a key figure; prominent features of his preaching were the direct address of different sections of the congregation according to their perceived spiritual state and the plain-spoken preaching of the 'terrors of the law' to the unconverted. Frelinghuysen in turn influenced the Presbyterian Gilbert Tennent (1703–64) who, like many of his congregation, had brought elements of the Ulster revivalist tradition across the Atlantic. Tennent became an effective evangelist himself, and was to influence Whitefield.

As in Frelinghuysen's ministry, Evangelicalism made a sharp distinction between the converted and those deemed merely nominal Christians. From 1662 many churches of English origin, especially among the Independents (now becoming known as Congregationalists), had introduced a 'Half-Way Covenant'; their initial insistence that applicants for membership should give a testimony to personal conversion, and that only such could have their children baptized, left them with a problem when, after a generation, these children grew up, married, and had children of their own. As things stood they could neither join the church nor have their children baptized, and so a kind of associate membership was introduced. It did not require applicants to have been converted, nor did it allow them to take communion, but it placed them under the discipline of the church and allowed them to present their children for baptism. Applicants had simply to own the baptismal covenant which had been made by their parents on their behalf. Dispute over the Half-Way Covenant was often furious and protracted, and the Great Awakening led many Congregational and Presbyterian churches to abandon it because of their desire to purify the membership of the church. The new style of preaching also led to schism among Presbyterians, something which was to be a recurrent feature of their denominational life over the next century under the impact of successive waves of religious excitement.

The best-known eighteenth-century American Evangelical is Jonathan Edwards (1703–58), pastor of the Congregational church in Northampton, Massachusetts.[25] His grandfather, Solomon Stoddard (1643–1729), had pastored the same church and had reaped five 'harvests' of converts during a ministry which lasted from 1672 until his death. Stoddard abandoned the Half-Way Covenant as ineffective in securing conversions. What was needed, he felt, was to bring as many as possible to a state of preparedness to receive the gospel, so that revival might come as the law and then the gospel were preached. Such preparation (which might be a lengthy process, although conversion itself was instant) took place as individuals made diligent use of means such as Bible reading and prayer, but also the sacraments: Stoddard, like the Wesleys, opened the communion table to such people, deemed to be those who attended church regularly and led an outwardly upright life, rather than restricting it to those with an assured faith. His approach was therefore closer to the idea of a national church than to the 'gathered church' often seen as a hallmark of Congregationalism, and may owe something to the fact that Congregationalism enjoyed established status in the state until 1833. So here we may have an example of Walls's argument that Evangelicalism represents a response to the problems raised by the context of Christendom.

The Great Awakening's symbolic beginning is 1734, when Edwards preached a series of sermons on what he regarded as the distinguishing doctrines of the Protestant Reformation, especially justification by faith alone. The result was revival in the local community, especially among the young. Ward explains that Edwards deliberately targeted this age-group, although he later had to discipline many of them and they failed to support him when he was dismissed by his congregation in 1750.[26] The harvest was not necessarily any more extensive than in previous awakenings, but it attracted worldwide interest because Edwards was asked to write it up, which he did in his *Faithful Narrative of a Surprising Work of God*, first published in 1737. Isaac Watts supported its republication in England, and it stimulated a desire for similar blessing throughout the English-speaking world.

As well as being an evangelistic preacher Edwards was a serious philosopher; his approach to the question of assurance has been seen as indebted to Locke, although it is debated whether this extends beyond terminology to substance. What was evident in Edwards's preaching was a shift from a sober religion understood primarily in intellectual terms to one which stressed the 'religious affections' – those inward inclinations which dictate how we feel, think, and act; the heart, emotions, and will. This is also visible in Whitefield's preaching. Both may be regarded as representatives of the Puritan tradition in terms of their understanding of conversion and especially of the role played by the divine grace in preparing the heart and drawing it to exercise faith in Christ, but their stress on sudden conversion and assurance of faith went beyond what many Puritans had experienced.

Edwards's own ministry ended in outward failure: attempting to throw out the Half-Way Covenant in 1750 and revert to the previous practice of requiring all intending communicants to testify to a personal Christian faith, his congregation, who saw this as threatening the idea of church membership as a cohesive force in society at large, dismissed him. He spent his remaining years at Stockbridge, seeking to minister to the Indians but mainly writing and thinking. Still, by his output he influenced a generation of Evangelicals and did much to set the agenda for American Protestant theology until well into the nineteenth century.

At a national level the Great Awakening has been seen as the first American event of national significance; much of this is due to the role played by Whitefield as what we would call today a 'networker'. He was at the heart of a developing international communication network which spanned the Atlantic and was kept in action through correspondence and a steady flow of publications giving news of awakenings and stimulating believers to concerted prayer. He visited America seven times from 1738, dying there while on a preaching tour.

Geographically speaking, Noll has argued that three patterns of colonial religion may be discerned in the three main areas, and that each was affected in different ways by the Great Awakening. By the 1730s New England churches expressed concern at the decline of orderly institutional religion; those in the Middle Colonies were learning to live together in a pluralist society; and in the South religion (in this case Anglican, as Dissenters did not gain much of a foothold here until the 1750s, when Baptists began to provide a highly successful alternative) was seen as legitimating the existing social order. The awakening resulted in a cleavage of the New England churches between supporters and opponents, the latter party preferring a more enlightened approach to religion which in time would give rise to American Unitarianism. Furthermore, those influenced by the new movement often rejected the church–state link and adopted believer's baptism: the number of Baptist churches in the region thus grew from 25 in 1740 to 312 by 1804. In the Middle Colonies all denominations were affected in similar ways, and several experienced division between those who advocated the revival and those who opposed it; the result was thus a sense of cross-denominational unity between those touched by revival currents. In the South it created an alternative to Anglicanism where none had existed before.[27] Overall the statistical impact seems to have been a surge in applications for church membership, followed by a dip; over the long term, it may have made surprisingly little difference numerically, though its significance in shaping American Protestantism was epochal.

The impact of the revival was patchy: where there were other forces at work to create social cohesion it made little difference, but in unstable urban and frontier environments, where population mobility was a major factor, it was much more effective.[28] This helps to explain why revivalist Evangelicalism has often been seen as 'frontier religion'. On the other hand Anglicanism also profited from the awakenings: although it was largely unresponsive to them, it provided a home for those who reacted against Whitefield's preaching. Even where Evangelicalism was not accepted, it did much to shape the thought of other Christian traditions as they reacted to issues which it raised. We shall see in the next part of the book just how far this was the case during the nineteenth century.

Questions for thought

1 Which of the interpretations of Evangelicalism we have discussed do you find (i) most convincing, and (ii) least convincing, and why?

2 How far do you think Welsh Evangelicalism was a response to the threat of assimilation by England?

3 Contrast the roles of John Wesley and George Whitefield in the development of Evangelicalism in the English-speaking world.

4 If you had been an eighteenth-century bishop in the Church of England, what would your concerns have been if Evangelicalism appeared in your diocese?

5 In what ways do you think Evangelicalism was (i) drawing on Enlightenment thinking, and (ii) reacting against it?

6 Do you detect any differences between North American Evangelicalism and its British counterparts during this period?

Further reading

D.W. Bebbington, 1995, *Evangelicalism in Modern Britain: A History from the 1730s to the 1980s*, 2nd edn, London: Routledge, chs 1–2.

Ted A. Campbell, 1994, *The Religion of the Heart*, Columbia, SC: University of South Carolina Press.

Kenneth Cracknell and Susan J. White, 2005, *An Introduction to World Methodism*, Cambridge: Cambridge University Press.

David Hempton, 2005, *Methodism: Empire of the Spirit*, New Haven, CT: Yale University Press.

Kenneth Hylson-Smith, 1989, *Evangelicals in the Church of England 1734–1984*, Edinburgh: T. & T. Clark, part 1.

Mark A. Noll, 2004, *The Rise of Evangelicalism: The Age of Edwards, Whitefield and the Wesleys*, A History of Evangelicalism, Leicester: IVP.

W.R. Ward, 2006, *The Early English Evangelicals, 1670–1789*, Cambridge: Cambridge University Press.

W.R. Ward, 1992, *The Protestant Evangelical Awakening*, Cambridge: Cambridge University Press, chs 7–8.

Notes

1 See Elie Halévy, 1971, *The Birth of Methodism in England*, ed. and trans. Bernard Semmel, Chicago: University of Chicago Press.

2 See E.P. Thompson, 1968, *The Making of the English Working Class*, Harmondsworth: Penguin.

3 Campbell, *Religion of the Heart*.

4 Ward, *Protestant Evangelical Awakening*, p. 353.

5 Ward asserts that the outbreak of the Seven Years' War (1756–63), which looked as if it was the long-expected renewal of religious conflict, was followed by revival in England and Wales (*Protestant Evangelical Awakening*, p. 350).

6 Walls, *Missionary Movement*, p. 83.

7 Noll, *Rise of Evangelicalism*, p. 144.

8 Ward, *Protestant Evangelical Awakening*, p. 316.

9 Williams is best known in the English-speaking world as author of 'Guide me, O thou great Jehovah'.

10 For a valuable discussion of communion seasons as occasions for religious revival, see Leigh Eric Schmidt, 2001, *Holy Fairs: Scotland and the Making of American Revivalism*, 2nd edn, Grand Rapids, MI: Eerdmans, ch. 1.

11 The motif of resistance to assimilation is apposite here, since in their origins these gatherings derived much of their impact from their significance as expressions of protest against the attempted imposition of episcopacy on the Scottish Church which continued to a greater or lesser extent until 1690. For those who had been evicted from their charges by Charles II (as 300 ministers were in 1660) because of their allegiance to the Solemn League and Covenant and the resulting distrust of his intentions which led them to refuse him political support, these gatherings were the only way of meeting because the churches were closed to them.

12 On John Wesley, see R.P. Heitzenrater, 1995, *Wesley and the People called Methodists*, Nashville, TN: Abingdon; H.D. Rack, 1989, *Reasonable Enthusiast*, London: Epworth; the best edition of his works is appearing from Oxford University Press (35 volumes are projected). Charles has been less studied, but

primary sources and historical introduction are usefully combined in John R. Tyson (ed.), 1989, *Charles Wesley: A Reader*, New York: Oxford University Press.

13 *Journal*, 24 May 1738 (this is available in many editions and also (in an abridged version) on the Internet at www.ccel.org/ccel/wesley/journal.html).

14 This is perhaps a more accurate description than simply calling it his 'conversion', since in his *Journal*, at the point where he records his conviction that he who had gone to America to convert others was not converted himself, he adds a terse footnote: 'I am not sure of this' (*Journal*, following 1 February 1738). He actually said relatively little about this experience, preferring to cite his self-dedication in 1725 as the start of his active Christian life. It has been suggested that this may be a consequence of his rejection of Moravianism, since it was through the Moravians and their ideas that his 'Aldersgate Street experience' had come about: when he rejected Moravianism he turned to the Anglican spiritual tradition to understand what had happened to him over the years (Cracknell and White, *World Methodism*, p. 15).

15 See George Whitefield, 1960, *George Whitefield's Journals*, ed. Iain H. Murray, London: Banner of Truth; Harry S. Stout, 1991, *The Divine Dramatist: George Whitefield and the Rise of Modern Evangelicalism*, Grand Rapids, MI: Eerdmans.

16 Journal for 27 April 1739, in *George Whitefield's Journals*, p. 259.

17 Rupp considers that the roots of Wesley's system are to be found in his practice in Georgia (Gordon Rupp, 1986, *Religion in England 1688–1791*, Oxford History of the Christian Church, Oxford: Clarendon, p. 355; cf. Wesley, *Journal*, 17 April 1736).

18 For an exposition of Methodist polity, see Frank Baker, 'The People called Methodists – 3. Polity', in Rupert Davies and Gordon Rupp (eds), 1965, *A History of the Methodist Church in Great Britain*, vol. 1, London: Epworth, pp. 211–55.

19 Quoted by J.R.H. Moorman, 1973, *A History of the Church in England*, 3rd edn, London: Adam & Charles Black, p. 299.

20 It was in 1784 that Samuel Seabury secured episcopal ordination from the Scottish Episcopal Church with the aim of ministering in the United States.

21 Coke was already an ordained Anglican clergyman, but wanted some kind of affirmation of his authoritative position. John Wesley was horrified, though, when Coke accepted the title 'Bishop'.

22 Though Doddridge has been seen as inadvertently contributing to the spread of Unitarian views by refusing to impose any tests of religious belief on applicants to the academy which he founded in 1730.

23 See Frank Rinaldi, *The Tribe of Dan*, Carlisle: Paternoster, forthcoming.

24 Gerald R. Cragg, 1970, *The Church and the Age of Reason 1648–1789*, Pelican History of the Church 4, Harmondsworth: Penguin, p. 181.

25 On Edwards, see Stephen R. Holmes, 2000, *God of Grace and God of Glory: An Account of the Theology of Jonathan Edwards*, Edinburgh: T. & T. Clark; G.M. Marsden, 2003, *Jonathan Edwards: A Life*, New Haven, CT: Yale University Press. Edwards's works are appearing in a multi-volume edition from Yale University Press.

26 Ward, *Protestant Evangelical Awakening*, p. 278. In response to the falling

away of many of his converts, he had attempted to insist on a strict testimony to conversion and change as a pre-requisite to church membership.

27 Mark A. Noll, 1992, *A History of Christianity in the United States and Canada*, London: SPCK, pp. 90, 98–100.

28 Ward, *Protestant Evangelical Awakening*, p. 295.

PART 2   1789–1914

Timeline: World Events, 1789–1914

1800	Camp Meetings spark off 'Second Great Awakening' in USA
1801	Concordat between the Vatican and France
1807	First Protestant missionary to China (Robert Morison)
1810	American Board of Commissioners for Foreign Missions founded
1813	Missionaries allowed to enter East India Company's area of influence
1814	Jesuits restored
1815	Treaty of Vienna
1817	Union of Lutherans and Reformed in Prussia and elsewhere
1821	Greece rebels against Ottoman rule, the first of several Eastern European countries to seek independence
1830	Latter-Day Saints founded
1835	David Strauss, *Life of Jesus*
1848	*Communist Manifesto* published
1854	Immaculate Conception declared to be an article of faith by Pius IX
1858	Apparitions at Lourdes
1861–5	American Civil War
1864	*Syllabus of Errors*; first black Anglican bishop (Samuel Ajayi Crowther)
1865	China Inland Mission founded
1867	First Lambeth Conference
1868	White Fathers founded
1869–70	First Vatican Council defines doctrine of papal infallibility
1870	Franco-Prussian War
1872	German *Kulturkampf* begins
1872	First 'Ethiopian' church founded
1886	Student Volunteer Movement for Foreign Missions founded
1891	Leo XIII in *Rerum Novarum* offers landmark statement of Catholic social teaching
1901/06	Pentecostalism begins in North America
1902	Philippine Independent Church secedes from Rome; Ecumenical Patriarch issues an encyclical advocating efforts towards Christian unity
1907	Papal condemnation of Catholic Modernism
1908	US Federal Council of Churches of Christ founded
1910	World Missionary Conference at Edinburgh
1910–15	*The Fundamentals* published
1914	World War I begins

7

Orthodoxy

Russia

Orthodoxy in nineteenth-century Russia may have appeared to be in an unpromising state of organizational subservience to the civil power, but in fact this was an age of spiritual renewal and creative theology. After Catherine the Great died in 1796, monastics returning to Russia brought with them hesychast spirituality and the idea of spiritual fatherhood. As a result, the nineteenth century became the great age of the *starets* (plural *startsy*), the equivalent of the Greek *gerōn* ('elder'). These were spiritual guides who exercised a great deal of influence on those who sought their counsel.[1] They could be men or women, and were often monastics; some were priests, and others were lay people, but they tended to function as a kind of alternative or supplementary spiritual leadership. This was partly because the priesthood was seen as closely linked with the interests of the state (and hence often as morally compromised) and its role was thought to be primarily that of dispensing the sacraments and conducting public worship. A noted centre for this ministry was the monastery at Optina in the north of the country, whose elders exercised an influential ministry to the thousands of pilgrims who came seeking counsel, until the monastery was closed by the Bolshevik authorities in 1923.

The first of the *startsy* is often said to have been St Seraphim of Sarov (1759–1833). He spent 16 years in a monastic community and 20 as a hermit before beginning to receive a stream of visitors, who testified to his spiritual discernment. His disciple Nicholas Motovilov recorded that on one occasion he could not bear to look at Seraphim, whose face had been radiantly transfigured – a visible expression of Orthodox belief in deification (transfiguration into the likeness of God) as the goal of the believer.[2]

One who served as a parish priest was St John of Kronstadt (1829–1908), a naval town near St Petersburg. He was known for his life of prayer and his passionate manner of celebrating the liturgy (he was forced to revive the practice of public confession of sins because too many came to him for their confessions to be heard privately, and he saw this as a means of conversion), as well as his spiritual direction and his concern for the poor (among other things, he initiated what might now be called a job-creation scheme which employed several thousand people).

It should be noted that both the practice of seeking counsel from an elder and the cultivation of hesychast-type spirituality were not reserved for the higher ranks of church or society, but formed significant aspects of popular devotion. One writing which became enormously influential was the anonymous work *The Way of a Pilgrim*, which describes how one simple pilgrim journeyed throughout Russia during the 1850s seeking to learn how to pray. The spirituality he advocated was centred on the 'Jesus Prayer', 'Lord Jesus Christ, have mercy on me', and its exposition in the *Philokalia*. Monasticism also flourished after its near-extinction during the mid-eighteenth century: between 1850 and 1912, numbers of male religious rose from 10,000 to over 21,000, and those of female religious from 8,500 to over 70,000.

One spiritual leader who also held high office in the institutional church was St Philaret (1782–1867), Metropolitan of Moscow from 1821; he sought to re-present Orthodox teaching in an authentically Russian manner which contrasted with previous tendencies to Latinization under the Enlightenment-influenced regimes of Peter and Catherine. A growing disapproval of modern Western thought was more widely evident, along with a measure of intellectual renewal: the 'Slavophil' movement represents a response to the large-scale apostasy of the Westernized Russian upper classes. An important concept in its thinking was that of *sobornost*, which could be translated as 'individual diversity in free unity'.[3] The most influential exponent of this was the layman A.S. Khomiakov (1804–60), who saw it as combining the elements of catholicity and conciliarity, or unity and freedom. Catholicism had unity, but in the form of papal despotism; Protestantism had freedom, but it had run to anarchy: a balanced combination was needed, which could be found in Orthodoxy alone. Rome located authority in the papacy, and Protestantism in the Scriptures; but Orthodoxy, Khomiakov asserted, had retained the vision of the whole Church as guided by the Holy Spirit and therefore authoritative. His vision was of an Orthodoxy freed from the recent tendency to derive its arguments and opponents from the Western tradition, because it could draw upon its own theological resources. Among the Slavophils the 'Third Rome' ideology experienced something of a revival; some of them saw Russia as having a decisive role to play in a coming crisis of Western civilization, as the main scene of the battle between Christian and non-Christian forces. But this was no slick triumphalism: the Church, they believed, would be called to suffer. The Slavophil movement prepared the way for a return to Christianity among many Russian intellectuals in the decades before the Revolution.

At the same time as the Church's organizational centre in Moscow was stagnating because of its suffocating links with the state, mission flourished in a manner as remarkable as that experienced by Roman Catholicism. The renewal of Russian missionary vision appears to have derived its dynamism from the resurgence of Orthodox spirituality. As so often, the way was often opened by colonization, as Russian government spread eastwards throughout Siberia and Alaska. Much nineteenth-century expansion was resourced from Kazan, where a theological academy (1842, one of only four in Russia) and missionary training centre (1854) were founded. In 1870, the Orthodox Missionary Society was founded by Innokenti Veniaminov (1797–1879), who had been a missionary bishop in the Far East before his appointment as Metropolitan of Moscow; the society was intended to enable mission to become the activity of the whole Church, and not just of a few pioneers. Before 1900 the liturgy had been translated into 22 languages or dialects, and so much Bible translation had been undertaken that calls began to be made for the Scriptures to be translated into Russian. A notable example of missionary adaptability was Nikolai Ilminsky (1822–91): perplexed at the spread of Islam among tribes along the Volga and in the Urals, he concluded that their written languages were so infused with Muslim theology that preaching should switch to using their spoken languages, a move which resulted in a number of conversions.

Orthodox and Protestant 'sects' remained a significant feature of Russian life. The Old Believers increased by at least six times between 1764 and 1825; one stream gained its own bishop in 1846 and hence was able to restore a hierarchy and resume a full sacramental life. Apart from the Old Believers, the eighteenth-century groups already noted continued active (and continued to divide), and a number of churchmen began to fear the danger presented by the heterodox. The century also saw the establishment from 1867 of a thriving Russian Baptist community, which prospered in Ukraine and drew many former Molokans to receive believer's baptism. Also in Ukraine were the Stundists (so named from the German *Stunde*, 'hour', a reference to their small group meetings). They had come into existence around 1860 under Mennonite and Protestant influence, and gradually moved towards adopting Baptist views. Other evangelical groups also appeared, such as the 'Evangelical Christians' or *Radstokisty*, so named from one of their progenitors, Lord Radstock; from 1870 these gained a number of converts among the Westernized upper classes, especially in St Petersburg. Thus when these groups came together in the twentieth century, varying roots were the cause of some measure of internal tension among Russian and Ukrainian Baptists.

Under the visionary Tsar Alexander I (1801–25), an unusual measure of freedom was allowed to agencies such as the Bible societies, a Russian one being founded in Moscow in 1812. He himself was a non-doctrinal, non-sacramental, Bible-reading individualist, attracted to both Pietist-type mysticism and freemasonry. His breadth of outlook is evident from the leading role he played in the 'Holy Alliance' formed in 1815; in it Orthodox Russia, now one of the great powers after defeating Napoleon in 1812, joined with Catholic Austria and Protestant Prussia to stand against the threat posed by the godless ideology of revolutionary France.

Such openness to the West did not continue: Nicholas I (1825–55) forbade the circulation of vernacular editions of the Bible (the New Testament had been translated into contemporary Russian), although the Bible Society restarted in 1831, focusing on non-Russian ethnic groups. The later nineteenth century saw the government basing its authority on the three pillars of Orthodoxy, autocracy, and nationality.[4] The Church appeared to enjoy a privileged position, but in reality it was in enforced subjection to the state. Effectively controlled by state officials at every level, it was unable to speak freely as books and sermons had to be officially approved. Only after the early 1880s was it allowed any role in education apart from the provision of seminary training (and that not infrequently turned pupils without a vocation to the priesthood into anti-religious revolutionaries). The last procurator, Konstantin Pobedonostsev (1828–1907), who served from 1880 to 1905, was one of the most repressive: not only did he oppose Protestantism, but he also regarded the Orthodox Church as a state department whose functions included the propping up of the tsarist regime.

With the end of Pobedonostsev's rule it became possible to grant religious equality to all Russian citizens. Since non-Orthodox groups (including the Old Believers) then acquired legal status and the right to self-government, it was only logical that the same privilege should be restored to Orthodoxy. Preparations therefore began for a church council, although renewed state oppression meant that it would not take place until 1917. Among the topics mooted for discussion were the raising of educational and economic standards for the clergy and a restoration of the female diaconate which had existed in the early Christian centuries.

Ottoman domination and its legacy

Even after centuries of conversions to Islam, by the nineteenth century a third of the population of the Ottoman Empire remained Christian; the great majority were Orthodox but about 10 per cent were Roman Catholic (including the Eastern-rite churches).

The 1820s saw systematic persecution of Christians by the Ottomans, in part sparked off by growing nationalist sentiments in various quarters of the Empire. At Easter 1821 the Ecumenical Patriarch was hanged, still in his liturgical robes, and 30,000 Greeks killed in retaliation for the uprising. However, in due course secularization brought a measure of relief in some areas as Christians began to be treated equally with Muslims. But it also led to an erosion of the power of the Ecumenical Patriarch, as a number of Christian communities became recognized as *millets* in their own right, among them the Syrian Catholics (1830), the Melkite Catholics (1838), and the Chaldeans (1845). Christians gradually acquired an increasing measure of civil and political rights during the century, but they remained liable to suffer a backlash because of the sultans' suspicion that the diplomatic activity of Western powers on their behalf involved the Christian population in disloyalty to the Empire. In addition, there was often jealousy of Christians because the provision of better educational and health-care facilities among them by Western missions enabled them to modernize more effectively than non-Christian groups, and to develop their national consciousness. This was especially evident among the Armenians, among whom some of the worst persecution of Christian ethnic groups occurred from the 1890s, as when 3,000 Armenians were burnt alive in the cathedral at Urfa (the ancient Edessa) in 1895.

In 1908 the reformist Young Turks seized power and a constitution was proclaimed, but massacres continued, now as part of a policy of enforced mass deportation. This culminated in the genocide of the remaining Armenian population during the early twentieth century and the massacre of large numbers of ethnic Greeks living in Turkey just after the First World War. Between 1915 and 1923 an estimated 1.5 million Armenians died. By this point many Christian communities in the Middle East had begun to lose large numbers of members through emigration, especially to North America. Ironically, it was the education provided by the missions which often enabled local people to raise their expectations, and so it can be argued that mission ultimately and inadvertently contributed to the dispersal of ancient Christian populations.

For many nations under Ottoman rule the relationship between Orthodoxy and nationalism became an extremely close one, and this explains many of the attitudes shown by Orthodox in south-east Europe today. In earlier times Orthodox Christians had been conscious of belonging to something much larger than their own ethnic group, an outlook fostered by belonging to the Byzantine Empire. After its collapse, its legacy of religious internationalism gradually faded, and by the nineteenth century we see in most countries the identification of religious allegiance and ethnic identity to the exclusion of any sense of belonging to something transcending ethnic boundaries. From being a local manifestation of 'ecumenical' Orthodoxy (that is, a faith which was diffused throughout the *oikoumene*, the inhabited world), each jurisdiction became a central pillar of the emerging nation states, providing an ideology to unify it and legitimate its rulers. Autocephaly 'emancipated national churches from Constantinople only to deliver them up to the control of secular states'.[5]

The Ottomans had treated the Ecumenical Patriarch as head of all Christians within their dominions but, as Kallistos Ware has pointed out, 'as Turkish power declined, the frontiers of the Patriarchate contracted'.[6] It became possible for nations to struggle for ecclesiastical as well as political independence; that involved challenging not only the Ottomans but also the Greek-dominated ecclesiastical leadership. In a number of former Ottoman dominions political independence was secured by leaders with a secularizing and modernizing outlook which brought them into collision with national hierarchies. A less positive result of this process was that although Orthodoxy might be recognized as the state religion, it was also liable to be regarded as a state department responsible for carrying out government policy: one kind of servitude had perhaps been exchanged for another.

An uprising in Greece from 1821, supported by monks on Mount Athos as well as many of the bishops and other clergy, resulted in independence being declared in 1832. The following year the Church declared its independence from Constantinople, setting a pattern in which political independence was followed closely by ecclesiastical, and reinforcing the role of the Church as the bearer of national culture and the tendency to identify the Church with the nation. Greek church–state relations followed the German-inspired model adopted by Peter the Great in Russia, with secular authorities being required to ratify major decisions. Also paralleling Russian events, many monasteries and nunneries were suppressed in 1833. As was to happen so often during the century, Constantinople was slow to recognize the newly autonomous church; in this case, it refused to do so until 1850 because autonomy had been sought (or rather, unilaterally declared) in a manner deemed uncanonical. The Ecumenical Patriarch was, of course, in a delicate situation, in that he could not be seen by the Ottomans to be giving approval to movements for independence by recognizing national churches in areas where these were active, but throughout the century the patriarchate was also concerned to uphold the wider vision of a transnational communion. Unfortunately, this was made more difficult by the suffering and martyrdom which were the lot of a number of the hierarchy during the independence struggle; their acclamation as 'ethnomartyrs' contributed to the process of narrowing of Orthodox vision.

A similar, if less bloody, sequence of events occurred in Romania; it became politically independent in 1877, although Transylvania was not added to the nation until 1918, when the Austro-Hungarian Empire was dismembered. In 1864 the Romanian Orthodox Church, which included Transylvania and so provided a focus for nationalist aspirations, declared its independence from Constantinople, a move which only received patri-

archal recognition in 1885. As in Greece, the Church was treated virtually as a state department, and as in Russia the Westernized intelligentsia
tended to look down on the priesthood.

The most intractable problem was presented by Bulgaria: because the
Bulgarian wish for ecclesiastical independence preceded national independence, it lacked a canonical basis, and it has been called 'a substitute
for a political liberation movement'.[7] The Ottoman Empire recognized
the Church's independence in 1870, but two years later Constantinople
cut off relations because independence had been sought on ethnic grounds
rather than political ones. It alleged that the Bulgarian church was guilty
of the heresy of *phyletism*, 'maintaining that ecclesiastical jurisdiction
is determined ethnically rather than territorially',[8] and hence identifying
the Church's interests too closely with those of a particular ethnic group.
The picture is complicated by the fact that the Church was struggling to
end the dominance of Greek-speaking clergy installed by Constantinople.
Political autonomy came about in 1878 and full independence in 1908,
thus removing the barrier to seeking a regularization of the Church's
status, but feelings were such that this was not done until 1945. Until
that point, the Bulgarian church was deemed to be in schism and so was
out of communion with the Ecumenical Patriarch.

Serbia provided the only exception to this pattern. It became politically
independent in 1878, having been a Russian protectorate since 1817. The
Serbian church achieved autonomy in 1831 and autocephaly in 1879.
On each occasion, the request was readily granted by the Ecumenical
Patriarchate because it was consistent with canonical provisions for such
matters. In the same way, various Orthodox jurisdictions in the new
state of Yugoslavia were amalgamated without patriarchal opposition
in 1919.

Churches in the Middle East felt the impact of Western missionary
expansion. From 1810 onwards, Western agencies began to make contact with churches in the East of the Ottoman Empire and beyond, especially in Egypt, Lebanon, Syria, Armenia, Iraq, and Persia (modern Iran).
Often this followed the development of economic and diplomatic (or at
least protection-seeking) relationships between Middle Eastern communities and Western colonial powers. This included the Church of the East,
by this point restricted to what is now northern Iraq; when rediscov-
ered by the West early in the century, they were seen as 'Protestants of
the East' because of their rejection of icons (a feature common in non-
Chalcedonian churches) and their opposition to the papacy; a number of
Western Protestant denominations therefore worked among them.

The Turkish Armenian population also proved particularly responsive, not least because their precarious position left them in especial need
of foreign protection and advocacy. Eschatological considerations had
motivated the newly founded American Board of Commissioners for

Foreign Missions (ABCFM) to begin work in the East in 1810 (they were present in Constantinople from 1819); their objective was to reach the Muslim world by stimulating reform in the Eastern churches. As elsewhere in the world, Bible translation was seen as crucial, along with literature production and training preachers and teachers (including local clergy and bishops); the mission published the Scriptures first in classical Armenian, and then in the modern vernacular. The response generated led to more concentrated missionary efforts, including the setting up of schools despite the Armenian patriarch's protests.

Inevitably, from the 1840s new denominations emerged from these churches as groups found themselves so influenced by Western theology and practice that they were unable to continue worshipping in their existing congregations, which were showing increasing hostility to Protestantism (although Protestant-type congregations were allowed to remain as part of the Church of the East until 1871). Thus in 1847 Armenian Evangelicals were granted *millet* status by the sultan, a request supported by Prussia, Britain, and the USA (an example of the interplay between Protestantism and politics in the region during this period). Some agencies, such as the American Presbyterians who worked in Cairo from 1854, made the creation of separate churches their aim from the beginning.

Among the main agencies were the Church Missionary Society (CMS), the London Society for the Promotion of Christianity among the Jews, and the American Board of Commissioners for Foreign Missions; all aimed to establish a presence in strategic locations. By the end of the century Russian Orthodox missionaries were also engaging in proselytism among the 'Nestorians'. By contrast the CMS adopted the policy of seeking to assist those churches to renew themselves rather than to proselytize: it provided education and health care, and advocated their cause in Western political circles. The resulting institutions frequently achieved high reputations locally for their quality and proved valuable when many missions, taking advantage of interest in Western culture and a measure of toleration resulting from Western diplomatic pressure, switched their focus late in the century to evangelizing the Muslim population. This had been their initial objective in the 1830s, but the state of the Eastern churches had been believed to present an obstacle to the credibility of Christianity, hence the focus on assisting them so that they, rather than foreigners, could evangelize local Muslim populations.

Western input could on occasion cause problems for the ancient Eastern churches. For instance, in South India the CMS sought to assist the ancient and indigenous 'Thomas Christians' by teaching and translating. A notable figure in this was Claudius Buchanan (1766–1815), who also campaigned to open the domain of the East India Company to Christian missions. Nevertheless, the impact of Western influence was such that the

Thomas Christians experienced half a century of tension culminating in a split in 1889; the breakaway body, the Mar Thoma Church, incorporated elements of Protestant practice in its worship and rejected ancient cultural elements deemed tainted by association with Hinduism.

In response to Western Protestant successes Rome redoubled its efforts in the Middle East, especially in strengthening the Uniat communities. These experienced varying fortunes under the different empires of the period: in the Austro-Hungarian Empire they flourished; in Russia they were suppressed; and under the Ottomans they were by turns tolerated, protected, and massacred. Like the Orthodox they often provided a means for the expression of nationalist aspirations. In Ukraine in particular, the 'Greek Catholics' played an important role in the formation of a national consciousness and enabled the population to resist assimilation by Polish and then Hungarian culture. Relations with the Orthodox were always particularly difficult: under the *millet* system they were placed under Orthodox jurisdiction, and elsewhere Uniatism represented a kind of treason against their ethnic group because it involved submission to a different ruler, the pope.

However, under Leo XIII (1878–1903) relations between Rome and Eastern-rite jurisdictions improved considerably, and his 1894 encyclical *Orientalium Dignitas* laid the foundation for a new way of relating to one another. He forbade the reception of Orthodox converts into Latin-rite Catholic jurisdictions (in all Orthodox countries there are Western-rite Catholics as well as Eastern-rite communities) and founded a Vatican commission in 1895 which developed into the Congregation for the Oriental Churches (1917).

But it was not only Western powers which sought to colonize the Middle East. Russia, too, was anxious to strengthen its control of the Black Sea area and the regions to the south of its borders, and to that end played up its role as protector of Orthodoxy, the only free Orthodox power. Russian missionaries were therefore active in Armenia, for example, from the late nineteenth century. Even Mount Athos did not escape Russian attention; by 1900 there were more Russian than Greek monks in residence, and it has been suggested that the Tsar intended to use it as a foothold from which to secure control of the Bosphorus and even to take the Ecumenical Throne, although such a move was blocked.

Western activity did indeed bring about the reawakening of Eastern Christianity, though not always in the ways which had been expected. In Egypt, for instance, Napoleon's invasion in 1798 was a watershed in the history of the Coptic Orthodox Church.[9] The following century saw it reintegrated into national life. Rome sought to gain control over the Coptic church, and from 1854 Protestant missionaries were active in Cairo; they soon switched from work among Muslims to proselytizing the Coptic population. The challenges thus presented by the West helped to precipitate the awakening of the Coptic church, which developed an extensive educational arm under Patriarch Cyril IV (1854–61). Even today it is considerably in advance of other Orthodox jurisdictions in its educational work.

Lest the impression be given that most Orthodox jurisdictions could see no further than their own borders, ecclesiastical as well as geographical, an encyclical of 1902 from the Ecumenical Patriarch invited Orthodox leaders to reach a consensus on relationships with Western Christians, Protestant as well as Catholic. This was to prove to be one of the most significant steps towards the modern ecumenical movement, even though the Patriarch was aware that Western Christians were seeking to proselytize among Orthodox populations.[10]

Questions for thought

1 How do you think the state of health of the Russian church in the nineteenth century compared with that of the eighteenth?

2 Why did the desire of East European Orthodox to achieve ecclesiastical independence cause such problems for the Ecumenical Patriarchate?

3 Compare and contrast the attitudes towards local culture and religious expression shown by Protestant and Catholic missions during the nineteenth century.

Further reading

The period between 1453 and 1917 is not well served for historical accounts in English, but some material may be gleaned from general histories of various Eastern European and Near Eastern nations, especially the numerous works on Russia.

Michael Angold (ed.), 2006, *Cambridge History of Christianity*, vol. 5: *Eastern Christianity*, Cambridge: Cambridge University Press, chs 10, 14–15.
Wil van den Bercken, 1999, *Holy Russia and Christian Europe*, London: SCM Press, ch. 8.
G.P. Fedotov (ed.), 1950, *A Treasury of Russian Spirituality*, New York: Harper & Row, especially 'The Conversation of St. Seraphim with Nicholas Motovilov' (pp. 266–79) and St John of Kronstadt, 'My Life in Christ' (pp. 350–416).
C. Frazee, 1969, *The Orthodox Church and Independent Greece 1821–1852*, Cambridge: Cambridge University Press.
Sheridan Gilley and Brian Stanley (eds), 2006, *Cambridge History of Christianity*, vol. 8: *World Christianities c.1815–c.1914*, Cambridge: Cambridge University Press, chs 25, 28.

Philip Walters, 1999, 'Eastern Europe since the fifteenth century', in Adrian Hastings (ed.), *A World History of Christianity*, London: Cassell.

Nicolas Zernov, 1961, *Eastern Christendom: A Study of the Origin and Development of the Eastern Orthodox Church*, London: Weidenfeld & Nicolson, ch. 6.

Notes

1 For a picture of such an elder, see the portrayal of the elder Zosima in Dostoyevsky's novel *The Brothers Karamazov*.

2 On Seraphim, see Valentine Zander, 1975, *St Seraphim of Sarov*, London: SPCK.

3 Walters, 'Eastern Europe', p. 301.

4 Nicholas also resumed severe persecution of the Old Believers, and suppressed Eastern-rite Catholicism throughout Russia; 1839 saw the forced conversion to Orthodoxy of 1.67 million Greek Catholics in former Polish territory.

5 Paschalis M. Kitromilides, in Angold (ed.), *CHC*, vol. 5, p. 248.

6 Timothy [Kallistos] Ware, 1997, *The Orthodox Church*, rev. edn, Harmondsworth: Penguin, p. 91.

7 Kitromilides, in Angold (ed.), *CHC*, vol. 5, p. 241.

8 Walters, 'Eastern Europe', p. 306.

9 On Coptic Orthodoxy, see Christine Chaillot, 2005, *The Coptic Orthodox Church: A Brief Introduction to its Life and Spirituality*, Paris: Inter-Orthodox Dialogue.

10 For a translation of the encyclical, see Gennadios Limouris (ed.), 1994, *Orthodox Visions of Ecumenism: Statements, Messages and Reports on the Ecumenical Movement 1902–1992*, Geneva: WCC, pp. 1–8.

8

Rome, Revolution, and Reaction

The period between the French Revolution and the First World War was to see a strengthening of the Catholic Church's position in areas where it had been oppressed or had been hindered by restrictive legislation, but outbreaks of opposition to it in areas where it had hitherto been dominant (for example, France and parts of Latin America). Overall, we may say that it gained spiritual authority but lost temporal power. This chapter examines the impact on Catholicism of the French Revolution and of contemporary currents of thought, an impact which expressed itself in surprisingly diverse ways.

Revolution

The French Revolution, 1789–1815

The events of the French Revolution are confusing, and a brief summary will be helpful before we assess its impact on the Church.[1] It began with an attempt by French nobility to usurp the power of the monarch, expressed in terms of a new constitution affecting both church and state (by 1789, the latter was close to bankruptcy).

Parish clergy were open to the idea of moderate reform and mostly welcomed Louis XVI's reluctant calling of the States-General, which had not met since 1614. The 'Third Estate' (that is, the commoners, the first two estates comprising the nobility and the higher clergy) declared itself to be the National Assembly to the exclusion of the others, though they later joined it. Under the initial reforms, the number of dioceses was reduced from 130 to 83, with boundaries coterminous with the civil *départements*; church lands were to be nationalized and sold, but clergy were to be paid by the state; and monasteries were dissolved. Motivation for such changes was not so much hostility to religion itself as resentment at the wealth of the Church coupled with the pressing need to do something about the parlous condition of state finances. Protestants were to be given the same freedoms as Catholics, and religious toleration was extended to Jews in 1791 (uniquely for this period). Under the influence of Enlightenment thought, sovereignty was vested in the people rather than the monarch, whose authority was to be constitutional rather than absolute; institutions thus derived their authority from the nation, and so could be regarded as departments of state – including the Church. At this stage, rank and file clergy were keen to make the most of their new freedom to be fully involved in government.

The Civil Constitution of the Clergy (1790) provided for the election of bishops and clergy by parliament and local electors respectively, and required clergy to swear to uphold its provisions. The oath was enforced from November 1790 but by the following April only 55 per cent of clergy had taken it. This was not because it was anti-Catholic in itself, but because many clergy objected to its imposition without any attempt to consult the Church, which they saw as amounting to state interference in church affairs. Many therefore would only swear it with certain qualifications, which in the eyes of the authorities amounted to not swearing it at all. The result was a split between those clergy willing to swear the oath as it stood (the constitutional clergy) and those who were not (the non-jurors).

Things took a sharp turn for the worse from 1791, when a new Legislative Assembly came to power which was more anticlerical. By the time war was declared on Austria (which was allied with Prussia) in April 1792, the pope had condemned the *Declaration of the Rights of Man* (published in August 1789, this had affirmed the equality of all before the law), the Civil Constitution, and the underlying principles of the revolution. From both sides there appeared to be no way in which the clergy could work with the revolutionary state. Early in 1793, too, there was a religiously motivated peasant uprising in Brittany and the Vendée. Not surprisingly, therefore, the regime turned up the pressure on the Church. During the 'Reign of Terror' (1793–4), which climaxed in the execution of Louis XVI, between 2,000 and 5,000 priests were executed, as were many female religious. The constitutional clergy were not exempted from persecution; the state had treated Christians as opponents of the revolution, even though many were not at first, and now Christianity had become a powerful motivating force for counter-revolutionary feeling, with some priests taking a commanding role in counter-revolutionary guerrilla warfare. (Note that it was religion, and not royalist sympathies, which fulfilled this role.)

A concerted attempt was made to replace Catholicism with a new religion, the cult of Reason. This even extended to the introduction of a new calendar in 1793, dated from 22 September 1792 (the date when a republic was declared), with new names for days, months, and seasons, and new festivals to replace the old ones, which were associated with religion. The cult of Reason proved unpopular, and was briefly replaced in 1794 by the cult of the Supreme Being.

The dechristianization campaign drew on Enlightenment thought and popular anticlericalism, but it may be seen more as an expression of something negative – grievances against the Church – rather than as offering any serious positive alternative. Although the campaign was undertaken by the army rather than being primarily a spontaneous manifestation of majority opinion, the Church was dealt a devastating blow; whole areas saw the disappearance of any form of public Christian worship, and in many religious observance never recovered to pre-revolution levels. A generation grew up without any religious training. Where worship was maintained, it was not infrequently conducted by lay people, resulting in a reversal of the Tridentine attempts to bring a measure of order, decorum, and centralization into the chaotic mess of local observances: pilgrimages and observance of local saints' days, which the clergy had tried to suppress, now reappeared with a vengeance. Women bore a major role in the preservation of the faith. It must be remembered that from 1792 onwards, 25–40,000 priests fled the country (a law of 26 August had required non-juring clergy to do so), though many returned after 1801. About 7–10,000 ended up in Britain (including the Channel Islands), 6–8,000 in Spain, and up to 5,000 in Rome, where the pope had offered them sanctuary.

To many onlookers, it seemed as if the revolution had overthrown not only the French church but also the papacy itself. It was 'the most inimical onslaught by any government against organised religion for nearly 1,500 years',[2] a Christian state turning against Christianity. Small wonder that among Catholics as well as Protestants many thought that the end-times foretold by the book of Revelation had arrived. Their apocalyptic pessimism neatly counter-balanced the millennial language used by some of the more naive supporters of the revolution. We shall see this polarity of eschatological attitudes again when we look at developments in the English-speaking world, as evangelical millennialism of various types was decisively shaped by the French Revolution.

At the same time as the revolution was being worked out in France, French forces were engaging in a series of military conquests abroad, where they carried out the same dechristianizing programme as part of the process of setting up satellite republics. In 1796, they set up a republic in Rome and forced Pius VI into exile (he died at Valence, south of Lyons, in 1799). Elsewhere French forces engaged in religious persecution: in Spain, Belgium, and the area west of the Rhine in Germany. During the late 1790s a number of popular counter-revolutionary movements emerged which drew on Christian imagery; areas affected included France, Belgium, and northern Italy. Because the clergy played a leading role, French reprisals were often directed at the Church.

At home, however, a coup in 1794 allowed the moderates to regain power, resulting in a let-up of the pressure on the Church; worship was once again allowed and proved very popular. Non-juring clergy began to return to France, celebrating the sacraments in secret and sheltering in a network of safe houses. Paradoxically, it was not until in 1795, just as the worst was ending, that the Catholic Church in France was formally disestablished. A brief recurrence of dechristianization from September 1797 ended after the seizure of power by Napoleon Bonaparte (1769–1821), the youngest general in the French army, in 1799. He was a realist, and while not a religious man himself, like many eighteenth-century French thinkers he believed that religion could play a useful social role as an instrument of domestic policy. He therefore sought to implement whatever religious policy was deemed most acceptable to the population (and thus most conducive to social order) in each area of his dominions. In Egypt this favoured Islam; but in France it involved rebuilding the Church, and in particular reuniting those who had refused the oath and those who had sworn it. He made a concordat with the papacy in 1801, which was formally promulgated in churches at Easter 1802 (with the unilateral addition of 67 Organic Articles of a rather Gallican complexion, to the papacy's dismay), regulating church–state relations in France, in which the state took over church property but agreed to pay clerical stipends. More remarkably, in 1804 he asked the pope to anoint him as Emperor, thus conferring an increased legitimacy on his rule and countering his opponents' claim to be the true supporters of the Church. This was no relationship of humble submission, though: from 1808, he tried to break the pope, occupying Rome, incorporating the Papal States into the French Empire the following year, and deporting the pope to France.

The concordat of 1801 had laid down that all bishops, whether from the 'constitutional clergy' appointed after 1790 or from those who had refused to swear the oath, should resign and replacements be appointed. They were to be nominated by Napoleon but instituted to their sees by the pope. However, the deep division between the constitutional clergy and the non-jurors made schism inevitable: some bishops and clergy refused to recognize the provisions of the concordat and formed the *Petite Église*, centred on Lyons. Deadlock also ensued over the refusal of Pius VII to institute the bishops nominated by Napoleon; eventually the latter offered to restore the temporal power of the papacy, but Pius refused to negotiate until restored to Rome and freed from his captivity. This ensued in 1814 with the defeat of Napoleon by a coalition including Austria, Great Britain, Prussia, and Russia; on his return to Rome the pope also restored the Jesuits, thus demonstrating his determination not to be dominated by the demands of European governments. Unquestionably the pope's principled resistance to Napoleon had raised the spiritual authority of the papacy and attracted considerable public sympathy, so helping to prepare the way for the dominance of Ultramontanism in nineteenth-century Catholicism as a reaction against political aggression.[3]

By 1815, when the Treaty of Vienna ended the Napoleonic wars, there were in Europe about 100 million Catholics, 40 million Protestants, and the same number of Orthodox, but it was the non-Catholic powers (Great Britain, Prussia, and Russia) who were stronger in political and military terms. The treaty restored the Papal States, which had been occupied by Napoleon in 1808, but the papacy had great difficulties in balancing its role as a temporal power (which was seen as guaranteeing its independence of judgement in the international arena) with a commitment to political neutrality, especially when its temporal interests were threatened.

Nationalism and anticlericalism

It is noteworthy that the later years of the century saw anticlerical policies being adopted in many European Catholic countries. Factors behind this included reaction to the heightened claims being made for papal authority and to Roman opposition to liberalism, and the need for states to establish a distinctive identity which would secure the loyalty of their people. While some anticlericalists sought to continue the suppression of public Christianity which had been attempted during the French Revolution, the Catholic Church was unwilling to withdraw from the public sphere because of its sense of divine vocation to reconstruct the social order according to Christian principles, and its commitment to education as a primary mode of instruction in the faith.

In France anticlericalism was to surface in various forms during the century. The restored hierarchy were highly royalist in their sympathies, but their lack of understanding of contemporary realities provoked hostility. Under the rule of Charles X (1824–30) the alliance of Catholicism and the old aristocracy experienced a revival, provoking opposition from the more liberal-minded middle classes. This was to endure, and as they came to exercise increasing political power it was to have important consequences for relations between church, state, and society. These were most evident later in the century: 'laicization' was seen as a policy which could unite the republican coalition which came to power in 1879, and so the state attempted to secularize education, this being recognized as a key aspect of the Church's hold on the population: priests and religious were banned from teaching in state schools, and religion was removed from the curriculum. In addition, religious elements were removed from state ceremonies and Sunday work was permitted. These measures were followed in the 1900s by legislation against monasticism. In 1905 the government annulled the concordat of 1801, severed diplomatic relations with the papacy, and separated church and state, confiscating much of the Church's property in the process. Church property was to be transferred to lay 'cultural associations'; however, although most bishops and clergy were ready to comply, Pius X forbade the formation of such bodies during his reign, and the Church's consequent failure to act led to much ecclesiastical property being converted to secular use.

Church and state continued to clash in Italy from the restoration of the Papal States in 1815 until their incorporation into Italy in 1870, the Church finding itself on the wrong side of the growing nationalist movement. When revolution engulfed Italy in 1848 (as it also did Germany and France), Pius IX rejected its democratic principles, and went into exile until 1850. Late in the century Leo XIII's lack of sympathy with Italian nationalism also helped to strengthen anticlerical and anti-Catholic feeling, leading to government restrictions on church activities.

The mid-1830s saw the dissolution of monastic orders in Portugal and Spain and the appropriation of their property by the state, repeating Napoleon's actions in 1808–9 (see below). (Most Spanish bishops had been exiled then, and French reprisals had created martyrs and strengthened popular loyalty to the Church.) The Church was to recover, and after the reintroduction of religious orders they grew rapidly: in 1860 there were 1,683 men and 18,819 women in orders in Spain, and by 1910 the figures had risen to 13,359 and 46,357 respectively. Nevertheless, relations with the state were unsettled and at times turbulent, and this continued until the Civil War of 1936–9, a major factor in which was the antagonism between political liberals and right-wing clergy.

The dominance of Prussia in German affairs, secured by the unification of Germany in 1870, was followed by a concerted attempt to marginalize the Catholic Church, whose loyalty to a foreign leader (reinforced by the declaration of his infallibility resulting from the Vatican Council of 1869–70) was seen as suspect. German nationalism was seen as a Protestant phenomenon; the enemies recently defeated (Austria in 1866 and France in 1870–1) had been Catholic. The state took control of education, including seminaries, and expelled most religious orders. Prussian legislation in 1875 removed Catholic constitutional freedoms; by the following year all Prussian bishops were in prison or had fled abroad, and a third of parishes were left without priests. The conflict, labelled the *Kulturkampf* ('struggle for culture / civilization'), came to an end when relations with Rome were restored from 1882 and anti-Catholic legislation was thereafter moderated because of the need to secure Catholic support in the face of the threat presented by the National Liberals and the Socialists. (Bismarck, the Prussian leader, opposed Socialism because it, like Catholicism, was seen as a transnational phenomenon.)

Latin America also saw an upsurge of anticlericalism in several newly independent nations. The continent had been divided up between Spain and Portugal at the end of the fifteenth century, and their crowns had retained control over church appointments. When invasion by Napoleon in 1808–9 resulted in the introduction of anticlerical republican government at home, it was only to be expected that Spanish and Portuguese colonies should seek independence over the following three decades, and that similar sentiments should shape the form taken by independence movements. But why did these countries, which had been colonized by Catholic powers, turn so violently anticlerical on gaining independence? One explanation lies in the recognition that liberal political and social thought existed in various forms, which related to religion differently. In Northern Europe the Catholic Church was allowed to open or re-open schools, churches, and monasteries, often by Protestant-leaning governments. By contrast, in Southern Europe (with which we may include France) and Latin America, liberals sought freedom from perceived ecclesiastical domination of society and so closed such institutions as part of their attempt to exclude the Church from public affairs. Church and state were formally separated in Colombia (1853), Brazil (1891), Cuba (1902), Uruguay (1909), and Portugal (1911).

Initially, however, the new governments were usually concerned to uphold Catholicism as the state's religion and to seek papal recognition and direct relationships with Rome, and it can be argued that anticlerical measures represented not persecution but reform. Just as the Spanish and Portuguese rulers had decided church affairs, so too their successors believed it appropriate to do the same. The slowness of the papacy to recognize the new governments, due partly to their perceived lack of legitimation because they had come into being through revolution, may have made a number of South American states more genuinely anticlerical: papal recognition only began with Colombia (1835) and Mexico (1836).

In East Asia, church–state relations were also challenging. Korean Catholics were persecuted from the start because of their refusal to participate in Confucian ancestral rites (the fact that they did refuse indicates the changed outlook of missionaries, Jesuits in seventeenth-century China having allowed participation until it was condemned by Rome). Persecution culminated in the period 1866–71, when 8,000 out of 15,000 Korean Catholics were martyred; by 1881, however, it had ended, due to the state's desire to establish good relations with Western powers. Thereafter the Catholic community grew to 73,000 by 1910. Martyrdom was also the lot of 30,000 Vietnamese Catholics between 1848 and 1860, but thereafter the community grew from 400,000 to 870,000 by 1915, in spite of the loss of 130,000 more martyrs. In Japan the Catholic community had gone underground since its proscription in the early seventeenth century; when Western missionaries began to visit the country once again from the 1860s, they were amazed to discover that this community still survived, centred on Nagasaki, even though it had had no clergy for over two centuries. Anti-Christian edicts were abolished in 1873, and a measure of growth followed, although the perceived backward status of the *Kakure Kirishitan* ('hidden Christians') presented an obstacle to educated Japanese interested in the new faith. Similarly, about 200,000 Catholics survived in China at the end of the eighteenth century, although with very few priests; persecution was renewed early in the nineteenth century, but Western involvement in China would lead to greater freedom and hence to growth.

By contrast Poland provides an example of nationalism and Catholicism reinforcing one another. In 1795 the old Polish–Lithuanian state was partitioned between Prussia, Austria and Russia. The nineteenth century saw a lengthy struggle to regain independence and reunite the nation. Catholics were oppressed by Protestant Prussia and Orthodox Russia, and Uniats were distrusted by the Austrians because they were identified with Ukrainian nationalist aspirations. Resisting attempts to assimilate them, Poles attached a symbolic significance to the continuing use of their own language; Polish identity became tightly bound up with allegiance to Catholicism (to the extent that over 90 per cent of them were observant Catholics), an outlook which easily withstood the post-1945 period of Communist rule, and which was earlier exported to the United States, where millions of Poles settled from the end of the nineteenth century.

Reaction

The growth of Ultramontanism

The century was marked by changing understandings of the papacy and of authority in the Church, and the greatly increased stature of successive occupants of the papal throne. Much of the underpinning for these developments was provided by the development of Ultramontanism, which we defined earlier as a particularly strongly Rome-centred form of Catholicism which saw the authority of Rome as above that of nation states. One of its first modern advocates was Joseph de Maistre (1754–1821), who argued that ultimately the papacy was the basis of all legitimate political sovereignty, since the moral and religious foundation truths for society had been divinely revealed and were handed on in the Church. His work *Du Pape* (1819) has been regarded as a key exposition of this outlook.

Another advocate of Ultramontanism was the French priest F.R. de Lamennais (1782–1854). For him the social utility of Christianity derived from its being true; however, this was not discovered by the exercise of individual reason, for truth was a matter of the common consent of humanity to universal divine revelation (which he equated with Catholicism): 'the individual is dependent on the community for his knowledge of the truth'.[4] Since papal authority was both absolute and infallible, the papacy needed to regain its right to intervene in world affairs as supreme ruler, and guarantor of the freedom of Christians. In this way it could establish brotherly relationships between nations. Individual national churches were too liable to state control, and so de Lamennais advocated the separation of church and state because formal relationships between the two served only to hinder religion; in place of church–state ties, he called for an alliance between the Church and democracy. Such views might not be thought of as characteristically ultramontane, and he met with an unsympathetic response from Rome, which saw any alliance between the Church and liberalism as unnatural and condemned his views in two encyclicals, *Mirari vos* (1832) and *Singulari nos* (1834). It was unusual for an individual's views to be denounced explicitly in this way, and in due course he left the Church.

Ultramontanism was to mark Roman thinking for the rest of this period and was a catalyst for anticlericalism in various countries. Gradually it took on more of a defensive twist, as the papacy came to be (and to see itself as) the rock of defence against modern intellectual and political trends. For much of the century, too, 'the papacy insisted on confronting new problems with past solutions'.[5] An example of this is provided by Gregory XVI (1831–46); although he laid much of the foundation for the expansion of nineteenth-century Catholic missions, as a monastic he did not really understand the impact of industrialization and modernization, and in *Mirari vos* he condemned de Lamennais's version of the liberal programme for society. Incidentally, it has been suggested that Roman opposition to democracy sprang in part from a fear that its introduction in the Papal States would run counter to their theocratic government; the popes 'universally condemned movements in the world at large which seemed similar to those causing difficulties within their own dominions'.[6]

In Germany Ultramontanism proved attractive to the Church's hierarchy as a way of preserving the Church's independence as well as enhancing episcopal authority, especially to those who had formerly been prince-bishops (the last of whose domains had disappeared in 1803). Under more or less hostile Protestant rule for much of the time, the bishops looked to Rome rather than to their own state for support for their authority and a guarantee of their independence.

Pius IX (1846–78) was a liberal thinker in some respects, and early in his reign he was warmly applauded for his approval of modern technology and his expressed determination to take such steps as introducing railways to the Papal States. He was also willing to explore the scope for convergence between religion and liberal ideals of progress. However, the revolutionary events of 1848, which resulted in his exile from Rome until 1850, led him to drop thoughts of political reform; he seems to have thought his actions partly to blame for the Italian unrest. Religiously and theologically, too, Pius was a traditionalist in his views. He was responsible for the definition of the dogma of the Immaculate Conception, the belief that Mary was conceived without original sin. In 1849 an encyclical to church leaders invited their views on the subject. Receiving majority approval, he had a draft definition prepared by two Jesuits, which the bishops meeting in Rome modified. The dogma was then solemnly proclaimed in the bull *Ineffabilis Deus*, on 8 December 1854, the Feast of the Immaculate Conception. Significantly, it was defined on his authority, and not that of a council of the Church, and it was based on the consensus of the Church at that time, rather than the testimony of Catholic tradition.

Pius was able to capitalize on the Ultramontanist vogue and to exercise an extraordinary degree of influence on the shape of contemporary Catholicism because of the length of his reign, his appointment over a long period of bishops who would support his outlook, and his personal charisma. He was the first of the modern 'superstar' popes, thanks to the increase in pilgrimage to Rome and the assiduous use by the Vatican of the developing media network. The loss of the remaining Papal States in 1870 coincided with an increased emphasis on the pope as spiritual rather than political leader; Pius himself exemplified this style both by his personal bearing and by leading a catechism class each Sunday. Coppa sums up his outlook incisively:

> Pio Nono's claim to be God's representative on earth, and his assertion that the church had to instruct, direct and govern the Christian world, clashed with the liberal demand for popular sovereignty and the nationalist call for the omnipotence of the state. He judged the triumph of liberalism and nationalism attained at the expense of the faith and the enslavement of the church. . . . He likewise disdained the liberal call for individual self-maximization, in place of God's harmonious society.
> . . . Liberal Catholics came in for a special condemnation from the pope, who charged they undermined the spiritual unity of the church while championing a false liberty.[7]

For Pius, Christendom had apostatized, and he advocated a kind of defensively counter-cultural Catholicism which would unite the faithful in loyalty to the pope (as the visible centre of the Church) and separation from the world. The emphasis on the Church as an alternative society thus paralleled (and was reinforced by) the Church's exclusion from temporal power.

The idea of the Church's existence apart from the world gave strength to conservative opposition to new intellectual currents. In the encyclical

Quanta Cura and the attached *Syllabus of Errors* (1864), the Vatican notoriously condemned 'liberalism', as well as rationalism, freemasonry, religious toleration, Bible societies, and the separation of church and state, culminating in the rejection of the idea that 'The Roman Pontiff can, and ought to, reconcile himself, and come to terms with progress, liberalism and modern civilization.'[8] Such pronouncements, which effectively sought to put the Church on a war footing, occasioned some deft footwork on the part of bishops and other Catholic opinion-formers in the attempt to show that the words should be taken in a restricted sense rather than a general one.

Curiously, the dependence on the contemporary consensus of the Church rather than its doctrinal tradition which underlay *Ineffabilis Deus* was also to nourish an approach to doctrine which would in time result in a far more open attitude to contemporary thought. The catalyst for this was John Henry Newman (1801–90), who converted to Rome. In an *Essay on the Development of Doctrine* (1845), Newman argued that the Church was as subject to development and change as any other institution or individual (he had reason to know this, having been an Evangelical and then an early liberal before becoming a high churchman).[9] However, continuity was evident in the way that Roman Catholic doctrine had developed, thanks to the supervision provided by the divine institution of the papacy, so that later doctrines were always in harmony with those elucidated earlier, even if this was not capable of logical demonstration. The full fruit of Newman's approach would be seen in the Second Vatican Council (1962–5), which we shall examine in Chapter 20.

The significance of Vatican I

Undoubtedly the main achievement of Pius IX was the formal definition of papal infallibility. On 8 December 1869, the Vatican Council opened in Rome, convoked by the pope as an ecumenical council. About 700 bishops attended, including over 100 from America and 60 from Eastern-rite churches. Orthodox and Protestants had been invited to return to Rome, but neither tradition sent representatives.

We have already noted that loss of temporal power was paralleled by an increasing stress on the papacy's spiritual power as part of the process of withdrawal from the world (one might even describe this as 'ghettoization'). Papal infallibility in matters of faith and morals was very widely accepted, but there were a number of bishops who, for various reasons, felt that this was not an opportune time for a formal definition of it as a dogma binding on the faithful. Germans faced pressure at home, some North Americans feared it would hinder the conversion of Protestants, and Eastern bishops were sensitive to the likely impact on relations with the Orthodox. About 80 of them, including the Uniats (who had protested at the council's failure to understand Eastern Christian traditions), therefore left the council before a vote was taken.

The definition of papal infallibility was set out in the dogmatic constitution *Pastor Aeternus*, which declared that:

> faithfully adhering to the tradition received from the beginning of the Christian religion . . . with the approval of the sacred council, we teach and define that it is a divinely revealed dogma that the Roman Pontiff, when he speaks *ex cathedra*, i.e., when exercising his office as pastor and teacher of all Christians he defines, by his supreme apostolic authority, a doctrine of faith or morals which must be held by the universal Church, enjoys, through the divine assistance, that infallibility promised to him in blessed Peter and with which the divine Redeemer wanted His Church to be endowed in defining doctrine of faith and morals; and therefore that the definitions of the same Roman Pontiff are irreformable of themselves and not from the consent of the Church.[10]

This was a much more centralized understanding of authority in the Church than many either wanted or thought timely, although it must be conceded that in practice the pope has only once spoken *ex cathedra*, when defining the dogma of the bodily assumption of the Blessed Virgin Mary in 1950. The constitution was accepted by 535 votes to 2, but the council was later suspended because of the Italian occupation of Rome. Thus the majority of its agenda was never discussed, and an opportunity for reform lost. It was on returning from Rome that the English Catholic historian Lord Acton expressed the view that 'power tends to corrupt; absolute power corrupts absolutely'.

The fall-out, though less than might have been expected (which is a testimony to the nature of the bishops appointed by Pius), was still significant. A prime instance was the Munich theology professor Ignaz von Döllinger (1799–1890). Döllinger, who wished to avoid setting up a further obstacle to rapprochement with Anglicans and Orthodox, argued that the dogma of papal infallibility lacked antiquity, universality, and consent, and that it thus contravened the fifth-century Vincentian Canon, which set up as a yardstick for Christian belief that which has been taught 'always, everywhere, and by all'. Excommunicated for his views, Döllinger played a leading role in the organization into a coherent body (which he never formally joined) of those Austrian, Swiss, and German Catholics who likewise rejected the Vatican Council's definitions of papal infallibility and universal primacy. Although the German authorities were ready to offer every kind of assistance to the 'Old Catholics', as they became known, they failed to attract much support, remaining the church of a small, if select, minority. From 1889 they were formally united with the Church of Utrecht, the Jansenist-inspired body which had split from the Catholic Church in 1723.

A more moderate approach to papal authority was adopted by Leo XIII. His strength was in the area of social thought (see Chapter 13); his background accounted for this, as he had served in Belgium in 1843–6 as a papal nuncio (a kind of ambassador), where a Catholic government had introduced much legislation dealing with social issues. He also opened the Vatican archives to scholars in 1881, arguing that the Church had nothing to fear from the truth; and he sought to relate to all types of government, asserting that Catholic teaching did not require belief in one as inherently more Christian than all others.

Catholic Modernism

Another example of the Church's tendency to react conservatively to changing ideas was its fierce opposition to the phenomenon of Catholic Modernism. This label covers a range of views, united by the underlying conviction that the Church needed to accommodate itself to the modern world in its theology and socio-political outlook. Its centre was France, though English and German Catholicism also contributed. The controversy came to a head in the early years of the pontificate of Pius X (1903–14). Pius was unusual among popes in not having aristocratic roots; he was also less diplomatic than his predecessor had been, and more concerned to insist on the Church's authority and its rights. His intransigence undoubtedly helped precipitate the separation of church and state in France in 1905.

In spite of the dogmatic definitions already noted, the eighteenth and nineteenth centuries were not a time of great theological creativity for Roman Catholicism and many theologians preferred to rehash traditional teaching rather than explore its implications or develop it in new ways. One reason for this was the tendency to emphasize the unchanging nature of Catholic tradition over against the novelties of both Protestantism and contemporary society. In its own eyes, Rome was the Church which affirmed those things which had been believed 'always, everywhere, and by everyone'. This attitude both provoked and was reinforced by the conflict over Catholic Modernism.

Modernists accepted the methodology and conclusions of contemporary critical scholarship regarding the Bible. Related to this was the idea that what mattered for faith was not the origins of Christianity (about which they were often extremely sceptical) but its ultimate development as seen in the worship and practice of the contemporary Church.

Reacting against the renewed emphasis on the study of scholastic philosophy which followed Leo XIII's encyclical (1879), they saw Christianity as being about life rather than doctrine; some expressed sceptical views regarding traditional understandings of Christ's divinity and his bodily resurrection. At about the time of the movement's condemnation, it was claimed that Newman was the grandfather of Catholic Modernism by virtue of his theory of the development of doctrine and his dislike of Thomist scholasticism. The idea has some truth in it, for he had no trouble in accepting Darwin's theory of evolution when it came to public notice, but he would not have shared the scepticism of the advanced modernists.

The French Jesuit Alfred Loisy (1857–1940) argued that since the Bible was a record of the teaching of the early Church rather than that of Jesus himself, it was possible to reject the Protestant emphasis on the Bible in favour of stressing the contemporary Church as the authoritative interpreter of truth. Other key thinkers included another Jesuit, George Tyrrell (1861–1909), and Baron Friedrich von Hügel (1852–1925). Rome's reaction was uncompromising. The decree *Lamentabili* (1907) condemned a syllabus of Modernist errors regarding biblical interpretation and the Church's ministry and sacraments; Modernists, it was claimed, asserted that 'Modern Catholicism can be reconciled with true science only if it is transformed into a non-dogmatic Christianity; that is to say, into a broad and liberal Protestantism.'[11] The encyclical *Pascendi dominici gregis* (also 1907) portrayed an 'ideal type' of Modernism composed of a variety of heresies in different intellectual disciplines, but in reality the movement was never as coherent as the encyclical claimed. A clampdown took place, bishops being urged to adopt a range of measures to prevent the publication of Modernist works and to discipline those known to hold such views. Loisy and Tyrrell were excommunicated, but von Hügel survived. An anti-Modernist oath to be taken by clergy and seminarians was introduced in 1910 and remained in force until the 1960s.

Popular piety

Revolution acted as a catalyst not only for secularization but also for religious awakening. In the years immediately after the French Revolution a new mood was evident in the pulpit; whereas eighteenth-century Catholic sermons had tended to stress the reasonable nature of Christian belief, as had many of their Protestant counterparts, the Romantic emphasis on mystery fostered a heightened supernaturalism – again, something shared with many Protestants. Miracles, rather than being minimized or explained away, were now something to be gloried in. This may help to explain the occurrence of apparitions of the Virgin during this period. Also in parallel with Protestant developments, affective piety took on revivalist overtones.

Confession and regular reception of the sacrament became more frequent features of the average Catholic's life, and a range of new (or newly popular) devotions helped to keep their piety fervent. Among them were the rosary, the Stations of the Cross, devotion to the Sacred Heart, observance of May as Mary's month, and Benediction. Confraternities and other agencies were founded to promote these devotions. The officially approved status of these rites, and the fact that most of them normally took place in church and were thus under clerical supervision, helped to further the post-Tridentine attempt to eliminate local observances (which were deemed frequently to be superstitious). Rome-centredness was thus evident in this sphere as it was in that of church government. But this should not be overstated: the new devotions were genuinely popular, and the Vatican's role was more that of evaluating and approving, rather than imposing. Part of the Vatican's influence in this area was undoubtedly due to a change in the way lay Catholics viewed the papacy: rather than being a distant leader of whose actions and pronouncements they were unaware, the pope became 'the Holy Father', his face was familiar to them though mass-produced pictures and photographs, and his words were read by millions in the burgeoning number of Catholic newspapers and magazines. A prime example is the Vatican newspaper *Osservatore Romano*, founded in 1860 to inform the faithful of papal opinion.

The status of the clergy was rising too, partly because of the devotional developments, but also due to improvements in clerical training and a more professional view of the priesthood. In France, for example, many of the priests ordained after 1830 were ordinary people with a real sense of vocation. Perhaps the most famous was Jean-Baptiste Vianney (1786–1859), the Curé d'Ars, a village near Lyons. He became known for his saintly life and devoted parish ministry, which attracted people from all over France and beyond who sought spiritual counsel. Canonized in 1925, he was made the patron of parish priests in 1929. The social background of the clergy in time effected a change in the episcopate: whereas the eighteenth-century French bishops were almost all from the upper classes, by 1900 only 4 out of 90 were from the nobility. This would have been a significant factor in bringing the Church closer to the people, but the humble and rural origins of many of the clergy meant that they were less likely to favour liberal opinions and so the French church became marked by an anti-liberalism which caused repeated clashes with the state. Even the new forms of religious devotion were co-opted in support of right-wing politics: the Sacred Heart was adopted as a symbol of the Catholic vision of what France should be.

Both apparitions and pilgrimages were particularly prominent in

French Catholicism. Among the most important pilgrimage sites were La Salette (1846); Lourdes, where Mary appeared to the young Bernadette Soubirous (1858); Knock in Ireland, where Marian apparitions occurred in 1879; and Fatima in Portugal (1917). Lisieux became popular because of its association with the nun St Theresa (1873–97), again an example of precocious spirituality. Some of the apparitions can be related to periods or contexts of crisis, and all reflected and fostered the 'feminization' of Western Christian piety. The practice of pilgrimage changed quite radically, especially after the railways made travel so much easier and faster. No longer was there a long journey offering opportunities for penance or fleshly diversion as part of the pilgrimage experience. More importantly, pilgrimage became concentrated on fewer destinations (with many local pilgrimage sites dying out), but these saw vastly increased numbers of visitors; this reinforced the contemporary trend towards centralization.

While the above offers a general description of what the majority of observant Catholics were doing, it must also be noted that there were considerable and longstanding regional variations in the level of observance. These were affected by such factors as stability of the population, age, occupation, and gender (the feminization of Catholicism was aided by the appeal of the new devotions to women and the growth of political and social organizations offering men other places to interact). Another factor was the patchy nature of clerical provision in some areas; in Spain, for example, rural parishes often found it hard to secure a priest, and there was a wide disparity in the level of observance between the north and the south of the country.

The 'churchly' nature of lay piety fitted well with the tendency for Catholics to segregate themselves from non-Catholics as an alternative society. It seemed as if the Church was doing all it could to go contrary to contemporary trends: apparitions of the Virgin challenged the claims of science to dominance; ultramontane spirituality encouraged many to stress their links with Rome, the 'Eternal City', rather than the (sometimes hostile) state in which they lived; papal condemnations of contemporary thought were sweeping and unsparing. In the short term, one result was a certain triumphalism, which was reinforced by inspiring news of Catholic missions to many parts of the globe.

In view of the quasi-monastic tone of much lay Catholic spirituality of the period and the Church's emphasis on detachment from the world, it is small wonder that the religious orders saw considerable growth in their numbers, especially those for women[12] and those dedicated to mission. Many new orders were founded, such as the Sisters of Mercy, the Sisters of St Vincent de Paul, and the Marist Brothers. Most were involved in teaching, mission, or practical 'works of mercy'. In France almost four hundred new religious orders were founded between 1800 and 1880, and 200,000 women took religious vows; between 1851 and 1901, the numbers of men and women in religious orders increased from 37,000 to 162,000. In Chapter 14 we shall see that as a result this period saw achievements in Catholic overseas mission as remarkable as those of the Protestant missionary force.

Questions for thought

1 Looking at the last two chapters, how would you account for the fact that in some countries during the nineteenth century the relationship between Christianity and national aspirations was positive, while in others it was negative?

2 Did the attempt to replace Catholicism with the cult of Reason in 1792 testify to the importance of religion as a binding factor in French life, or to its insignificance?

3 Drawing on Chapter 3 and this chapter, review the development of the relationship between church and state in France to 1914. How would you relate to this the movements of spiritual renewal such as Jansenism, the apparitions at Lourdes, or the revival of monasticism?

4 What changes do you notice from the eighteenth century to the early twentieth in the factors which fuelled French anticlericalism? What significance would you attach to such changes?

5 Did the growth of Ultramontanism strengthen or weaken the Church's position in the nineteenth-century world?

6 Compare and contrast the two ways of relating to the contemporary world followed by Ultramontanism and Modernism.

7 How convincing do you find the argument that the nineteenth century witnessed the 'feminization' of Catholic piety?

8 How would you relate the triumphalism evident in much Catholic piety at the end of the nineteenth century with the defensiveness which marked the condemnation of Modernism?

Further reading

Nigel Aston, 2002, *Christianity and Revolutionary Europe c.1750–1830*, Cambridge: Cambridge University Press, part 2.

Nicholas Atkin and Frank Tallett, 2003, *Priests, Prelates and People: A History of European Catholicism since 1750*, Oxford: Oxford University Press, chs 2–4.

Stewart J. Brown and Timothy Tackett (eds), 2007, *Cambridge History of Christianity*, vol. 7: *Enlightenment, Reawakening and Revolution 1660–1815*, Cambridge: Cambridge University Press, chs 27–8.

Owen Chadwick, 1998, *A History of the Popes 1830–1914*, Oxford History of the Christian Church, Oxford: Oxford University Press.

Owen Chadwick, 1980, *The Popes and European Revolution*, Oxford History of the Christian Church, Oxford: Oxford University Press.

Frank J. Coppa, 1998, *The Modern Papacy since 1789*, Longman History of the Papacy, Harlow: Longman, chs 1–9.

Sheridan Gilley and Brian Stanley (eds), 2006, *Cambridge History of Christianity*, vol. 8: *World Christianities c.1815–c.1914*, Cambridge: Cambridge University Press, chs 2, 5, 14–17, 23–4.

J. Derek Holmes and Bernard Bickers, 2002, *A Short History of the Catholic Church*, with a postscript by Peter Hebblethwaite and final chapter by Peter Doyle, London: Burns & Oates, ch. 6.

Notes

1 For a fuller but clear summary of events, see Brown and Tackett (eds), *CHC*, vol. 7, chs 27–8.

2 Aston, *Christianity and Revolutionary Europe*, p. 211.

3 Cf. Stephen Neill's comment about Napoleon that 'By humiliating the Pope, he had elevated the papacy' (Stephen Neill (revised by Owen Chadwick), 1986, *A History of Christian Missions*, The Pelican History of the Church 6, Harmondsworth: Pelican, p. 398).

4 *ODCC*, art. 'Lamennais, Félicité Robert de'.

5 Coppa, *Modern Papacy*, p. 74.

6 Holmes and Bickers, *Short History of the Catholic Church*, p. 235.

7 Coppa, *Modern Papacy*, p. 116.

8 Proposition 80, *Syllabus of Errors*, downloaded from http://www.papalen cyclicals.net/Pius09/p9syll.htm, 17 January 2007.

9 Among the voluminous literature on Newman, see especially Sheridan Gilley, 1990, *Newman and his Age*, London: Darton, Longman & Todd; Brian Martin, 2000, *John Henry Newman: His Life and Work*, London: Continuum. Newman's sermons, works, letters, and diaries are appearing in a multi-volume edition from Oxford University Press.

10 *Pastor Aeternus*, ch. 4, downloaded from http://www.cin.org/docs/pastorae. html, 17 January 2007.

11 Proposition 65, *Lamentabili sane*, downloaded from http://www.papalen cyclicals.net/Pius10/p10lamen.htm, 17 January 2007.

12 The resurgence of the female religious life, which was centred on France and Belgium, probably, like the Marian apparitions, played a major role in the 'feminization' of Roman Catholicism.

9

European Protestantism during the Nineteenth Century

Paradoxically, the nineteenth century was a time marked by two opposites, secularization and religious revival. On the one hand, new intellectual currents challenged traditional Christian explanations of the physical order and states sought to limit the power of the churches in the civil and political spheres; on the other hand, several waves of revival served to reinforce the widespread religious earnestness which was visibly manifest in relatively high levels of religious observance. The challenge for scholarly interpreters is to explain how these tendencies could coexist. This chapter offers the evidence for you to synthesize into an argument.

The challenges of modern thought

Science

The most obvious example of a challenge to traditional belief is the theory of evolution, especially as formulated by Charles Darwin (1809–82), although the nature of the impact of his work on the churches continues to be hotly debated. Theories of evolution had been around for some years before Darwin, and the anonymous *Vestiges of the Natural History of Creation* (1844; written by Robert Chambers, the encyclopedist) applied evolution to the origin and development of all forms of animal life, doing away with any concept of a special divine creation. Darwin's most influential works were *The Origin of Species* (1859) and *The Descent of Man* (1871). The original part of his case was his explanation of the appearance of different species by means of the process of natural selection; in this he was indebted to the clergyman and economist T.R. Malthus (1766–1834), who claimed that the natural world could be explained in terms of a struggle for survival. The argument from design, which had been beloved by eighteenth-century apologists, was fatally undermined, although it has since reappeared on various occasions in mutated forms, the most recent being those of the 'anthropic principle' and 'intelligent design'.

It has been suggested that Darwin's theories were valued more for what they appeared to claim for contemporary Western civilization than for their contribution to an understanding of biology.[1] Marxists and capitalists both deployed them in support of their theories, the former in support of a particular view of the historical process and the latter as justifying the practice of *laissez-faire* economics and the working of the law of competition, by which the weakest companies went to the wall.

It is a popular myth that the relationship between science and religion is fundamentally one of 'warfare';[2] some scientists have claimed this, and many religionists have given colour to it by the way they have responded to scientific challenges. But during the nineteenth century the picture was somewhat more complex, and much Christian response was quite positive, although many theologians sought to resist the philosophical implications drawn from Darwin's theories.[3] Although an agnostic, Darwin was buried in Westminster Abbey, and most Protestant churchmen, including (initially at least) many English-speaking Evangelicals, rapidly adopted his ideas. Indeed, it almost seems as if more of a furore was raised by developments in Old Testament criticism than by Darwin and other proponents of evolutionary theory. What did happen, however, was that natural theology (that is, the investigation of the extent to which God could be known from his works in creation by the use of reason alone) and the apologetic argument from 'evidences' declined in popularity.

Clearly a process of evolution such as Darwin outlined required that the earth be much older than Christians had previously thought. No longer could most accept the chronology put forward by Archbishop Ussher of Armagh in 1652, which posited the creation as occurring in 4004 BC. The way had been prepared for a new approach to this question by the development of the science of geology. By the beginning of the twentieth century, geologists were developing techniques for dating rocks based on the decay of radioactive material, which showed that the age of the earth could be measured in terms of billions, and not mere thousands, of years.

From a different direction came the challenges presented by the rise of the discipline of anthropology. Drawing heavily on contemporary exploration and colonization, the latter part of the nineteenth century saw the rise of the discipline of comparative religion and the scientific study of religious experience, as well as the beginnings of the sociology of religion. For many, the existence and conclusions of these disciplines supported the belief that religion was fundamentally a human construct.

Archaeology, which also came to prominence during the century, also fostered this approach; new discoveries added a great deal to understanding of ancient Near Eastern religions, making it possible to locate the religion of Israel in context. By 1914, however, a reaction was setting in, as scholars inveighed against the tendency among members of the German 'History of Religions school' (*Religionsgeschichtliche Schule*) of New Testament scholars to look for parallels to Christian beliefs and practices derived from a comparative study of religion at the expense of their Old Testament antecedents.

Taken together these scientific disciplines presented major challenges to Christian theology as traditionally formulated, and it has become commonplace to speak of a 'loss of faith' among educated classes throughout Europe during this period. However, we should not overstate this, nor ignore the fact that a number of conversions from secular to Christian viewpoints occurred (in countries as diverse as England, France, and Russia), as well as those in the opposite direction.[4] Neither should we attribute the loss of faith simply to the impact of scientific discoveries (or, more precisely, to popular dissemination – and occasional misrepresentation – of the fruits of scientific research); major social changes, such as social dislocation arising from urbanization and industrialization, the growth in leisure opportunities, and the disconnection of religion and politics all contributed to a complex process of secularization, whose nature, time-span, and impact continue to be debated by scholars.

Philosophy and theology

The following section deals with a range of philosophical and theological issues which may be difficult to grasp at first reading, but a grasp of the basics of nineteenth-century thought in these disciplines helps us to understand more recent theological trends and developments.

Part of the response to new scientific discoveries and theories was the development of liberal Protestant theology (which was paralleled by Catholic Modernism), not to be confused with political liberalism. This approach sought to reconstruct Christian theology in the light of modern thought; since traditional doctrinal formulations were no longer regarded as fixed and authoritative, liberal theologians also sought to rediscover the essence of Christianity at the heart of these formulae and to give this expression in ways which would maintain the credibility and attracting power of Christianity. Drawing on Enlightenment thought, liberal theologians worked on the basis of the authority of reason over the Bible or the Church's tradition, and regarded human history as essentially a story of progress.

While liberal theology was rooted in Enlightenment perspectives, it also drew on a response to the Enlightenment known as Romanticism. This emerged late in the eighteenth century, and had its main influence on the churches during much of the nineteenth. Reacting against the reductionism and rationalism of the Enlightenment era, it stressed the limits of reason and the value of the imagination as a means of perceiving truths which were hidden to reason, and the value of the aesthetic senses. Admission of human inability to understand the world gave rise to a sense of mystery: Romantic artists and writers loved the mysterious aspects of the world, and in some quarters this was given expression in a heightened supernaturalism or an increased stress on divine transcendence in the conduct and content of worship. A high-profile example of this in Britain and Germany was the Catholic Apostolic Church, whose origins were bound up with an outbreak of charismatic manifestations such as tongues, healing, and prophecy in Britain from 1830, but whose worship in its developed form was marked by a sense of the mysterious and a love of beauty.[5] Linked with aspects of Romanticism, and offering a means for its expression, was the renewal of interest in the medieval period which derived strength from the post-revolution desire in much of Europe to reconnect with the past.

One result of Romanticism's tendency to stress the aesthetic and poetic aspects of religion, as opposed to the dogmatic ones, was the 'de-dogmatization' of nineteenth-century Protestantism. This took up the Pietist emphasis on experience, and a widespread renewal of affective religion followed. The fact that Romantic values were seen as countering those of the Enlightenment and the French Revolution gave this renewal, which was at its peak in the 1810s, further strength in countries such as Prussia.

One outgrowth of this was the thought of the German theologian and pastor F.D.E. Schleiermacher (1768–1834),[6] which the twentieth-century theologian Karl Barth, himself a major figure in the development of Protestant theology, saw as inaugurating a new era in the history of theology. Brought up in an intense Pietist atmosphere, Schleiermacher rebelled against its narrowness while retaining its stress on the importance of religious experience. He became a professor at Halle and then Berlin, where he also preached regularly to large congregations. Drawing on Kant's rejection of natural theology, he saw Christianity as being about the spiritual world within rather than the natural world without, a matter of experience rather than doctrine or ethics. The Bible thus became a record of religious experience; theology became an account of corporate religious experience rather than an exposition of divine revelation; doctrines expressed truths of experience rather than objective realities. For him, the essence of religion was a 'feeling [sense or intuitive awareness, translating the German *Gefühl*] of absolute dependence' which was universal to humanity, and the uniqueness of Jesus Christ lay in his being the one in whom that sense of dependence was perfectly realized. Salvation was about entering into Christ's perfect God-consciousness. Schleiermacher's epochal significance, then, lies in his recasting of theology so that it speaks of subjective realities rather than objective ones; subsequent theologians often focused on developing his ideas or on reacting against them.

By grounding theology in experience, 'Schleiermacher went on from where Kant left off: from the moral consciousness to the religious consciousness.'[7] Kant had argued that the only knowledge available to us by reason is of things as we experience them, not of things as they are in themselves. That being so, traditional arguments for God's existence can no longer be accepted, because they claim to give knowledge of God as he is in himself: no metaphysical system, philosophical or theological, can give us knowledge of things beyond our experience. Yet every person is conscious of moral imperatives, which only make sense if there is a God who can lay these down. In addition, since we cannot achieve moral perfection in this life and human society is imperfect in that evil is not always punished nor good rewarded, there must be a life to follow it which will include rewards and punishments, hence we can affirm human immortality. Such a version of religion removes it from the field of scientific or historical scrutiny, while maintaining its basis in a reality beyond ourselves.

Another important philosophical outlook to appear during this period was Idealism. Its basic theme was the priority of the mind and the spiritual over the material: reality is ultimately spiritual rather than physical, hence the importance of consciousness, as in the thought of Kant and Schleiermacher. The most important exponent of Idealism, however, was the German philosopher G.W.F. Hegel (1770–1831). Against Kant's rejection of the possibility of rationally based knowledge of things as they are in themselves, Hegel argued that all reality must be knowable – if there are things which are unknowable, how could we know that? Ultimately, the universe represents the outworking or progressive realization of the rational principle of spirit: 'a self-consciousness which manifests itself in the difference of self and not-self, that through this difference and by overcoming it, it may attain to the highest unity with itself'.[8] Through nature and history, spirit realizes itself, becoming self-conscious in human beings. It manifests itself in forms which conflict with one another and are then reconciled – his famous dialectic of thesis, antithesis, and synthesis, in which antithesis conflicts with thesis to produce a synthesis, which becomes the new thesis, and in this way human thought progresses. On such an account, God is entirely immanent within the universe. Hegel sought to reinterpret the whole edifice of Christian theology in line with his scheme, and in doing so did much to set the agenda for nineteenth-century thought, partly because his scheme could be interpreted in terms consonant with evolutionary theory. But while some utilized his thought in defence of Christianity, others built on it a case for atheism, such as the philosopher Ludwig Feuerbach (1804–72), who argued that there was no transcendent dimension to reality and so religion was nothing other than a projection of human values. His thought was to influence people as diverse as the composer Richard Wagner and the philosophers Friedrich Nietzsche and Karl Marx (though Marx was more influenced by Hegel).

Nietzsche (1844–1900) asserted that since God did not exist, it was for humanity to create its own system of values; he was hostile to those of Christianity because he saw them as hindering the emergence of his 'superman' who exemplified the will to power which Nietzsche saw as the heart of life. Marx (1818–83) was the son of a Jewish lawyer who had felt himself compelled by circumstances to convert to Lutheran Christianity in order to avoid the antisemitic prejudice which was widespread in Europe at the time. In Marx's worldview, ideas are responses to material reality; therefore, if we change social and economic conditions, beliefs will alter as a result. Religious ideas, too, represent projections of human concerns about social and economic alienation; they offer consolation, but it is illusory. The tendency of religion is to drug the masses into accepting their unhappy conditions instead of changing them; religion must therefore be eradicated by dealing with the conditions in which it flourishes.

Biblical criticism

An important process which continued throughout this period was the disconnection of exegesis from dogmatics. Biblical interpretation was less and less subject to the controlling influence of confessions of faith and, in line with the canons of historical criticism, biblical documents were increasingly studied as sources rather than as authorities, with attention being paid to their original contexts and readership. This had implications for church history, historical theology, and dogmatics, as it fostered a certain distance from the idea that the biblical writings were divinely inspired throughout. The problem was that determining the original context, readership, and purpose was often not very easy; the documents themselves did not always give clear indications of these, and so scholars tried to reconstruct them and to date the documents according to a particular theory of how biblical religion developed. Of course, to many this was less than exciting, and some feared the results. Romanticism met both concerns by approaching the Bible as literature rather than as science or history, seeing its authority in terms of its power to change lives. This approach fitted well with the turn inward that we have already noted in connection with Schleiermacher's theological method.

Old Testament criticism: the evolution of religion

The development of the idea of evolutionary progress, and its application to human society and history as well as to biology, offered the possibility of a new way of understanding the Old Testament documents, as scholars attempted to reconstruct the development of Israelite religion according to an evolutionary hypothesis. Initially this was a relatively crude affair, postulating a development from simple to complex and arguing that the more complex worldview required by monotheism made this a fairly late development, but over the decades it was refined and became the mainstream approach to the Old Testament.

Arguably the most important aspect of this was the formulation of the documentary hypothesis regarding the development of the Pentateuch, which viewed these writings as coming from a number of hands over a long period of time, rather than all being written by Moses. Its classic exposition was offered by Julius Wellhausen (1844–1918) from 1878, who 'sought to establish the development of Hebrew religion from a nomadic stage through that of the Prophets to the religion of the Law'.[9] The hypothesis, which achieved enduring popularity, postulated four documents underlying the Pentateuch: J, originating in ninth-century BC Judah; E, from eighth-century BC Israel (in which there were many sanctuaries and no centralized priesthood or sacrificial law); D, from Josiah's seventh-century reforms of Temple worship (advocating centralization of worship); and P, from the period following the return from exile (marked by a concern with issues of atonement and ritual purity).

In terms of their impact on the churches, such views were highly controversial. William Robertson Smith (1846–94), professor in the Free Church of Scotland, provoked a storm of controversy by some articles for the *Encyclopaedia Britannica* in which he upheld Wellhausen's evolutionary model of the development of Old Testament religion. In 1881 he lost his professorial chair for heresy after a lengthy inquiry; but his was to become the dominant viewpoint. The pastoral intent of his scholarship should be noted: he saw himself as clearing away obstacles preventing people from believing the Christian gospel, and a critical approach as essential to the defence of the Old Testament as the Word of God. He also claimed to accept the teaching of the *Westminster Confession*, the defining doctrinal statement for conservative Presbyterians, and in spite of his own fate his work did much to secure acceptance of critical views by a wider public.

New Testament criticism: the 'Quest for the Historical Jesus'

In its earliest form the 'Quest for the Historical Jesus' represented a response to the perceived discrepancy between what emerged from the process of interpreting the New Testament and what could be known of Jesus by means of the techniques of historical study. In an age which valued rationality and downplayed the supernatural, this was deemed vital to saving Christianity. The starting-point for the Quest is often seen as the publication of the rationalist views of H.S. Reimarus (1694–1768) by Lessing in a series of pamphlets, the *Wolfenbüttel Fragments* (1774–8). Among other things, these portrayed Jesus as a religious reformer who was misled into thinking that the kingdom of God as a political entity was about to appear, and who decided to force its appearance by his triumphal entry into Jerusalem; his death was the inevitable result, and he died believing that God had deserted him. The disciples invented the story that he had risen from the dead and that the kingdom of God would in fact appear when Jesus returned. Reimarus, drawing on English Deist writers, argued that the real Jesus, the Jesus of history, was not the same as the Christ portrayed in the Gospels, and sought to elucidate the nature of the real Jesus; from that point, this has been a central preoccupation of theological and biblical scholarship, right through to the present and the North American 'Jesus Seminar'.

The Quest gave birth to a number of important lives of Jesus, each illustrating changing trends in New Testament scholarship. Kant's stress on moral values and Hegel's stress on timeless principles rather than historical events together helped to ensure that many of these works portrayed him as an ethical teacher rather than a divine saviour. What mattered was what he taught rather than who he was or what he did, about both of which many writers felt that little could be known. The application of the techniques of historical criticism to the New Testament documents cannot be said to have been objective, however: many used it to filter out those aspects which they found unacceptable, most notably the supernatural and the assertions of Christ's divinity.

In 1835 the German D.F. Strauss (1808–74) produced a *Life of Jesus* which argued that the supernatural elements conveyed spiritual truths, and were the means of expressing those truths within a particular world-view, but should not be taken literally. The Gospels were mythological rather than historical documents, in the sense that they gave expression to timeless truths but in a concrete rather than abstract form, suited to the needs of the first Christians. This was not simply a matter of re-interpreting individual supernatural events such as the resurrection, but of the character of the Gospels as a whole. Following Hegel, 'he saw Christianity as an expression of eternal truths: the historical setting was of secondary interest'.[10] When the radical cantonal government of Zurich

proposed to appoint him to a chair of theology there in 1839, the resulting public outcry brought about the fall of the cantonal administration.

F.C. Baur (1792–1860) applied the idea of the resolution of thesis
and antithesis by synthesis to New Testament interpretation, although
it is not certain that he got it from Hegel; he postulated a resolution of
Judaistic and Hellenistic outlooks, represented by the Twelve and Paul
respectively, in a second-century 'early Catholicism' exemplified by Acts,
in which he found no evidence of internal tension. The various documents
were then dated according to the place which he thought they occupied in
this scheme and the Christology which they contained. Interestingly, Baur
saw the synthesis as evidence of decline rather than of progress as Hegel
had claimed. Baur came to be regarded as the founder of the 'Tübingen
school', which followed Strauss in adopting a non-supernaturalist viewpoint from which to interpret the New Testament writings along the lines
indicated by Baur.

While the French writer Ernest Renan (1823–92) also produced a de-
supernaturalized life of Jesus in 1863, he did so in a different way, painting a vivid picture of the human Jesus as an itinerant Galilean teacher.
The book was immensely popular, although its author later admitted
that it was merely one portrayal of how things might have taken place.
In 1865 a similar work appeared in English from the pen of the young
historian J.R. Seeley (1834–95), *Ecce Homo*, which portrayed Jesus as a
moral reformer and was likewise widely read.

A reaction to the Tübingen stress on historical study set in under
Albrecht Ritschl (1822–89). Ritschl saw faith as founded on value judgements rather than on established facts about Jesus. Things in themselves
were knowable (*pace* Kant) in terms of their effect on us. Theological
statements were therefore to be regarded as value judgements based on
the impact of things on us, rather than factual assertions concerning the
nature of these things in themselves; as such, they required personal commitment and were not capable of objective assessment. The evidence on
which they were based was the material found in the Gospels, through
which Christ speaks to human beings and enters into a relationship with
them. To call Christ 'God' was to make the value judgement regarding
his significance for the individual's salvation that he perfectly embodied
the values of the kingdom of God, a community marked by brotherly
love. Jesus' work was to inaugurate the kingdom as the sphere in which
human beings experience salvation, and so Ritschl emphasized Jesus'
teaching about the kingdom, understood as an ethical reality – the sphere
in which Jesus' ethic is followed. Such an interpretation, which continued
the earlier stress on Jesus' ethical teaching rather than his miracles, would
feed into the developing Social Gospel movement in the English-speaking
world (see Chapter 13).

The Strasbourg theologian Albert Schweitzer (1875–1965), in his *The*

Quest for the Historical Jesus (*Von Reimarus zu Wrede*, 1906), provided a shock to the liberal system by his assertion that the Quest had got its understanding of Jesus wrong because it had failed to recognize that his teaching was fundamentally apocalyptic in character. All that it had produced was a series of reconstructions of Jesus in the image of their authors. For Schweitzer, the kingdom was an eschatological entity, whose imminence Jesus proclaimed; passages such as Mark 13 and the Apocalypse thus assumed renewed significance. Jesus' ethical teaching was based on the conviction that it would not be long before the kingdom appeared, and his death came about because he attempted to force the coming of the kingdom. Schweitzer became a medical missionary in French Equatorial Africa from 1913, where he worked out the implications of his belief in 'respect for life'.

Wilhelm Wrede (1859–1906) expounded the idea of the 'Messianic secret' (Jesus never claimed to be the Messiah, but the early Church read such a claim back into his ministry, hence the idea in the Gospels that Jesus forbade those who recognized his Messiahship to speak of it), in order to explain why belief in Jesus as Son of God only appeared after the resurrection. Wrede was sceptical regarding the possibility of establishing a historical foundation for belief; Martin Kähler (1835–1912) went a step further in his claim that what mattered for faith in any case was not the historical Jesus but the preached Christ. The Quest was both unnecessary and impossible, since the only historical sources, the Gospels, could not be accepted as sufficiently reliable from a historian's point of view.

The patristic scholar Adolf Harnack (1851–1930), in his *History of Dogma* (1886–9), posited a discontinuity between Jesus and Paul, arguing that the religion *of* Jesus had been changed by Paul into a religion *about* Jesus, a process which was continued by the early Church, which was influenced by Hellenistic thought-patterns in its formulation of fundamental doctrines such as that of the incarnation. In this he followed Ritschl's opposition to metaphysics. A series of popular lectures were published as *What is Christianity?* (1900), in which he expounded the essence of Christianity as the fatherhood of God, the brotherhood of human beings, the worth of each human soul, and the higher righteousness based on love rather than law-keeping. It was to refute his work that Loisy wrote *The Gospel and the Church* (1908), a key Catholic Modernist text.

In the end, what tended to emerge from the Quest was, as Schweitzer asserted, a Jesus who looked remarkably like contemporary liberal Protestants. The Catholic Modernist Tyrrell spoke of Harnack's Christ as the reflection of a liberal Protestant face at the bottom of a deep well. The attempt to ground Christian faith in human experience had been intended as a way of sidestepping the problems raised by adherence to traditional sources of belief (Scripture) and traditional doctrinal formulations (such as concerning Christology), and of reshaping theology so that it could speak to contemporary people; but in the end the liberal project raised just as many questions of its own, and we shall see that the First World War raised serious questions about its inability to make sense of the experiences which were the lot of millions of combatants and civilians during those years.

As for textual scholarship, the century saw considerable advances, both in refinement of methodology and in discovery of manuscripts such as the Codex Sinaiticus (found in portions from 1844 in St Catherine's Monastery in the Sinai desert). From 1895 the researches of Adolf Deissmann (1866–1937) demonstrated that the Greek of the New Testament was not unique as had often been thought but was the common (*Koine*) dialect of the day. It is not possible to outline them here, but such advances increased the pressure for new translations to be produced which were based on the best possible manuscript evidence. In the English-speaking world, the *Revised Version* (OT 1881, NT 1885, Apocrypha 1894) owed much to the textual work of the Cambridge scholars B.F. Westcott (1825–1901) and F.J.A. Hort (1828–92).

How did all this touch the ordinary person? Well, for most people it was not so much intellectual factors which would make them cease to believe or to attend church as social ones – moving away from the village where church attendance was part of the regular routine, or discovering alternative leisure pursuits. Middle-class men in particular were being lost to the Church. In some German cities, church attendance was extremely low for the period. In Berlin, for example, only 5 per cent of the population attended church in 1858. Furthermore, whereas in the confessional era the great divisions had been between the various Christian confessions, we now see fault-lines running across them; thus conservative Lutherans and Catholics, for example, might have more in common with one another than with liberal members of their own communion. To some extent this was a result of the stress now laid on experience, but it also owed much to the immense range of theological views now being heard.

Church and state

In the years immediately after 1789, many European Protestant churches went out of their way to stress their loyalty to the state, even where the state had sought to keep them under strict control. The establishment of religion became useful once again, as rulers asserted the divine legitimation of their rule. Almost all states, Catholic as well as Protestant, were 'concerned to foster (and supervise) the growth of belief and practice rather than restrict it, seeing in the Churches the most important forces for stabilising the foundations of the Restoration order'.[11] On the other hand, this had to take place within strict limits: 'the attack on the power and influence of the official churches was an integral part of any attack on the existing political and social order, and the demand for religious freedom and equality became an essential part of any programme of liberal reform'.[12] Several countries therefore saw schisms within Reformed churches, as currents of spiritual renewal in established churches ran up against theological and institutional opposition: apart from Scotland (1843), which we shall examine in the following chapter, such divisions occurred in the Swiss cantons of Vaud (1845), Geneva (1849), and Neuchâtel (1873); and in Holland (1834 and 1886). Reformed theology was more likely than Lutheran theology to fuel such schisms, partly because of the somewhat different conceptions of church–state relationships elaborated within each tradition during the Reformation era, and partly because Reformed theologians had a more fully developed doctrine of the right of resistance to rulers who overstepped the bounds of their authority.

The case of Germany illustrates many of the issues and tensions surrounding church–state relationships. The Congress of Vienna (1814–15) completed the replacement of the old imperial structures with a confederation of German states (34 monarchies and four free cities). This saw a Protestant ascendancy from the beginning of the century, culminating in the *Kulturkampf*, which followed hard on the reunification of Germany in 1871. Actually, this was a Prussian takeover as much as anything: northern Germany had effectively become a federal state a few years earlier under Bismarck, and the southern states, which were largely Catholic, were now incorporated.

The tendency among German Protestant churches was for the head of state to be the head of the church within his bounds; Luther's 1520 appeal to the German princes as 'emergency bishops' had achieved a more permanent form than he had envisaged. The Erastian nature of Prussian religion, which suffered from frequent interference by the nation's rulers, is demonstrated by the fact that although many Protestants were taken up with Romantic values and opposed Enlightenment thought, they were nevertheless willing to support the state's agreement with Napoleon in 1812. On the other hand, Christianity fuelled a national rising in Prussia the following year, with clergy urging support for the armed forces. In 1817, a union between Lutherans and Reformed was imposed by Friedrich Wilhelm III (1797–1840) in Prussia without the consent of the churches or their leaders. In the year when the 300th anniversary of Luther's posting of the *Ninety-Five Theses* was being celebrated, this was an inept move, and it provoked a great deal of opposition, with a body of conservative Lutheran congregations insisting on remaining outside the union. From 1839, thousands migrated to North America, where they formed the nucleus of the highly conservative Lutheran Church – Missouri Synod. Similar unions took place in some smaller German states, but with better reception as they accorded with the will of the people. Prussian tolerance of other religious groups tended to be limited: Friedrich Wilhelm II (1786–97) prohibited public gatherings of Moravians, Mennonites, and Jews and enforced Protestant orthodoxy.[13]

A rather different pattern is illustrated by Holland, where church–state relationships developed from the late nineteenth century according to a pattern known as 'pillarization'. Different confessional and ideological outlooks were represented by churches, political parties, and educational institutions designed to cater for all aspects of the life of their followers, a strategy whose implementation was made easier by the fact that the Catholics were concentrated in the south, the conservative Protestants in a belt running across the middle from south-west to north-east, and the liberals and non-religious in the north and east. Catholics, conservative Protestants, liberals, and socialists were all represented. It became possible for individuals to live their lives without any contact with those of other outlooks, although the different 'pillars' consulted with one another at national level. The restoration of the Catholic hierarchy in Holland in 1853 had provoked rioting and brought down the government, but it became clear over time that Catholics and orthodox Calvinists shared a number of policy objectives: extension of the franchise, subsidies for religious education, and protection against state intrusion. In 1901, therefore, they formed a coalition government under the Calvinist theologian Abraham Kuyper (1837–1920).

Renewal movements

As early as the 1790s, religious revival followed the Reign of Terror in France, as those weary of the revolution, and convinced that the resultant sufferings had been a divine judgement on them for rejecting the Church, returned to it. This was as evident among aristocrats (who had their own social and political reasons for supporting the Church) as among peasants. This particular wave of renewal had affected the Catholic Church, but further outbreaks of 'anti-revolutionary' religious revival in various parts of Europe from the 1810s mainly affected the Protestant churches. In spite of their wide diffusion, too much should not be claimed for the impact of these movements, which was patchy and often mainly rural.

Renewal not only strengthened the hand of the established churches and stimulated the formation of missionary societies, but also gave rise to a variety of Protestant sects. A prime example would be the Brethren (often known as the Plymouth Brethren). Although originating in Ireland and Britain around 1830, they quickly spread to Switzerland, and later to France, Germany, Holland, Spain, Italy, and late in the century to various parts of Eastern Europe.[14] To some extent this was the result of missionary work from Britain and Switzerland, but they also linked up with similarly structured groups of local origin. Another example would be the Baptists, who drew on Pietist traditions of spirituality to establish themselves in Scandinavia, Germany, and France (as well as Central and Eastern Europe) from the 1820s.[15] In these and other cases, expatriate and local agents of the British and Foreign Bible Society and similar agencies often played significant roles.

In Switzerland renewal followed a turbulent course, not unrelated to the political unsettlement which was a feature of the first half of the nineteenth century. The renewal movement which broke out in 1817, as the result of the activity of Moravians and then British Evangelicals in Geneva, became known as the *Réveil*.[16] The Swiss canton of Vaud provides an example of how religious dissent could on occasion profit from the unpopularity of the state church. Under the government of the German-speaking canton of Bern, Protestant ministers of the established church were seen as the mouthpieces of a 'foreign' power. As a result many people were apathetic towards the established church and open to dissent. As well as a Free Church, a number of smaller dissenting groups emerged, and Protestant cantons provided relatively fertile soil for groups with an international spread such as the Brethren and the Catholic Apostolic Church.

Pietist-type renewal probably achieved its widest diffusion during this period in Scandinavia. In Denmark, from 1824 N.F.S. Grundtvig (1783–1872) helped make revivalism 'mainstream' rather than sectarian, combining an emphasis on personal spiritual experience with advocacy of the Church's sacraments as the locus for this by virtue of the presence in them of the risen Christ. Although Pietism has often been a shorthand for a narrow and exclusively 'religious' kind of faith, it is noteworthy that Grundtvig was a major figure in Danish educational and cultural history as an expert on Anglo-Saxon and Norse writings. At the opposite end of the churchly spectrum was the philosopher Søren Kierkegaard (1813–55), whose thought was neglected until the twentieth century; we shall refer to it more fully later, therefore. In Norway (politically united with Sweden from 1814 to 1905), the itinerant layman H.N. Hauge (1771–1824) was the main revivalist preacher, though he was frequently imprisoned for his activities. The awakening's main impact was in rural areas; although dissent was legal from 1845, awakened believers preferred to remain in the national church, in which Pietism became a dominant influence. Similar movements occurred in Sweden, although here dissent played a larger part (having been legalized from 1860), and Finland (which was under Russian rule from 1809 to 1918). Throughout the region, as individuals were converted and began to lead disciplined, thrifty lives, a new middle class emerged, a phenomenon which has parallels in Britain.

In Germany, renewal took a more socially concerned form, in the 'Inner Mission' movement. A deaconess institution was established at Kaiserswerth in 1836, for Protestant women who felt a sense of religious vocation. Interestingly, the British nurse Florence Nightingale (1820–1910), who became famous through her activity tending the wounded during the Crimean War (1854–6), spent some time in training there during 1851. A prominent figure in the Inner Mission was J.H. Wichern, who achieved note as a social reformer, and instigator of the *Kirchentag* or church congress, held annually from 1895 and still an important event on the German Protestant calendar.

In conclusion, we return to the question with which this chapter began: how could the impulse to secularization coexist with that to religious revival? Hugh McLeod suggests that religion ceased to provide a focus of social unity (one which had been imposed from above) and became instead a basis for the distinctive identity of subgroups within society, in which class and ethnicity often played a defining role. The character and social role of religion changed, under pressure from trends towards liberalization, urbanization, and the development of capitalism.[17] Such an interpretation can take account of irreligion as well as religion, for it can be argued that different classes stopped going to church for different reasons. In the next two chapters we shall examine what happened in Britain and Ireland, and how the Church responded.

Questions for thought

1 How would you characterize the relationship between the sciences and religion during the nineteenth century? Do you think that it changed significantly?

2 How does Schleiermacher's use of religious experience compare with that of Zinzendorf?

3 Why did so many of the developments in nineteenth-century philosophy and theology take place in the German-speaking world?

4 To what extent can some of the approaches to Christology and biblical criticism which we have looked at in this chapter be seen as expressions of their time, and to what extent might they represent perennial tendencies in theology?

5 With reference to conceptions of the relationship between church and state, what points of comparison or contrast do you notice between ultramontane Catholicism and German or Prussian practice?

6 Can you formulate alternative explanations to that offered by

McLeod for the coexistence of secularization and religious revival? What evidence would you adduce in support of your argument?

Further reading

Gerald Bray, 1996, *Biblical Interpretation Past and Present*, Leicester: Apollos, chs 7–8.

Colin Brown, 1990, *Christianity and Western Thought: A History of Philosophers, Ideas and Movements*, vol. 1: *From the Ancient World to the Age of Enlightenment*, Leicester: Apollos, ch. 17.

C[olin] Brown, 'Historical Jesus, Quest of', in Joel B. Green *et al.* (eds), 1992, *Dictionary of Jesus and the Gospels*, Leicester: Inter-Varsity Press.

Sheridan Gilley and Brian Stanley (eds), 2006, *Cambridge History of Christianity*, vol. 8: *World Christianities c.1815–c.1914*, Cambridge: Cambridge University Press, chs 11–12, 18, 20–1.

R. M. Grant and D. Tracy, 1984, *A Short History of the Interpretation of the Bible*, London: SCM Press.

Nicholas Hope, 1995, *German and Scandinavian Protestantism 1700–1918*, Oxford: Oxford University Press, part 2.

Alister McGrath, 1986, *The Making of Modern German Christology*, Oxford: Blackwell.

Hugh McLeod, 1997, *Religion and the People of Western Europe 1789–1989*, Oxford: Oxford University Press.

Stephen Neill and N.T. Wright, 1988, *The Interpretation of the New Testament 1861–1986*, Oxford: Oxford University Press.

Steve Wilkens and Alan Padgett, 2000, *Christianity and Western Thought*, vol. 2: *Faith and Reason in the Nineteenth Century*, Leicester: Apollos.

M. J. Wintle, 1987, *Pillars of Piety: Religion in the Netherlands in the Nineteenth Century 1813–1901*, Hull: Hull University Press.

Notes

1 E.g. by Mary Heimann, in Gilley and Stanley (eds), *CHC*, vol. 8, pp. 496–7.

2 Cf. Andrew D. White's work, *History of the Warfare of Science with Religion* (1893), online at www.infidels.org/library/historical/andrew_white/Andrew_White.html.

3 For a lucid summary of recent thinking, see Nicolaas Rupke, 'Christianity and the sciences', in Gilley and Stanley (eds), *CHC*, vol. 8, pp. 164–80. Cf. also D.N. Livingstone *et al.* (eds), 1999, *Evangelicals and Science in Historical Perspective*, New York: Oxford University Press; J.R. Moore, 1979, *The Post-Darwinian Controversies: A Study of the Protestant Struggle to come to terms with Darwin in Britain and America 1870–1900*, Cambridge: Cambridge University Press.

4 For a recent corrective to the view of the nineteenth century as an era char-

acterized by 'loss of faith', see Timothy Larsen, 2006, *Crisis of Doubt: Honest Faith in Nineteenth-Century England*, Oxford: Oxford University Press.

5 On the Catholic Apostolic Church, see Columba Graham Flegg, 1992, *'Gathered under Apostles': A Study of the Catholic Apostolic Church*, Oxford: Oxford University Press.

6 On Schleiermacher, see Keith W. Clements, 1987, *Friedrich Schleiermacher: Pioneer of Modern Theology*, London: Collins. His most important works in English are *On Religion: Speeches to its Cultured Despisers* (1799) and *The Christian Faith* (1821); the latter has been described as 'the most important Protestant theological text since Calvin's *Institutes*' (J.B. Webster, in *NDT*, art. 'Schleiermacher, Friedrich Daniel Ernst'). An interesting if inconsequential connection is that Schleiermacher prepared Bismarck for confirmation.

7 Alec R. Vidler, 1971, *The Church in an Age of Revolution*, Pelican History of the Church 5, Harmondsworth: Pelican, p. 24.

8 W.T. Stace, *The Philosophy of Hegel*, p. 43, quoted in Vidler, *Age of Revolution*, p. 29.

9 *ODCC*, art. 'Wellhausen, Julius'.

10 Vidler, *Age of Revolution*, p. 101.

11 Aston, *Christianity and Revolutionary Europe*, p. 297.

12 Hugh McLeod, 1981, *Religion and the People of Western Europe 1789–1970*, Oxford: Oxford University Press, p. v.

13 It has been said that 'A number of wolves donned sheep's clothing but few genuine conversions took place' (A.L. Drummond, 1951, *German Protestantism since Luther*, London: Epworth, p. 194).

14 On the Brethren, see Tim Grass, 2006, *Gathering to His Name: The Story of Brethren in Britain and Ireland*, Milton Keynes: Paternoster; Fred[erick] A. Tatford, 1985, *That the World may Know*, vol. 8: *West European Evangel*, Bath: Echoes of Service.

15 On the Pietist roots of European Baptists, see Ian Randall, '"Pious wishes": Baptists and wider renewal movements in nineteenth-century Europe', *Baptist Quarterly* 38 (1999–2000), pp. 316–31.

16 On the Swiss movement and its impact on British and Irish Evangelicalism, see Timothy C.F. Stunt, 2000, *From Awakening to Secession: Radical Evangelicals in Switzerland and Britain 1815–35*, Edinburgh: T. & T. Clark.

17 McLeod, *Religion*, pp. v–vi.

10

The Churches in Nineteenth-Century Britain (I): Church and State in England and Wales

The significance and extent of nineteenth-century developments for the British churches and their place in society is such that the topic needs to be split over two chapters. In this chapter we shall focus on the way in which church–state relationships in England and Wales moved from being conceived in terms of the state's duty to uphold the Anglican establishment to a broader approach which saw all the main Christian traditions as having a role to play in society. Such a transition was not achieved without considerable controversy regarding such matters as the state's role in education. This was also a century in which the religious landscape became considerably more variegated as new groups emerged and old denominations underwent changes in doctrine, practice, and organization. We shall therefore examine the rise of denominations and of 'parties' within denominations (especially Anglicanism).

A little social background may be helpful for understanding the factors impinging on the development of church–state relationships. The moral earnestness which had appeared during the late eighteenth century left a deep imprint on Victorian society; one reason for its widespread reception was fear that the nation might otherwise be headed for a fate like that of France. In time, 'seriousness'[1] became respectability, partly because of the inevitable operation of a principle sometimes described as 'redemption and lift': as individuals were converted, they developed habits of thrift and diligence which ensured their economic improvement, as well as aspirations to a way of life which set them apart from many of their peers. This was reinforced during the latter part of the century by a rise in the real value of wages, and a consequent growth in the size of the lower middle-class constituency (to be 'middle class', you had to keep at least one servant). Social respectability was also made possible by the removal of barriers to the full integration of Dissenters in the spheres of politics and education. To serve the lower classes a number of new religious groups appeared, but it is debatable how successful they were.

Timeline: Events in Britain and Ireland, 1789–1914

1791   Catholics granted freedom of worship in England and Wales
1792   Particular Baptist Society for the Propagation of the Gospel among the Heathen (later the Baptist Missionary Society) founded
1795   Methodist Conference allows societies to observe the sacraments
1798   Widespread unrest in Ireland
1801   Ireland comes under direct rule from Westminster; Church of Ireland united with the Church of England
1804   British and Foreign Bible Society founded
1829   Roman Catholic Emancipation Act
1833   Tractarian movement begins
1843   The 'Disruption' results in the formation of the Free Church of Scotland
1845   Newman converts to Roman Catholicism
1846   Evangelical Alliance founded
1850   Gorham Judgement; Catholic hierarchy established in England and Wales
1851   Census of Religious Worship
1859   Charles Darwin, *Origin of Species*
1860   *Essays and Reviews* published
1865   Christian Mission (later Salvation Army) founded
1867   First Lambeth Conference
1871   Church of Ireland disestablished
1873–5 Moody and Sankey tour Britain
1878   Catholic hierarchy established in Scotland
1881   *Revised Version* New Testament inaugurates flow of modern translations
1889   *Lux Mundi* published
1891   Particular Baptists unite with the New Connexion of General Baptists
1907   First Pentecostal church in Britain
1914   Parliament approves disestablish in Wales
1914   World War I begins

Roman Catholicism

By contrast with the eighteenth-century trend toward integration of Catholics into society (which drew on such factors as toleration, indifference to doctrinal details, a decline in fear of popery, and Catholic emphasis on beliefs held in common with Protestants), the nineteenth century saw a gradual move towards stressing the differences between Catholicism and British culture, in line with the ultramontane vision of the Church as an alternative society. As on the Continent, this was in part a response to external hostility and bore fruit in the creation of a 'safe' alternative network of social and educational institutions; this, coupled with the success of Catholicism at retaining the working-class ethos in this network, ensured the retention of most Catholic immigrants and their children. By the end of the century, Catholics would once again be seen by many as a race apart, their separate identity marked out by marriage rules (if they married a non-Catholic, the children were to be brought up in the Catholic faith) and a school system which had been built through the sacrificial giving of a community which was not, for the most part, wealthy.

In the aftermath of the French Revolution the thousands of Catholic priests who took temporary refuge in England functioned as ambassadors for their cause. Anglican congregations took up collections to relieve their physical needs, and the evident spirituality of these men, coupled with their status as victims of a godless regime, did much to allay residual fears of Catholic intentions. Anti-Catholicism was relatively weak during these years, not least because the papacy was seen as mortally wounded; only with its revival did anti-Catholicism in turn revive from the 1820s. It was given strength by apprehension at developments in Ireland, where Daniel O'Connell established himself as an effective leader and did much to fuse the notions of Catholicism and Irishness.

The Catholic Emancipation Act of 1829, signed with reluctance by George IV, allowed Catholics to fill all but a few political offices, although they had to swear an oath denying that the papacy had power to depose monarchs or exercise any temporal jurisdiction within Britain; Catholics were also allowed to vote. While this weakened the claim that Britain was constitutionally a Protestant nation (and some believed that it risked exposing the nation to divine wrath), it strengthened (by reaction) popular anti-Catholicism, and there were to be periodic outcries at any government move which appeared to be giving ground to Rome. Several societies were founded to defend Protestant liberties and alert the populace to the perceived evils of Romanism: the Reformation Society (1827), the Protestant Association (1835), the National Club (1845), the Scottish Reformation Society (1850), and the Protestant Alliance (1851).

Debate about Catholic Emancipation had fuelled anti-Catholic sentiment, but its strongest public expression came in the wake of the restoration of the Catholic hierarchy in 1850. This replaced the system of vicars-apostolic with a metropolitan archbishop and twelve suffragan bishops, although England remained a missionary territory until 1908. Furious controversy followed an ill-timed pastoral epistle *From out the Flaminian Gate* by the community's first head, Archbishop Wiseman, which came just when the Church of England was being shaken by the Gorham controversy (see below) and which was understood as implying that the Catholic Church was about to attempt the reconversion of England. Legislation was rushed through Parliament in 1851 forbidding Catholic bishops to assume titles of existing English sees, although it was never actually applied. Wiseman himself hastened to assure the nation that Catholics like Dissenters sought only the right to practise their religion freely as an integral part of the English community, but in some areas of high Catholic immigration and consequent economic competition suspicion died hard. Legally, however, the process of emancipation continued, Catholics being granted equal rights with other denominations in 1909.

Immigration, most notably to urban parts of Lancashire, was the main factor behind the growth of the Catholic community from under 100,000 in 1800 to 750,000 by 1850, although it is argued that a measure of growth would very probably have occurred anyway as Catholics engaged in mission.[2] There had been tensions between French refugees and the English Catholic community in the early 1790s; now more enduring tensions appeared. With the changing make-up of the Catholic community tensions became evident between established Catholic families, converts, and the poor. New devotional practices such as adoration of the Sacred Heart and the use of the rosary were introduced by Italian missionary orders active in England from the 1840s, providing a Catholic counterpart to popular Protestant revivalism; these contrasted with the restraint of the old English Catholics, who feared that the Church was becoming too ultramontane for them to retain their position in society. They wanted something as much like the Church of England as possible, whereas the converts and the immigrants wanted something visibly different from it. In addition, leadership of the community was passing from aristocrats and gentry to the clergy. Whereas the gentry had tended to settle for peaceful coexistence, from the 1830s the hope of England's reconversion to Rome was rekindled by the zeal of the converts. Under Archbishop Manning (1808–92), himself a former Anglican archdeacon, the three strands gradually integrated, although they have continued to remain visibly distinct to the careful observer.

Anglicanism

Legal and administrative change

The sixteenth-century Anglican Richard Hooker's vision of church and state as a harmonious whole had been placed under severe strain by the enforced ejection of Puritan clergy in 1662 and the Toleration Act of 1689. With the end of the war with France in 1815 the repressive conservatism of the war years came under pressure from a range of groups committed to reform, in church as well as state; repeal of the Test and Corporation Acts in 1828 opened the way for Dissenters to sit in Parliament, followed by Catholic Emancipation in 1829. The remarkable change in the ethos of the established church during this century owed much to the administrative reform in which, sometimes reluctantly, it engaged. It was the government which set up an Ecclesiastical Commission in 1835 to advise on administrative reform of the Church of England; two years later this was made a permanent body. Its recommendations lay behind some of the legislation passed during the next few years to address establishment abuses and Dissenting grievances. Reform may be assessed at the levels of parish and clergy, the episcopate, and the national church.

At the beginning of this period, the parish structure of the Church of England remained essentially that of the medieval period, in spite of the significant changes in settlement patterns. Thus rural Norfolk had 731 parishes, while urbanized Lancashire had but 70. Large cities such as Birmingham, which in the 1820s had a population of 120,000, might still form one parish: it was clearly impossible to exercise a meaningful parish ministry in such circumstances. In spite of the rapid urbanization of large parts of England, parish boundaries continued to require an Act of Parliament to change them until the Church Building Act of 1843; the only option, therefore, was to build privately funded 'chapels of ease' or 'district churches' in populous areas, always assuming that the incumbent of the parish was in sympathy. Parliament provided grants towards church-building in 1818 and 1824, and hundreds of new buildings were put up: according to one calculation, 308 in the 1820s, 600 in the 1830s, and 929 in the 1840s.[3] The first batch were intended as a kind of national monument celebrating military victory at Waterloo, and all were intended to help counter the threat of the spread of revolutionary sentiments among the masses. Even after the 1843 Act many urban parishes built mission halls or schools, but the motivation was now that such buildings, because they were less ecclesiastical in character, were less intimidating for unchurched people to enter, and allowed a greater freedom in the services which could be conducted.

One of the main problems confronting reformers was the prevalence of clerical pluralism and non-residence: in 1831, only 44 per cent of parishes in England and Wales had a resident incumbent; 33 per cent of beneficed clergy (that is, those serving a parish as rector, vicar, or perpetual curate) held more than one living. Many churches were served by curates, who did the work while the non-resident rectors enjoyed the income from tithes, but many parishes (1,000 in 1812) had no Anglican clergyman resident. The Pluralities Act of 1838 helped to deal decisively with this.

Clergy became regarded as a professional body, with higher expectations of them and a more systematic approach to training. The first Anglican theological college, at St Bees in Cumberland, was founded in 1816 and the first diocesan theological college (Chichester) in 1839. This development drew on the post-Tridentine Catholic system of diocesan seminaries. At the same time lay people also took on increasing responsibilities in the range of new organizations and outreach initiatives; many urban Anglican congregations were beginning to function in a manner not unlike those of the Dissenters: individuals came to church because they chose to, and committed themselves to working for it.

The episcopate, too, changed almost out of recognition. Whereas during the eighteenth century many, perhaps most, bishops had been court hangers-on, often neglecting their dioceses for months or years on end, the archetypal mid-nineteenth-century bishop was a hard worker, an efficient organizer of the diocese, a tireless spokesman for Anglican Christianity, and a father to his clergy. There was a new sense of diocesan identity and purpose as Anglicans banded together to respond to the evangelistic and social challenges of the age, and new dioceses were created (ten between 1880 and 1914).

At the national level the Church of England asserted its independence in the face of a Parliament which was no longer exclusively Anglican, restoring its own mechanisms of government. Convocation had been suppressed by the government in 1717, fearful that the clergy would seek to undermine the Hanoverian royal succession and offer support to Stuart claims; it was restored in 1854 (the province of Canterbury) and 1861 (the province of York), enabling the Church to undertake internal reform; from 1861 an annual Church Congress provided a debating platform for consideration of the issues of the day.

A major change in Anglicanism during the mid-nineteenth century was the transition from being primarily an English church to becoming an international family of churches. From 1841 it became possible for English bishops to consecrate bishops for overseas dioceses without the requirement to swear the oath of allegiance to the British Crown, something which had been possible for bishops in the United States since 1787. The Colonial Bishoprics Fund was established immediately in order to finance such appointments. By the mid-1860s many new dioceses had been created, and in many parts of the British Empire (and beyond) the church was functioning independently of the mother church in England.

A vital role was played in this process of internationalization by the Lambeth Conferences, to which Anglican bishops from all over the world were invited. These were not official councils passing binding legislation, but opportunities for leaders to consult together and reach a common understanding on pressing matters. The first Lambeth Conference took place in 1867, and further meetings occurred at intervals of ten years from 1878.

The development of the high church party

A development which did much to change the face of Anglicanism was the emergence of distinct parties, 'High', 'Low', and 'Broad'. This was evidence of the increasing strain being put upon the Church of England's comprehensiveness, and ran parallel to the emergence of Nonconformist denominational bodies and modern-style political parties. More broadly, they may also be compared with a revival of confessional spirit evident in Lutheran and Reformed circles in mainland Europe from fairly early in the century, which produced such diverse results as a renewed attachment to the theology of Calvin and a distinctively high-church strain of German Lutheranism. Party lines were drawn initially on theological grounds, and should not be seen as hard and fast, but in time differences in worship and ritual came to be regarded as indicative of party affiliation as the boundaries became set in stone.[4] Party allegiance was further crystallized by the establishment of a range of para-church agencies – missionary societies, publishing houses, evangelistic organizations, philanthropic bodies – many of which were identified with particular outlooks. We shall now examine each party in turn.

High churchmanship during this period underwent a succession of what amounted almost to reinventions. From the 'High and Dry' and the Hackney Phalanx of the beginning of the century, dominance passed to the Oxford Movement (also known as Tractarianism). From the middle of the century, Ritualism expressed the changing concerns of many high churchmen, and the period ended with the movement becoming widely known as Anglo-Catholicism.

Traditional high churchmen had emphasized the apostolic succession of the Anglican ministry, the threefold order of ministry of bishops, priests, and deacons. They also asserted the Church's independence of state control, which was balanced by acknowledgement of the monarch as ruling by divine right. Early in the nineteenth century their dynamism was provided by the Hackney Phalanx, a network of related clergy and laity centred on the parish of Hackney, then a suburb north-east of London. They were responsible for the founding of the National Society (1811) to fund schools providing an Anglican education, the Incorporated Church

Building Society (1818), and the Additional Curates Society (1837). However, their restrained style of churchmanship failed to attract a younger generation which was influenced by the Romantic stress on the mysterious and the medieval, and the baton passed to a movement which began in early 1830s Oxford. To tell its story, we need to set the scene.

In 1833 it became known that a reformist government planned to suppress ten Anglican bishoprics in Ireland and divert their income to other causes. This may appear to us as a sensible piece of ecclesiastical rationalization, but to many Anglican clergy who believed that the Church was not a department of state but an apostolic entity founded by Christ and possessing his authority, this seemed like unwarrantable interference in church affairs. Moreover, the government was pledged to reform, and further tampering with the Church's prerogatives looked inevitable. On 14 July 1833 John Keble (1792–1866) preached a sermon on 'National Apostasy', arguing that the government was seeking to cast off religious restraints, as demonstrated by its intent to suppress Irish bishoprics and its Erastian attitudes and disrespect to the bishops, among other things. This has been portrayed as the start of the Oxford Movement, but more significant was a small clerical conference a fortnight later at Hadleigh, Suffolk, which agreed that only a government ignorant of the true nature of the Church could contemplate such action, and that the challenge was to remind the public of the Church's divine authority and consequent independence of state control.

Among other early leaders were the ex-Evangelical John Henry Newman, then vicar of St Mary's in Oxford, and E.B. Pusey (1800–82), Regius Professor of Hebrew at the University. Their initial protest was against the state's failure to fulfil its duty to uphold the established church and the interference of non-Anglicans in the affairs of the Church of England (with which the Irish church was at this time united), on the basis of belief in apostolic succession as the foundation for the Church's authority. What distinguished them from older high churchmen was that they looked only to the early Fathers of the undivided Church, and not also to the Protestant Reformers, as their sources of inspiration, and therefore they did not share the anti-Roman sentiments of the older men (sentiments which were, indeed, held by the great majority of Englishmen, who identified Englishness with Protestantism). As in the late seventeenth century, 'the Church in danger' was their passionate concern. As a reaction against an unsympathetic state, it may be paralleled with Ultramontanism in France and Germany.

To publicize the movement's views, ninety *Tracts for the Times* appeared from September 1833 until their abrupt termination in 1841 after Newman had argued that the Thirty-Nine Articles were capable of interpretation consistently with Roman Catholic doctrine. By this time he had been challenged by the argument that the Church of England was in a similar situation to the fourth-century Donatists: whatever the correctness of its doctrine and order, it was out of communion with the centre of Christianity and confined to a limited part of the globe. This, coupled with the ferocious opposition provoked by *Tract 90*, culminated with his becoming a Roman Catholic in 1845; a number followed him and with their departure the movement's 'Tractarian' phase may be said to have terminated.

The next phase of the movement saw its centre of gravity shift from Oxford to London, and its emphasis move from academic to pastoral. It also introduced the term 'Anglo-Catholic', first used by Newman in 1838, a term which in its original usage referred not primarily to ritual but to ecclesiology. The Tractarians made the term 'Anglican' common currency as part of their 'branch theory' of the Church: for them, it had equal status with Rome and Orthodoxy as branches of the true Church of Christ, hence they could describe themselves as 'Anglo-Catholics'. The Church of England was not merely one denomination among many, but the continuation of the apostolic Church; Nonconformists, of course, were in effect unchurched as they lacked episcopal government and ordination in the apostolic succession.

Initially Evangelicals had sympathized with most of the main Tractarian concerns: the quest for holiness, the advocacy of frequent reception of communion, the fear that political reform amounted to an attack on the Church's divine prerogatives, and the belief in the Church's apostolicity. However, this changed once it became evident that many Tractarians were looking to Rome for inspiration and rejecting the Reformation heritage which meant so much to Evangelicals. Such developments as *Tract 90*, the republication of works by the Caroline Divines and others in the *Library of Anglo-Catholic Theology*, and the steady trickle of secessions to Rome were met by the founding of the Parker Society to translate and republish works by sixteenth-century English and Continental reformers, works of controversial theology upholding evangelical principles. There was a growing suspicion of Tractarianism as the first step to Rome and hence as an ominous portent of the fulfilment of biblical prophecy concerning the spread of apostasy and the rise of the False Prophet (Revelation 13). By the time of the Gorham controversy, therefore, Evangelicals and Tractarians saw themselves as being on opposing sides, a polarization which did much to poison intra-Anglican relationships for the rest of the century. The controversy in question was precipitated in 1847 by the refusal of the high-church Bishop Phillpotts of Exeter to institute an Evangelical, G.C. Gorham, to a living in his diocese because Gorham did not uphold the doctrine of baptismal regeneration in the form taught by the Book of Common Prayer. A lengthy legal battle ensued, with judgement being given in Gorham's favour in 1850 by a judicial committee of the Privy Council which included the two Archbishops and the Bishop of London, on appeal from the Church's own courts. What scandalized high churchmen was not so much the verdict, though this was objectionable enough in itself, as the fact that a secular authority was claiming the right to pronounce on matters deemed to be the Church's prerogative (in this case the limits of acceptable doctrine); this seemed proof positive of the irredeemable Erastianism of the Church of England. Several seceded to Rome, but it is arguable that if the judgement had gone the other way a number of Evangelicals would have seceded in the opposite direction. For much of the century many Evangelicals upheld the principle of state involvement in church affairs on the basis of an understanding of the Reformation as asserting the rights of the laity in the form of the godly ruler, regarding Parliament as the defender of Anglican doctrine and polity against the threat of unrestrained episcopal authority. However, Evangelicalism was becoming increasingly fractured, and throughout the century there was a trickle of clerical secessions in protest at what was regarded as the confusion of the Church and the world which resulted from establishment and from the parochial system.

Ritual had not been a concern of the original Oxford high churchmen, save insofar as they sought a more reverent approach to the conduct of worship as part of their quest for individual and corporate holiness. However, this changed for many under the influence of Romanticism, which revived the study of medieval church architecture and ritual as part of a broader idealization of medieval culture. A major influence in this field was the Cambridge Camden Society (later the Ecclesiological Society), founded in 1839 to study church architecture and ritual. Clergy adopted Roman Catholic ritual and vestments, and introduced such things as lighted candles on the altar and the use of incense. They faced east (and so away from the congregation) at the altar, which opponents saw as indicative of a belief in the sacrificial nature of the Eucharist, and by the end of the century had begun to introduce the practice of reserving the consecrated elements, mainly in order to be able to take communion to the sick and dying, but in some cases also as the focus of services of adoration (since they believed that the consecrated elements became the body and blood of Christ). Perhaps the most controversial practice of all to be introduced was that of private confession to a priest, which opponents saw as placing a man between the believer and God and hence subjecting Christians to a new form of priestly tyranny. Bitter late-nineteenth-century controversies about ritual and the system of belief which it was perceived to represent struck at the heart of the idea that England's Christian identity was fundamentally Protestant and demonstrated that the Church of England could no longer enforce liturgical uniformity, as it had done since 1662; and the loss of liturgical uniformity made it more difficult to contain the increasing theological diversity.

Having begun in part as a protest at the weakening of the church–state relationship resulting from legislative reform, high churchmen had moved to assert the Church's independence of (hostile) state control arising from its apostolic foundation. By the late nineteenth century, they were frequently taking an independent standpoint over against the state.

Since ritualist clergy were rarely welcome in established parishes, they frequently served in the newer urban ones. Often ministering to the poorest sector of society, they established a reputation as 'slum priests', sometimes living in community, like missionaries or Catholic monks. Such a ministry was not merely a necessity but also an outworking of their belief in the incarnation as a model for Christian living and as the central point of Christian belief (contrasting with the Evangelicals' focus on the cross); mission was conceived in terms of 'presence' and not merely 'proclamation'. The need for visual presentation of the faith provided them with a further argument in favour of colourful ritual, although it is questionable how effective this actually was: it can be argued that in many cases those who were attracted were middle-class Anglicans seeking a religious outlet for their aesthetic sensitivities, especially in southern England. The Evangelicals' appeal to Parliament to curb ritual excess lost credibility after the Public Worship Regulation Act (1874), which resulted in the prosecution of several clergy who became regarded as martyrs, most notably the saintly Bishop King of Lincoln in 1888.

In the 1820s and 1830s Pusey, who had studied under Schleiermacher in Germany, was one of a handful of people in Britain who were aware of Continental developments, and spent his life opposing them in the field of Old Testament scholarship. However, one wing of high churchmanship came to accept a judicious use of biblical criticism. *Lux Mundi* (1889), edited by Charles Gore (1855–1932), exemplified in this outlook; its telling subtitle *A Series of Studies in the Religion of the Incarnation* indicated where the centre of gravity of the movement's theology now lay. This wing fused high churchmanship with social concern and an acceptance of moderate biblical criticism, and was to dominate Anglicanism for the first half of the twentieth century.

The rise and decline of Evangelicalism

Low churchmanship, which in the previous century had been primarily a political category, became increasingly identified during this period with Evangelicalism. In the conservative climate following the French Revolution, Evangelicals found it expedient to stress their loyalty to the establishment and its value in upholding a Christian social and moral order. By the 1830s they were becoming deeply attached to the established church. Their loyalty to it was no longer suspect, and they saw it as both a defence of principles which they held dear as constitutional

Protestants and a means for the instruction and pastoral care of every English person through the parochial system. However, from the 1820s Evangelicals experienced a fragmentation which left them ill-equipped to respond to the succession of challenges presented by government legislation. In opposition to more moderate Evangelicals, an increasingly vocal group of radicals articulated a vision of the Church's place in the state and society which seemed in some ways to hark back to the era of the confessional state; with this they coupled a strong critique of the contemporary Church, especially in its established forms, and frequently a gloomy prognosis concerning its future (pre-millennial eschatology first received widespread public expression among the radicals).[5]

The outstanding evangelical leader during the first half of the century was Charles Simeon (1759–1836), Vicar of Holy Trinity, Cambridge from 1782 until his death.[6] Not only did he succeed in living down the opprobrium to which Evangelicals were frequently subjected, but he proved a gifted trainer of clergy in the days before theological colleges were widespread. He combined zealous Evangelicalism with a heartfelt attachment to the forms and structures of the Church of England, encouraging many to express their evangelistic vision within the context of a regular parish ministry rather than by itinerating beyond it. No great theologian, and certainly no friend of excessive systematization of theology (at a time when divisions between Arminian and Calvinist Evangelicals ran deep), it was nevertheless said of him that his influence was greater than that of any Anglican primate.

As the movement grew and its respectability became evident, it made greatest headway among the middle classes. Thus its complexion was somewhat different from that of contemporary Dissent, in which the working classes formed a larger proportion of members than had been the case a century earlier. Watering places such as Bath, Cheltenham, and Tunbridge Wells became centres of Evangelical influence by 1850. Indeed, in some quarters Evangelicalism could almost be described as fashionable, although in the later generations of the movement earnestness was prone to degenerate into affectation, as portrayed by novelists such as Dickens and Trollope.

The Evangelicals' greatest influence in the Church of England came during the third quarter of the century, once their numbers were sufficient but before the full impact of biblical criticism on the beliefs of parish clergy. The first evangelical bishop was appointed in 1815 (Henry Ryder, to Gloucester), and the first evangelical Archbishop of Canterbury in 1848 (J.B. Sumner); from 1855 to 1865 Lord Palmerston appointed a number of Evangelicals as bishops, drawing on the advice of a relative, the evangelical layman Lord Shaftesbury (of whom more later). There was a congruence between the ethos of Evangelicalism and that of contemporary culture which enabled the movement to spread easily. This was to lessen later in the century, with a trend to emphasize the incarnation rather than the atonement which could be harmonized with developments in scientific and philosophical thought.

In terms of corporate worship, high churchmen and Evangelicals both contributed to the restoration of the Eucharist to a central place in worship (though Evangelicals later tended to downplay this). Both also made full use of hymns in worship, once these had been declared permissible in 1819; rival collections were produced expressing each movement's distinctive theology. These, and the growth of congregational involvement in the liturgical responses, made congregations into participators rather than spectators, which helped to foster a sense of seriousness and reverent devotion. Other changes during the century included the replacement of bands of musicians (usually seated in a gallery at the west end of the building, hence the genre of 'West Gallery' psalmody) by organs, and the general cleaning up of church interiors. Harvest Festivals, first celebrated in 1842, became one of the great feasts of the church's year, especially in rural areas.

The emergence of the broad church

The term 'broad church' came into use about 1850 to designate an outlook which advocated the comprehensiveness of the Church of England in a manner not unlike that of the Latitudinarians. It saw Christianity as presenting a moral ideal, supremely in the example of the incarnate Christ, and shared the contemporary belief in human ability to progress. One of the main intellectual ancestors of this outlook was the writer S.T. Coleridge (1772–1834), a former Unitarian who became an Anglican. In *Aids to Reflection* (1825), he argued that rationalistic apologetic for Christianity was inadequate; he proposed a turn inwards, leading people to feel their need of faith rather than seeking to argue them into it. The authority of Christianity lay not in its susceptibility to logical demonstration but in its power to meet the deepest human needs. Coleridge was to influence a range of thinkers, including Edward Irving (1792–1834), a Church of Scotland minister in London who was found guilty of heresy for allegedly asserting that Christ took sinful human nature at his incarnation and who did much to pioneer the new outlook on biblical prophecy, F.D. Maurice (of whom more below), and some later high churchmen. Evangelicals, too, adopted a similar approach in their evangelistic proclamation.

Biblical criticism was slow to catch on in England; after the French Revolution, the country had retreated somewhat into intellectual isolationism and conservatism. Isolated figures such as Coleridge were aware of it, but it was broad churchmen who were most aware of German developments and who mediated them to the British public. In the same way, it was a trio of Cambridge men who may perhaps be associated with the broad church who did much to respond to the more extreme developments in New Testament scholarship, establishing a tradition of cautious criticism, careful exegesis, and devout exposition: J.B. Lightfoot (1828–89), Westcott, and Hort. The first two became bishops, and all three exercised a determinative influence on the relationship between scholarship and the Anglican pulpit.

Essays and Reviews (1860), which helped to popularize Darwin's thinking, was an attempt by a group of scholarly writers to challenge the Church of England to accommodate itself to modern scientific discoveries. The controversial dictum of one contributor, B.H. Jowett (1817–93), 'Interpret the Scripture like any other book', was perhaps what most horrified contemporary clergy. By it he meant adopting a common-sense hermeneutical approach paralleling that applied to other ancient writers, seeking to know what it meant to the first hearers or readers; this was linked with the idea that the Bible was not to be viewed as a divinely revealed unity which was timeless in nature, but as a record of the progressive religious development of humanity and hence not all of equal value. He went on to explain that through such an interpretation, it would become evident that in many respects it was unique. But it was enough that he appeared to be treating the Scriptures as a collection of human writings rather than a divinely integrated whole. However, a petition against the book was signed by 11,000 clergy and 137,000 laity, and in 1861 it was solemnly condemned by the bishops. Similar condemnation was offered of the biblical writings of J.W. Colenso (1814–83), Bishop of Natal in South Africa since 1853; he had denied the doctrine of the eternal punishment of the wicked, and argued that the atonement was an objective matter and that the missionary's task was not to seek conversions but to tell people that they were already redeemed and to work for the christianization of culture. He also challenged the historical accuracy of the Pentateuchal account of Israel's journeyings and conquest of Canaan, drawing on his background as a mathematician. The lengthy and complex legal wrangles surrounding attempts to have him deposed were a major factor in establishing the principle that where a territory had its own legislative assembly, its church had the right to function independently of the Church in England. His teaching also precipitated a request by the Canadian bishops in 1865 for an international gathering, which bore fruit in the form of the 1867 Lambeth Conference.

Which party was dominant? As the century progressed, the prominence of Evangelicalism began to give way to high churchmanship as the former decayed and the latter gained in maturity and public sympathy. It was high-church influences that restored the Eucharist to the central place in the parish's weekly diet of worship (by reaction, Wesleyanism, which had begun with a high view of the Eucharist, progressively downplayed its importance during the nineteenth century, as did other evangelical denominations). But it should also be noted that many clergy and bishops could not be easily pigeonholed in any of the categories of high, low, or broad: among them were notables such as F.W. Robertson (1816–53), one of the best-known Anglican preachers of the century, C.J. Blomfield (1786–1857), the tireless and efficient Bishop of London from 1828 to 1856, and the hymnwriter William Walsham How (1823–97), whose final episcopal appointment was to the see of Wakefield.

From Dissenters to Nonconformists to Free Churchmen

Changes in self-understanding

Unitarians such as Joseph Priestley welcomed the French Revolution as the dawning of the biblical millennium, as did some other middle-class Dissenters: it was seen as analogous to the Glorious Revolution of 1688, and as justified on the basis that an oppressed people may depose a tyrannical ruler. When it seemed as if the papacy had been dealt a fatal blow (coupled with the earlier suppression of the Jesuits), the way appeared open for mass conversions of Catholics and a global revival to usher in the millennium. However, enthusiasm cooled rapidly as the anti-Christian aspect of the revolution became clear, and in the politically apprehensive climate of the later 1790s most Dissenters found it expedient to stress their loyalty to the powers that be. (By this point, some Anglicans were paralleling the execution of Louis XVI with that of Charles I.) As war with France dragged on, and other potential forces for revolution came to the fore, a number of Evangelicals explored an alternative eschatology in which the entire fabric of European Christian civilization and social order was written off as doomed to destruction. This was known as pre-millennialism, because in it the return of Christ (preceded by a range of cataclysmic events) was seen as occurring before the millennium: the older view, postmillennialism, had applied the eighteenth-century belief in human progress to eschatology, postulating a gradual improvement in society coupled with increasing success for the gospel, culminating in the return of Christ to a world thus made ready for him.[7]

A change in self-designation during this period is indicative of changes in self-understanding. The traditional term 'Dissenter' came to be seen by many as unduly negative in tone; for Wesleyan Methodists, whose attachment to the establishment persisted at the higher levels of the denomination, it was also somewhat inaccurate: in 1843, the denominational leader Jabez Bunting (1779–1858) commented that in one sense they were not Dissenters but Nonconformists. The latter term became widely used, deriving some of its popularity from commemorations in 1862 of the bicentenary of the 'Great Ejection', when almost 2,000 Anglican clergy had been evicted from their livings because of their refusal to conform to the requirement that the Book of Common Prayer be used in worship. However, nomenclature was to change again: by the end of the nineteenth century, the designation 'Free Church' had come to be the preferred label for non-Anglican Protestants as more positive in tone and as expressing the equality with the establishment to which they now aspired. It received formal acknowledgement in the title of the National Council of Evangelical Free Churches, founded in 1896 to give expression to their sense of kinship (based on a broader understanding of the doctrine of the Church) and to assist in planning united outreach.

A similar progression was evident in the terms used to describe the buildings in which they met. Wesley had called the first Methodist buildings 'preaching houses' to indicate that he was not seeking to draw people away from the parish churches; other Dissenters had used the terms 'meeting' or 'meeting house'. As they drew apart from the establishment, Methodists adopted the term 'chapel' (confusingly, in northern England this also designated a Roman Catholic place of worship); other Dissenters followed them in this early in the nineteenth century. The great religious divide running through many English and Welsh communities thus became that between 'church' and 'chapel'. By late in the century, they began to use 'church', as did Anglicans, to describe their buildings. This was not merely a matter of labels: worship in some congregations took on a more liturgical flavour, and the buildings themselves were increasingly 'church-like' in design.[8] Whereas Dissenters had tended to prefer a classical style for their larger buildings (such as C.H. Spurgeon's Metropolitan Tabernacle in London), many urban congregations now adopted the Gothic style popularized by the Tractarians and eventually beloved by Anglicans of all types.

Antagonism to Anglicanism's established status

As for the spheres of relations with the civil authorities and political involvement, the century saw Dissenters shed much of their introversion and achieve redress of a number of longstanding grievances; sociologically speaking, the outlook of most developed from 'sectarian' to 'churchly'.

In an age when Anglican Evangelicals stressed the benefits of establishment, relationships between them and Dissenting Evangelicals were frequently strained. Persecution of Dissent was by no means unknown in rural areas, though this was not instigated by Evangelicals. The repeal of the Test and Corporation Acts in 1828, followed by the Municipal Corporations Act (1835), allowed Dissenters to play a full part in government at local and national levels (although annual indemnity Acts had allowed Dissenters to sit as Members of Parliament before this). Far from assuaging their sense of unjust treatment, Dissenters were emboldened to seek not merely toleration but full equality with the Church of England, and even the latter's disestablishment. Their political militancy contrasted sharply with Anglican social conservatism. Something of the deep anti-establishment sense felt by many comes over in these words of the Congregationalist Edward Miall in 1842:

> Our strength lies in aggression, rather than in defence. The system which at present obstructs the free working of Christian principles, and the general diffusion of Christian truth, must be smitten with the sword of sharp rebuke, and pursued with all the determination of purpose which should sustain the minds, and brace up the energies, of men who are aiming at the overthrow of antichrist. Whatever there is of real good, mingled with the mass of corruption and evil, will survive the system which it now helps to sanctify, and by which its own elasticity and usefulness are well nigh destroyed. Upon all national churches is enstamped, in deep and indelible characters, the mark of the beast. All kind of alliance with them, the genius of Christianity strictly prohibits. 'Come out and be separate' is the only command which, in reference to these institutions, we are permitted to regard. Homage, even the most indirect, paid to the state church is, in essence, the recognition of falsehood and the worship of a lie.[9]

In 1844 Miall founded the British Anti-State Church Society, later known as the Liberation Society, to press the government to accord equal status to Dissenters. It achieved wide support among non-Wesleyans; in the 1860s Spurgeon allowed it to use the Metropolitan Tabernacle for a time. But after the failure of several bills seeking disestablishment, interest waned; in any case, a substantial proportion, possibly half, of Dissenters (including most Wesleyans) either opposed disestablishment or stood apart from controversy over political issues. The last real upsurge of anti-establishment feeling among Nonconformists was provoked by the Education Act of 1902, which proposed official funding for denominational schools; this was seen as state subsidy for Anglican propaganda and as especially obnoxious in rural areas where the only school was a church one. Over the following four years 70,000 Nonconformists received court summonses for non-payment of part of their rates.[10]

Dissenters' grievances began to be addressed soon after the electoral reforms of 1832. From 1836 Nonconformists were allowed to marry in their own chapels (since 1753 only marriages conducted in Anglican churches had been legally recognized, unless the parties were Quakers or

Jews). Until the introduction of civil registration in 1837, Anglican baptismal registers offered the only official record of births, but now an alternative system of records was put in place. In 1868 compulsory church rates (levied on the population of a parish in order to finance the running and repair costs of its church) were abolished; these had been a particular cause of grievance because Dissenters felt that they were already paying to build and maintain their own places of worship, and should not have to bear the additional expense of the upkeep of a building which was to be used by others. In 1871 the Universities' Tests Act abolished all religious tests for the universities, except for degrees in theology and fellowships at Oxford and Cambridge. In 1880 Nonconformists won the right to conduct funeral services for their own people in Anglican graveyards according to their own rites. Yet for much of this period, removal of grievances was paralleled by an increase in Nonconformist agitation, as they set their sights on full equality rather than mere removal of disabilities.

By contrast, the Evangelical Alliance (EA) was founded in 1846 to unite Dissenting and Anglican Evangelicals at a time when such pan-denominationalism was under pressure as a result of debates such as that surrounding establishment.[11] One major unifying factor was positive – a shared understanding of the gospel; another was negative – opposition to 'popery' and 'Puseyism', which derived some of its force from the agitation concerning a government grant to the Catholic seminary at Maynooth, near Dublin, from 1845.

In Wales the century saw a hardening of divisions between traditional Anglicans and Methodists, followed by the massive expansion of all forms of Dissent, especially in newly urbanized industrial areas in the south. In 1811 the Calvinistic Methodists (later known as the Presbyterian Church of Wales) effectively seceded from the established church when they ordained a number of lay preachers to administer the sacraments because of the shortage of Anglican clergy in the movement (as had happened in the United States).[12] They grew rapidly, to the extent that in the 1851 Religious Census, 87 per cent of worshippers attended Nonconformist places of worship; Nonconformity dominated industrial and urban areas. Revival from 1858 benefited the Nonconformists far more than the Anglicans, with Calvinistic Methodists increasing their membership from 59,000 in 1850 to over 90,000 in 1861 (though not all of this gain was permanent). The differences were not solely religious: 'the tension between church and chapel was not only theological and ecclesiastical but was profoundly political and social'.[13] Its ethos was relatively democratic until late in the century, and the established church had an inadequate network of parishes in industrial areas and (for the first half of the century) cumbersome mechanisms for remedying the deficiency. Yet by 1900 the Anglicans were again the largest single religious body in the principality, thanks to vigorous extension efforts. In addition the role of Nonconformity as a bearer of Welsh language and culture was somewhat eroded as Anglicans worked from mid-century to shed the image of 'the English church'. Disestablishment was inevitable, however, in part because Anglicanism was seen as an English religion; the legislation received parliamentary approval in 1914, although its implementation was delayed by war until 1920. Thereafter the Church in Wales was fully independent of Canterbury.

The rise of modern Nonconformist denominations

A key development in nineteenth-century Nonconformity was the emergence of the modern denomination. One powerful motivating factor for this was the upsurge of evangelistic concern which was evident from the 1790s and reinforced by the recognition that, if it was possible to organize and plan for mission overseas, the same thing could be done to facilitate mission at home. Congregationalists founded a home missionary society in 1797 (refounded 1819), and Baptists did so in 1821. Dozens of similar local bodies were founded in various parts of the country. Such agencies, like the seventeenth-century associations of Dissenting churches, were able to adopt a more strategic approach to the planting of new churches than any individual congregation could do, though the primary agents remained local churches. Congregations were extremely active themselves setting up 'preaching stations' in local communities, with the objective of establishing regular Sunday worship and eventually a self-supporting church. One example is the Particular Baptist church in the village of Grundisburgh in Suffolk, itself formed as recently as 1798, which saw eight churches established through its activity during the first half of the nineteenth century. Such expansion was made possible by the widespread use of lay preachers, who would conduct services wherever they could gain an entrance; here the Methodists had led the way. Such preachers were hardy individuals, often walking ten miles or more to a preaching engagement, and liable on occasion to experience verbal or even physical abuse, especially in the tense social climate of the 1790s.

Other factors in the move to establish denominational structures included (i) the wish to provide a means of financing new buildings without the need for ministers to undertake long preaching tours to raise money, wearing themselves out and neglecting their flocks in the process; (ii) a concern to establish central funds for the support of ministers; and (iii) the commencement of publishing agencies to produce periodicals and books inculcating denominational principles. From the 1830s, denominational agencies were also seen as playing a role in maintaining the civil rights of Dissenters.

The emergence of a plurality of denominations suited an age which played up the values of competition and free trade; as Watts comments, 'Nonconformity flourished in an atmosphere of free trade and competition in religion.'[14] Yet at the same time denominations became increasingly aware of what they had in common, initially in the quest for redress of political grievances, but later in a more catholic understanding of the Church and a concern to join in combating the growth in irreligion.

Most Nonconformist causes saw a shift in focus during the century from piety to fellowship.[15] From the 1870s the amount of leisure time available increased and so did the range of venues where it could be passed. Finding themselves having to compete with alternative attractions, churches began to offer a whole range of leisure activities in an attempt to retain the allegiance of younger members of their community, and in response to the trend towards a marginalization of their social role. Musical, dramatic, sporting, and debating societies all made their appearance in chapel life, offering a sharp contrast with the previous programme of Sunday services and midweek prayer meetings. Leisure was no longer seen as an occasion of temptation, but as a means whereby the churches could make (or retain) contact with people; such a development did not pass without criticism from conservatives such as the influential Baptist minister C.H. Spurgeon (1834–92), whose Metropolitan Tabernacle functioned well enough without such diversions from what Spurgeon saw as its 'spiritual' priorities. But Spurgeon and his church were thoroughly involved in a related trend, which was the development by many larger urban churches of a network of affiliated institutions responding to local social needs; a prime expression of this was the Central Halls of Methodism, established as part of the late-nineteenth-century 'Forward Movement' to provide popular worship and engage in social work, but it was evident in most Nonconformist denominations, and in many Anglican churches also. Parallel developments were evident in Northern Europe, in the 'Inner Mission' movements of Germany and Scandinavia.

As Nonconformist denominations matured, and became more institutionalized and less sectarian in their relations with the world, new groups emerged seeking to recapture a radicalism which they believed had been let slip. A prime example is the Salvation Army. This began when William Booth (1829–1912), a revivalist who had ministered among the Wesleyans and then the Methodist New Connexion, concluded that these denominations were too respectable to reach those at the bottom of the social ladder. In 1865 he founded his 'Christian Mission' in Whitechapel, East London. It was not until the late 1870s that the movement adopted its trademark quasi-military identity, expressing the conviction that it was engaged in a war for souls. In a jingoistic society the Army's uniforms, brass bands, processions, and military-style structure and discipline proved highly attractive; no theoretical justification was offered for its ecclesiology, merely the pragmatic one that it worked. Even observance of the sacraments was abandoned, in part because in view of the likelihood of objections to female officers celebrating communion it was deemed better to give up communion than lose the ministry of preachers whose effectiveness had been proven. By 1900 there were an estimated 100,000 Salvationists in England alone, and the movement had spread to various parts of the Commonwealth and beyond. Yet it has been argued that the Army failed in its attempt to win the very poor; new recruits understandably aspired to a more 'respectable' lifestyle and so tended to lose touch with their peers; its insistence on temperance, too, would have presented a major obstacle to success in working-class areas whose culture centred largely round the public house.[16]

The newer groups entered their most fruitful period in the late nineteenth century, at a time when the growth rate of the older denominations had slowed. To some extent we can argue that each new generation's sectarian movements represent a response to the tendency to institutionalization which appears as older movements become established, but Gilbert has argued that the slowing growth of older denominations came about in part because there was simply less demand for the hot religion which Dissenters had traditionally provided.[17]

We should also note the attraction of another radical movement, Mormonism,[18] in depressed rural areas, such as parts of Norfolk. In the 1851 Census there were more Mormons than Quakers. Most were former Methodists, and the two groups used similar revivalist methods. However, during the 1850s most British Mormons emigrated to the American Mid-West, drawn by the promise of an earthly millennium, and the introduction of polygamy hastened the movement's decline; not until well into the twentieth century did numbers recover fully.

Methodists began this period as the odd men out among Dissenters, because their close kinship with Anglicanism made them gravitate towards Toryism. On John Wesley's death in 1791, they had 72,500 members, with 470 preaching houses (chapels) organized into 114 circuits and served by 289 itinerants, mostly laymen with a few Anglican clergy. It was perhaps inevitable that the drift away from Anglicanism should continue, the more so as an increasing proportion of their members would have had no meaningful experience of Anglican worship. In 1795, therefore, the Plan of Pacification, approved by the annual Conference, allowed the administration of the sacraments in Methodist buildings if so desired by local societies. In addition, it was acknowledged that services might now be held at times which conflicted with those of the parish church, although congregations which did so were requested to use the Book of Common Prayer or John Wesley's abridgement of it. Methodism could now make complete provision for the corporate Christian life of its members.

It was not long before tensions between conservatives and radicals erupted into open conflict. The first schism occurred in 1797, leading to the formation of the Methodist New Connexion. Many of these schisms were fuelled by a desire for more democratic church government in the face of a tendency towards clericalism in the parent body. In Wolffe's words, they 'owed something to the legacy of a revivalistic tradition that had given ordinary Methodists a sense of spiritual dignity and empowerment, leading them to confront the perceived authoritarianism of the connexional leadership'.[19] Others were fuelled by a desire to recapture the evangelistic passion which was believed to have marked early Wesleyanism. The Primitive Methodists developed a separate existence because the Wesleyans forbade the holding of 'camp meetings', all-day evangelistic outreaches employing a number of preachers and exhorters, held in a rural location and drawing large crowds, such as that at Mow Cop in Staffordshire in 1807. Another group with similar concerns to the Primitive Methodists were the Bible Christians, who began in Cornwall during 1815. Wesleyans were sensitive to the need to demonstrate that they were not a threat to the social order at a time when there were those in authority who wished to restrict Dissenting itinerancy as potentially seditious (England was at war with France until 1815), and so they tended to clamp down firmly on what were seen as disorderly manifestations. The fear was that large meetings could be regarded as potentially subversive, and also that Parliament would react by banning all itinerant preaching. This was what Lord Sidmouth tried to do in 1811–12, with a Bill which would have refused official recognition of ministerial status (and exemption from such things as military or jury service) to those who were not settled in a congregational charge. Another factor making tension worse was that under the leadership of Jabez Bunting, whose outlook may be gleaned from his assertion that Methodism was as opposed to democracy as it was to sin, Wesleyanism was placing increasing stress on a recognized clerical ministry rather than relying quite so extensively on lay workers. Perhaps some of the tension had always been latent within the Methodist ethos, and was coming into the open as the result of new challenges and contexts.

During the nineteenth century, the evangelistic schisms in particular were marked by a strong sense of belonging to the Dissenting community, something which was slow to develop among the original Wesleyans. Such groups grew rapidly, whereas those which originated in disputes over church government (such as the Wesleyan Reformers, who took almost a quarter of the English Wesleyan membership in 1849) grew more slowly if at all. To some extent the evangelistic schisms proved better able than the increasingly staid Wesleyans to reach those of lower social classes, not least because they tended to be movements *of* the poor rather than *to* the poor.

On the theological fringes of Dissent, Unitarians suffered from the sharpened sense of denominational identity which marked the early nineteenth century. The Trinity Act of 1813 freed them from legal penalties, but a number of court cases contested their control of trusts originally intended to benefit Presbyterian causes; Trinitarian Dissenters drew away from them and they were forced out of the General Body of Protestant Dissenting Ministers in 1836, and it began to appear that they would be turned out of many ex-Presbyterian chapels. (An explicitly Trinitarian Presbyterian Church of England was formed after 1836, including those congregations which had remained orthodox.) However, their continued existence was secured by the Dissenters' Chapels Act of 1844, which allowed them to remain in possession of buildings which they had occupied for the previous 25 years, unless the trust deeds were explicitly Trinitarian. Unitarians experienced a theological shift as well as a change in their legal position: by the 1820s the older biblicist Unitarianism was fading away, to be replaced by a more liberal outlook stressing the authority of reason and conscience. Later in the century, something of a rapprochement with Trinitarian Nonconformity occurred as James Martineau (1805–1900) sought to assimilate Unitarian worship to that of the Church of England (and in his devotional writings influenced a generation of liberally minded Nonconformists); this development was reflected in the 'parish church' style of some buildings erected from the 1860s onwards. Unitarians, like many other Nonconformists, were attracted by the aesthetic qualities of contemporary high Anglican worship with its sense of mystery.

The century was also pivotal in the transition of England (and Wales) from a confessionally Anglican state to a pluralistically Christian one, and in the next chapter we shall explore the process by which this was achieved.

Questions for thought

1 Review the developments in the relationship between the Roman Catholic community and society.

2 In what ways do you think legal and administrative changes within Anglicanism reflected wider social trends?

3 Why did the Oxford Movement make such an impact on religious life in England?

4 What reasons would you offer for the eventual decay of Anglican Evangelicalism during this period?

5 Compare and contrast the approach to Christian doctrine of the broad church and Catholic Modernism.

6 What aspects of earlier Dissenting self-understanding were left behind in the nineteenth century, and why do you think this was?

7 Why do you think Dissent became so much more politically active during this period? What changes in other aspects of Dissent might have facilitated this?

8 To what extent were the new Dissenting groups giving expression to new concerns, and to what extent were they seeking to readdress old ones?

Further reading

David W. Bebbington, 2005, *The Dominance of Evangelicalism: The Age of Spurgeon and Moody*, A History of Evangelicalism, Leicester: IVP.

D.W. Bebbington, 1995, *Evangelicalism in Modern Britain: A History from the 1730s to the 1980s*, 2nd edn, London: Routledge, chs 3–5.

David W. Bebbington (ed.), 2006, *Protestant Nonconformist Texts*, vol. 3: *The Nineteenth Century*, Aldershot: Ashgate.

John Bossy, 1975, *The English Catholic Community 1570–1850*, London: Darton, Longman & Todd, part 3.

Owen Chadwick, 1987, *The Victorian Church*, 2 vols, London: SCM Press.

Horton Davies, 1961, *Worship and Theology in England: From Watts and Wesley to Maurice, 1690–1850*, Princeton, NJ: Princeton University Press, part 3.

Horton Davies, 1962, *Worship and Theology in England: from Newman to Martineau, 1850–1900*, Princeton, NJ: Princeton University Press.

(The above volumes were reissued in 1996 as *Worship and Theology in England: From Watts to Martineau, 1690–1900*, Grand Rapids, MI: Eerdmans.)

Sheridan Gilley and W. J. Sheils (eds), 1994, *A History of Religion in Britain: Practice and Belief from Pre-Roman Times to the Present*, Oxford: Blackwell, part 3.

Kenneth Hylson-Smith, 1997, *The Churches in England from Elizabeth I to Elizabeth II*, vol. 2: *1689–1833*, London: SCM Press, parts 3–4.

Kenneth Hylson-Smith, 1998, *The Churches in England from Elizabeth I to Elizabeth II*, vol. 3: *1833–1998*, London: SCM Press, part 1.

James R. Moore (ed.), 1988, *Religion in Victorian Britain*, vol. 3: *Sources*, Manchester: Manchester University Press.

Edward Norman, 1986, *Roman Catholicism in England: From the Elizabethan Settlement to the Second Vatican Council*, Oxford: Oxford University Press, chs 4–5.

Geoffrey Rowell, 1983, *The Vision Glorious: Themes and Personalities in the Catholic Revival in Anglicanism*, Oxford: Clarendon.

Nigel Scotland, 2004, *Evangelical Anglicans in a Revolutionary Age 1789–1901*, Carlisle: Paternoster.

Michael R. Watts, 1995, *The Dissenters*, vol. 2: *The Expansion of Evangelical Nonconformity 1791–1859*, Oxford: Clarendon.

John Wolffe, 2006, *The Expansion of Evangelicalism*, A History of Evangelicalism, Leicester: IVP.

Notes

1 On this attitude, see Ian Bradley, 1976, *The Call to Seriousness: The Evangelical Impact on the Victorians*, London: Jonathan Cape; reprinted 2006, Oxford: Lion.

2 For this argument, see Bossy, *English Catholic Community*.

3 It is often overlooked that grants were also made in 1818 to the Church of Ireland (£1 million) and the Church of Scotland (£350,000) for similar purposes.

4 For an illuminating contemporary account, see W.J. Conybeare's article 'Church Parties' (*Edinburgh Review*, October 1853), reprinted in Stephen Taylor (ed.), 1999, *From Cranmer to Davidson: A Church of England Miscellany*, Woodbridge: Boydell Press for the Church of England Record Society.

5 On divisions and secessions within the Church of England, see Grayson Carter, 2001, *Anglican Evangelicals: Protestant Secessions from the Via Media, c.1800–1850*, Oxford: Oxford University Press.

6 On Simeon, see: William Carus, 1848, *Memoir of the Life of the Rev. Charles Simeon*, London: Hatchards; Hugh Evan Hopkins, 1977, *Charles Simeon of Cambridge*, London: Hodder & Stoughton; Charles Smyth, 1940, *Simeon and Church Order*, London: SPCK.

7 The third main eschatological viewpoint is known as amillennialism; it teaches that the biblical millennium is not literal but symbolic (usually of the church age); its main progenitor was Augustine of Hippo, and it became the dominant viewpoint in the Western Church during the medieval and early modern periods.

On British nineteenth- and twentieth-century millennial views, see Crawford Gribben and Timothy C.F. Stunt (eds), 2005, *Prisoners of Hope? Aspects of Evangelical Millennialism in Britain and Ireland, 1800–1880*, Carlisle: Paternoster; Stephen Hunt (ed.), 2001, *Christian Millenarianism from the Early Church to Waco*, London: Hurst; W.H. Oliver, 1978, *Prophets and Millennialists: The Uses of Biblical Prophecy in England from the 1790s to the 1840s*, Auckland, New Zealand: Auckland University Press / Oxford University Press; E.R. Sandeen, 1970, *The Roots of Fundamentalism: British and American Millenarianism 1800–1930*, Chicago: University of Chicago Press. For works on North American millennialism, see Chapter 12, note 3.

8 A useful visual introduction to nineteenth-century ecclesiastical architecture is James Stevens Curl, 1995, *English Heritage Book of Victorian Churches*, London: B.T. Batsford. There is also a superbly illustrated series (covering earlier centuries as well) by Christopher Stell, 1986–2002, *Nonconformist Chapels and Meeting-Houses*, 4 vols, Swindon: English Heritage.

9 E. Miall, 1842, *The Nonconformist's Sketch Book*, p. 280, in John Briggs and Ian Sellers (eds), 1973, *Victorian Nonconformity*, Documents of Modern History, London: Edward Arnold, p. 127.

10 For tensions between Anglicans and Free Churchmen over education, see Chapter 11.

11 On the Evangelical Alliance, see Ian Randall and David Hilborn, 2001, *One Body in Christ: The History and Significance of the Evangelical Alliance*, Carlisle: Paternoster.

12 Similarly, from 1816 Irish Methodist lay preachers were allowed to administer the sacraments, and the majority of the movement withdrew from the Church of Ireland.

13 E.T. Davies, 1965, *Religion in the Industrial Revolution in South Wales*, Cardiff: University of Wales Press, p. vi.

14 Watts, *Dissenters*, vol. 2, p. 158.

15 For this argument, see Charles D. Cashdollar, 2000, *A Spiritual Home: Life in British and American Reformed Congregations, 1830–1915*, University Park, PA: Pennsylvania State University Press, 2000.

16 On the Salvation Army, see Robert J. Sandall and Arch J. Wiggins, 1947–68, *The History of the Salvation Army*, 5 vols, London: Salvation Army; Pamela J. Walker, 2001, *Pulling the Devil's Kingdom Down: The Salvation Army in Victorian Britain*, Berkeley, CA: University of California Press; and its official historical website: http://www1.salvationarmy.org.uk/heritage. As recently as 2004, the Salvation Army was refused permission to operate in Moscow on the ground that it was a military organization.

17 A.D. Gilbert, 1976, *Religion and Society in Industrial England: Church, Chapel and Social Change, 1740–1914*, London: Longman, p. 44.

18 Their preferred nomenclature is 'The Church of Jesus Christ of Latter-Day Saints'.

19 Wolffe, *Expansion*, p. 90.

11

The Churches in Nineteenth-Century Britain (II): Growth and Division

The previous chapter concentrated on the organizational life of the English and Welsh churches and their relationships with the state; in this chapter we shall broaden the focus to include Scotland and Ireland, and look at the extent of, and reasons for, the growth of the non-established churches.

The 1851 Religious Census[1]

Only once has the United Kingdom government attempted to collect data concerning the religious allegiance of its citizens: in 1851. (Other unofficial censuses were undertaken in London by the *British Weekly* in 1886–7 and the *Daily News* in 1902–3, the latter of which may well have been the most accurate of all.) In the 1851 Census, as well as the decennial population census, a vast army of local enumerators collected data about the attendance at every known place of worship on a particular Sunday, 30 March. Coverage was not complete. About 7 per cent of Anglican churches failed to submit a return, often because the clergy objected to the census in principle. A somewhat higher proportion of Dissenters was omitted, mainly because the flexibility which enabled them to start new causes by holding house meetings meant that they were not infrequently overlooked by enumerators. This was particularly so for denominations such as the Primitive Methodists, Baptists, and Brethren. In addition, reliance on statistics provided by the clergy themselves, of varying standards of accuracy, makes it unwise to place too much weight on the detail of the data. Nevertheless, the main lines of the picture can be trusted, and historians have developed techniques for minimizing the degree of error in statistical analysis of the returns.

Table 11.1: Denominational allegiance in England and Wales, 1851.[2]

Denomination	England – congregations	England – estimated attendances	Wales – congregations	Wales – estimated attendances
Roman Catholic	558	288,305	12	3,725
Anglican	13,098	3,415,861	979	112,674
Presbyterian	160	58,762	–	–
Unitarian	202	34,110	27	2,901
Independent	2,604	655,935	640	132,629
Baptist	2,349	499,604	440	92,344
Quaker	363	16,783	8	115
Wesleyan	6,151	924,140	428	58,138
Other Arminian Methodist	4,323	565,054	105	8,352
Calvinistic Methodist	48	unknown	780	160,671
Mormon	(Eng + W) 222	19,792		3,368
Total attendances		6,618,538		580,109

NB: Not all groups are shown.

The main aspects of the census findings which shocked contemporary Britain were (i) the proportion of the working-class population in England (not in Wales) who did not attend a place of worship, even though much of the century's Nonconformist growth had been among the poor, with a resulting change in the social composition of the Baptists and, to some extent, the Independents; and (ii) the proportion of attenders who went to Nonconformist services. (Attenders would have outnumbered members, often by several times, especially in areas where the culture was predominantly Nonconformist, as in industrialized South Wales.) Nonconformist growth was among those denominations which owed their origins to the eighteenth-century evangelical movement; others barely held their own, or (in the case of the Quakers) were declining. Many in the established church were shocked at the extent of Dissent and feared that Dissenters would make capital out of it in their campaign against establishment, but it was Nonconformist opposition which ensured that the exercise was not repeated in 1861. As for working-class non-attendance, this had drawn comment since the mid-eighteenth century, but the unsettled political climate of the 1830s and 1840s made those in authority somewhat more sensitive to it. The official report on the Census, compiled by Horace Mann, put it down to dislike of the maintenance of social distinctions in church by such means as the system of pew rents[3] (which reinforced a working-class sense of inferiority), indifference of the churches to the needs of the working classes, perception of ministers and clergy as doing a job because they were paid to rather than out of conviction, inability to afford to dress appropriately for worship, and a lifestyle which left little time for church attendance because of the need to work long hours to earn enough to survive. Such arguments have provided the parameters for much subsequent debate concerning the relationship between the working classes and the churches, although they have been challenged in more recent years on the basis of other statistical data.

The effectiveness of outreach

The population of England and Wales grew from 8.9 million in 1801 to 36.1 million by 1911. Anglicans did not find it easy to respond to rapid urbanization within their existing structures, although the number of parishes in England did double between 1850 and 1900, but Nonconformist flexibility and strategic planning meant that between 1772 and 1851 the number of their congregations increased tenfold.

Growth was due to the convergence of a number of factors: apart from the success of Nonconformist evangelism and educational and philanthropic work, in many areas social circumstances were favourable to new forms of the old faith. As a result the numbers of new congregations being registered in England increased dramatically; there were 1,405 from 1781 to 1790, 4,245 from 1791 to 1800, and 5,434 from 1801 to 1810. Nonconformists flourished better in some environments than others. Villages where the parson and squire (as chief landowner) between them exercised a tight degree of social control were unlikely to prove fertile soil for Dissenting groups, since villagers would have had pressure put upon them to ensure that they attended the parish church. By contrast, where land ownership was split among a number of people, there was more variety in occupation, a greater measure of independent action was possible, and it was easier to find a cottage in which to hold meetings or land on which to build a chapel. Dissent also seems to have done relatively well in smaller industrial communities such as coal-mining villages in Durham and South Wales, not least because workers were no longer dependent on the squire for employment and housing. It should be noted that growth of Dissent is not necessarily an indication that the Church of England was failing in its duty of education and pastoral care (though this was not infrequently the case): Watts argues that Dissent often reaped where the establishment had sown, benefiting from an acquaintance with Christianity gained at school or church. Where the Church of England's parochial system had never really become firmly established, as in sparsely populated upland areas or large-scale industrial conurbations, Dissent too was unlikely to do well.[4]

For much of the century a chief means of outreach was the Sunday school, which taught poorer children to read (so that they could read the

Scriptures and be converted) and often initially also taught writing, basic numeracy, and other useful skills. In the late 1790s Dissenting Sunday schools had grown exponentially, leading to Anglican fears that they were nurseries of sedition and agencies of proselytism. As the evangelistic objective came to achieve precedence over the educational ones, fears concerning their seditious potential lessened. By 1851 2.1 million children were enrolled in Sunday schools in England, over half of them run by Nonconformists; by 1900 an estimated three-quarters of children in England aged between 5 and 15 were attending Sunday schools. However, the effectiveness of Sunday schools in recruiting new church members has been widely questioned; in many urban areas it seems that people made the Sunday school their 'church', rather than going on to join the churches themselves. There has been debate about whether Sunday schools were a means of imposing middle-class values on the working classes, or whether they expressed working-class aspirations to that most Victorian of virtues, respectability.[5] The truth is probably somewhere between the two: whatever the intent of the founders and leaders, these institutions would not have flourished as they did unless they offered something which their attenders (or their parents) wanted. In any case, it has been suggested that the most proletarian denominations were those least likely to provide Sunday schools – especially the Primitive Methodists, the Bible Christians, and the Roman Catholics.[6]

An evangelistic response to urbanization was the city mission, an inter-denominational agency which established mission halls and employed missionaries to conduct services, visit their 'patch' and employ whatever means were practicable in order to bring people to personal Christian faith. The first is reckoned to have been that founded in Glasgow in 1826, but it was soon followed by others in such places as Belfast (1827), Dublin (1828), Liverpool (1829), New York (1830), and London (1835; the largest, and still in existence as the London City Mission). A national co-ordinating body, the City and Town Missionary Society, was founded in 1837; it employed missionaries in many locations where there was no local agency.[7]

As well as the regular outreach of the churches, there were periods when a heightened sense of spiritual concern was evident. It was believed that such 'revivals' were divinely originated, although human, and even demonic, agency might well vitiate the purity of these occurrences (cf. Jonathan Edwards' defence of them in the previous century). It is noticeable that they occurred most often among communities engaged in hazardous occupations such as mining or fishing, or at periods of insecurity, such as the cholera epidemic of 1832 which killed 32,000 people in Britain. The most widespread of these revivals was that which began in the United States in 1858 and spread to Scotland, Ulster, and Wales, lasting until 1860. Revival in Wales during 1904–5 was more significant for the knock-on effects as far away as India and the United States; in both cases, as in Wales, it prepared the way for the emergence of Pentecostalism.

Attempts to perpetuate the blessing, to express it in a distinctive form of spirituality, and to induce it in other areas, have been described as 'revivalism'. These were evident throughout the century, especially among those who were not committed to the Calvinist belief in the sovereignty of God in salvation, which was traditionally seen as precluding such efforts. In time, theoretical underpinnings and practical methodologies were developed for such activity, especially by the American revivalist Charles Finney (1792–1875; see the following chapter), whose *Lectures on Revivals* appeared in 1835 and immediately sold throughout the evangelical world; by 1838 they had been published in Britain, and the following year they were translated into Welsh. Other American revivalists who were influential in Britain were Lorenzo Dow (1777–1834) and James Caughey (c.1810–91). Dow's visit to Britain from 1805 to 1807 was the catalyst for the emergence of the Primitive Methodists, while Caughey, who was active in Ireland and then Britain from 1841 to 1847, was especially influential among Methodists in northern England. The largest revivalist effort, however, was probably the mission of the American evangelists D.L. Moody (1837–99) and Ira D. Sankey (1840–1908) to Britain during 1873–5, which resulted in an estimated 100,000 professions of faith; but even at the time there was vigorous debate as to whether such campaigns were really effective in reaching those who did not attend church, or whether they merely harvested those on the fringes. It is noticeable, too, that revivalism, like Nonconformist church life generally, was becoming respectable; Moody's campaign has been described as 'a model of middle-class respectability and religious order'[8] and he took care to involve the clergy in the meetings and to feed the converts back to the churches rather than founding new congregations. That respectability fitted with a business-like and lay ethos which contrasted with traditional conceptions of churchliness.

Later in the century the first signs of decline in Nonconformist membership (as well as attendance) became evident: broadly speaking, growth had outstripped population growth in the period before 1840; from then until the 1880s it more or less kept pace with population growth; thereafter it grew more slowly than the population until the late 1900s, before beginning a decline which has seen only brief intermissions until the present. All the same, decline began from a high point: in 1901 an estimated 15 per cent of the population of England and Wales would have identified in some way with one or other of the Nonconformist denominations, a percentage which far exceeded that in Germany (1 per cent in 1925) and which represented a more diverse array of allegiances than the nearest European parallel, the Netherlands (12 per cent in 1899). Decline affected urban congregations, but it is less often recognized that rural ones also suffered: the number of agricultural labourers in England and Wales declined by almost 40 per cent between 1851 and 1891, as many migrated to the cities or went abroad because of the depressed state of British agriculture. And those who left were often the sort who had played key roles in chapel life. Elsewhere Nonconformity became increasingly a middle-class suburban religion, with the growth from the 1870s of the modern suburb. Some members continued to travel in to their traditional place of worship, but many inner-city congregations declined sharply in line with the depopulation of their catchment areas. In many localities, it was the Church of England which remained to minister to the poor.

One issue which has continued to excite scholarly debate concerns the relationship between the churches and the working classes.[9] We have already noted the shaping influence of Mann's assessment of the significance of the results. When modern researchers began to investigate this topic, they concluded that the urban poor were never in the chapels; further evidence indicated that in fact skilled workers did attend chapel; research into particular localities suggested that congregations tended to reflect the social composition of the locality; and the most recent view is that while the majority of the working class did not attend worship, the minority regularly present at chapel was still a sizeable one.[10]

Even among non-attenders, a diffuse form of Christianity remained widespread, in spite of Mann's fear that many were 'unconscious Secularists'.[11] It mixed aspects of Christian teaching and practice (especially prayer, acquaintance with a not-inconsiderable body of hymnody, and the observance of 'rites of passage' such as baptisms, marriages, and funerals) with elements of indigenous superstition, and proved able to incorporate some of the leading ideas of contemporary political radicalism. The result was a mix which stressed the importance of 'practical Christianity': living a good life and being kind to others, these being seen as the criteria which would be applied by God in the Final Judgement.[12] Thus non-attendance at church should not be taken as indicating a secularized outlook on life. However, belief in what amounted to salvation by good works meant that many were resistant to the evangelical message of justification by faith alone. Nonconformist sabbatarian opposition to Sunday leisure pursuits did not go down well with those who had little other opportunity for relaxation. An emphasis on what might be called 'group solidarity' made many suspicious of church-goers for setting themselves up as apart from, and better than, their peers and neighbours. Overall, taking attenders and non-attenders together, the extent of alienation from Christianity was considerably less in England than in Germany, and McLeod has argued that much of this is due to the effectiveness, variety, and unique strength of Protestant Dissent in England.[13] The argument could doubtless be extended to Scotland and Wales.

The tendency for much of this period until 1914 was to focus on the perceived alienation of the working classes from the churches. Yet it can be argued that the most significant losses were from the middle classes: the nineteenth century had seen their dramatic expansion, and the prosperity of Nonconformity had been closely linked with it. This loss became increasingly visible from late in the nineteenth century; new forms of leisure coupled with the erosion of traditional Christian certainties meant that churches lost numbers of those upon whom the burden of leadership and activism had often devolved. The departure of many from the middle classes came just when evangelistic activity was making greater use of approaches which would have been more acceptable to them and churches were erecting buildings which needed to be funded by middle-class giving. Churches were seeking to appeal to the middle classes, yet they were losing them.

The changing roles of women

In all this, what roles were played by women? The ratio of men to women was better among attenders than members, indicating a degree of reluctance on the part of men to commit themselves; throughout the period covered by this chapter, about two-thirds of members were women.[14] Quakers had long allowed women to be travelling ministers, and by 1835 twice as many women as men served in this way. The Wesleyans effectively prohibited women from preaching in 1803, although John Wesley had recognized their ministry and they had often led evangelistic meetings in cottages; however, among the Primitive Methodists and the Bible Christians they served as local or itinerant preachers (the latter were influenced by Quaker practice in this). When revival broke out in Ulster, Scotland, and Wales from 1859, women once again assumed public roles, with some becoming itinerant evangelists; a number of them were associated with the growing network of undenominational mission halls. Theoretically the Salvation Army placed women on an equal footing with men as officers. The justification offered in both cases was typically pragmatic – the novelty of a woman preaching was more likely to draw a crowd. In practice, therefore, women found the doors of opportunity closing as revival fires cooled, movements became institutionalized and moved up the social scale, ministry became increasingly professionalized and formal training was required, and the notion of 'separate spheres' became a dominant way of thinking about the respective roles of men and women in family and society. This encouraged women to stay at home and give their best attentions to housekeeping and motherhood. The last female Primitive Methodist preacher retired in 1862, and whereas in 1829, 21 out of 83 travelling preachers among the Bible Christians (whose understanding of ministry owed something to Quaker thinking) had been women, only one remained by 1872. Ordination was not on the horizon for women in any denomination during this period. Nevertheless, women were active in church life, especially in philanthropy (though some men even opposed this), home visiting, and missionary fund-raising. Several denominations gave official recognition to the ministry of women by introducing deaconess orders modelled on those established in Germany from 1836, including the Church of England (1866, formally recognized as an order of ministry in 1914) and the Wesleyans (1890). Furthermore, as churches introduced an array of leisure activities in order to meet new challenges presented by contemporary social trends, and a range of agencies designed to reach out to every conceivable group within society, women were needed as part of the burgeoning workforce.

The growth of non-Anglican Christianity in Ireland

The year 1782 saw the achievement of legislative independence from Westminster. However, in 1798 rebellion fuelled by sectarian tensions resulted in 30,000 deaths; Irish Catholics saw the French troops who landed in the country as potential religious liberators, a striking contrast to the image they had in the rest of Europe. The British government, then at war with France, was therefore intent on bringing the situation under firm control, and in 1801 the Act of Union was imposed, bringing Ireland under Westminster rule. As part of the unification process, the Church of Ireland was amalgamated with the Church of England, though in practice it continued to function independently. The government had wished to include Catholic emancipation as part of the Act of Union, but George III blocked this, insisting that to sign such legislation would contravene the oath to uphold Protestantism which he had sworn as monarch. Irish patriotism now became associated with Catholicism, especially as a result of the popular appeal of Daniel O'Connell during the 1820s (he was elected to Parliament in 1828 and a leader in the campaign to secure Catholic rights): he saw that the clergy must be given a central role if moves to secure greater freedom for Catholics were to gain widespread popular support, and so he founded the Catholic Association. At the same time widespread and well-funded attempts were made by Evangelicals to convert Roman Catholics, although relatively little was achieved in this way, as the Catholic community was growing in confidence and enjoying a higher standard of pastoral care. All the same, regular Mass attendance does not appear to have become the norm among the poor until the second half of the century. After the potato famine of 1845–50, which resulted in a decline in population of approximately 1.7 million through death or emigration, there were more priests to serve fewer people; a 'devotional revolution' ensued, in which new types of church-based and clerically controlled religious observance became widespread.

One way of grasping the overall religious situation in Ireland is to examine the results of a census of religious affiliation (rather than attendance) undertaken in 1834. This showed that just over 80 per cent of the population were Catholic, and 8.4 per cent (nine-tenths of them in Ulster) Presbyterian; only 10.7 per cent were Anglican, and apart from Ulster and the area around Dublin, in large tracts of the country the Anglican presence was all but nominal. It was the religion of the 'big house', not that of the masses. At the start of the century the Church of Ireland was marked by a worrying degree of non-residency and lukewarmness in performance of clerical duties: a survey in 1807 found that half the beneficed clergy were non-resident and a quarter were pluralists. This changed within a few decades, partly as a result of evangelical activity and partly in response to a fear of assimilation by Catholicism: by 1832, only a quarter of clergy were still non-resident. Fear also fuelled the proselytizing activity of 'the Second Reformation' from 1822 onwards, although this made little headway in converting Catholics and indeed may have helped to polarize the situation further. Even the building of hundreds of new churches (633 from 1808 to 1829 alone) could do little to alter the situation. Suppression of the Irish bishoprics in 1833 (as part of a package of legislation intended to allay Irish unrest and release church revenues for re-application) was followed by disestablishment (and separation from the Church of England) from 1871. This was again intended to settle Irish Catholic apprehensions, at a time when the country was economically depressed, depopulated, and prone to outbreaks of nationalist violence.

Presbyterianism saw controversy over the presence of Arianism within the denomination as Evangelicals achieved a position of dominance and called for the imposition of subscription to the *Westminster Confession*; the Non-Subscribing Presbyterians therefore withdrew in 1829. The '1859 Revival'[15] was most fruitful among the Presbyterian community, which had been prepared for a harvest by evangelical dominance, although the revival may represent a response to the threat of assimilation by Roman Catholicism in society at large. (The Church of Ireland and the Methodists also benefited considerably.) But the Presbyterians lost as well as gained through the revival: ministers expressed intense opposition to revivalism, principally because it was essentially a lay movement, and Evangelicals joined in the condemnation, as they did in Scotland, not least because their congregations were often severely affected when groups such as the Brethren set up independent congregations. Any rise in church membership was short-lived, and the gains were largely among the churches' existing constituencies.

Division and pluralism in Scotland

At the beginning of this period, the ecclesiastical landscape was dominated by the Church of Scotland and its Presbyterian offshoots, which accounted for the allegiance of an estimated 97 per cent of Scots, the Kirk claiming 85 per cent and the others 12 per cent. Apart from Roman Catholics and Episcopalians, both concentrated in particular parts of the country, there were a few radically biblicist congregations (such as the Glasites or Sandemanians, which began after 1730 when their founder, John Glas, was deposed from the Church of Scotland ministry on account of his opposition to the Kirk's established status). By the end of the period, things looked very different, with a range of Presbyterian denominations and a bewildering variety of Protestant Dissent encompassing everything from the Brethren and the Churches of Christ through to the Catholic Apostolics, as well as a considerably increased Roman Catholic presence. Religious pluralism thus came to Scotland quite suddenly, but it is noticeable that there were not the widespread calls for disestablishment which were evident elsewhere in Britain, perhaps because the Church of Scotland enjoyed a greater measure of independence. However, there were tensions between 'voluntaries', who believed that the Church should be entirely separate from the state, and 'establishment men', who upheld the principle of state support for religion.

Patronage had been a running sore in Scottish church affairs, and represented a key point of difference between Moderates and Evangelicals, not least because it symbolized two different attitudes to the social function of religion: for the Moderates, the basic building-block of the Church was the parish, in which the leading landowners played a determinative role; for Evangelicals, it was the congregation. Evangelicals argued that congregations should have the right to reject unsuitable candidates presented by the patron. Controversies over patronage in the 1830s raised parallel issues to those being debated by Anglicans: the question of the right of the state to determine church policy, and thus the nature of the Church – was it a divine creation or a legal one?

In 1834 Moderates lost control of the Church of Scotland's General Assembly to the Evangelicals; it passed a Veto Act giving the right of veto on unsuitable candidates to heads of households in a congregation, and authorized the creation of new *quoad sacra* parishes (that is, ecclesiastical parishes which did not reflect the boundaries of civil parishes). The Evangelicals proceeded to undertake a vigorous campaign of church extension, erecting over 220 new buildings and creating new parishes. However, the Veto Act was judged to contravene civil law, and in 1842 the Court of Session ruled that the new parishes had no status in law, which meant that their ministers and elders (who would usually have been Evangelicals) were denied the right to sit in the Assembly and other church courts. Evangelicals were thus driven to the conclusion that if evangelism and the pastoral care of the urban masses were to be hindered in this way, they were better out than in. They were strengthened in their conviction by an outbreak of revival which began during a communion season at Kilsyth, in the central part of the country, in 1839, and by the sacrificial example of the ministry of such men as R.M. M'Cheyne (1813–43), who wore himself out to remarkable effect at Dundee. A party convinced by such events that God was blessing their course would be in no mood to risk losing that by compromise.

Things came to a head on 18 May 1843 at the General Assembly. No fewer than 451 evangelical ministers withdrew, three-eighths of the denomination's ministers, and set up the Free Church of Scotland (about a third of those who remained were also Evangelicals). A third of the church's membership also withdrew. Thomas Chalmers (1780–1847), the leader of the Evangelicals, who had defended the established church as an instrument for evangelizing the whole nation, now took his place as leader of the seceders. He ensured that the Free Church remained committed to the principle of establishment of religion, and it set about replicating the parochial structure and educational provision of the Church of Scotland as far as possible. It was no mean feat for the seceders to erect 470 new churches within their first year, and to add 163 new charges and 238 preaching outposts during its first two years, although funds had been collected and preparations made since Autumn 1842; by 1847 over 700 congregations were worshipping in their own buildings, few of which had been taken over from the Church of Scotland. The 1851 Religious Census recorded 32.2 per cent of attendances in Scotland at the Established Church and 31.7 per cent at the Free Church, and in many parts of the Highlands the Free Church more or less swept the board. One reason for this was resentment at the 'clearances', which saw numbers of families evicted from their cottages in order to allow the landowners to engage in more profitable but less labour-intensive forms of land use. While it might be overstating things to say that 'social and economic change was the begetter of ecclesiastical schism',[16] it was certainly a major factor, the importance of which has often been underplayed by denominational historians.

The data of the 1851 Census are not as detailed for Scotland (the original returns are no longer in existence), and also more inaccurate, since a third of Church of Scotland clergy made no return. Nevertheless, it has been calculated that only 32 per cent of attenders went to the Church of Scotland, against 59 per cent attending other Presbyterian congregations. However, from that point it does appear that the establishment slowly won back lost ground, as it did in England. Part of the reason for this was the widespread waning of old antagonisms between church and state, and between church and church, and the addressing of old grievances. The abolition of patronage finally came in 1874, as the congregation gained the right to appoint its own minister. This cleared the way for the voluntaryist United Presbyterian Church to merge in 1900 with the establishmentarian Free Church, to form the United Free Church of Scotland; this had 1,112 congregations, compared with 1,447 belonging to the Church of Scotland. One consequence was the speedy closure of a number of duplicate causes left under-supported by migration from the cities to their suburbs. Another was that, as so often, merging two denominations produced three: Free Kirk Highlanders mounted a legal challenge to the union and in 1904 the House of Lords gave its judgment in their favour. The following year, Parliament had to pass a measure apportioning property between the United Free Church and the Free Church.

Doctrinal revisionism was to cause major problems for the Church of Scotland in the 1830s, although it did ultimately result in a loosened attachment to the *Westminster Confession*. Three men took a leading role: John McLeod Campbell (1800–72), Edward Irving, and the layman Thomas Erskine (1788–1870).[17] For Campbell, Christ's death was not merely a punishment but a manifestation of God's attitude to sin. As one with us he made the perfect confession of sin; as one with God he offered the perfect condemnation of sin; in place of anxious introspection to determine whether one was numbered among the elect Campbell substituted the proclamation that all were already redeemed by Christ, and needed only to enter into the conscious enjoyment of their status. Irving was deposed for teaching that in the incarnation Christ assumed *fallen* human nature; perhaps more of a problem for many was his espousal of claims to a restoration of spiritual gifts of tongues, prophecy, and healing, which had resulted in his eviction from his church in London's Regent Square in 1832 on the ground that he was allowing unauthorized persons to speak in public worship (the Kirk was at this time opposed to lay preaching, which was seen as likely to beget heresy and schism). Erskine came to the belief that all would ultimately be saved.

One fruit of this revisionism, with its gentler understanding of the Christian faith and more optimistic estimate of human abilities, was the Evangelical Union, an anti-credal and largely working-class denomination formed in 1843, ironically on the same day as the Free Church of Scotland. This adopted congregational rather than presbyterian church order, and espoused a Finneyite approach to revivalism, which ran completely counter to the traditional idea that God was sovereign in the conversion of sinners.

Further debates regarding the extent to which subscription to doctrinal standards should be required ensued in the Robertson Smith case, which we noted in Chapter 9. This affected the Free Church, and in 1892 a Declaratory Act allowed diversity of opinion within that communion on matters not deemed to form part of the substance of the Reformed faith; this provoked a small Highland-based conservative secession, the Free Presbyterian Church, in 1893.

After the death of Charles Edward Stuart in 1788, the Episcopal Church transferred its allegiance to the House of Hanover; in 1792, therefore, it was granted full toleration. This was followed in 1804 by formal union of the Episcopalians of the north-east (whose sympathies had been with the Jacobites) with those lowland congregations whose ministers had sworn allegiance to the Hanoverian monarchy. However, the church did not share in the nineteenth century's growth until quite late on, partly because it was too catholic for some of the immigrants who belonged to the Church of Ireland but mainly because it was perceived, with some justification, as being the church of the landowners. Later on it mounted an effective outreach to the working classes in the urban west of Scotland from the 1870s, but in the perception of many it continued to be hindered by the dominance of English clergy and ideas, and was often regarded as 'the English church'. As for the Catholics, 1878 saw the restoration of the hierarchy in Scotland, but popular anti-Catholicism continued to manifest itself in a way which was rare south of the border. From the 1820s to the 1860s there was also tension between Scottish priests and Irish laity who felt that their interests were being ignored.

All churches struggled to cope with the challenges presented by population growth. Population tripled between 1801 and 1911, rising from 1.6 million to 4.8 million, although there was also large-scale emigration (perhaps as many as two million from 1830 to 1914). Scotland was the European country in which urbanization was most marked: in 1700 just 5.3 per cent of the population lived in towns larger than 10,000; by 1850 the proportion had risen to 32 per cent. The bonds which operated in smaller communities to keep people within the orbit of the established church could not withstand the pressure, and dissent, whether Presbyterian or other, grew rapidly. It should be noted that people often chose dissent rather than non-attendance: there is no clear evidence that across the country rates of attendance were significantly lower in urban areas than in rural ones. Lay preaching was nothing like as important in Scotland as it was in England and Wales; until about 1800 almost all Dissent was Presbyterian in nature and shared the Church of Scotland's emphasis on the need for an educated ordained ministry. However, the Society for the Propagation of the Gospel at Home, founded in 1798, was responsible for the planting of a number of Independent and later Baptist congregations, and from the 1850s groups such as the Brethren and the Churches of Christ grew rapidly, especially in the central lowlands.

Overall, the British religious landscape was very significantly different in 1914 from what it had been in 1789: viable alternatives had arisen to the established churches in all four nations. Nevertheless, that landscape was still more or less entirely Christian, apart from a small Jewish presence, mostly in larger cities. It was thus possible for the majority of the population to unite in support of a broadly Christian moral consensus. Radical as these changes were to many at the time, they were to be outstripped by developments after 1914.

Questions for thought

1 Why, in your opinion, did the nineteenth-century churches lose the working classes? To what extent had they gained working-class allegiance in the first place?

2 Compare the attitude of the middle classes to organized Christianity in Catholic France, Protestant Germany, and Britain.

3 Why and how did English Nonconformity change during the nineteenth century? What internal and external factors were at work in this process?

4 Compare and contrast the relationship between Catholicism and nationalism in nineteenth-century Ireland and Poland.

5 What do you think was the impact of the Disruption on church life in Scotland? What evidence would you offer for your view?

6 Compare and contrast the reasons for the growth of pluralism in England and Scotland during this period.

Further reading

(See also the bibliography to Chapter 10.)

Callum G. Brown, 1997, *Religion and Society in Scotland since 1707*, Edinburgh: Edinburgh University Press, chs 4–5.

Andrew L. Drummond and James Bulloch, 1973, *The Scottish Church 1688–1843: The Age of the Moderates*, Edinburgh: St Andrew Press, chs 6–12.

Andrew L. Drummond and James Bulloch, 1975, *The Church in Victorian Scotland 1843–1874*, Edinburgh: St Andrew Press.

Andrew L. Drummond and James Bulloch, 1978, *The Church in late Victorian Scotland 1874–1900*, Edinburgh: St Andrew Press.

Nigel Yates, 2006, *The Religious Condition of Ireland 1770–1850*, Oxford: Oxford University Press.

Notes

1 For discussion of the task of interpreting the Census data, see Michael R. Watts, 1995, *The Dissenters*, vol. 2: *The Expansion of Evangelical Nonconformity 1791–1859*, Oxford: Clarendon, Appendix I. A valuable guide to discussions of the Census is Clive D. Field, 'The 1851 Census of Religious Worship: A Bibliographical Guide', *Local Historian* 27 (1997), pp. 194–217. See also Frances Coakley, 'The 1851 Religious and Educational Censuses', www.isle-of-man.com/manxnotebook/methdism/rc1851/index.htm. The returns for Wales and for many English counties have been published; sadly, those for Scotland have long been lost.

2 Figures are drawn from Robert Currie, Alan Gilbert, and Lee Horsley, 1977, *Churches and Church-Goers: Patterns of Church Growth in the British Isles since 1700*, Oxford: Clarendon, pp. 216–18; Watts, *Dissenters*, vol. 2, pp. 23, 28. To obtain totals of attenders, Watts took the best-attended service for each denomination in each of the 624 registration districts and added a third of the total attendances at other services (Watts, *Dissenters*, vol. 2, p. 27).

3 Pew rents were one of the chief means by which Nonconformist chapel-building was financed, although they were also a feature of Anglican and Catholic churches. As in a theatre, the higher the rent you paid, the better the seat you obtained; some pews were usually left for occupation free of charge, but often these were clearly demarcated from the rest.

4 Watts, *Dissenters*, vol. 2, ch. 1, section 8. For geographical analysis of which types of Dissent flourished where, see John D. Gay, 1971, *The Geography of Religion in England*, London: Gerald Duckworth; K.D.M. Snell and Paul S. Ell, 2000, *Rival Jerusalems: The Geography of Victorian Religion*, Cambridge: Cambridge University Press.

5 Ironically, respectability may also have been one of the factors inhibiting many among the working classes from attendance at worship; concern to overcome this obstacle lay behind attempts from the 1850s to put on services of a more popular nature, and to develop new forms of church life with a popular appeal, such as the Salvation Army. Respectability was also a factor in the growing divergence between rural or industrial congregations, which were predominantly working-class, and town-centre congregations, which experienced a degree of upward social mobility as members prospered and looked to better themselves. Other signs of growing respectability included a decline in lay preaching and a concomitant emphasis on a professional trained ministry, the marginalization of women's public roles, and even (for Baptists) the building of indoor baptisteries to replace the use of streams and ponds. The gap left by the upward move of many congregations was filled by newer groups such as the Brethren, as well as the multitude of undenominational mission halls.

6 Snell and Ell, *Rival Jerusalems*, pp. 299–300. However, the argument needs refining since it does not take account of the possibility that Methodists and Catholics may have had substantially different reasons for not running Sunday schools, related to the differing ways in which children were integrated into the life of the church and the contrast between Methodist emphasis on conversion and Catholic sacramental initiation.

7 On city missions, see the paradigmatic study of London by Donald M.

Lewis, 2001 (first published 1986), *Lighten their Darkness: The Evangelical Mission to Working-Class London, 1828–1860*, Carlisle, Paternoster.

8 Janice Holmes, 2000, *Religious Revivals in Britain and Ireland 1859–1905*, Dublin: Irish Academic Press, p. 55.

9 A standard older work is K.S. Inglis, 1963, *Churches and the Working Classes in Victorian England*, London: Routledge & Kegan Paul. See also Hugh McLeod, 1974, *Class and Religion in the Late Victorian City*, London: Croom Helm; Snell and Ell, *Rival Jerusalems*.

10 Cf. David W. Bebbington (ed.), 2006, *Protestant Nonconformist Texts*, vol. 3: *The Nineteenth Century*, Aldershot: Ashgate, p. 1. For statements of the four viewpoints see, respectively: E.R. Wickham, 1957, *Church and People in an Industrial City*, London: Lutterworth; A.D. Gilbert, 1976, *Religion and Society in Industrial England: Church, Chapel and Social Change, 1740–1914*, London: Longman; Mark Smith, 1994, *Religion in Industrial Society: Oldham and Saddleworth 1740–1865*, Oxford: Oxford University Press; Watts, *Dissenters*, vol. 2.

11 Horace Mann, [1854], *Census of Great Britain, 1851. Religious Worship in England and Wales*, abridged and revised edn, London: George Routledge, p. 93.

12 One important discussion of working-class religiosity is Jeffrey Cox, 1982, *The English Churches in a Secular Society: Lambeth 1870–1930*, Oxford: Clarendon.

13 Hugh McLeod, 'Dissent and the peculiarities of the English, c.1870–1914', in Jane Shaw and Alan Kreider (eds), 1999, *Culture and the Nonconformist Tradition*, Cardiff: University of Wales Press, p. 126.

14 On women in Victorian churches, see Clive Field, 'Adam and Eve: Gender in the English church constituency', *Journal of Ecclesiastical History* 44 (1993), pp. 63–79.

15 On Ulster revivalism, see Holmes, *Religious Revivals*.

16 Callum G. Brown, 1993, *The People in the Pews: Religion and Society in Scotland since 1780*, Glasgow: Economic and Social History Society of Scotland, p. 29.

17 On Campbell, see Peter K. Stevenson, 2004, *God in Our Nature: The Incarnational Theology of John McLeod Campbell*, Carlisle: Paternoster; on Erskine, see Don Horrocks, 2004, *Laws of the Spiritual Order: Innovation and Reconstruction in the Soteriology of Thomas Erskine of Linlathen*, Carlisle: Paternoster; on Irving, see Mrs M.O.W. Oliphant, 1862, *The Life of Edward Irving*, 2 vols, London: Hurst & Blackett. My own biography of Irving is due to be published in 2009.

12

Christianity in the United States

Given the declared intent of this book to provide something approximating to a global focus, it is necessary to justify devoting a chapter to the United States of America. That can best be done in terms of the significance for world Christianity of the religious developments in this nation during the nineteenth century. Evangelicalism was decisively shaped by its American incarnation, and the results became evident globally as the result of revivalist and missionary activity. The Puritan vision of 'a city set on a hill' fuelled both evangelical eschatological expectations and (in more or less secularized form) the development of the nation's sense of 'manifest destiny' as a world power. Movements such as Mormonism, Pentecostalism, and what would later become known as Jehovah's Witnesses emerged, and went on to spread throughout the world. The course of relationships between black and white Protestants, and the development of separate black-led churches, would be a factor in the rise of locally instituted churches in South Africa and elsewhere from the late nineteenth century. Protestantism wrestled with some of the major issues thrown up by the growth of capitalism and industrialization, phenomena which affected many other nations too. As the result of mass immigration, the Eastern churches developed their first large communities in the West, and began to face a range of problems which still trouble them today. Roman Catholicism had its first taste of accommodation to a modern democratic society in which church and state were separated. Such a society, it has been argued, also provided the right conditions for the emergence of denominations in their modern form, and hence for the growth of institutional ecumenism. So the story of nineteenth-century North American Christianity is, in a sense, integral to that of the subsequent development of Christian traditions throughout the world.

The development of religious pluralism

The religious legacy of the American Revolution was a clear separation between church and state. In recent decades American writers have debated vigorously the extent to which America could or can claim to be a 'Christian nation' in terms of the ideology underlying its constitutional documents, but several of the early presidents were Unitarians or Deists, and they had no interest in establishing orthodox Christianity as the religion of the nation. Rationalists and Evangelicals agreed that religion was a matter for the individual and that churches were to be voluntary communities. The United States was the first predominantly Christian nation in the modern era in which the Church had no official link with the state, and which therefore offered a 'level playing field' for denominational competition. It has therefore been argued that the American experience was crucial for the emergence of the modern denomination, halfway between an all-embracing church and an exclusive sect. The prevailing ethos in religious matters was democratic, voluntaryist, pragmatic, optimistic, and expansionist. These characteristics were not unique to the USA, but they were hallmarks of North American religion. The result of all this has been an unparalleled diversity of Christian traditions, a phenomenon which owes as much to the cultural and political context as it does to the oft-asserted fissiparous nature of Protestantism. The arrival of migrants from many different ethnic groups and churches, the unparalleled freedom and equality accorded to all forms of religious expression, the demise of the last of the old religious establishments (Massachusetts Congregationalism in 1833), and the distinctive frontier mentality combined to make it easy for new movements to establish themselves.

Somewhat behind the development of pluralism came its counterpart, institutional ecumenism. The ground was prepared by interdenominational bodies such as the Young Men's Christian Association (YMCA; 1844 in London, 1851 in Canada and the United States) and Young Women's Christian Association (1866), and the Evangelical Alliance (1867 in the United States). In 1908, the Federal Council of Churches of Christ in America came into being, the first such body in the world to be constituted by denominations as opposed to individuals or local churches. We shall see in Chapter 19 that the course of twentieth-century ecumenism was to be shaped decisively by American thinking, which was itself shaped by the pluralist and non-established status of the churches (a factor which would cause problems for Christians from a different milieu, such as the Orthodox in Eastern Europe).

The churches and the black community

After the revolution, hopes that blacks could achieve equality with whites faded fairly quickly. It became clear that if blacks were to attend the same churches as whites, they would be treated as second-class citizens, even by committed abolitionists. Even where they continued to do so, their main religious inspiration often came from meeting apart, in settings where their faith could be given appropriate cultural expression. And in any case, many slave owners feared that Christianity could act as a catalyst for rebellion, and discouraged slaves from meeting for worship; thus it was common for gatherings to take place clandestinely.

The first black churches developed fairly soon: the first African Methodist Episcopal (AME) church was founded by Richard Allen (1760–1831) in Philadelphia in 1793. But it was after the Civil War that these denominations really took off; the AME Church grew from 20,000 in 1860 to 450,000 in 1896, and the similar AME Zion Church from 4,600 to 350,000 during the same period. Most of this expansion took place in the South. In spite of the figures just quoted, the Baptists, who saw separate black congregations founded from the 1860s onwards, were easily the largest family of black denominations, with 3 million worshippers by 1915, most in the National Baptist Convention. There was a commensurate increase in numbers of black clergy in these denominations (though not in denominations which remained racially integrated), who frequently exercised leadership roles in the community as well as the Church.

Churches rapidly assumed centre stage in black corporate life; they provided education and practical help, as well as giving voice to the social concerns of the black Christian community; their congregations amounted to extended kinship networks as a result of intermarriage; and their affairs allowed black Christians a rare opportunity of self-determination. Moreover, many Northern and Western congregations helped escaping slaves along the 'underground railroad' to freedom.

Although these denominations differed little from their white counterparts in theological terms, a distinctive black Christian spirituality developed in which the biblical motif of exodus from slavery and journey to the promised land featured prominently. Putting their own spin on what they had been taught by white missionaries, black preachers sometimes portrayed their people as the chosen. Some saw Christianity as offering other-worldly consolation, but others applied it in terms of justifying rebellion. Revivalism was popular, not only because of the freer nature of its corporate expression, but also because it implicitly put blacks and whites on a level as having the same need of salvation.

Black churches soon began to look outward; as early as 1784, a black Baptist (George Liele) founded a church in Jamaica which developed into a flourishing denominational community. Further afield, black missionaries went to West Africa (especially Liberia and Sierra Leone) and by the end of the nineteenth century to South Africa, where they were one of the stimuli for the formation of locally instituted churches (see Chapter 14).

Adapting to the American context

One of the most important features of the American context was the rapidity of population growth, from 2.5 million in 1776 to 31 million in 1860 and over 99 million by 1914. Much of that growth came through immigration, though some was the result of the 'Louisiana purchase' of territory in the South and Mid-West formerly held by France (1803), the accession of the short-lived republic of Texas (1845), and the cession by Mexico of many of what became the Western states (1848). Inevitably, a plethora of denominations established a North American presence, and even in churches which remained united (such as Roman Catholicism), ethnic differences were a factor in the development of divergent outlooks within the Church.

Protestantism

In the colonial era, Episcopalians had dominated American Protestantism. However, their position in the revolutionary struggle was ambiguous: on one hand, most of the signatories to the Declaration of Independence were Episcopalians; on the other, every Anglican priest in the United States had sworn allegiance to the British Crown at ordination and many ceased to conduct worship rather than drop the prayers for the King from the liturgy. As a result, they lost their leading role in American Protestantism, partly because they were associated with loyalty to the British and partly because their structures and ethos were ill-adapted to reaching out to the communities developing as the frontier of white settlement was pushed steadily westwards (although they would appoint missionary bishops from the early nineteenth century to spearhead the Church's advance into the Western states). To shed the image of a British church, it was essential for the Episcopalians to become self-sufficient, and to that end they secured their first bishop, Samuel Seabury, in 1784 (through the Scottish Episcopal Church, thus avoiding the need to swear the Oath of Allegiance). In 1789 further bishops were consecrated in England, and American Episcopalianism achieved ecclesiastical independence.

It is estimated that around 1790 only 5–10 per cent of the population were members of a particular church (although up to half the population may have attended church before Independence); the churches were thus starting the process of expansion from a relatively low point. But we should not minimize their success in translating adherents into members and making them activists. Noll argues that the most successful denominations were those which were best at translating their message into an American cultural idiom and becoming 'churches of the people'. Table 12.1 is taken from his work.[1]

Table 12.1: Share of church adherents for the main denominations.

Denomination	1776	1850
Baptists	16.9%	20.5%
Congregationalists	20.4%	4.0%
Disciples	–	1.8%
Episcopalians	15.7%	3.5%
Lutherans	?	2.9%
Methodists	2.5%	34.2%
Presbyterians	19.0%	11.6%
Quakers	?	1.6%
Reformed (German/Dutch)	?	1.9%
Roman Catholics	1.8%	13.9%
Unitarians/Universalists	–	1.9%

These figures show that the Methodists and Baptists were most successful, their lay ethos and relative flexibility enabling them to expand in newly settled areas. Leaders such as the Methodist superintendent Francis Asbury (1745–1816) emphasized the importance of itinerant ministry, which was more appropriate to the frontier setting than was the settled pattern of New England. By contrast the Congregationalists and Episcopalians, whose roots were in the older-established areas of population and who hankered after establishment status, both declined as a proportion of the church-going public. Roman Catholics, Lutherans, and Reformed grew by virtue of immigration, each finding expression in a range of ethnically based congregations and (in the cases of Lutherans and Reformed) whole denominations which acted as bearers of ethnic identity.

Denominations reacting against Evangelicalism also grew. Apart from the Episcopalians, Unitarianism developed as a distinct denomination after 1815 before merging with the Universalists, who had been Trinitarian. Prominent spokesmen for the Unitarian-Universalist viewpoint included the former Evangelical W. E. Channing (1780–1842) and the writer Ralph Waldo Emerson (1803–82), who combined Unitarianism with Romanticism to produce a current of thought labelled Transcendentalism. This stressed the importance of a warm experience of the spiritual realm, which could be known by intuition, by contrast with the cold and rationalistic approach to religion which was believed to have marked eighteenth-century Deism.

Catholicism

In 1776 there were just 25,000 Catholics in the United States; by 1916 the number had grown to approximately 16 million, largely through immigration. In the process, its ethnic make-up changed profoundly, from English and French to a much greater variety, in which Hispanics, Irish, Germans, and later Italians and East Europeans vied with one another for influence, although leadership tended to be concentrated in Irish hands. At first Catholicism was seen as a threat to the broad Protestant unity of the new nation (especially as Catholic immigration increased markedly from the 1830s), and as something to be resisted, but by the 1860s it became the country's largest single Christian tradition. The United States remained under the jurisdiction of *Propaganda* as a missionary territory until 1908, although it had developed a Catholic hierarchy from the late eighteenth century onwards, with the first bishop being appointed as early as 1790, just a few years after the first Anglican bishop.

In the 1890s United States Catholics were divided into two main groups, conservatives and progressives. On the progressive side the Paulist Fathers had been founded in 1858 by the ex-Methodist turned Redemptorist priest Isaac Hecker (1819–88), who wished to establish Catholicism in the United States as a model for the Church worldwide. Their aim (as that of the Redemptorists had been) was to preach, publish, and educate, but in such a way as to win American converts. He sought to accommodate Protestant and scientific thought in his version of Catholicism, and earned the suspicion of many conservatives. Controversy from the 1880s centred on such matters as the legitimacy of the American pattern of separation of church and state, democracy, social and religious activism, and new methods of outreach. At the bottom was the issue of how far American society offered congenial soil for Catholicism: should the Church adapt to the host culture or pursue a counter-cultural line? Those who had settled and assimilated tended to argue the former position, whereas newer immigrant communities favoured the latter. Tensions to some extent reflected those between various ethnic groups, especially the Irish (who dominated the national hierarchy) and the Germans. (These tensions were one factor in the establishment of 'national parishes', each catering to a particular ethnic group, in larger cities.)

It was a biography of Hecker which kindled an explosion after it was translated into French in 1897. Conservatives denounced liberals to Rome, and in 1899 Leo XIII condemned what he called 'Americanism' (the idea that the Church should adapt itself to the pluralist and democratic context, the assertion that the Church should relax the requirements laid on converts and emphasize those things it held in common with other Christian traditions rather than those which set it apart, and the emphasis on activism at the expense of cultivating interior virtues) in the apostolic letter *Testem Benevolentiae*. Americanism was alleged to be a 'phantom heresy'; Leo was careful to explain that he did not necessarily believe that anybody held the whole set of opinions condemned, and those in the firing line were equally careful to explain that they did not hold these opinions either!

Orthodoxy

From 1794 Russian missionaries were active in Alaska, with considerable success. Although the territory was purchased by the United States in 1867, the Russian Orthodox Church has maintained a significant presence, especially among indigenous ethnic groups. The latter half of the century saw large-scale immigration of Orthodox laity from Eastern Europe and the Middle East. Each ethnic community founded its own parishes: as with Protestantism and Catholicism, these served as bearers of culture and language and hence they tended to be grouped under different jurisdictions on an ethnic basis. The Russians had arrived first, establishing missions in what is now California from the eighteenth century; but other communities were usually reluctant to come under their wing, and the result was a plethora of jurisdictions. Although they were catering for different groups and thus not really in competition with one another, their inability to find ways of working together during this period undoubtedly helped to slow the process of Orthodox integration into American society.

Theological developments

Modifications to Calvinism

It was Jonathan Edwards himself who sowed the seeds for later theological developments, notably in his thinking regarding the freedom of the will, and the distinction he made between natural and moral inability to turn to God: he argued that sinners were in the latter condition, whereas traditionally Calvinists had tended to assume the former. From the 1820s the theological faculty at Yale propounded a system known as 'New Haven theology', which offered a theological rationale for the 'New Measures' adopted in revival by Finney and others. It asserted human capability to respond to God in a way which was unacceptable to more traditional Calvinists, thus carrying on the modification process begun by Edwards, as well as introducing a more rational understanding of God, as moral governor of the universe. Among its leaders were the Yale theological professor Nathaniel Taylor (1786–1858) and the New England pastor, theologian, and social reformer Lyman Beecher

(1775–1863). Taylor was to influence Finney, as can be seen in the latter's *Systematic Theology* (1846–7), in the direction of a 'governmental' understanding of the atonement. This differed from the traditional evangelical emphasis on Christ's death as a substitute for sinners by interpreting the cross primarily as an affirmation and demonstration of God's moral government which required him to punish sin, and of his willingness to forgive.[2]

Conservative Calvinists also made modifications, not so much to their beliefs as to the justification which they offered for them. At Princeton Seminary (founded in 1812), a school of theology grew up which provided intellectual underpinning for conservative thinking about Scripture. Prominent spokesmen for this outlook included Charles Hodge (1797–1878) and B.B. Warfield (1851–1921). It drew on eighteenth-century Scottish 'Common Sense' philosophy, which taught that individuals could use their senses to gain reliable knowledge not only of the physical world, but also that (through the 'moral sense') there were certain moral and spiritual truths which could be intuitively perceived, such as the existence of God and of the external world.

The Bible 'as originally given' was seen as the inerrant word of God; in Warfield's words, 'what Scripture says, God says'. This view should, however, be distinguished from any kind of 'dictation theory' holding that the human writers were merely amanuenses; Warfield was quite clear that human agents wrote as free agents, God having so ordained the circumstances of their lives and their intellectual development that in a given situation they would write what he wished to be written. Whereas earlier Reformed writers had argued that persuasion of the Bible's divine authority was the work of the Holy Spirit within the individual, the Princetonians sought to demonstrate it by rational arguments. A corollary of this approach was the assertion that discovery of any error in the Bible would make it impossible to accept its divine authority, and so writers of this school came to devote considerable attention to apologetic argument against biblical critics and others who claimed that error was present in Scripture; once again, the confidence in human reason is evident. The importance of 'Princeton theology' lies in the seminal role it played until recent decades in English-speaking evangelical thought.

The rise of Dispensationalism[3]

Dispensationalism has become a high-profile and controversial version of American Evangelicalism. Its roots lie in the widespread interest in biblical prophecy in the English-speaking world from the late eighteenth century onwards. Several schools of thought emerged, differing over such matters as:

1 whether it was possible or appropriate to work out a chronology from biblical prophecy whose fulfilment could be discerned in current events (historicism, which generally taught that a day in biblical prophecy could be equated with a year in human history; thus the 1,260 days of the book of Daniel represented 1,260 years, and so on) or whether all the events foretold in Revelation 4–22 were as yet in the future (futurism);

2 whether there would be a return of the Jewish people to their ancestral land; and

3 whether there would be a 'rapture' of true Christian believers to heaven before the great outpouring of judgement on earth which was expected by premillennialists to precede the millennium (pre-tribulationism).

Repeated failure of historicist predictions resulted in the ascendancy of futurist premillennialism.

The basic idea underlying Dispensationalism is a hermeneutical one with a pedigree stretching back at least to Origen (185–254), if not to the New Testament writings themselves: that the Bible portrays a God who works according to a pattern which is repeated in successive periods of salvation history. Thus events in one period or 'dispensation' may be seen as corresponding to events in another, a principle which is believed to throw additional light on the meaning of Scripture and the ways of God. What was distinctive about the dispensationalist use of this concept was the belief that each dispensation saw the obedience of humankind tested by God in a unique way appropriate to the manner in which God related to humanity during it, and that each ended in human failure. Here was the seed of later fundamentalist separatism. In addition, Dispensationalists have postulated not one plan of salvation history but two, one relating to God's earthly people, Israel, and the other to his heavenly people, the Church. (The traditional view since patristic times had been that the Church replaced Israel as the people of God.) The church age represents a hiatus in God's dealings with Israel, which will be resumed at the end. This explains why Dispensationalists have been strong supporters of the modern state of Israel.

The self-contained hermeneutical system offered by Dispensationalism has enabled it to sidestep the challenges presented by successive generations of biblical critics, and the best-known dispensationalist work is the *Scofield Reference Bible* (1909), so named because its compiler was the American layman C.I. Scofield (1843–1921). Much of the teaching in this work can be traced back to J.N. Darby (1800–82), a clergyman who seceded from the Church of Ireland and was one of the founders of the Brethren movement around 1830. Darby visited North America extensively from 1862, and his eschatological views became widely accepted among Presbyterians and Baptists in the post-Civil War climate, which was marked by a decline in the optimism which had earlier been such a force in the development of American society.[4]

The roots of evangelical Fundamentalism[5]

The term 'Fundamentalism' was first coined with reference to a move-ment within American Evangelicalism. Its birth as a distinct movement is often dated to the appearance of a series of tracts on *The Fundamentals* (1910–15), distributed free to every minister in the United States in an effort to counter the growth of unbelief and affirm evangelical doctrine. However, the main planks of the fundamentalist platform – the verbal inspiration and inerrancy of Scripture, the deity of Christ, the Virgin Birth, the substitutionary understanding of the atonement, and Christ's resurrection and bodily Second Coming – had all been adumbrated by a conference of Evangelicals in 1895 at Niagara. Almost from the start, Fundamentalists found that they shared considerable common ground with the Princetonians, especially regarding their view of Scripture, their confidence in rational apologetic, and (paradoxically) their pessimism concerning human ability in salvation. Thus Warfield and others contrib-uted to *The Fundamentals* even though they did not espouse fundamen-talist eschatology, which was usually dispensationalist. But from about 1900 the alliance weakened, largely because unity of belief concerning Scripture did not extend to agreement concerning prophetic interpre-tation. The legacy has been a tendency within much North American Evangelicalism to disparage Evangelicals who do not hold dispensation-alist views, and to treat such matters as being of the essence of the faith.

American religious creations

The unique environment offered by the nineteenth-century United States fostered a number of developments which went on to have a global impact. In addition to the development of revivalism as a means of bring-ing people into the churches, movements emerged which have achieved an international spread, although not all have been accepted by main-stream Christian traditions as theologically orthodox.

Revivalism[6]

In the traditionally Christian societies of Europe the question of how to make converts was slow to arise. It was widely assumed that every individual born in such societies was 'Christian' in some sense, even though, as Anabaptists, Pietists, Evangelicals, and others insisted, they might need to experience a personal religious awakening. In the United States the combination of the separation of church and state with a positive estimate of the value and social function of religion meant that, for the first time in modern history, personal commitment assumed greater social significance than community allegiance.

The 1790s and 1800s saw a second 'Great Awakening', more widespread than the first but following a similar pattern of itinerant preaching calling for immediate response to the gospel. This was followed by further waves of revival and revivalist activity until about 1860. It spawned a range of societies for mission and social reform, such as the New York Missionary Society (1796), the American Board of Commissioners for Foreign Missions (1810), the American Education Society (1815), the American Bible Society (1816), and the American Tract Society (1825). It ensured that voluntaryism rather than establishment became the dominant form of American religious expression, and elevated activism as a chief Christian virtue.

This awakening took somewhat different forms in New England and the Western frontier. In the former, as befitted a well-established and settled pattern of community life, it was sober and decorous, influencing many through the regular pattern of congregational worship, as well as through ordained clergy who exercised an itinerant ministry in a particular area, such as the Congregationalist Asahel Nettleton (1783–1844) in New England and New York. On the other hand, some of its leaders were open to a sober application of new methods in evangelism and thus co-operated with the leading revivalist of this period, Charles Finney (see below).

On the frontier, however, things were radically different. Because the frontier of settlement was moving steadily westward over and beyond the Appalachian mountains, an established pattern of community and church life was only just beginning to emerge. A different type of ministry was called for, one in which preachers had to be willing to travel far more, to cover a greater area, and to adapt to a rural rather than urban setting. Religion was more of an individualistic affair, and often intensely emotional in its expression. No tradition had a monopoly or any kind of social advantage over others, and so all could compete on equal terms.

It was during this period that large outdoor 'camp meetings' lasting several days took shape. These had their roots in the Presbyterian 'communion seasons' as observed by settlers from Scotland and Ulster. The first camp meeting was held in Kentucky during 1800 in association with a communion season, under the leadership of James McGready, a Presbyterian minister of Ulster stock. A notable one occurred at Cane Ridge, Kentucky, in 1801, which was marked by intense preaching, physical reactions such as falling to the ground, and the overleaping of denominational barriers as preachers from various traditions shared in the work. Blacks as well as whites were involved, with the result that Evangelicalism became a dominating force in black Christian culture. Baptists and Methodists were the main agents in this aspect of the awakening because their structures offered greater scope for adaptation to the frontier environment and they were not restricted by rigid adherence to Calvinist doctrinal standards.

Following the second Great Awakening the professional revivalist appeared as an agent for the perpetuation of revival blessings. This development was facilitated by the modifications to Calvinist theology which we noted earlier, which allowed greater scope for human agency in the spiritual realm. Finney offers a personal paradigm of the progressive revivalist outlook. Converted in 1821, he ministered extensively in the North-East from 1824 to 1835 as a Presbyterian missionary, moving from place to place holding intensive evangelistic 'campaigns'. He worked on the basis that revival was something for which churches could pray and prepare, and for which they did not need to wait passively. It was not a miracle, but part of God's regular providential oversight of human affairs. Since conversion was, for Finney, primarily a matter of the will (individuals possessed the power within themselves to believe the gospel but would only do so when the Holy Spirit worked on the will to induce them to respond), the revivalist system sought to create an environment in which the will would be most likely to respond positively to the gospel. That involved preaching for a verdict, something which Finney's legal training qualified him to do with great effect. His methods became known as the 'New Measures', and included daily meetings over a sustained period, massed choirs, preaching which called for an immediate response, 'altar calls' for those wishing to respond to go to the 'anxious bench' at the front of the congregation, the deployment of counsellors to assist those responding, and prayer meetings in which sinners were prayed for by name. None of these were necessarily new in themselves, but their combination as a systematic evangelistic methodology was. From the late 1830s Finney's approach became influential in Britain and Ireland as well as in North America, and its legacy remains in the work of Billy Graham and other practitioners of 'mass evangelism'.

Baptists and Presbyterians tended to make greatest use of the 'New Measures'; series of revivalist meetings became annual features of the life of many congregations. Methodists, however, persisted with the camp meeting format, although it became institutionalized in the form of permanent camp grounds where believers could go each summer for such gatherings. A few continue today in Holiness and Fundamentalist circles.

Not all approved of these developments. Conservative Calvinists such as Nettleton challenged the view of human freedom to respond underlying Finney's approach (in this, they had the tradition of Whitefield and Edwards behind them). Unitarians and others of a liberal outlook despised what they saw as the irrationalism and enthusiasm of religion, often failing to distinguish between its various forms. Another group of theologians, centred on the German Reformed seminary at Mercersburg in Pennsylvania, reacted from the mid-1830s by stressing the importance of the incarnation (and not merely the atonement) in salvation history, and the role of the visible Church as the mediator of Christ's life to believers. Their best-known representatives were the church historian and ecumenist Philip Schaff (1819–93) and the theologian John Williamson Nevin (1803–86), whose work *The Anxious Bench* (1843) evaluated Finneyite revivalism critically.

The Mercersburg outlook stressed the process of nurture in the faith through teaching and participation in the sacraments, by contrast with the alleged unhealthy individualism of the revivalist emphasis on crisis conversions. The stress on nurture was taken further by theologians who placed it in opposition to treating children as sinners in need of a sudden conversion. The Connecticut Congregationalist pastor Horace Bushnell (1802–76) gave this viewpoint definitive expression in his *Christian Nurture* (1847), which asserted that children should be able to grow up and be taught in a Christian environment, never knowing themselves to be anything other than Christian. His approach stressed experience just as much as did the revivalists, but his debt was more to Coleridge than to the likes of Jonathan Edwards. This form of reaction to revivalism was ultimately the most influential, as it led to education assuming increasing significance in the programme of local congregations.

Nevertheless, revivalism experienced another massive boost when much of the English-speaking world was affected by a heightened sense of spiritual concern during the period 1857–60, which resulted in large numbers of conversions and accessions to church membership on both sides of the Atlantic. It began in New York with daily prayer meetings provoked by financial crisis and concern about mounting tension over slavery. In this revival we see the communications network operating most effectively to ensure the spread of the latest revival news through books, periodicals and newspaper coverage. Even more than before, interdenominational co-operation was a marked feature, and this was to continue in connection with Moody and a host of other full-time revivalists. In addition, this awakening saw the emergence of full-time female revivalists in Britain and the United States, although as the fires cooled their ministry gradually became less acceptable.

The revivalist impetus was not confined to Protestants, but was to affect many Catholic parishes. A major problem confronting the American hierarchy was the fact that many immigrants ceased to practise their faith. Parish missions, comprising daily meetings over a period of a few weeks, was the strategy adopted in order to reclaim the lapsed. These had begun after the Council of Trent (although they were rooted in the late-medieval practice of preaching orders such as the Franciscans and the Dominicans), and initially were used as a way of reclaiming converts to Protestantism; religious orders such as the Jesuits, the Oratorians, and the Redemptorists specialized in the conduct of these missions. In North America they were re-invented from the 1830s in a form which combined Finney's 'New Measures' and the guidelines for parish missions laid down by the Italian Alphonsus Liguori (1696–1787). Specialist Catholic revivalists made their appearance, one of the best-known being the convert and priest Clarence Walworth (1820–1900), and they travelled throughout the country conducting missions. As with Protestant revivalism, the aim was to secure a personal response to the message (which was marked by a similar stress on the affective side of Christian commitment, as well as a parallel emphasis on temperance), but in a Catholic context conversion was demonstrated and ratified by participation in the sacraments, especially confession and the Eucharist.

New religious movements

Revivalism had become the dominant expression of American Protestantism from the Independence era onwards, and its non-hierarchical ethos fitted well with the individualism of the frontier spirit and with the Enlightenment emphasis on the authority of universal human experience. It is therefore not surprising that, in a climate which encouraged each person to read the Bible for themselves and make up their own mind regarding its truth and interpretation, a host of new movements should have appeared. Many took root in the 'burned-over' district, a rural part of New York state where Finney had been active and which displayed unusual openness to new forms of religion and social experimentation (for example in communal living). Whereas many groups of European immigrants sought to maintain their inherited religious traditions as a means of shoring up their sense of ethnic identity, those who had become assimilated to the New World and its lack of traditions frequently adopted a primitivist attitude in religious matters, primitivism being the belief that it is both possible and desirable to recreate New Testament church life today.

Christian Church (Disciples of Christ)

Sometimes known as Restorationists (and not to be confused with a British movement bearing the same name which emerged from late-twentieth-century charismatic renewal), the Disciples of Christ developed a church order which was strikingly similar to that of the early Brethren, emphasizing plural leadership, weekly observance of the Lord's Supper, and the autonomy of local congregations. Also similar were the two main goals of realizing the unity of all believers and submission to the Bible as sole authority in religious matters.

Barton W. Stone (1772–1844) was a Presbyterian preacher who led the Cane Ridge meeting in 1801. He was already developing an emphasis on the Bible as sole authority, which led him to challenge that of confessional standards such as the *Westminster Confession*. His revivalism created further tensions with the denomination, and from 1804 he and several colleagues seceded and determined to be guided by the Bible alone. In 1807 they adopted the practice of believer's baptism.

The other key figures were also seceders from Presbyterianism, Thomas Campbell (1763–1854) and his son Alexander (1788–1866); they had migrated from Ulster in 1807 and 1809 respectively. They argued that unity could only be achieved as all Christians returned to the New Testament as their guide in faith and practice. Athough the movement grew by individual secessions of those convinced by such an argument rather than by reuniting congregations formerly estranged from one another, Disciples were to become extensively involved in twentieth-century ecumenism.

The Campbells founded an independent congregation in 1811 and associated for some years with the Baptists before parting company with them in 1825. The majority of Stone's movement merged with the Campbellites from 1832, having picked up several smaller groups with similar aims along the way. However, the insistence that churches should not go beyond what was prescribed in the Bible in regard to doctrine or church practice resulted in disagreements and divisions over the legitimacy of such things as missionary societies (1849) and the use of musical instruments in worship (1859). Nevertheless, the movement grew rapidly because its primitivist revivalism flourished in contemporary frontier culture.

Mormonism

In some ways Mormonism (properly called 'The Church of Jesus Christ of Latter-Day Saints') can be viewed as a quintessentially North American religion: optimistic, pragmatic, activist, adventuring, and possessed of a sense of 'manifest destiny'. The church was founded in 1830, after Joseph Smith (1805–44) claimed to have seen visions telling him where to dig up tablets containing the story of the ten lost tribes of Israel, who had migrated to America; these were published as *The Book of Mormon*. On the basis of further revelations, he produced additional books which the church also accepts as divinely inspired and on a level with the Bible, *Doctrine and Covenants* and *The Pearl of Great Price*. Mormons emerged in the 'burned-over district', sharing the belief in human perfectibility which gave rise to communitarian experiments such as the Oneida community, as well as the widespread interest in millennial views and the longing for a restoration of the primitive Church. Gradually the focus of their expectation came to centre on a restored earthly Zion; they saw this place of refuge from the coming cataclysmic judgements as being set up in America, and it is noteworthy that most early British Mormons were sufficiently attracted by this prospect to emigrate.

In its early decades Mormonism was fiercely opposed by the surrounding society on account of its practice of polygamy, its co-operative approach to land acquisition and farming which enabled it to outperform individual farmers in the frontier context and thus enjoy increasing prosperity, and the members' practice of living in exclusively Mormon settlements and having as little as possible to do with non-Mormons or 'Gentiles'. They were thus forced to migrate westwards, seeking land which was not already occupied by others in order to establish a secure habitation. After Smith was killed by a hostile mob at Nauvoo, Illinois, Brigham Young (1801–77) led the movement and established their headquarters at Salt Lake City in Utah in 1847; only after polygamy was forbidden in 1890 was Utah admitted to the union, in 1896.

Seventh-Day Adventism

The New England Baptist farmer William Miller (1782–1849) developed a historicist scheme of prophetic interpretation which included predictions of the date of the Second Coming. When this twice failed to occur (in 1843 and 1844), his followers almost all disappeared, but his predictions were given a spiritual interpretation by Ellen G. White (1827–1915). In many ways she was the real architect of Seventh-Day Adventism, and was regarded by members as a prophet: visionary experiences (she clamed to have had at least two thousand visions from 1844 onwards) led her to propagate such distinctives as observance of Saturday rather than Sunday as a day of worship, and dietary regulations intended to promote physical health (two famous cereal manufacturers, J.H. Kellogg and Sylvester Graham, were Adventists). The movement established a national organization in 1863, and by the end of the century had missionaries on all continents.

Christian Science

In 1866 Mary Baker Eddy (1821–1910) experienced healing from back pain after a study of the healing miracles in the Gospels. This led her to devote her life to healing, study, and teaching, and her discoveries were published in *Science and Health* (1875). Its main argument was that God is the only reality; matter, sickness, and evil are illusions, and healing comes as individuals recognize these things for what they are. The first 'Church of Christ, Scientist' was founded in 1879, and the movement made Boston its base of operations. Its message was spread by lectures and by the practice of healing by recognized 'practitioners'. The importance of Christian Science is not so much in its size or spread (it remained very largely restricted to the United States) but its illustration of the widespread interest in alternative therapies and explanations of spirituality which intersected at various points with traditional Christianity. The interest in healing would also be taken up in the Pentecostal movement and within mainstream churches in North America and Europe.

Jehovah's Witnesses

The organization known since 1931 as Jehovah's Witnesses was founded in Pennsylvania in 1884 by Charles Taze Russell (1852–1916) as the Zion's Watch Tower Tract Society. His experience of loss and recovery of faith, and his dissatisfaction with the teachings of existing churches, led him to set up his own network of Bible study groups marked by rejection of traditional doctrines such as those of the Trinity and the deity of Christ, insistence on the nearness of the end, and an attempt to predict the date of Christ's return. Ostracism by other ecclesiastical communities was reciprocated with strongly worded denunciations of Christendom as apostate and doomed. In 1909, the growing movement established its headquarters in Brooklyn, New York. Under Russell's successor, 'Judge' J.F. Rutherford (1869–1942), the movement assumed a clearly defined organizational shape.

While insisting that the Bible should be seen as verbally inspired and the final authority for belief, Russell's interpretations, disseminated through a magazine, *Zion's Watchtower* (1876) and the seven-volume work *Studies in the Scriptures* (1886–1917), were regarded as authoritative because of his status as a prophet in receipt of divine revelation (a status which has been transferred to the organization which he founded). Their refusal to participate in government, politics, or warfare marked them out for hostile attention in times of crisis, but the antagonism they experienced from colonial authorities ensured that they found a hearing among the people. Thus in several Southern African countries they rapidly achieved a large following, and their teachings left a significant mark on local millennial expectations.

Holiness movements

Perfectionist theology was particularly associated with Oberlin College in Ohio, an evangelical institution which from 1835 adopted a clear abolitionist and integrationist standpoint. Its president from 1835, Asa Mahan (1799–1889), built on John Wesley's understanding of sin as 'voluntary transgression of a known law' to portray holiness as a matter of the will, and hence to affirm the possibility of believers experiencing freedom from sin. Mahan's successor Finney continued this emphasis, as well as the college's advocacy of causes such as the peace movement and equality of educational opportunity for women. During this phase the movement had a keen social cutting-edge; one social reformer who was influenced by Holiness teaching was the Swiss Henri Dunant (1828–1910), founder of the Red Cross. However, this aspect of the message soon disappeared, at a time when it was also disappearing from much of the rest of American Evangelicalism.

Perfectionism in its later form taught the eradication of all sin from the sanctified believer's heart through a spiritual crisis experience. Christians were encouraged to seek such an experience and taught that it represented a distinct stage or 'second blessing'. Such thinking derived strength from grass-roots concern that existing Wesleyan denominations were becoming lukewarm and worldly (their opposition to Holiness teaching being taken as evidence of this). Denominations were founded to uphold such teaching, notably the Church of God (Anderson, Indiana) in 1881 and the Church of the Nazarene in 1895. Prominent teachers such as Phoebe Palmer (1807–74) and Robert Pearsall Smith (1827–98) and his wife Hannah Whitall Smith (1832–1911) spread the message in North America and in Britain, where (in a toned-down version, speaking of sin being kept under rather than totally eradicated) it resulted in the formation of the Keswick Convention (1875), and thus influenced several generations of middle-class British Evangelicals, especially in the Church of England.

Pentecostalism

Within the Holiness movement the late nineteenth century saw a quickened expectation of a worldwide outpouring of the Holy Spirit, and the appearance of the idea that the charismata should still be present in the Church. A post-conversion experience of 'baptism in the Spirit' came to be advocated, as conferring power to serve God. In addition, the idea that healing of body and soul was an integral part of the Church's ministry was becoming more widespread, not only in North America and Britain but also in Europe under such leaders as the Pietist J.C. Blumhardt (1805–80) and his son C.F. Blumhardt (1842–1919) at Bad Boll in Germany.

Such phenomena as speaking in tongues have occurred from time to time throughout Christian history, but much of the English-speaking movement has traditionally dated its birth to 1 January 1901, when speaking with tongues occurred after a Bible study at a small Bible College in Kansas run by the Holiness preacher C.F. Parham (1873–1929). Its occurrence was taken as confirming Parham's teaching that tongues were the visible evidence of having received the 'baptism of the Spirit'.

Under one of Parham's students, W.J. Seymour (1870–1922), tongues broke out in Los Angeles in 1906; Seymour took over a building at Azusa Street in the city and meetings continued for several years, initially daily, attracting seekers from Europe as well as North America. This was one of the major catalysts for the spread of Pentecostalism worldwide, partly through an informal network of contacts. A key figure was the Cornish-born Methodist minister T.B. Barratt (1862–1940), who visited Azusa Street while on a preaching tour of North America during 1907; receiving the baptism of the Spirit, he returned to his charge in Oslo and began to spread the Pentecostal message in Scandinavia. It was from Barratt that the movement's English pioneer, the Sunderland Anglican clergyman Alexander Boddy (1854–1930) heard the Pentecostal message and entered into the experience; he gave the movement a 'shop window' through annual Whitsun conventions at his church (1908–14) and the publication of a magazine, *Confidence* (1908–26).

While sharing the Fundamentalists' acceptance of the Bible as the inspired and accurate Word of God, the two movements did not make common cause. For one thing, Fundamentalists, like other Evangelicals, categorically rejected the new movement: in Germany, for example, an interdenominational evangelical grouping issued a condemnatory statement which was not retracted until 1995. Thus in many contexts Pentecostals were forced to develop apart from existing denominations. In addition the Pentecostal emphasis on experience, which represented a development of that found in the Wesleyan and Holiness traditions, did not sit well with the more rational fundamentalist approach to doctrine.

Traditional white accounts of Pentecostal origins have seen the movement as beginning in one place, Azusa Street, and (by implication) treating the theological understanding developed within the family of churches which sprang from it as normative, most notably in regarding speaking in tongues as the 'initial evidence' that an individual has been baptized with the Holy Spirit. However, more recent research has tended to support the idea of several largely independent originating centres. For example, independently of events in America, there was an outbreak of speaking with tongues in India (others had occurred during the previous century) in 1906 among a group led by Pandita Ramabai (1858–1922), who was active in women's education; this appears to have been stimulated by news of the Welsh Revival of 1904–5, an event which Pentecostals frequently saw as continuing within their own movement. In Chile, a Methodist missionary couple named Hoover read a pamphlet describing events in India, corresponded with Barratt and others, and began to preach and experience Pentecostal phenomena, resulting in the creation of a separate Methodist Pentecostal denomination in 1910. Seeing the movement as beginning in several places more or less at once requires us to accept the presence of greater theological variety within the movement, and challenges the tendency to privilege the North American and European wings. It also makes it harder for us to distinguish Pentecostalism from certain locally instituted churches, especially in Africa, which claim similar phenomena.

Seymour was black, and Pentecostalism drew to a significant extent on currents in black Christian spirituality; we should not therefore regard it simply as a development of the Holiness tradition. The early meetings were noted for their inter-racial character (which earned the disapproval of the racist Parham), but within a few years the movement split, partly along racial lines although this was bound up with division over the doctrine of the Trinity and differing models of Christian experience. We shall take up the story in Chapter 18.

Questions for thought

1 What problems arising from, and responses to, their arrival in an alien cultural context were shared by all three Christian traditions examined in this chapter? Were any responses unique to one or other of these traditions? If so, how would you account for their failure to appear in the other traditions?

2 How would you compare the ethos of North American religion during this period with that of England or Scotland?

3 What parallels do you notice between Catholic Modernism and Americanism? How far might this account for papal condemnation of the latter?

4 In what ways do you think the American cultural context influenced the course of the main theological developments noted in this chapter?

5 What were the implications of a primitivist outlook for attitudes of newer movements towards existing churches?

Further reading

(See also the section on North America in Suggested Further Reading at the end of the book.)

Sheridan Gilley and Brian Stanley (eds), 2006, *Cambridge History of Christianity*, vol. 8: *World Christianities c.1815–c.1914*, Cambridge: Cambridge University Press, ch. 22.

Robert T. Handy, 1976, *A History of the Churches in the United States and Canada*, Oxford History of the Christian Church, Oxford: Clarendon, chs 5–11.

Mark A. Noll, 1992, *A History of Christianity in the United States and Canada*, London: SPCK, parts 3–4.

John Wolffe, 2006, *The Expansion of Evangelicalism*, A History of Evangelicalism, Nottingham: IVP.

Notes

1 Noll, *Christianity in the United States and Canada*, p. 153. Noll draws on Roger Finke and Rodney Stark, 'How the upstart sects won America', *Journal for the Scientific Study of Religion* 28 (1989), p. 31, and the 1850 population census.

2 The roots of this theory lie in the thinking of the Dutch jurist Hugo Grotius (1583–1645), and it was popular among the early European Arminians.

3 On millennialism and the history of Dispensationalism in North America, see Paul Boyer, 1992, *When Time Shall Be No More: Prophecy Belief in Modern American Culture*, Cambridge, MA: Belknap Press; E.R. Sandeen, 1970, *The Roots of Fundamentalism: British and American Millenarianism 1800–1930*, Chicago: University of Chicago Press; Timothy P. Weber, 1979, *Living in the Shadow of the Second Coming*, New York: Oxford University Press.

4 In Britain, Anglicans had been the most receptive denomination, though some seceded to join the Brethren.

5 On Fundamentalism, see the writings of George M. Marsden, including his 1991 work *Understanding Fundamentalism and Evangelicalism*, Grand Rapids, MI: Eerdmans.

6 On revivalism, a standard work is Richard Carwardine, 2006 (first published 1978), *Transatlantic Revivalism: Popular Evangelicalism in Britain and America 1790–1865*, Milton Keynes: Paternoster.

13

Western Christian Social Thought to 1914

In this chapter, we shall survey some of the most significant nineteenth-century Western Christian responses to social change: Roman Catholic social thought; the German and Scandinavian 'Inner Mission'; British thinking as seen in (i) the Evangelicals, (ii) the broad church / Christian Socialist traditions, and (iii) Nonconformity; and finally the North American 'Social Gospel'.

Roman Catholic social teaching

The nineteenth century saw the development of Catholic social teaching, drawing on the Thomist theological tradition. Thomist philosophy was declared normative by the 1879 encyclical *Aeterni Patris*. This led to a flowering of its study, but it also had implications for Catholic social teaching, for which scholasticism was believed to provide a metaphysical basis. Aquinas had stressed the idea of 'natural law', that is, the existence of a body of moral principles written on each human heart by God and knowable through the use of reason, which were thus accessible to, and valid for, all. The Catholic Church was seen as the guardian of this deposit, and hence the custodian of right social and political thought. These ideas coalesced to give Rome a sense of having a message for all people, not just the Catholic faithful, a conviction which has continued to colour the Vatican's social pronouncements.

By the 1850s Catholic theologians were beginning to address the challenges of the new industrial order. Wilhelm Ketteler (1811–77), bishop of Mainz in Germany, drew on Thomist teaching in his critique of socialism and liberalism. In 1881 Leo XIII established a commission to examine possible solutions to the challenges presented by social change and the increasing gap between the Church and the urban poor. The result was the 1891 encyclical *Rerum Novarum*, the first of a succession on social issues. It was a landmark in Catholic social teaching because it did not restrict itself to advocating personal charity but considered structural issues. As summarized by Sheridan Gilley, its teaching was that

Church and state are distinct, each divine in origin and sovereign in its own particular sphere. Whether Christian or pagan, the state derives its sanction from God. Democracy is as tolerable as other forms of government as long as it acknowledges its divine foundation and the special realm of sovereignty of the church. States are bound by the natural law, which requires controls on the expression of moral and religious error. Ideally, in a Christian society, education and the regulation of public morals belong to the church, while the family is, as much as church and state, a sacred institution, also of divine origin, which the state is bound to protect. Voluntary association is a positive good. . . .

This is traditional Catholic teaching. The original twist was Leo's consistent denunciation of the two rival systems of unregulated liberal *laissez-faire* capitalism and socialism, which he held to be wrong in teaching an autonomous secular doctrine of society and the state, placing both beyond religious discipline and the natural law.[1]

The main features included the unique dignity of individuals, the family as the basic social unit, and the right to humane labour conditions and a fair wage. A moderate form of trade-unionism was deemed acceptable, and thereafter associations for Catholic workers grew rapidly in several European countries. Leo's approach, for which Ketteler's thought had proved seminal, offered a middle way between socialism and liberalism, neither of which was deemed compatible with Catholic teaching.

At the same time Catholics were active in practical ways. One of the best known was St John Bosco (1815–88) of Turin, who established homes where boys could be trained and receive a spiritual formation. In 1859 he founded an order, the Salesians, inspired by the example of the Genevan St Francis de Sales (1567–1622), to educate poor youths with the hope that some would enter the priesthood. Also founded to do acts of charity and campaign on social issues was the Society of St Vincent de Paul (1833), an association of lay people which rapidly spread from Paris throughout much of the Western world.

German and Scandinavian Protestantism responds to social need

In the new order which obtained following the adhesion of many German states to the Reformation, the burden of provision for the poor fell on the Protestant parish. This arrangement proved inadequate to meet the stresses imposed by the wars ensuing on the French Revolution and then the onset of rapid industrialization and urbanization. It became clear that a parish-based approach was not only overwhelmed by the scale of the need (such as the numbers of children left orphaned and homeless by war) but was also not geared up to deal with the challenges posed by large-scale internal migration. It was proving virtually impossible to subdivide urban parishes which might in extreme cases contain 30,000 or more people; this meant that in large cities a generation was growing up which had little meaningful contact with the churches. Non-parochial agencies were needed, and since the idea that the state should be responsible for the needs of the urban poor was slow to catch on, it was the churches (or, more particularly, concerned individuals within them) who must meet the challenge.

There was a well-established Moravian and Pietist pattern of voluntarily funded philanthropic institutions, which fed into the first responses during this period. In 1833, the Hamburg Protestant J.H. Wichern (1808–81) founded a home for destitute boys, the *Rauhes Haus*, influenced by the contemporary trend towards a more positive attitude towards children (as seen, for instance, in the work of the educationalist J.H. Pestalozzi (1746–1827)). Wichern formed an order of 'brothers' to care for the children and from 1844 publicized this and other 'works of saving love' through a periodical, *Der Fliegende Blätter*. In 1848 the German Protestant churches held their first national *Kirchentag*, at which Wichern suggested co-ordinating such works on a national basis under the banner of 'Inner Mission' ('Outer Mission' being that undertaken overseas). This came to be the designation for a range of voluntary and non-parochial social, philanthropic, and evangelistic work undertaken by the churches, all with the objective of reclaiming and restoring those who had wandered or fallen. Similar agencies appeared in Scandinavian countries, and the North American Social Gospel movement also owed something to German developments.

A somewhat different approach was pursued by Theodor Fliedner (1800–64), a Protestant pastor at Kaiserswerth in the Lower Rhineland. His thinking about charitable work was shaped by his contact with that undertaken by the Dutch Reformed Church and also with the institutions founded by English Quakers and Evangelicals. In 1836 he and his wife founded an institution to train women to nurse and minister to the poor as deaconesses (though he disliked that term). Florence Nightingale was profoundly impressed by the institution when she visited it in 1850 and 1851, though appalled at the poor hygiene in the hospital. Hundreds of women were trained at Kaiserswerth, daughter institutions began to be founded overseas from 1849, and the deaconess became (and has remained) a prominent figure in the German local church set-up.

The revolutionary year of 1848 saw another influential response to German social conditions, when Marx and Friedrich Engels (1820–95) issued their seminal *Communist Manifesto*. Engels had lived some years in Britain, and drew on his acquaintance with the condition of the working classes in Manchester. Marxist thought has sometimes been seen as a Christian heresy, and the reason why becomes clear when we compare the main outlines of the two respective systems. Both have a sequence of thought which runs from 'creation' though the experience of fall / alienation to redemption (undertaken by the proletariat in Marxism) to the eschatological goal. Furthermore, both systems share the principle of economic redistribution which Marx expressed in the phrase 'from each according to his ability, to each according to his need'. However, Marx was strongly anti-religious and critical of the inadequacy of Christian responses to contemporary social problems.

By contrast with Marx, Wichern tended to be identified with political conservatism and desired to see the restoration of a moral order based on Protestant principles. In his thinking, he focused on character formation rather than addressing the context in which the needy lived, and gave no place to the question of legislative reform. He was anti-socialist and developed close links with Friedrich Wilhelm IV and leading politicians and nobility.

The tendency towards a conservative approach was even more starkly demonstrated by developments in Denmark; there the Indre Mission became a significant moral influence in the late nineteenth century, especially in smaller communities. But it drew on that strand of Lutheran thought which opposed good works, and on Pietist renewal to stress a narrow approach to ministry which focused more or less exclusively on saving souls.

In the event the 'Inner Mission' proved incapable of meeting the massive challenges posed by late-nineteenth-century Berlin, where by 1875 only 20 per cent of marriages took place in church and only 60 per cent of children were baptized. Many German church leaders concluded that theology and pastoral work must begin to address the matter of legislative social reform, and call on the state to take this matter seriously. Wichern always resisted the idea that Inner Mission should get involved in such campaigning, which meant that, due to his close alliance with the ruling powers, the movement tended to be seen as upholding the status quo. The rapidly growing German Socialist Party (the SPD) saw the churches as part of the establishment which it sought to challenge. Protestant clergy, who in 1890 had been granted permission to involve themselves in politics, found this permission withdrawn in 1895. However, from about 1900 theologians began to develop a thought-out approach to such issues, influenced in part by the notion formulated by Ritschl and others of the Kingdom of God as an ethical reality.

British Christian social thought

The Anglican Evangelicals

The best-known example of evangelical involvement in social issues is undoubtedly the 'Clapham Sect' (although there were non-Evangelicals associated with them). This was a group which came together during the 1790s, centred on Clapham, then a village outside London. Its rector from 1792 was John Venn (1759–1813), who combined a commitment to parish life with a broad missionary vision. The group included clergymen and politicians, journalists, and officers of societies such as the British and Foreign Bible Society. Hannah More (1745–1833) was also a member of the group, although she lived in Somerset, where she founded a number of charity schools and wrote popular tracts inculcating evangelical religion and a due sense of deference to social superiors as part of the reaction against the French Revolution.

Members of Parliament sharing the Sect's outlook were known as the 'Saints'; they did not always align themselves with a political party, preferring the freedom of an independent standpoint (most other Evangelicals in Parliament were Tories). The best-known, William Wilberforce (1759–1833), was MP for Hull; he took up the anti-slavery cause in the late 1780s, receiving the encouragement of John Wesley, whose *Thoughts on Slavery* (1774) was one of the earliest works on the subject by an Evangelical. Several of the Sect were active in the abolitionist cause, notably Granville Sharp (1735–1813), who was active in the anti-slavery cause by 1772, when a legal judgement laid down that slaves on British soil had the status of free men and could not be returned to masters overseas against their will. Others included an Anglican with Quaker sympathies, Thomas Clarkson (1760–1846), who devoted his life to anti-slavery campaigning after writing a prize Latin essay on the topic at Cambridge. The campaigners pioneered modern political pressure-group techniques such as lobbying members and amassing evidence to support their case. Many Evangelicals, however, were unhappy about the Sect's political involvement because they believed that Romans 13 prescribed submission to 'the powers that be'. In Parliament, advocates of abolitionism faced many defeats, and could do nothing for some years from 1793 because of the likelihood that their cause would be seen as revolutionary at a time when Britain was at war with France. In 1807 Parliament voted to abolish the slave trade in British territories, and Wilberforce initially hoped that the condition of the slaves would gradually improve thereafter; when that did not occur, he came to the conviction that emancipation was the only solution. In 1823 serious campaigning restarted with the founding of the Anti-Slavery Society. The burden of parliamentary work was taken over by the brewer Thomas Fowell Buxton (1786–1845), an evangelical

Quaker. After a further decade of campaigning, an act was passed in 1833 to replace slavery with a system of apprenticeship (which was itself abolished in 1838 as it seemed to be making little practical difference) and compensate former slave-owners. Thereafter Sierra Leone became a landing-place and refuge for former slaves as the Royal Navy patrolled the area for illegal slave ships.

Evangelical discussion of 'anti-slavery' has tended to overlook the role played by freed slaves themselves. A considerable impression was made by Olaudah Equiano (1745–97), whose best-selling *Interesting Narrative* (1789) and speaking tours of Britain enabled many to begin to understand what slavery was like for those trapped in it. Similarly, Quobna Ottobah Cugoano's *Thoughts and Sentiments on the Evils of Slavery* (1787) offered an exegetical justification for opposing slavery. Moreover, other groups were also active in the abolitionist cause. Many Quakers had come over to it from the mid-eighteenth century, some such as the American John Woolman (1720–72) adopting the principles of abstaining from consumption of goods produced by slave labour and paying slaves for their services when staying in houses where they were kept. Another Quaker abolitionist was Anthony Benezet (1713–84), who sought to influence Evangelicals to take up the cause (he succeeded with John Wesley). Enlightenment thinkers also included convinced abolitionists, and their arguments were widely adopted. Conversely, not all Evangelicals supported abolition. In Britain, radical Evangelicals such as Edward Irving and the erstwhile MP Henry Drummond (1786–1860) opposed it as interference with the divinely appointed lot of the negroes.[2]

In the United States the irony of white Americans claiming liberty from British dominance but refusing to grant such liberty to the black population came to be widely recognized; the Northern and Middle states began to abolish slavery from 1777, and the import of slaves was abolished throughout the nation in 1808. However, from the 1820s some Evangelicals, particularly in the Southern states, openly defended the institution of slavery on biblical grounds (as Edwards had done): they saw abolitionism as subversive of social order and biblical authority. In response, other Evangelicals argued not merely that slavery provided occasion for sin on the part of unjust slave-holders, but that it was in itself sinful for one human being to claim ownership of another.[3] The issue split several American denominations. Presbyterians (1837–8), Methodists (1844), and Baptists (1845) all divided, the Northern wings opposing slavery and the Southern ones allowing it. An American branch of the EA was not founded until 1867 because of disagreement over slavery. In the Civil War (1861–5), Evangelicals fought on both sides; revivals occurred in both camps, and theologians claimed biblical justification for opposing positions. After the war ended Southern Evangelicals continued to assert the legitimacy of slavery. With the end of the period of 'Reconstruction'

(1865–77), blacks found the whites abandoning anti-slavery activity for other causes; discrimination remained, and many blacks were consigned to existence on the margins of society, as were many European immigrants, with whom they competed for employment.

'The evangelicals' crusade for the reform of British manners and morals in the early nineteenth century would be indebted to the moral capital the Clapham Sect first accrued during the campaign against the slave trade.'[4] The other main aspect of Wilberforce's vision, which may help to explain why his campaign for the abolition of slavery met with widespread public support, was the reform of public morals. He believed that this could help to create a godly and stable society, a vision which contrasted strikingly with the chaos evident in revolutionary France. This vision found expression in his *Practical View of the prevailing Religious System of Professed Christians in the Higher and Middle Classes in this country contrasted with Real Christianity* (1797); its appeal to the middle classes ensured that it was a best-seller, and it was a significant factor in the conversion of Thomas Chalmers to evangelical faith.

We do not find much sustained ideological critique of industrialization or the growth of capitalism among mainstream Protestants, but a prime example of response to the problems thrown up by such developments was provided by Anthony Ashley Cooper, seventh Earl of Shaftesbury (1801–85). A Tory MP from 1826, he campaigned for a range of causes which included factory reform (limiting the hours worked by children), the treatment of lunacy, public health, and the 'ragged schools'. At his memorial service, which was held in Westminster Abbey, no fewer than 189 religious and charitable organizations were represented. Yet this activist was constantly preoccupied with the prospect of the imminent Second Advent of Christ, and in that respect he serves as something of a bridge between the earlier, more socially active Evangelicalism and that of the later part of the century, which was more introverted, seeing holiness more exclusively in terms of individual spirituality and withdrawing from social engagement under the influence of its eschatology.

The era's preferred mode of philanthropic operation was the formation of voluntary societies to address specific issues. Education, prisoners' welfare, care of orphans, medical outreach, reclamation of 'fallen women', and animal welfare all saw agencies appear to publicize the needs, campaign for change, and take practical action. Such specialization both hindered the development of, and sprang from the lack of, an overall social vision. Most voluntary philanthropic societies during this period were evangelical in their inspiration: in Bradley's words, 'The Evangelicals established the voluntary charitable society as the characteristic vehicle for philanthropic activity in Victorian England.'[5] It is often alleged that the Evangelicals' response to social issues failed to go beyond alleviation of the symptoms by such means. For most this was undoubtedly the case; their ultimate concern was not so much to transform society as to save souls; only later did a significant proportion of them conclude that the former was an essential prerequisite to the latter. The issues on which Evangelicals focused were often those deemed to be obstacles to the spread of the gospel (such as illiteracy) or substitutes for the gospel (which could cover everything from anti-Catholicism to teetotalism). Opposition to sin (which was often reduced to opposing particular sins) meant that they sometimes appeared more concerned to eliminate an evil than institute a good, and there were not lacking those, mostly members of the working classes, who saw the institutional churches as blind to the evils of middle-class society.[6] Furthermore, most Anglican Evangelicals retained the traditional belief in society as a hierarchy in which the places of individuals were divinely ordained and should not be tampered with. Nevertheless, they achieved a great deal, and many of today's leading charities owe their origins to nineteenth-century Evangelicalism.

The Broad Church / Christian Socialist tradition

The pioneer of Christian social thought in broad church circles (though they were not then known as such) was F.D. Maurice. His work *The Kingdom of Christ* (1838) was an exposition of the Thirty-Nine Articles which owed much to Coleridge's social thought. Maurice's underlying Platonic sense of the unity of all things, his belief in God as the source of human social order, and his conviction that Christ's work had been to restore the world to a right relationship with God, led him to stress that social regeneration had to be grounded in God, and that the Church was the chief sign and foretaste of the unity of all humanity.

The Christian Socialist movement made its appearance in 1848 as an alternative reaction to Chartism against the *laissez-faire* individualism which had become widespread. Initially, Christian Socialists were aligned with the broad church wing of Anglicanism. One of its leaders was the barrister J.M. Ludlow (1821–1911), who had witnessed the 1848 revolution in Paris, and was convinced that socialism must be Christianized or else it would shake Christianity. Maurice was also involved, as was the novelist and clergyman Charles Kingsley (1819–75). They set up workers' co-operatives (at a time when similar ventures were appearing independently in northern England) and issued publications aimed at the working classes, including a periodical, *Politics for the People*. Their movement petered out in 1854, but not before it had proved seminal in the formation of what was to become the Workers' Educational Association.

Later on there was the more pragmatically orientated Guild of St Matthew (1877), led by the Bethnal Green cleric Stewart Headlam, and the Christian Social Union (1889), which focused on fostering social thought within the Church of England. Both combined high church teaching (especially as modified in the light of the growing importance of the incarnation in contemporary theology) with the social outlook of Maurice, the former movement more provocatively than the latter.

While none of these movements was very influential in itself, they did lay the foundation for a tradition of Anglican social thought which was to become much more important during the twentieth century.

British Nonconformists

Exclusion from government and contempt from wider society had left many Nonconformists somewhat introverted, a mentality which was fed by the tendency to focus on questions related to individual salvation. It is therefore all the more remarkable that the second half of the nineteenth century should have seen so many of them develop such a keen social involvement so rapidly. When they did, their experience of exclusion made them highly critical of those in power.

Education became the biggest bone of contention between Anglicans and Nonconformists, both because of its importance as a means of inculcating religious principles and because of its status as symbolizing the fact of Anglican establishment.[7] Thus the campaign for disestablishment became inextricably linked with debate about education. In 1831, the Anglican National Society supported 2,002 schools, and the mainly Nonconformist British and Foreign Schools Society, founded in 1807 by Joseph Lancaster, just 191. Succeeding decades saw massive expansion in the number of Nonconformist schools as a means of outreach but also in order to ensure that their children did not come under Anglican teaching, especially with the growth of Tractarianism. Most of the main denominations were involved, and even groups such as the Brethren founded dozens of schools. At this stage, therefore, Nonconformists were committed to a voluntary system in which denominations bore the financial responsibility of providing education for their children, state aid being refused on principle. This proved to be too great a burden for Nonconformists to bear, and from the late 1860s many apart from the Wesleyans (among whom there lingered the ghost of an attachment to the principle of establishment) began to advocate universal state-funded secular education instead. They therefore supported the 1870 Education Act, which was intended to provide sufficient schools under the Board of Education, alongside existing schools run by voluntary agencies, to allow all children to have a place. Ultimately, however, Nonconformists wanted to secure one system for all, and their agitation for this culminated in the Edwardian era, as we saw in Chapter 10.

Another great campaigning issue for Nonconformists was temperance. The first denomination to grant official recognition to the temperance cause was the Primitive Methodists, who in 1841 ordered the use of unfermented wine at communion. Gradually teetotalism (abstinence from all alcohol) replaced temperance (abstinence from spirits), but the movement attracted some criticism because of the tendency to substitute 'signing the pledge' for experiencing an evangelical conversion, and for implying that individuals had the power to save themselves.

As well as the humanitarian motive and the opposition to drunkenness as a sin, campaigners may well have been motivated by a concern to remove obstacles to attendance at worship, which was widely regarded as a duty incumbent on all. The campaign was thus directed at what constituted the main rival to the chapels for working-class allegiance, the public houses. However, it rarely addressed underlying issues: in many parts of Britain, men went to public houses because they provided the only alternative social meeting-point to the churches and chapels. In addition, it tended to be unpopular because it amounted to condemnation of a key aspect of working-class culture, and so the campaign reinforced the perception of the chapels as distant and unsympathetic. Rather than removing an obstacle, it created one.

Nonconformist attitudes towards the contemporary industrial set-up were rather more ambivalent. Five of the six 'Tolpuddle Martyrs' sentenced to transportation in 1834 for trades union activities (and pardoned after mass demonstrations in various parts of England) were Methodists. The agricultural worker and union pioneer Joseph Arch (1826–1919) was a Primitive Methodist lay preacher, and there were strong links between Primitive Methodism and the mining unions in County Durham. As a result, some have argued for the primary importance of Methodism in the trades union movement.[8] Others, notably E. P. Thompson, have claimed that Methodism diverted energies from radicalism to religion. Closer examination indicates, however, that there was a significant gap between the conservatism of the leadership (reinforced among the Wesleyans by a 'no politics' rule for preachers) and the presence of more or less radical views among many lay preachers and members.

For the first two-thirds of the century, many Nonconformist factory owners were unsympathetic to the development of unionism, and their denominational leaders asserted that involvement in such issues was a distraction from the business of saving souls; poverty was due primarily to sin, and the way to improve society was to improve the individual by converting them. Until the 1870s it tended to be Anglican Evangelicals rather than Nonconformists who were active in reform, perhaps because among some of them a more interventionist outlook was present. Watts goes so far as to claim that 'The failure of the majority of Nonconformist leaders to support the working class on issues such as factory reform and the poor law constitutes the most glaring failure of compassion in the whole history of Dissent.'[9]

Things were to change during the final third of the century, with the articulation of the 'Nonconformist conscience'. This term was used to designate a complex of social, ethical, and political opinions widely held and vocally advocated by late nineteenth-century Nonconformists. It was coined in 1890, as part of the reaction to the revelation that the Irish politician Charles Parnell, whom they had tended to support, had been guilty of adultery; as the Methodist leader Hugh Price Hughes put it, 'What is morally wrong cannot be politically right.' (It was a combination of British Nonconformists and Irish Catholics which ended Parnell's political career.) It tended to focus on issues of individual morality: temperance, gambling, and sexual conduct. However, Nonconformists were also active in the field of education, as we have seen. Another area in which their contribution is often neglected is that of municipal reform, where they frequently called for improvements in areas such as housing, sanitation, and water supply. The Birmingham Congregationalist minister R.W. Dale (1829–95) was a prime example of this, co-operating closely with municipal government led by the Unitarian Joseph Chamberlain and contributing to education policy debates within the Liberal Party. However, it can be argued that the 'Nonconformist conscience' did not account by itself for any changes in Liberal policy. We should also note that a proportion of Nonconformists withdrew from, or stood apart from, political involvement, either because it was perceived as divisive in its impact on the churches or because it was a misguided substitute for the gospel, which they saw as the only hope of real improvement. The alliance between Nonconformity and Liberalism began to weaken from 1886, when the Liberals experienced a sharp division over Irish Home Rule. Nevertheless, the 1906 election saw 157 Nonconformist members returned to Parliament (in 1868, there had been 63).

It can be argued that Nonconformists were motivated by a conviction that their evangelistic strategy was proving ineffective among the poor. Such a concern undoubtedly lay behind the programme of social action laid out in William Booth's book *In Darkest England and the Way Out* (1890): K.S. Inglis has asserted that 'It was Booth's anxiety about the Army's lack of penetrating power among slum-dwellers that turned him towards social reform.'[10] In addition, it could be claimed that many Nonconformists were moving away from a tendency to put social problems down to human sin, and towards an approach which laid greater stress on the manifestation of sin in the formation and perpetuation of unjust social and economic structures. Recent debate has considered the extent to which Nonconformist social involvement was underpinned by a coherent theological perspective.[11] According to David Thompson, the two key changes in Nonconformist thinking were a broader concept of the remit of the state, and a broader understanding of the doctrine of redemption, which led to a shift of focus from securing redress of grievances to the promotion of social righteousness.[12] Nevertheless, the great majority of Nonconformists wished to retain their evangelistic concern alongside that for social reform, by contrast with those Christian Socialists who rejected traditional views concerning sin and individual salvation. Examples included the Baptists John Clifford (1836–1923) and F.B. Meyer (1847–1929) and the Methodist Hugh Price Hughes (1847–1902).

Yet it is true some were losing sight of the essential unity of the two and beginning to view ministry in terms of a choice between evangelism and social action. This was especially evident among conservative Evangelicals: widespread espousal of pre-millennial views, with their accompanying pessimism regarding efforts to better this world, led many to de-prioritize or abandon social action. At the opposite end of the spectrum, from about 1907 the Congregationalist R.J. Campbell (1867–1956) argued that the task of the churches was not to prepare individuals for heaven but to hasten the coming of God's kingdom on earth, a vision which to contemporary observers appeared almost identical with that of Labour politicians. His 'New Theology' provoked a storm and was extensively reported by certain daily papers, but in 1915 he renounced his views, bought up remaining copies of his books, and became a high church Anglican.

The 'Social Gospel' in North America

As in Europe, the late nineteenth century was a time of rapid social change: large-scale industrialization from the 1870s, immigration (in several waves between the 1830s and 1914), and movement from village to town and city all contributed to the development of seriously deprived urban areas. A financial panic in 1893 caused distress and hardship to great numbers. In spite of that, leading industrialists and financiers became fabulously rich, and some in industry and in the ecclesiastical hierarchies proclaimed a 'gospel of wealth' which offered spiritual legitimation for the pursuit and accumulation of material wealth. However, this did not go unchallenged: coupled with a new sense of the corporate dimension of human existence, many in the churches began to question the morality of what was going on and to elaborate alternative social visions. Thus in 1912 the Federal Council of Churches issued a 'Social Creed' embodying the Social Gospel vision and based on a statement prepared for the Methodists.

One ideological root for the Social Gospel movement, as it came to be known, was the Inner Mission. This was exported across the Atlantic with German emigrants and then copied by English-speaking churches. Better known are the movement's roots in liberal theology such as that of Ritschl (which viewed Jesus as primarily an ethical teacher rather than a divine Saviour, taught the perfectibility of human nature, and advocated rational reform) and American optimism (which drew on the secularized remnants of Puritan postmillennialism to offer a vision of achieving the kingdom of God on earth through human agency). Reacting against evangelical individualism and *laissez-faire* economic theories, its proponents offered comprehensive and progressive proposals for social reform, which they saw as integral to the establishment of God's kingdom on earth. The movement flourished from about 1880 until the onset of the Great Depression in 1929, and influenced most major Northern denominations.

Key thinkers included the pastor Washington Gladden (1836–1918), who produced a succession of books and articles applying his liberal understanding of Christianity to all areas of human corporate existence, and the seminary professor Walter Rauschenbusch (1861–1918), whose experience pastoring a church in a deprived part of New York known as 'Hell's Kitchen' shaped his approach to social problems and stimulated his attempt to provide the movement with a solid theological grounding. But perhaps the most widely read book to come out of this movement was a novel, *In His Steps* (1896) by Charles M. Sheldon, with its famous question, 'What would Jesus do?' It described the transformation which ensued in the life of a community when its members began to ask such a question.

While some Evangelicals were active in inner-city missions which combined evangelism and practical assistance, others had begun to develop close links with sympathetic businessmen which would have made any sustained or fundamental critique of contemporary business practice the more difficult. Whereas Finney had a keen social conscience, being a committed abolitionist and social reformer, Moody adopted a narrower approach to evangelism, seeing his task as being to rescue individuals from a world heading for disaster. His outlook was to prove the dominant one in English-speaking Evangelicalism, at least until the 1970s.

Questions for thought

1 Compare and contrast the thinking of the Catholic, 'Inner Mission', Broad Church, Evangelical, Nonconformist, and Social Gospel traditions on the respective roles of church and state in social reform.

2 How would you square the insistence that Roman Catholic social teaching was relevant to all and not merely to the faithful, with the

tendency of Catholics to withdraw from the world into an alternative society?

3 To what extent was Evangelicalism responsible for a rise in British moral standards during the nineteenth century?

Further reading

Sheridan Gilley and Brian Stanley (eds), 2006, *Cambridge History of Christianity*, vol. 8: *World Christianities c.1815–c.1914*, Cambridge: Cambridge University Press, ch. 10.

D.W. Bebbington, 1982, *The Nonconformist Conscience: Chapel and Politics, 1870–1914*, London: Allen & Unwin.

Kathleen Heasman, 1962, *Evangelicals in Action*, London: G. Bles.

Nicholas Hope, 1995, *German and Scandinavian Protestantism 1700 to 1918*, Oxford History of the Christian Church, Oxford: Oxford University Press, chs 16, 20.

John Wolffe (ed.), 1995, *Evangelical Faith and Public Zeal: Evangelicals and Society in Britain 1780–1980*, London: SPCK.

Notes

1 In Gilley & Stanley (eds), *CHC*, vol. 8, p. 21.

2 Drummond founded the chair of Political Economy at Oxford in 1826, hosted an important series of conferences at Albury (Surrey) for the study of biblical prophecy from 1826 to 1830, and became an apostle in the Catholic Apostolic Church.

3 For a dramatized presentation of contemporary arguments, see Willard M. Swartley, 1983, *Slavery, Sabbath, War and Women: Case Issues in Biblical Interpretation*, Scottdale, PA: Herald Press, ch. 1.

4 Christopher Brown, in Stewart J. Brown and Timothy Tackett (eds), 2007, *Cambridge History of Christianity*, vol. 7: *Enlightenment, Reawakening and Revolution 1660–1815*, Cambridge: Cambridge University Press, p. 528.

5 Ian Bradley, 1976, *The Call to Seriousness: The Evangelical Impact on the Victorians*, London: Jonathan Cape, p. 123. This work offers a valuable discussion of the role of Evangelicalism in shaping Victorian middle-class morality.

6 A middle-class exception would be the Congregationalist Edward Miall, author of *The British Churches in Relation to the British People* (1849): he argued that the gospel had become captive to middle-class values and that working-class people felt alienated from the churches.

7 Education had also been a cause of controversy in Ireland during the 1820s, not least because both Protestant and Catholic recognized its importance in reinforcing a sense of Catholic identity. Attempts by the Kildare Place Society (refounded in 1817 and supported by Catholics as well as Protestants) to allow able pupils to read editions of the Bible without notes were thwarted by Catholic priestly opposition, and a commission of inquiry set up in 1825 recommended

that separate religious instruction be provided for Protestants and Catholics.

8 E.g. Robert F. Wearmouth, 1937, *Methodism and the Working-Class Movements of England 1800–1850*, London: Epworth.

9 Michael R. Watts, 1995, *The Dissenters*, vol. 2: *The Expansion of Evangelical Nonconformity 1791–1859*, Oxford: Clarendon, p. 487.

10 K.S. Inglis, 1963, *Churches and the Working Classes in Victorian England*, London: Routledge & Kegan Paul, p. 197.

11 See, for example, R.J. Helmstadter, 1988, 'The Nonconformist conscience', in Gerald Parsons (ed.), *Religion in Victorian Britain*, vol. 4: *Interpretations*, Manchester: Manchester University Press, pp. 61–95; Ian M. Randall, 'The social gospel: a case study', in Wolffe, *Evangelical Faith and Public Zeal*, pp. 155–74; David M. Thompson, 1990, 'The emergence of the Nonconformist social gospel in England', in Keith Robbins (ed.), *Protestant Evangelicalism: Britain, Ireland, Germany and America, c.1750–c.1950*, Studies in Church History, Subsidia 7, Oxford: Blackwell, pp. 255–80.

12 Thompson, 'Nonconformist social gospel', pp. 257, 273.

14

Nineteenth-Century Expansion Outside Europe

It is one of the great paradoxes of church history that, just as Christianity was coming under severe pressure in Europe as a result of political and intellectual revolution, it was to experience a period of expansion outside Europe which had had no parallel since the Nestorian move eastwards during the seventh and eighth centuries. This process has continued to the present, increasingly independent of developments in Western Christianity. Missionary expansion is not the same thing as the expansion of Christianity, and this chapter attempts to offer insights into the historical outworking of each process and of the relationship between them. Although expansion during the nineteenth century was primarily in terms of numbers of missionaries, this laid the foundations for the twentieth-century expansion in numbers of Christians.

Where did Christianity expand?

Many areas which already had a sizeable and longstanding Christian community saw a greatly expanded missionary presence during the century, usually Protestant; examples include South India, Egypt, and even China.[1] Nevertheless, there were also previously un-Christianized parts of the world where the Church put down strong roots during this period, as in Siberia, large parts of East Africa, and the islands of the Pacific Ocean. This did not always occur in the way which the missionaries expected. In Polynesia, for instance, the pattern was established in the 1820s of mass conversions following the decision of a local chief to become a Christian, a pattern which had been widespread in Europe a millennium earlier but of which nineteenth-century missionaries would have had no experience. The dynamics of such decisions were often complex: while the missionaries valued the power and status which accrued from alliance with local rulers, the chiefs themselves used Christianity to strengthen and legitimate their own position. Mass conversions posed problems for Evangelicals because of the Enlightenment individualism which underlay their thinking and strengthened their tendency to seek individual conversions at the expense of considering the impact of Christianity on the dynamics of the community hearing the message. Converts seemed quite decided about becoming Christians, but did not show the characteristics which would have been expected in evangelical converts back home, such as a sense of repentance for sin. Some missionaries therefore adopted a two-stage model in which personal conversions of the evangelical type followed mass profession of Christian allegiance: if we recall Andrew Walls's interpretation of Evangelicalism as a protest movement against nominal Christianity which arose in a Christian society, this is not altogether surprising. Even so, personal narratives of indigenous converts often stressed factors which did not play a prominent role in nineteenth-century Western conversion narratives, such as the superiority of the Christian God over tribal deities. Mass movements were much less of a problem for Roman Catholics because of their different understanding of the relationship between initial conversion and growth in maturity and their tendency to stress the corporate aspects of Christianity, a tendency which meshed well with a parallel emphasis in many indigenous cultures.

Another pattern of church development was shown by Uganda, where Christianity took root and grew rapidly within a few decades from the late 1870s. Catholic White Fathers arrived first, followed by Anglicans from 1885. Although the Anglican party suffered the martyrdom of its leader, Bishop Hannington (probably because they arrived in the country by a route which exposed them to suspicion as likely invaders), converts were rapidly made among the ruling class. Almost a hundred converts were martyred in 1886, partly because of their refusal to engage in court homosexual practices, but there was never any intention to stamp out the Christian community as a whole. Tensions between Protestant and Catholic erupted in 1892–3, but once these were resolved it proved possible to establish strong churches enjoying widespread popular support, not least because Christians among the ruling class were able to secure a large measure of Christianization of the existing society, thus easing the religious transition for many. From the 1890s local Protestants and Catholics both engaged in vigorous church planting.

The expansion of the Christian community in a given area did not necessarily lead to its rapid indigenization. For example, the process of indigenization in West African Anglicanism was held up for six decades by the debacle in 1891 resulting from the elevation to the episcopate of Samuel Ajayi Crowther, which we shall examine later, and early in the twentieth century there was strong opposition to Roman Catholic attempts to appoint 'native' bishops. At the best, this represented a paternalistic attitude; at the worst, it was blatantly white supremacist. On the other hand, in many areas the chief agents in the dissemination of the Christian message were not missionaries but local converts, often teachers or catechists. From the 1830s, such individuals had been sent as missionaries from island to island in the Pacific, and by the 1840s the church in Polynesia was considerably stronger than that in Australia or New Zealand.

Even where people did not convert to Christian faith themselves, the advent of Christianity often left its mark on local culture and belief. Two different examples of this serve to demonstrate the variety of ways in which this impact could be experienced. In India, debate stimulated by Protestant critiques helped to fuel a reform movement within Hinduism, associated in particular with the founder of the Brahmo Samaj, the social reformer Ram Mohun Roy (1774–1833), who at one stage described himself as a Hindu Unitarian. This was an intellectual current of thought, but at a popular level it was not unknown for families to include Jesus among the deities to whom they offered worship, without actually converting. In South India there had been a longstanding tradition of Christians and Hindus supporting one another's ways of worship by gifts and attendance, and Christian and Hindu places of worship were frequently decorated in similar ways and using similar symbols. Only with the arrival of the CMS in the early nineteenth century did a more exclusive outlook gain ground among the Christian community, which gave rise to an equally exclusive Hindu reaction.

The second example of the impact of Christianity on local cultures is provided by the 'cargo cults' of Australasia and the Western Pacific, now often known as 'adjustment movements'. These enshrined belief in the material and technological superiority of the missionaries, often offering a material version of eschatological hope (especially in cultures which had traditionally associated religious and material well-being, developing complex rituals of gift exchange to express this), and sought to synthesize traditional ways of thinking about the world with aspects of missionary teaching.

The main types of agency

In recent decades missiologists have distinguished between two types of missionary agency, modalities and sodalities. A modality is a church active in mission as a mode of its existence, whereas a sodality is a voluntary society or missionary order within the Church. The latter was the chief vehicle for Western mission during this period, represented by Catholic missionary orders and Protestant voluntary societies (Orthodox mission, such as it was, is covered in Chapter 7).

During the eighteenth century Catholic mission had tended to languish; there were not the dramatic advances into fresh fields which had been seen in the previous two centuries, and the restrictions placed on monastic orders at home meant that they lacked freedom to continue preparing missionary recruits. Supply was also disrupted by the French Revolution and the growth of the Napoleonic empire. 'The vast pool of European religious almost disappeared while the structures of ecclesiastical command lay in fragments.'[2] So, for example, Angola saw the number of priests in the diocese decline from 100 in 1760 to just five by the 1850s. However, 1814 saw the restoration of the Jesuits, thus restoring one of Catholicism's most disciplined and dedicated missionary forces, and 1817 marked the re-establishment of *Propaganda*, through which mission could be strategically planned and directed. As with social action, one of the key roles played by the papacy and the Roman bureaucracy was to ensure a measure of direction, cohesion, and planning in Catholic mission, and Gregory XVI (1831–46) took these responsibilities very seriously. Technically Britain and the United States were both receiving countries so long as they remained under the jurisdiction of *Propaganda*, a status which contrasted with the dominant role played in mission by the Protestant communities of these countries. However, as part of a reform of the Curia, many territories in the Western world were removed from the jurisdiction of *Propaganda* (including Canada, the United States, Britain, and the Netherlands), which was thus left free to focus on areas outside Christendom.

During the century several new orders were founded which were devoted to missionary objectives. The most significant were in Africa, where Cardinal Lavigerie of Algiers founded the White Fathers in 1868 and the White Sisters the following year, in order to establish an indigenous Catholicism. This goal received further expression in the Verona Fathers, founded in 1867 with the objective of creating an African apostolate to evangelize the continent.

In the Protestant sphere, the same problem was evident with mission as had appeared with social engagement: the lack of an overall strategy allowed the appearance of a plethora of societies, each focusing on a particular area. The first was the Particular Baptist Society for the Propagation of the Gospel among the Heathen, founded in October 1792.[3] Its chief progenitor was a shoemaker and pastor from Northamptonshire, William Carey (1761–1834), who a few months earlier had set down the fruits of his researches into the religious condition of each part of the world, and his prescriptions for what Christians could do, in *An Enquiry into the Obligations of Christians to use means for the Conversion of the Heathens*,[4] and then preached a sermon on Isaiah 54.2–3 encouraging Christians to 'expect great things from God' and 'attempt great things for God'. The following year he and a few others sailed for India as missionaries, eventually settling at Serampore, near Calcutta. All this has often been seen as contrasting sharply with the traditional Protestant belief that the conversion of the heathen was God's affair, to be accomplished at the end of time, a belief which explains the famous rebuke Carey received from the elder John Ryland (1723–92), that when God wanted to convert the heathen he would do so without Carey's help. However, I would suggest that what was changing was not only the beliefs of the promoters (though these did change fairly significantly as Calvinism in Britain took on a more outward-looking cast) but also the circumstances to which they were responding: the events surrounding the French Revolution had convinced many Evangelicals that the end-times had now arrived, and that now was the time to turn interest (which had been rising since Jonathan Edwards published his *Humble Attempt* in 1748) into action.

The myth that Protestant mission began with Carey must be rejected; the *Enquiry* shows that he was well aware of the history of mission in the Western Church, and his vision was to see British Christians joining in a tradition of mission which had already become established in Germany as a result of Pietist activity. What was new about his work was the type of agency established to support it – the voluntary society. Founded on the model of a joint-stock trading company, it provided a channel for the growing missionary impetus and ensured that missionaries would receive the necessary back-up in terms of finances, equipment, and strategic planning. The new societies were initially slow to attract widespread interest but in time they became firmly established. By then most Nonconformist homes would have had a collecting box for mission, or taken a missionary periodical.

Societies soon began to appear in numbers.[5] In Britain the London Missionary Society (LMS) was founded in 1795 as an interdenominational body, but soon became mainly Congregational in its makeup. In 1799, the Clapham Sect took a leading role in the founding of the 'Society for Missions to Africa and the East', which later became known as the Church Missionary Society (CMS), to provide a channel for Anglican Evangelicals' interest in missions to the 'heathen' (they also encouraged Anglicans not to cease supporting the older agencies, the SPG and the SPCK, although these had somewhat different priorities and modes of operation). The first North American agency was the interdenominational American Board of Commissioners for Foreign Missions (ABCFM; 1810). The Netherlands Missionary Society was founded in 1797, the Basel Mission in 1815, the Danish Missionary Society in 1821, and the Berlin Missionary Society in 1824. Of course, German-speaking Pietists already had missionary agencies of an older type. It must not be thought that the formation of societies for mission was the exclusive preserve of the Evangelicals. Concurrent with the reinvention of high churchmanship in the 1830s, the SPG changed its focus of operations from ministry to the colonies to mission to the 'heathen', and switched its mode of finance from government grants to voluntary donations. In time, high church societies also made their appearance, most notably the Universities' Mission to Central Africa (1859). British Anglican mission was thus carried out through a range of societies, catering for different areas or different types of churchmanship. The result was that Anglicanism overseas rarely showed the full diversity of Anglicanism at home; one style was usually dominant, sometimes to the exclusion of others.

From the 1830s renewed confessionalism in many Protestant countries meant that the primary focus of mission moved from seeking individual conversions to planting churches, although these were not seen as mutually exclusive. Paradoxically, in Continental Protestantism missions tended to develop independently of churches; there was a parallel network of training institutions, and missionaries were ordained by the society rather than the Church.

During the middle of the century, interest in mission reached a plateau. Apart from the tendency to be preoccupied with internal controversies at home and the need of the urban unchurched, there was no longer quite the same sense of pioneering, and the postmillennial hope was giving way to a more pessimistic premillennialism. Experience was also showing that conversions were not occurring in the numbers that had been expected, and there was growing dissatisfaction with the approach that sought to civilize a people before Christianizing them. From the later 1860s, however, a second wave of missionary interest occurred, led by a new type of mission which reflected changing priorities and eschatologies – the 'faith missions', so called because they expected their workers to depend on God for financial and other provision rather than guaranteeing it themselves.[6] This enabled them to operate with the minimum of support structures, and thus made it easy for new missions to be founded for reaching particular territories.

Individuals had anticipated aspects of 'faith' thinking, most notably Edward Irving, who in 1824 had argued in a controversial sermon to the LMS that missionaries should go forth without visible means of support, trusting in God to provide for their needs, and the Brethren missionary Anthony Norris Groves (1795–1853), who put such views into practice as he served in Persia and India from 1830. But the most influential mediator of such views was Groves's brother-in-law, George Müller (1805–98), who founded a group of orphan homes in Bristol from 1834 on a 'faith' basis; interestingly, his primary motive was not humanitarian but apologetic – to demonstrate the reality of God to an increasingly sceptical age. All three men manifested a heightened supernaturalism which was characteristic of Romantic thought.

The largest of the faith missions was the China Inland Mission (CIM), founded in 1865 by the Englishman James Hudson Taylor (1832–1905). His own background was among the Methodists and the Brethren, but candidates were welcome from all denominations. In China he established a form of 'comity' (see below) whereby missionaries of particular denominational backgrounds were assigned to particular regions of the country. Among other things this resulted in the creation of the Anglican bishopric of Western China in 1895, to which a CIM missionary, W.W. Cassels, was appointed. The mission's force had grown to 641 by that year, comprising half of all Protestant missionaries in China. Taylor encouraged his missionaries to adopt Chinese dress, and his methodology was influenced by his friendship with John L. Nevius (1829–93), an American Presbyterian missionary who advocated the maximum measure of self-determination for the newly planted churches (see below).

Faith missions came to be dominated by a premillennial eschatology, and this affected their conception of the missionary task. They did not expect the conversion of the world, but affirmed the command to preach to it. Thus they were less concerned to concentrate on responsive areas, and indeed pioneered work in many previously unreached territories. But their pessimism meant that they had little time for adjuncts which could be seen as mere 'improvement': an educated sinner remained a lost sinner, and his deepest need thus remained unmet. Since human society was headed for judgement, there was no point trying to shore it up. And because the Second Coming might be expected any minute, long-term strategic planning tended to be looked down on in favour of a more short-term approach, which undervalued the importance of gaining a thorough understanding of local cultures and thought-patterns. That being so, recruits did not need an extensive training, nor did they need to be ordained or possess adequate intellectual qualifications: anybody with a divine call and good health could participate in the work of winning souls.

The later nineteenth century saw a narrowing of missionary vision as Evangelicals influenced by the world-denying spirituality of the Keswick Conventions began to appear on the mission fields in large numbers. From the beginning Keswick included a prominent missionary focus and many dated their 'call' to service abroad from such events. Their mission strategy focused on evangelism and Bible translation; medical work was acceptable as an adjunct to evangelism, but the establishment of indigenous churches and leadership took a lower priority than it had for the likes of Henry Venn (1796–1873), son of John Venn and secretary of the CMS from 1841 to 1872. Part of the reason for this was theological, in that they saw God's purposes in the world as centred on the salvation of individuals and believed that by taking the gospel to all peoples they were hastening the return of Christ (cf. Matthew 24.14), but there was also an element of belief in white superiority. The years from 1880 to 1914 may be seen as the golden age of 'high imperialism', when Western empires sought to divide the globe into spheres of influence in a manner reminiscent of the fifteenth-century division between Spain and Portugal adjudicated by the papacy. Indigenous peoples were often despised, and it was deemed unlikely that they would be able to assume church leadership in the foreseeable future. Not only so, but indigenous cultures were frequently condemned wholesale. What was needed was a process of civilizing (by which they meant Europeanizing) converts.

As well as the denominational societies and the faith missions, a third type of agency which developed during the nineteenth century was the mission with a specific objective, whether in terms of the work it did or the stratum of society it sought to reach. Some of the earliest missions of this type were involved with Bible translation and distribution. Because much missionary enterprise focused on areas of the world whose languages had not been reduced to writing or else had not seen many works printed, translation work was of primary importance. This was reinforced by the principle that 'faith comes by hearing, and hearing by the Word of God' (Romans 10.17), which had been emphasized by sixteenth-century Reformers, seventeenth-century Puritans, and eighteenth-century Moravians and Evangelicals alike. The first such society founded for a specific missionary objective was the British and Foreign Bible Society (1804). Not only did the advent of the book have a major impact on societies which had hitherto relied exclusively on oral means of linguistic communication, but Protestants believed that the Bible possessed an inherent power to convert open-minded readers, and asserted that their belief had repeatedly been confirmed by events. For example, in Madagascar, where the LMS had arrived in 1820, severe persecution broke out from 1835 to 1861 under Queen Ranavalona which necessitated the withdrawal of foreign missionaries. Nevertheless, the Church grew markedly during their absence because it had the Malagasy New Testament. By contrast, although Catholic orders such as the White Fathers produced able linguists and they often demonstrated a sensitivity to local culture which was superior to that of the Protestants, Catholic translations of the Bible were rare in missionary work.

Other such missions were engaged in medical work, often seen as a 'handmaid to the gospel'. Early generations of missionaries practised medicine as part of their work; they did not claim to be professionals, but it offered a way of demonstrating a concern for the whole person and thus commending their message. From the 1890s, however, with the trend towards professionalization in medicine, specialist medical missions appeared.

Yet other missions focused on reaching adherents of one particular faith. Christian mission has always been most successful among those societies which lacked a highly developed religious system such as Islam or Buddhism. While it was necessary, therefore, for missionaries to develop an apologetic engaging with established religious traditions, only Islam and Judaism saw agencies founded with the specific intent of reaching their adherents. We have already noted the eschatological motivation behind mission to the Jewish people; here we shall look briefly at work among Muslims. Optimism regarding the possibility of converting Muslims by means of rational argument and debate gave way as the nineteenth century progressed to a sense of apprehension at its expansion, especially in Africa, and increasing pessimism concerning the ability of the Eastern churches ever to serve as missionary agencies to surrounding Muslim populations. However, mission to Islamic peoples received a renewed impetus from the 1870s, as resurgent interest in prophecy combined with political crises in the Ottoman domains and extension of British rule in Muslim parts of Africa. Major conferences on Christian mission among Muslims took place at Cairo (1906) and Lucknow (1911). Agencies appeared which sought to reach parts of North Africa or the Middle East which were largely or exclusively Muslim.

By the end of the century, many missionaries were coming to a different understanding of the relationship between Christianity and other religions. Lacking the centuries of reflection on the subject which Catholicism had had, it took Protestants some while to develop a nuanced approach, although it is noteworthy that in India European missionaries rapidly deepened their grasp of existing cultures and religious traditions. Initially these traditions were regarded as idolatrous and as a degeneration from the original knowledge of God possessed by all human beings; their adherents were seen as lost and in darkness without the knowledge of Christ; this acted as a powerful motivating factor in drawing many to the mission field. Consequently, many missionaries sought to eradicate traditional religious customs and beliefs, although they were usually unsuccessful in this because converts tended to modify the missionary message in line with existing beliefs. In time, an approach developed which began with the insistence on the need to study indigenous traditions in order to understand the mindset of the local populace, and gradually some missionaries adopted the view that there was much of value in these traditions which should be conserved. It was from the early twentieth-century Indian context that the Scot J. N. Farquhar (1861–1929) elaborated the theory that all religions were to some degree divinely inspired, as preparing their respective adherents for the reception of the Christian gospel. Christianity should therefore be presented as the fulfilment of the aspirations contained in other faiths, and the best mode of doing this was dialogue rather than proclamation. With this often went the idea that the missionary task was not so much to convert individuals as to see society permeated with Christian values, a priority which entailed focusing educational work on the future opinion-formers rather than the masses.

The missionaries

At the start of the century few missionaries came from the middle classes or the clergy. For much of its early existence the CMS was dependent on German Lutheran personnel, no suitable British candidates being available. But as the imperial vision caught on with the population at large, British middle-class Christians began in the 1840s to consider a missionary vocation in the way that some of their compatriots contemplated a career in colonial administration: 'while a generation earlier the missionary had been at home an object of ridicule or mistrust, a low-class religious fanatic attempting the absurd if not the undesirable, now he was starting to be seen instead as the hero of both religious and secular achievement'.[7] This was reinforced by the impact of Moody's campaigns and the formation in the United States in 1888 of the Student Volunteer Movement for Foreign Missions (SVM), and its establishment in Britain in 1892. This agency fostered the study of missions by groups of students and others, encouraging individuals to pledge themselves to go overseas as missionaries.

Western accounts of the expansion of the Church have traditionally focused on the role played by white missionaries, but they were not always the only, nor even the most important, messengers of the gospel (hence relatively few are mentioned in this chapter). In early nineteenth-century Africa freed slaves played an important role in establishing Anglicanism. Much missionary work of various denominations in Liberia and Sierra Leone was undertaken by former slaves. Other non-Westerners who were active in mission were the catechists; Protestant and Catholic, active in much of Africa and Asia, they were already part of the local culture and understood its thought-forms, and so were able to communicate the Christian message to best effect.

Missionary strategy

Every society had to choose where it would work. For some the decision was influenced by knowledge of certain parts of the world then in the public eye. Captain Cook's travel diaries were widely read at the end of the eighteenth century and helped to draw attention to the needs of the Pacific islands; the LMS sent its first workers to Tahiti in 1797, partly because of this awareness and partly because communication networks in that part of the world appeared to be more reliable – an essential both for keeping the workers supplied with necessities and relaying news of the work. Other groups focused on India because of the strong links between Britain and this part of its developing empire. Conveniently, there was relatively little overlap between evangelical societies during the first few decades of the modern missionary movement. Thereafter, expansion was aided by improvements in transport (notably the development of the steamship) and peace between European nations for much of the century, and stimulated by the widening of imperial horizons. As territories filled up and competition between different denominations began to occur, it was increasingly recognized that the existence of different denominations in the 'mission field' presented a major obstacle to the acceptance of the Christian message by local people. The principle of 'comity' was therefore developed from the 1850s, according to which conferences of missionaries assigned different parts of a country to different missions or denominations. It was applied primarily in Asia (notably in India, China, and the Philippines), but also in parts of Africa and Latin America. So long as the majority of denominations agreed to abide by such agreements, the idea worked well enough as long as populations were stable, but once large-scale migration to cities began to occur, as happened in India, it broke down. Similar arrangements had developed from 1830 in the Pacific islands; they were aided by the pattern of Christianization in the area, which often saw Christianity being adopted as the religion of the people after a chief had declared allegiance to the new religion. In such circumstances, it often merged with traditional customs and strengthened traditional patterns of authority.

Protestants generally lacked the accumulated experience which Catholics had gained in dealing with such issues as how to help converts from other cultures and religious traditions fit into the Church. In addition postmillennial optimism may have made some of them underestimate the magnitude of the challenges they faced;[8] to this may be added the belief, increasingly widespread as the century wore on, in the superiority of Western civilization. Nevertheless, a great deal of thinking went on concerning the objectives of mission and the best ways of achieving them.

For example, Carey's strategy included preaching the gospel, Bible translation (he and his Serampore colleagues Marshman and Ward were responsible for translations of the whole Bible into six languages and the New Testament or portions into about thirty more, though many translations later had to be redone), establishment of local churches as early as possible, study of local cultures, and the development of an indigenous ministry. Developing a mission strategy involved a delicate balancing act because of the various interests which had to be considered: in this instance home supporters disapproved of the time spent on studying Hindu culture and translating Sanskrit religious writings, while Carey and his co-workers clashed with local culture over the custom of *sati* (the burning of a widow on her husband's funeral pyre), which they were instrumental in getting abolished in 1829.

Once churches began to be formed, the question arose as to the degree to which these should be independent of the agency through whom they had come into being. A seminal thinker here was Henry Venn. He advocated the 'euthanasia of missions', seeing them as scaffolding which could be dismantled once a fully functioning local church had been built and the missionaries had moved on. His three principles of self-government, self-support, and self-propagation were to be widely espoused in theory, partly because white missionaries faced language barriers and also frequently succumbed to an enervating climate and deadly diseases. However, they often proved more difficult to turn into practical reality and there was something of a drawing back from them after about 1870 when the shortage of missionaries eased greatly (partly because of the increased number of recruits and partly because medical advances ensured that they survived far longer) and the development of indigenous leadership appeared to be occurring more slowly than had been expected. Growing confidence in the superiority of Western civilization militated against a recognition of the validity of adopting local ways of 'doing church' which was implicit in Venn's model. In North American circles, Venn's approach found a parallel in the thinking of Rufus Anderson (1796–1880), secretary of the ABCFM, who advocated the 'three-self' model and insisted on disconnecting evangelism from the process of 'civilizing' non-Western peoples.

A later parallel to this approach was formulated by Bruno Gutmann (1876–1966), who served with the Leipzig Mission in what is now Tanzania from 1902. He developed a strategy in which the traditional structures and outlook of a people group were incorporated as far as possible into the way the Church developed in that area.

Evangelical missionaries sought to make individual converts and subsequently to gather them into churches, and then to establish a recognized leadership. In consequence they often lacked a strong sense of the wider Church, being concerned primarily with the work in which they were personally involved. This contributed to a tension in Anglican practice between the voluntary missionary society and episcopal church government; missionaries did not always welcome the establishment of a local hierarchy, fearing that it would lead to restrictions on their work. Such a tension mirrored that in Catholicism between the missionary orders and the bishops or the Roman bureaucracy. Venn, like most Evangelicals of his time, believed that the episcopate should emerge locally. The bishop was to be the keystone rather than the foundation of the indigenous church. High church societies, however, preferred to send out a hierarchy, including a bishop, and establish a worshipping community into which converts could be gathered, often as a community – not dissimilar to the Orthodox approach as practised in Siberia. Catholic strategy was in some respects closer to that of the Evangelicals.

In a number of areas local culture dictated that women could only be reached by other women. In India, for example, the number of women serving as Protestant missionaries grew from 479 in 1881 to 1,174 in 1900, many serving with 'zenana' missions such as the Church of England Zenana Missionary Society (1880). These were women's auxiliaries closely related to existing societies, seeking to reach women in cultures where the sexes were segregated. Such agencies were one way in which many women found greater opportunities for service than were open to them at home.

Missionaries not infrequently concluded that indigenous peoples had no religious tradition, and therefore presented a blank slate on which Christianity could easily be inculcated. To use an anachronistic image, indigenous religious traditions frequently failed to show up on the missionary radar screen, since they were looking for such phenomena as regular corporate worship. It was to be late in the nineteenth century before missionaries began to study what have often been called 'animistic' traditions seriously, and the newly emerging science of anthropology was to the fore in this development. This failure affected not only the presentation of the message, but the missionary understanding of the ways in which local people understood and appropriated it. From the sixteenth-century Philippines onwards, it was among such traditions that Christianity made its biggest advances, but also where it was most prone to cross the boundary between inculturation and syncretism, popular Catholicism in Latin America being a case in point.

Overall, the tension evident at home between reforming society and seeking individual conversions replicated itself overseas. If we regard Pietism and Evangelicalism as responses to the problem of nominal religion within Christendom, we can see that missions with roots in these movements might well be hard-pressed to choose in their priorities between the creation of a society permeated by assumptions derived from Christian theology and the establishment of voluntary churches comprised of converted individuals. The decision was all the more difficult because such individuals, by converting, would move outside their existing world of thought, and need a replacement in which to exist. The dilemma was resolved by some agencies through a shift in strategy which began to be evident around 1900, from converting individuals to transforming society. It can be seen as reflecting the renewed stress on the corporate which underlay the Social Gospel movement, and a good example of this is provided by Protestant mission in India. In reaction, other societies pursued a more narrowly evangelistic approach.

Missions and colonization[9]

Whereas in the late eighteenth century mission was the preserve of a small minority of enthusiasts, by about 1840 it had assumed a place at the heart of Protestant and Catholic church life. This transformation owed something to the contemporary interest in colonization (in the fifty years from 1860, over 7.6 million people emigrated from Britain and Ireland), but the relationships between that process and Christianity were complex.

Far from being the handmaids of imperial expansion, missions were guilty in the eyes of some churchmen of harbouring men with dangerous opinions. In the tense climate of 1790s Britain, the Church of Scotland's General Assembly in 1796 refused to give official approval to an evangelical scheme for sending out missionaries supported by local societies: the Moderates labelled its promoters as political radicals (there was good reason for this, since some English Dissenting missionaries were known to be radical or republican in their political views) but more fundamentally they argued that a certain level of civilization was a necessary prerequisite for the Christianization of any particular society. (By contrast, Evangelicals were at this point more likely to derive their sense of timing for initiating mission from a belief that biblical prophecy was being fulfilled in current events.) When the Kirk did become active in mission, a primary focus was India, because it was believed to be sufficiently civilized and thus likely to produce suitable Christian leaders. Education thus assumed primary importance in the Church of Scotland's Indian work.

A major factor in the move to colonize was commercial, especially the need to open up new markets and to source materials. The alliance between Christianity and commerce began as part of the anti-slavery campaign: as formulated by the British Evangelical Thomas Fowell Buxton the idea was that local populations could achieve economic independence through commercial development, thus obviating the need for chiefs to sell members of their tribe or prisoners of war into slavery. Economic development, it was hoped, would break the power of local rulers as effectively as industrialization had diminished the power of the British aristocracy. At the conclusion of a return visit to Britain in 1857, the missionary explorer David Livingstone (1813–73) told his hearers, 'I go back to Africa to make an open path for commerce and Christianity.'[10] Many followed him, and his call led to the formation of the Universities' Mission to Central Africa.

A different form of alliance between missions and commerce appeared in China, where the Opium War of 1839–42 had been concluded by a treaty which allowed the British free access to the Chinese market. Missionaries were guaranteed protection, and a treaty with the French promised that Catholic buildings would be restored to the Church.

Missionaries had already begun to investigate possibilities for opening work in China, and Catholics found a community of perhaps 200,000 remaining from earlier work. Chinese Catholics were not always keen on being reintegrated into the global Catholic network and giving up their autonomy; the ultramontane form which that network was taking did not help matters in a nation which had long regarded itself as superior to all others.

The advance of mission as part of the expansion of Western spheres of political and economic influence did not always proceed smoothly. European interests were not always sympathetic to the presence of missionaries, fearing that attempts to convert local peoples would pro- voke civil unrest. The British East India Company, which ruled India until 1858, would not allow missionaries to work (except as chaplains to the expatriate communities) in its areas of jurisdiction until 1813. Often they found it easier to work in areas outside colonial control, and so the earliest Baptist missionaries settled in the Danish enclave of Serampore. Missionaries were not infrequently thorns in the side of colonial govern- ments, as in the West Indies, where it was feared that missionary work would lead to insurrection. A *cause célèbre* occurred in Demerara in 1823, when John Smith, a missionary with the LMS, was imprisoned on the charge of fomenting rebellion among the slave community; he was sentenced to death but died from tuberculosis before the sentence could be carried out. In Jamaica missionary work was fiercely opposed because of the egalitarian principles on which congregations were run, culminating in the 'Baptist War' of 1831; the result was that missionaries who had begun determined to know nothing except the gospel became advocates of abolition in order to remove hindrances to its spread, and so found themselves in opposition to the dominant 'plantocracy'. Much of the missioning of the West Indies was in fact done by black Evangelicals from the United States; as early as 1842 Jamaican Baptists achieved independence from the Baptist Missionary Society, and the following year they began to send out missionaries to West Africa. However, appropria- tion of Christianity by the slave population did not always conform to evangelical norms, and movements such as the Spiritual Baptists com- bined aspects of black African religious traditions with Evangelicalism in a manner which was condemned as syncretistic.

Problems arising from the association of missionaries with Western interference in internal affairs might take a while to show themselves, but the effects could be devastating. The perceived association of Christianity with the Chinese opium trade, which the West sought to safeguard in the 1842 treaty, and on whose communication network missionaries often depended, did little to commend the Western religion to the Chinese, although the CIM consistently opposed the opium trade. Neither did a treaty of 1860 which ended further conflict over the opium trade and secured Protestant freedom to establish bases for work beyond the entry ports. (Missionaries poured in, and by 1890 there were over 700 Catholics and 1,300 Protestants: it was believed by many that the conversion of China would help to bring in the millennial reign of Christ.) Christianity was seen as undermining established traditions and threatening socio-religious harmony, a perspective which gained plausibility as a result of the Taiping Rebellion of 1849–64 in which as many as 40 million Chinese died: this was inspired by the 'God Worshippers' Society', an anti-idolatry movement which drew on some Christian concepts and whose ideas were confused with mainstream Christianity by many Chinese.[11] Sadly, nationalist feeling culminated in the Boxer (or 'Society of Harmonious Fists') riots of 1899–1900, in which missionaries were a particular focus of anti-European and anti-modernization sentiment. Possibly 30,000 Catholics were killed, along with 3,500 Orthodox and not quite 2,000 Protestants, figures which reflect the numerical dominance of Catholicism in Chinese Christianity.[12]

On the other hand, the opening up of countries to Western influence could work in favour of mission. When Japan began opening up to the West from the 1860s Catholic missionaries were astounded to discover a surviving community which, though it lacked a priesthood and manifested a somewhat distorted understanding of Catholic belief and practice, had nevertheless maintained the faith for 250 years since the expulsion of earlier missionaries. Of 30,000 people, at least half preferred to maintain their separate existence. Protestant mission proved successful principally because many converts had the makings of wise and zealous leaders and were of good social standing. Among them were such figures as Kanzo Uchimura (1861–1930), though he reacted against aspects of mission theology in his 'No-Church' movement (1893).

Korean attempts to maintain isolation from the outside world meant that Christianity was repeatedly persecuted until the 1870s. Once again the opening of frontiers was soon followed by the appearance of Protestant missionaries, although (as with Catholicism) the groundwork was laid by Koreans converted as a result of missionary work in Manchuria, beyond the country's borders. But, by contrast with other countries, Christianity became a means of expressing patriotism during Japanese occupation from 1910 to 1945. This identification laid some of the foundation for the rapid growth of the Korean Christian community during the twentieth century, but it was also important that in Korea the Church quickly achieved a high degree of autonomy from missionary direction. One of the chief architects of this policy was Nevius, whose strategy paralleled that of Venn and Anderson; from 1890 his approach was adopted by the main Protestant communities, and spectacular success followed, although this was not all due to methodological factors. As summarized by Neill,[13] it had four main planks:

1 Each Christian should 'abide in the calling wherein he was found', support himself by his own work, and be a witness for Christ by life and word in his own neighbourhood.

2 Church methods and machinery should be developed only in so far as the Korean church was able to take responsibility for the same.

3 The Church itself should call out for whole-time work those who seemed best qualified for it, and whom the Church was able to support.

4 Churches were to be built in native style, and by the Christians themselves from their own resources.

Another factor was the involvement of missionaries in education, which ensured that Christianity was seen as progressive by those disillusioned by traditional attitudes and convinced that Westernization was the way forward.

We must be careful not to over-simplify the relationship between missions and colonial expansion. For one thing, missionaries did not restrict themselves to areas being colonized by their government; for another, they might either precede or follow that government's establishment of colonial jurisdiction. They could take a range of attitudes towards that jurisdiction, ranging from uncritical support (rarer than might be thought, though late-nineteenth-century German missionaries received state assistance, colonization being portrayed as a Christian duty) through to principled opposition. Nevertheless, the conjunction is noteworthy of a renewed sense of missionary vision sparked off by Keswick and the SVM and the 'scramble for Africa' which resulted from the treaty concluded at Berlin in 1885 by which Africa was apportioned between Britain, France, Germany, Portugal, and other European nations. A similar 'scramble' took place in Asia, also involving the United States (culminating in their annexation of the Philippines in 1898). Colonization offered opportunities for missionary expansion just at the time when there were more candidates coming forward to mission agencies. Some of the new wave of missionaries shared their nation's imperial ambitions to a considerable extent, though they might hold colonial authorities accountable for the exercise of their governmental responsibilities. Thus Lavigerie stated on one occasion: 'We are working for France',[14] an outlook which was reciprocated in the willingness of the anti-clerical Third Republic (1871–1940) to look with favour on the work of French missionaries and orders overseas. In the case of British missionaries it was argued that the fact that providence had decreed that Britain, a nation founded on Protestant faith and civil liberty, should possess a great empire entailed a responsibility to spread the gospel in British dominions. By this point some British missionaries had come to view colonization as the most humanitarian approach on the basis that it guaranteed equality for all indigenous peoples and averted the possibility of rule by less sympathetic regimes.

For some, the expansionism of colonization had its spiritual counterpart in the famous watchword of the SVM, 'The evangelization of the world in this generation'. In the relatively peaceful late Victorian and Edwardian years, people really believed that this was possible, and laid plans to achieve it. This, like the faith missions, was a missionary thrust fuelled by hope, although for some it became a hope dependent on human achievement rather than on the return of Christ. Neill argues that in fact the watchword meant something else: 'that each generation of Christians bears responsibility for the contemporary generation of non-Christians in the world, and that it is the business of each such generation of Christians to see to it, as far as lies within its power, that the Gospel is clearly preached to every single non-Christian in the same generation'.[15] However, the watchword was popularized by A.T. Pierson (1837–1911), an ardent North American premillennialist who expected the imminent return of Christ, and it would seem at least plausible that he had in mind the fulfilment of Matthew 24.14 ('the gospel must first be preached to all nations') by his own generation as a means of hastening the Second Coming.

One of the consequences of the establishment of colonial jurisdiction in a territory was that missionaries tended to establish a network of institutions into which they withdrew, partly because government agencies saw missions as providing the infrastructure for education and medical care which they were unable or unwilling to do – imperial expansion was often carried out on a shoestring. This meant that they did not engage as thoroughly or consistently with the local cultures. It was in such situations, then, that indigenous teachers, catechists, and evangelists came into their own.

Of course, colonial government was not the only type of authority with which missionaries had to establish working relationships. There were local rulers, whether independent or subordinate to colonial powers, and plenty of scope for misunderstanding existed in such relationships. Missionaries might value royal protection, but local monarchs might see one function of missionaries as helping to legitimate their regime and so be unwilling to accept criticism of practices such as human sacrifice which the missionaries deemed immoral. In much of Southern Africa missionaries might have seen themselves as messengers, but the locals would have viewed them as rainmakers, this being a traditional function of holy men. Should missionaries go along with the expectations, pray for rain, and risk purchasing success at the price of misunderstanding, or should they resist and risk marginalizing themselves or incurring active hostility and so closing the door to their message?

The emergence of indigenous churches

One of the earliest Anglican attempts to implement Venn's idea of the self-governing local church took place in the Niger delta in West Africa.[16] In 1864 a Yoruba, Samuel Ajayi Crowther, was appointed bishop of those areas beyond British colonial jurisdiction (the latter remaining under an English bishop). It can be argued that Crowther was a classic example of the dedicated man in the wrong place, as he was ministering among a different people group rather than being appointed to work among his own people (the missionaries there did not want him), in an area which had little to bind it together except a river, without adequate logistical support, and in the face of the missionaries' refusal to accept his authority as bishop. But what really brought the experiment down was the arrival of a clutch of youthful recruits from England in the late 1880s. Influenced by a heady mix of Keswick theology and high imperialism, they adopted a starkly negative attitude towards local culture, and lacked sympathy with Crowther's approach and the shortcomings which they found in the local set-up, such as the deployment of men who were, in the missionaries' opinion, not sufficiently godly to serve as leaders. Their critical reports home led the CMS to conclude that the experiment had been a failure. Crowther retired in 1891, deeply saddened by what had transpired, and it was to be 1951 before another African was appointed as an Anglican diocesan bishop. For many, these events demonstrated that Africans were not ready for leadership, and the development of the Church towards maturity was retarded. Indeed, most societies abandoned the development of an indigenous ministry around this time; social Darwinism was doubtless a factor in this.

For many local Christians such events led them to conclude that the way forward lay in forming their own independent churches, albeit on European models. From 1872 until about 1920, therefore, the first wave of African-instituted churches began to emerge in South and (from 1888) West Africa in protest at continued white domination of the mission-founded churches. All Protestant denominations were affected by this phenomenon but the Roman Catholics saw few such bodies emerge. The Orthodox saw none, because they were not active in mission in Africa until the mid-twentieth century; in any case, they already possessed sound African credentials in the form of the ancient Ethiopian Orthodox Church, which served as an inspiration for many of the new groups.[17] Not only had it maintained its independence and resisted excessive foreign influence, but in 1896 the Ethiopian nation defeated Italian forces, providing political inspiration for Africans throughout the continent. The church's suspicious nationalism, which had made it resistant to other forms of Christianity ever since Catholic attempts to bring it under Rome in the early seventeenth century, enabled it to maintain a distinctively

African form of Christianity which served to inspire other movements seeking to inculturate the faith.[18] Furthermore, it was believed to be mentioned in Scripture (Psalm 68.31: 'Ethiopia shall stretch out her hands to God'), and it had long claimed Solomonic roots for its monarchy, based on the story of the Queen of Sheba's visit to the Hebrew king (1 Kings 10.1–13).

Not surprisingly, these locally instituted churches were often known as Ethiopian churches, 'Ethiopian' also being used as a generic term for all black Africans. They remained recognizably orthodox in doctrine and betrayed their denominational roots in their practice, but made more room for indigenous patterns of leadership and cultural values, as in their toleration of polygamy.[19] A second wave of locally instituted churches with a rather different shape and priorities, sometimes known as Zionist, would emerge from the 1950s.

Among the most important examples were the Harrists of the Gold Coast (Ghana). Around 1913 a Liberian Episcopalian, William Wade Harris (c.1865–1928), began to preach widely in West Africa upon his release from imprisonment for treason. In a vision the archangel Gabriel commissioned him as God's final prophet and instructed him to abandon European dress; he adopted the prophet's garb of a white robe and sandals. His message majored on monotheism, biblical authority, observance of the Ten Commandments, destruction of idolatrous fetishes, prohibition of adultery, and observance of Sunday as a day of rest and worship. He baptized tens of thousands, of whom some joined existing churches and some set up their own, and he exhorted converts to await direction from the missionaries whom he prophesied would come; ten years later Methodist missionaries arrived to find 45,000 following Harris's teachings. In 1998 this body joined the World Council of Churches (WCC).

Africa was not the only area to see locally instituted Christian bodies appearing. Two quite large examples were founded in the Philippines, in the wake of American colonization from 1898 and the period of unrest which followed. The Philippine Independent Church (1902) began as a schism from the Roman Catholic Church led by a priest, Gregorio Aglipay, and grew to 1.4 million by 1918. It adopted non-Trinitarian theology for a period before returning to traditional belief and entering into communion with the Episcopal Church in the USA. The non-Trinitarian Iglesia ni Christo (founded by Felix Manalo in 1912) has grown to several million; its members vote *en bloc* in presidential elections and its impressive church buildings create a strong and prosperous image in the public eye.

Edinburgh 1910[20]

As early as 1806 Carey had expressed the hope that a global conference of missionaries could be called at a convenient location such as the Cape of Good Hope; a similar proposal for 1810 was made by a Dutch missionary to South Africa with the LMS, Johannes van der Kemp (1747–1811). It was to be over a century before Carey's dream became a reality. Ecumenical conferences took place in New York (1854, 1900), Liverpool (1860), and London (1854, 1878, 1888). The importance of Edinburgh, therefore, was not that it was the first such conference (it was not), but that it was meticulously prepared for under the leadership of John R. Mott (1865–1955),[21] that it included a wider range of delegates than any previous conference, and that it appointed a continuation committee which would develop into the International Missionary Council (IMC; 1921), one of the main wings of the modern ecumenical movement. The intent of the conference was to enable mission leaders to consult together and formulate agreed strategies in response to the issues then deemed most pressing, and to develop a deeper sense of unity, both spiritually and in terms of practical co-operation.

As for the representation at the conference, the first thing to note is that it was drawn from missionary societies, not from churches. Second, the conference marked the start of Anglo-Catholic involvement in ecumenism. To secure their involvement, it was agreed that South America would not be regarded as a mission field from which delegates should be invited; the underlying division of the world on which this decision rested was that of evangelized and unevangelized areas.[22] There were no Roman Catholic or Orthodox delegates. Third, the conference was dominated by the Anglo-American axis: only 17 delegates were from non-Western backgrounds. But change was in the air. A moving and at the time controversial plea was made at the conference by V.S. Azariah, who in 1912 would become the first Indian Anglican bishop (of Dornakal): calling for Indian and European Christian workers to relate to one another as equals, he urged the Western world to send not labourers but friends. His call for partnership was, as we shall see, some time in being realized, but in time it would become the dominant way of understanding the relationship.

Overall, the nineteenth century saw Christianity put down roots in most parts of the world. Yet the initiative in expansion was still very much with Western missions, and global Christianity tended to be viewed through Western interpretative lenses and expressed in Western forms, certainly as far as officially sanctioned versions were concerned. Indigenization had begun but in many areas did not come to maturity until the following century, as Western influence declined and non-Western churches grew in confidence. That will be the leading theme of the third section of the book.

Questions for thought

1 If you are familiar with the story of Christian expansion in Northern Europe during the seventh to tenth centuries, compare and contrast the pattern of Christianization with that which operated in parts of the Pacific and elsewhere during the nineteenth century.

2 What do you see as the pros and cons of Protestant and Catholic ways of organizing for mission?

3 Review the various approaches to mission strategy which we have examined in this chapter. In which types of social and cultural context do you think each would have been most or least effective?

4 In what ways did eschatology shape missionary strategy and expectations during this period? How would you describe the interplay between eschatological belief and an imperially orientated worldview?

5 Compare and contrast the locally instituted movements emerging in Africa with those in the Philippines or even in nineteenth-century Britain.

6 The founding of the interdenominational London Missionary Society in 1795 was hailed as 'the funeral of bigotry'. Was this ever a realistic hope? What factors conspired to extinguish it, and what rekindled it?

Further reading

Norman Etherington (ed.), 2005, *Missions and Empire*, Oxford History of the British Empire Companion Series, Oxford: Oxford University Press.

Sheridan Gilley and Brian Stanley (eds), 2006, *Cambridge History of Christianity*, vol. 8: *World Christianities c.1815–c.1914*, Cambridge: Cambridge University Press, chs 26–7, 34.

Stephen Neill (revised by Owen Chadwick), 1964, 1986, *A History of Christian Missions*, The Pelican History of the Church 6, Harmondsworth: Pelican, chs 8–11.

Andrew Porter, 2004, *Religion versus Empire? British Protestant Missionaries and Overseas Expansion*, Manchester: Manchester University Press.

Brian Stanley, 1991, *The Bible and the Flag: Protestant Missions and British Imperialism in the Nineteenth and Twentieth Centuries*, Leicester: Apollos.

Brian Stanley (ed.), 2001, *Christian Missions and the Enlightenment*, Grand Rapids, MI: Eerdmans.

Notes

1 For key dates in nineteenth-century mission listed by country, see Franklin H. Littell, 2001, *Historical Atlas of Christianity*, 2nd edn, London: Continuum, pp. 358–63.

2 Adrian Hastings, 1994, *The Church in Africa 1450–1950*, Oxford History of the Christian Church, Oxford: Clarendon, p. 195.

3 The Methodist Thomas Coke had put forward a 'Plan of the Society for the Establishment of Missions among the Heathens' in 1783, and himself led groups of missionaries overseas from 1786, but he bore the primary responsibility for the direction and financing of the work himself; the Wesleyans did not found a denominational missionary society until 1818, though a denominational committee (headed by Coke) existed from 1804.

4 Carey's *Enquiry* is online at: http://www.wmcarey.edu/carey/enquiry/enquiry.html.

5 For a list by country of Protestant societies and Catholic missionary orders with dates of founding, see Littell, *Historical Atlas*, pp. 354–6.

6 On faith missions, see Klaus Fiedler, 1994, *The Story of Faith Missions*, Oxford: Regnum Lynx.

7 Hastings, *Africa*, p. 243.

8 A paradigmatic example for many was the *Life of David Brainerd* by the postmillennialist Jonathan Edwards, which portrayed Brainerd's vernacular preaching among the Indians as resulting in immediate conversions. This influential narrative doubtless led others working elsewhere to entertain similar expectations.

9 A landmark discussion of the relationship between mission, colonization and the growth of empires, as well as the scholarly debate, is Stanley, *Bible and Flag*.

10 As quoted by Elizabeth Isichei, 1995, *A History of Christianity in Africa: From Antiquity to the Present*, Grand Rapids, MI, and Lawrenceville, NJ: Eerdmans and Africa World Press, p. 138.

11 For an accessible brief account, see David Chidester, 2001, *Christianity: A Global History*, London: Penguin, pp. 476–82.

12 Unusually, the China Inland Mission (to which 79 of the 188 missionaries and children killed belonged) rejected the offer of compensation following the riots, believing that in not requiring this it could demonstrate a Christ-like spirit.

13 Neill, *History of Christian Missions*, p. 343.

14 David Bosch, 1991, *Transforming Mission: Paradigm Shifts in Theology of Mission*, American Society of Missiology Series 16, Maryknoll, NY: Orbis, p. 304.

15 Neill, *History of Christian Missions*, p. 394.

16 The first ordination of a black Anglican clergyman, Philip Quaque, took place in England in 1765, for ministry in the Gold Coast (Ghana).

17 On Ethiopian Orthodoxy, see Christine Chaillot, 2003, *The Ethiopian Orthodox Tewahedo Church Tradition*, Paris: Inter-Orthodox Dialogue.

18 As in the Middle East, Ethiopian encounters with nineteenth-century Protestantism were not positive. The CMS, who arrived in 1830, aroused hostility

by their declared intent to purify the church by disseminating the Scriptures and convincing the Ethiopians of their errors (in particular that of Marian devotion); later, around 1860, a reform movement emerged in Eritrea, in which Orthodox clergy and laity rejected certain practices such as Masses for the dead, and taught a doctrine of justification by faith, under Swedish Lutheran influence. Forced into exile, they founded a new church, the Evangelical Church Mekane Yesu.

19 Polygamy was one of the most intractable ethical problems facing Protestant missionaries in Africa. Often male converts were required to put away all their wives except one before they could be accepted for baptism, an action which Africans frequently regarded as heartless and immoral. Monogamy was sometimes criticized as a European pattern rather than a universal one. Even where polygamous men were accepted for baptism, they were excluded from leadership, on the basis of the command in 1 Timothy 3.2 that an elder should be 'the husband of one wife'. Easier to decide, but harder to root out, were the secret societies and rites of passage which were intended to cement society together and promote traditional moral codes. And then there were the traditional healers and others deemed to possess supernatural powers: converts might maintain a kind of double allegiance, attending church regularly but also visiting such people when family members fell sick.

20 A stimulating reappraisal of the significance of this conference is Brian Stanley, 'Edinburgh 1910 and the *Oikumene*', in Anthony R. Cross (ed.), 2002, *Ecumenism and History: Studies in Honour of John H. Y. Briggs*, Carlisle: Paternoster, pp. 89–105.

21 Mott was involved in the foundation of the Student Volunteer Movement, the World Student Christian Fellowship, and the International Missionary Council – quite a record!

22 Almost all the conference's attention was given to Asia; it was largely 'a gathering in which western Protestants talked to each other about the evangelization of the Orient' (Stanley, 'Edinburgh 1910', in Cross, *Ecumenism and History*, p. 100) – a valuable exercise, but by no means as comprehensive as later writers have tended to imply.

PART 3　1914 to the Present

Timeline: World Events, 1914–2007

1917	Russian Revolutions
1918	World War I ends
1919	Treaty of Versailles leads to formation of League of Nations (1920); Karl Barth, *Commentary on Romans*
1920	Lambeth Conference issues an 'Appeal to all Christian People'
1921	IMC founded; Kimbanguists founded
1925	First Life and Work conference
1927	Faith and Order founded
1934	Barmen Declaration; founding of Confessing Church
1937	Papal condemnations of Fascism and Communism
1939–45	World War II
1940	Bultmann publishes *The New Testament and Mythology*; Taizé community founded
1945–7	Communists take power in most Eastern European countries
1946	United Bible Societies founded; forcible merger of Eastern-rite Catholics with Orthodox in USSR
1947	Dead Sea Scrolls discovered; Church of South India comes into being
1948	WCC inaugurated; State of Israel established
1949	First missionaries expelled from China
1950	Papal infallibility invoked in the formal definition of the assumption of Mary
1950–3	Korean War
1951	Three-Self Patriotic Movement inaugurated in China
1960	Charismatic renewal begins in USA
1961	IMC incorporated into WCC
1962–5	Second Vatican Council
1965	Pope Paul VI and Patriarch Athenagoras lift mutual anathemas in place since 1054
1966	Chinese Cultural Revolution leads to severe persecution of Christians
1968	Martin Luther King assassinated; Latin American Catholic bishops meet at Medellín; *Humanae Vitae* condemns artificial contraception
1971	Gutiérrez publishes *Theology of Liberation*
1978	John Paul II elected as first non-Italian pope since 1523
1985	*Kairos Document* issued in South Africa
1989–91	'Collapse of Communism' in Eastern Europe

15

The Impact of Two World Wars

In many ways it was 1914 rather than 1901 which marked the beginning of the twentieth century. Certainly for the churches the advent of war was to change things out of all recognition, both in terms of its direct impact on church life and in terms of the political, social, economic, and intellectual changes which it set in motion. This chapter investigates the impact of World War I on the churches before turning to explore a theological development which was in part stimulated by the war – Neo-Orthodoxy. Examination of the impact of World War II is then followed by consideration of the closely related topic of Christian–Jewish relations during the century, focusing on two issues – the Holocaust and the establishment of the state of Israel.

World War I and the churches

It cannot be said that the outbreak of war in 1914 took the churches wholly by surprise. Britain and Germany had been building up their armaments for some years, and the churches had engaged in vigorous attempts to promote peace, as in the World Alliance for Promoting International Friendship through the Churches, whose foundation meeting at Konstanz in Germany was cut short by the declaration of war on 2 August.

Soldiers on both sides were motivated by being told that it was their Christian duty to fight, and assured that God was on their side. Preachers vied with one another to show their patriotism by presenting the national cause in absolute terms and deploying hyperbolic rhetoric. The Congregationalist preacher G. Campbell Morgan (1866–1943) declared from his pulpit in London's Westminster Chapel that 'the sign of the Cross is on every man that marches to his death'.[1] Nonconformists and Catholics in Britain may have done this as a way of demonstrating their loyalty to the establishment and their desire to be accepted as part of British society, and it can be paralleled with the outbursts heard over moral issues during the heyday of the 'Nonconformist conscience'; but Anglicans also engaged in this, which is a little harder to explain unless we recognize that all too often the churches reflected rather than shaped the prevailing national mood. Arthur Winnington-Ingram, Bishop of London, was deemed to be one of the most effective recruiting sergeants in the country.

Not all were willing to fight, however; even after the introduction in Britain of conscription in 1916 there were many who refused to participate in the war effort in any way, usually because their religious convictions led them to believe that taking life in any manner was wrong. During the Edwardian years, there had been a vocal pacifist lobby among Nonconformists, but when war arrived this was all but totally replaced by loud affirmations of the rightness of the British cause. Yet some maintained a witness for peace at great personal cost. In Britain, pacifism was especially widespread among the Quakers (although, in spite of the denomination's pacifist position, a third of members of military age did join up). 'Radical' groups such as Brethren, Christadelphians, and Pentecostals, while not taking a collective pacifist position, provided considerable numbers of conscientious objectors for the tribunals.[2]

Given that for most Christians on both sides the justification for war was self-evident, what explanations did they offer for its root causes? Some, especially in Britain, were sober enough to point to their own national sins as deserving of divine judgement: love of pleasure, moral laxity, and tolerance of heresy in the Church were among causes listed. As for German sins, for British writers these included unbridled militarism, acceptance of evolutionary theory, and the stress on the survival of the fittest which was found in the writings of philosophers such as Nietzsche. French Catholics saw war as divine judgement on the anti-clericalism of the Third Republic. German thinkers portrayed the war as a struggle for civilization against barbarism, for faith against the godless forces of Russia and France. In 1916, Harnack portrayed its objective as the promotion of the Kingdom of God by means of securing Germany's role in international affairs. Many combatants saw themselves as fighting for one form of faith against another, whether it was British Protestants fighting against Austro-Hungarian Catholics, or Russian Orthodox fighting against Turkish Muslims; of course, this convenient over-simplification overlooked the fact that most armies included men of varying religious traditions in their ranks, but like most over-simplifications it convinced and motivated many. From an avowedly neutral standpoint (which made him suspected by each side of sympathy with the other), Pope Benedict XV in November 1914 put the war down to the absence of mutual love, contempt for authority, class conflict, and grasping materialism. His concern was for the suffering, and he made persistent efforts to suggest ways forward for a diplomatic solution to the conflict, although these proved largely ineffectual.

We turn now to consider the impact of war on the churches. Many on all sides hoped that war would lead to a return to the churches, but an initial rise in attendance was not sustained. When the bishops of the Church of England led a National Mission of Repentance and Hope in 1916, it produced little result. Many claimed to be Christian but dissociated this from the world of church life, preferring to say their prayers, wear religious medals, carry a New Testament, and otherwise express their faith in individual rather than corporate ways. It became clear to chaplains and others that the Christianity of most average soldiers bore little relation to that promulgated by the churches. Even 'official' Christianity was to find itself forced to adapt in response to particular pastoral needs: the chief impact of war on the level and type of religious practice lay in the area of concern for the dead. During the late nineteenth century many churches, especially among the Nonconformists, had shifted the emphasis of their programme from preparation for the next life to the enjoyment of this one, developing extensive social, sporting, and cultural activities, and the establishment on earth of God's kingdom. The catastrophic loss of life during the war ensured the return of the afterlife to centre-stage in British theology, but this was not a return to traditional views of the four last things (heaven, hell, death, and divine judgement). Instead, there was a dramatic upsurge of interest in spiritualism as the bereaved sought for comfort concerning their loved ones, and prayer for the dead became more widely accepted. This gave considerable impetus to Anglo-Catholic attempts to introduce the practice into Anglican worship. As for the theology of the afterlife, there was a widespread popular perception that those who died for their country were to be regarded as Christian martyrs, and even as following Christ's example (as exemplified by the quotation of John 15.13 on many war memorials: 'Greater love hath no man than this, that a man lay down his life for his friends'); this contributed to the further weakening of the link perceived between explicit Christian faith and entrance into heaven. Only in this way could many make sense of the appalling and apparently pointless loss of life which occurred on the battlefields in engagements which seemed to make little if any difference to the overall balance of power.

When the fighting was stopped, it was by an armistice; formal cessation of hostilities had to await the signing of a treaty at Versailles in 1919. In this the Germans were forced to acknowledge that they were the ones who had started the war; coupled with the vindictive insistence of some of the Allied powers on exacting reparation from the German economy, this bred a festering resentment which would pave the way for the rise of Nazism and its doctrine of Aryan superiority as a way of restoring German national self-esteem. Benedict XV saw that this would be the consequence of such a harsh treaty, but few were as prescient, nor did they care: they were simply relieved to be able to put the war behind them and live for present joys.

The rise of Neo-Orthodoxy

For some, their experience of war and of the suffering which resulted led them to abandon belief in God, but the same experiences also provoked an equal and opposite reaction. Many concluded that war showed the inadequacy of all human attempts to solve the world's problems, and Christian theology thus saw a renewed stress on the divine transcendence which contrasted with the liberal preference for speaking of divine immanence. Both extremes represented reactions to the liberal theological tradition which had become influential in much of the Western Protestant world.

It has often been said that World War I dealt a deathblow to liberalism, which was shown to have no answers to the problems thrown up by the conflict between so-called Christian nations. The American Neo-Orthodox theologian Richard Niebuhr (1894–1962) once summarized the liberal message as being that 'A God without wrath brought men without sin into a kingdom without judgement through the ministrations of a Christ without a cross.'[3] However, such an interpretation needs to be nuanced: in fact, liberalism continued to flourish in the English-speaking world during the 1920s, feeding off the climate of optimism, hope, and determination never to become embroiled in such a conflict again which had given birth to such entities as the League of Nations (created at Versailles in 1919). Indeed, even a second war failed to extinguish the liberal tradition totally. Yet it remains true that many Christian thinkers did conclude that liberal theology was bankrupt; the alternative which many of them were to adopt began with a Swiss pastor, Karl Barth (1886–1968), himself an ex-liberal, whose commentary on Romans (1918, revised in 1921) 'fell like a bombshell on the playground of the theologians' (the verdict of the Roman Catholic scholar Karl Adam).[4] What had shaken him was the declaration of support for the German war effort as a fight to preserve national culture issued in October 1914 by 93 leading intellectuals, including prominent theologians.

The fundamental idea of Neo-Orthodoxy (also known in its early manifestations as 'dialectical theology' or the 'theology of crisis') was that Christian theology was first and foremost a response to the Word of God, rather than to the human situation or to human questions. The subject of Christian theology was to be God, not humankind; hence the attempt to ground faith in what was historically provable (as in the Quest for the Historical Jesus), or in human experience, was misdirected. In speaking about God, it was impossible to remain confined within either the positive dogmatic assertions of the theologians or the negatives of the mystics; rather, there was a dialectic (hence the name) between what could be said and what could not, because God who transcended all human attempts to describe him had made himself known in the incarnate Christ. A key source was the Danish thinker Søren Kierkegaard (1813–55), whose concept of God as 'wholly other' contrasted with the liberal tendency to emphasize the immanence of God. For Kierkegaard, God could only be known by a leap of faith into the dark, and Neo-Orthodox, whatever their disagreements on other matters, united in stressing the importance of faith as response to God's self-revelation.

The 'orthodoxy' on which its exponents drew was that of the Protestant Reformers, whose theology was marked by the same emphasis (and it is not without significance that Luther's theology in particular had also been forged in a setting of conflict and unrest). While continuing to utilize the tools and results of biblical criticism (hence the prefix 'Neo-'), Neo-Orthodox theologians were scathing about the liberal insistence that theology must accommodate itself to contemporary concerns and attitudes. For Barth the revealed Word of God, which exists in three forms, Christ and the witness borne by Scripture and the preached word, was to be the sole basis for Christian theology, although his dialectical approach led him to insist that God's self-revelation was not to be identified with a set of propositional statements. In 1934 he therefore opposed the attempt of another Neo-Orthodox theologian, Emil Brunner (1889–1966), to find a 'point of contact' by which God could make himself known to humanity: God could be known only insofar as he revealed himself. There was a contemporary relevance to this because Barth was coming to oppose the ideological project of the pro-Nazi 'German Christians' (see next section). Similarly, he disagreed with the New Testament scholar Rudolf Bultmann over the extent to which contemporary philosophy could define the shape of Christian theology. It was Barth whose formulation of Neo-Orthodoxy was to prove most influential, not only in the German-speaking world but also in Reformed circles in Scotland and North America. The movement's thought also exercised a shaping influence on the first two decades of the WCC and on the thinking of the IMC. While it was eclipsed in the 1960s by movements which it had helped to beget, it has proved more enduring than some of these and remains widely studied.

Christians, Jews, and Nazis in inter-war Europe

The longstanding Christian tradition of regarding the Jews as Christ-rejecters and therefore as hated by God was to come to catastrophic fruition in the events of the Holocaust or *Shoah*. In popular form (and mixed with resentment at perceived Jewish economic power) it made it easier for many throughout the West to close their eyes to the suffering of Jewish people as antisemitism became more aggressive in 1930s Germany. One root of German antisemitism was in the late-nineteenth-century attempts to respond to the challenges of the burgeoning cities. Adolf Stoecker (1835–1909) had argued that the biggest threat to the Protestant moral order came from the alliance of urban liberalism and secular Judaism.

Nazi policy towards the Jews did not go unchallenged. As early as 1928 a group of Protestant leaders including Barth, then a professor at Münster, signed a statement condemning it. In 1933 a Pastors' Emergency League was set up by the U-boat commander turned Lutheran pastor Martin Niemöller (1892–1984), opposing legislation expelling Jews from the civil service and attempts to do the same in the churches in the 'Aryan paragraph', which prohibited those of Jewish descent from holding office in churches. The motivation for opposition to the government was not so much concern for the Jews (Niemöller openly admitted his antisemitic views, but argued that exclusion of Jews from the churches ran counter to the effect of baptism) as disapproval of state interference in church affairs. The following year saw the promulgation of the Barmen Declaration, drafted by Barth, which asserted the sovereignty of Jesus Christ over all national considerations. It was the basis for the newly formed Confessing Church,[5] comprising those parishes and regional churches (*Landeskirchen*) which rejected the ideology of the German Christians as contaminated with paganism. Barmen was an uncompromising assertion of the Church's independence and a rejection of all attempts to derive Christian principles from human reasoning, interests, or concepts (and not, therefore, motivated by humanitarian considerations), but even Barth was forced to admit that the prevalence of antisemitism in the Confessing Church made it impossible to discuss the status of the Jews. His own views appear to have been broadly in line with the ancient tradition that the Church replaced the Jews as the New Israel, the people of God (an outlook more recently designated 'replacement theology').

Barth was forced out of Germany in 1935 but resistance continued; sadly, the majority of Protestants supported the Nazis, not least because of their shared opposition to Communism and approval of nationalism. German Protestant churches had a long tradition of political conservatism arising from close links with the state, and scholars continue to debate the extent to which this was grounded in Luther's political thought. Certainly the Nazis drew on Protestant antisemitism, republishing Luther's tract *On the Jews and their Lies* as part of a selection of his writings in 1936. Catholics, whose ultimate allegiance to a foreign power made them suspect, were prepared to speak out on issues affecting the Church's freedom, but in neither tradition were many willing to risk their necks by standing up for the Jewish community. One of the great missed opportunities of church history came in 1938: Pius XI asked a group of theologians to draft an encyclical opposing antisemitism, which would have appeared under the title *Humani Generis Unitas*, but the draft appears to have been lost in the system or else suppressed by Pius XII after his accession the following year. Sincere Christians simply withdrew into their own private lives; even among the 20,000 Protestant pastors, by 1936 only about 2,000 belonged to the German Christians and 6,000 to the Confessing Church; most were broadly neutral, perhaps conditioned by the Lutheran theological stress on obedience to the higher powers.

An iconic example of resistance to evil, however, was that of the German pastor Dietrich Bonhoeffer (1906–45); on a lecturing trip to America at the outbreak of war in 1939, he felt it his duty to return to Germany even though he was already a marked man by virtue of his leadership in the Confessing Church. After the discovery of a plot to assassinate Hitler in which he was secondarily implicated, he was imprisoned in 1943, finally being executed in April 1945 just a few days before the Allies liberated the camp where he had been confined. Because he was not able to develop his thought about what he called 'religionless Christianity' in a systematic manner, it has excited considerable interpretative debate. However, his stress that the Church existed for the world and not for itself (which may have been a reaction against the Confessing Church's preoccupation with its own affairs and rights), just as Christ was 'the man for others', proved seminal in the post-war development of ecumenical social thought.

World War II, the Holocaust, and the churches

When war broke out again in 1939, the churches' response was considerably more restrained. For one thing, they were not on the 'high' that they had been during the Edwardian years, having already expended a great deal of energy in ministering to those affected by the economic downturn which began in 1929. For another, the previous decade had been overshadowed by the threat of war: there had been more time to prepare, and society at large had fallen prey to a growing sense of foreboding as the advances of Communism and Fascism impressed themselves on the minds of many. This note is detectable in the statements issuing from ecumenical gatherings during the late 1930s (for example, the Life and Work conference held at Oxford in 1937) as they responded to the challenges of totalitarianism. In addition, because conscription was already in place when the war commenced, recruitment campaigns conducted from the pulpit were superfluous. Although there were almost four times as many conscientious objectors (59,000 as against 16,500 in World War I), they received a much lower profile. The tribunals were better conducted than had been the case first time round, and the authorities avoided making martyrs for the pacifist cause.

This war saw vastly more destruction of church buildings and loss of civilian life than had been the case in the previous one. The resulting dislocation was to be something from which churches never completely recovered; many replacement buildings were erected (in Britain, much of this work was overseen by the War Damage Commission, whose wheels ground with enervating slowness as it took up to ten years to deal with applications from churches for compensation), but large-scale loss of residential property had led to massive outmigration to new suburban developments, where the Church would struggle to establish itself.

Churches in many countries faced the perils of occupation. The Bishop of Oslo in Nazi-occupied Norway, Eivind Berggrav (1884–1959), earned international respect after the war for his courageous formulation of a distinctive Lutheran theory of resistance to unjust rulers (historically, such thought had been far more extensively developed in Calvinist circles ever since the 1550s). With his fellow-bishops he led the established church in declaring itself independent of the state from 1942 to 1945, becoming in effect a 'folk church' enjoying the allegiance of the people but not established. Elsewhere in the world, a number of missionaries lost their lives under Japanese occupation of parts of South-East Asia, Indonesia, and Australasia, although the development of indigenous churches was hastened by the loss or withdrawal of missionary leadership. Occupation of Hong Kong and the consequent lack of access to clerical ministrations resulted in the ordination of the first female Anglican priest, (Florence) Li Tim Oi, in 1944. Although her bishop was severely criticized for his action and she offered to resign when the occupation ended, this act has been accorded landmark status by advocates of women's ordination; in 1971 Hong Kong became the first Anglican province to ordain women as priests.

But all these troubles pale into insignificance when compared with the Holocaust. Discrimination and violence against Jews had been gathering pace since 1933, and official killings had been going on since 1939. At least by the summer of 1941 the 'final solution' formed part of Nazi policy. In Britain information regarding the Nazi extermination camps began to filter through fairly soon after that. However, those in authority were slow to credit what they were told, partly in reaction against the tendency in the previous war to invent or exaggerate reports of enemy atrocities. While individuals such as George Bell, Bishop of Chichester, did all they could to persuade officials to act on what they were hearing, there were none in positions of sufficient authority to be able to have much effect on government policy. In any case, even in Britain there was an element of half-conscious antisemitism which made many less concerned about the fate of the Jews. Even when in 1942 the WCC and the World Jewish Congress issued a statement about what was happening, it was not taken seriously.

By the time it ended in 1945 six million people, two-thirds of European Jewry, had lost their lives, almost a quarter of these at Auschwitz. Others had also suffered, among them Roma (gypsies), mentally handicapped, and homosexuals. It was one of the largest mass exterminations in human history, and the more shocking because of the high proportion of the target group who were killed.

How far have the churches faced up to antisemitic aspects of their own history? Led by Niemöller, who had spent 1937–45 under arrest, Confessing Church leaders issued a declaration at Stuttgart in the autumn of 1945, admitting their nation's guilt in the war. Such an action made the re-establishment of international and ecumenical contact much easier, and contrasted with the reluctance of some to take similar action after 1918. Niemöller himself was to play a leading role in the ecumenical movement as an inspirational figure, if less qualified as an administrator. Similarly, Anglicans in Japan issued a confession of war guilt in 1984. Others have been less open; the New Apostolic Church, for example, has said little so far about its support for Hitler, and many smaller evangelical groups in Germany have also found it difficult to come to terms with the role they played, if only by withdrawal from 'worldly' affairs.

Since 1963 there has been vigorous debate about the role of the papacy during World War II, and in particular its alleged failure to do all that it might have done to avert the Holocaust or rescue Jewish people. Pius XII, as a diplomat, was slow to speak out, possibly fearing the consequences which doing so might have for Catholics under Nazi rule. He tended to leave public criticism to local leaders, and the German church was more outspoken in opposing Nazi policy than any other national institution. His concern to maintain Vatican political neutrality (which had enabled Benedict XV to help the suffering on both sides during the 1914–18 war) may also have hindered him in acknowledging and responding to the moral dimensions of what was happening. And his tendency to anti-Communism (which owed something to a Marian apparition at Fatima in 1917, warning against the Communist threat) and the Church's to anti-semitism would also have made it more difficult for him to recognize the evil of what was happening. His silence continued after the war, during a time of immense political significance as Russian Communism expanded its dominion to include much of Eastern Europe. Yet it must also be acknowledged that during the German occupation of Rome in 1943–4, several thousand Jews found sanctuary in monasteries and convents at the direction of the Vatican. The pope had also opposed the forced conversion of Serbs from Orthodoxy to Catholicism in Croatia, and worked with the hierarchy in Slovakia to stop the deportation of Jews in 1941.

Since 1945 Christians have been more ready to engage in dialogue with Jews, a process which many on both sides have seen as fruitful. In Britain William Temple was the stimulus for the founding of the Council of Christians and Jews in 1942, which has always drawn support from all major Christian traditions. The Roman Catholic Church, in the Vatican II decree on non-Christian religions *Nostra Aetate* (1965), formally absolved the Jews as a people of guilt for the Crucifixion, condemned its own history of anti-Judaism, and affirmed the continuing status of the Jews as a covenanted people of God. This has paved the way for a more positive relationship between Catholicism and Judaism expressed through dialogue. Yet inevitably the central issue, of how a just God believed to be active in human history could have allowed or ordained such an event, has received no widely accepted answer.

Since the war, relationships have been further affected by the establishment of the state of Israel in 1948.[6] Perhaps a sense of guilt at complicity or inaction during the Holocaust has been one of the factors in Christian support for this. Rather more significant since then, however, has been the influence of Dispensationalism. Because this postulates a continuing history for the Jewish people on earth concurrent with that of the heavenly Church, and sees their ultimate restoration and blessing as foretold by biblical prophecy, Fundamentalists have generally offered uncritical support for Israeli political and military actions. This has been a significant factor shaping United States foreign policy, enabling successive administrations to secure the support of a large bloc of voters. By contrast, most other Christians have been more critical, partly because of their desire to be impartial and partly because the Palestinian community contains a sizeable Christian minority.

Many who read this event in eschatological terms did the same thing with the growth of Communism, especially during the Cold War era; in the next chapter we turn to examine how the churches fared under Communist rule.

Questions for thought

1 How would you explain the churches' support for World War I, given that they had previously been seeking to promote peace? Do you think that any theological factors might have played a part (for example, their understanding of the kingdom of God)?

2 We have said that the suffering in World War I provoked opposite reactions – loss of religious faith and a heightened stress on divine revelation. How can historians avoid overlooking the possibility that other events might also have provoked widely varying reactions? Is there a risk that we may approach the evidence assuming that people all reacted in a similar way? How can we guard against that?

3 If you had been a Christian during the 1930s, would you have reacted any differently from most in Germany? How easy do you find

it to step into the shoes of these people and view things from their perspective?

4 Compare and contrast the responses of the churches to the end of the war in 1918 and in 1945.

Further reading

Hugh McLeod (ed.), 2006, *Cambridge History of Christianity*, vol. 9: *World Christianities c.1914–c.2000*, Cambridge: Cambridge University Press, chs 8, 15.

Klaus Scholder, 1987–8, *The German Churches and the Third Reich*, 2 vols, London: SCM Press.

Alan Wilkinson, 1986, *Dissent or Conform? War, Peace and the English Churches 1900–1945*, London: SCM Press.

Notes

1 Quoted in Wilkinson, *Dissent or Conform?*, p. 25.

2 On pacifism and conscientious objection, see Martin Ceadel, 1980, *Pacifism in Britain, 1914–1945*, Oxford: Clarendon; John Rae, 1970, *Conscience and Politics: The British Government and Conscientious Objection to Military Service 1916–1919*, London: Oxford University Press.

3 Quoted in Alec R. Vidler, 1971, *The Church in an Age of Revolution*, Pelican History of the Church 5, Harmondsworth: Pelican, p. 213.

4 For a valuable compressed introduction to Barth and especially to his *Church Dogmatics*, see Daniel Hardy's chapter (1), in David Ford with Rachel Muers (eds), 2005, *The Modern Theologians: An Introduction to Christian Theology since 1918*, 3rd edn, Oxford: Blackwell, and the sources there listed.

5 Initially it was known as the Confessional Church, referring to their desire to remain faithful to the classic Reformation confessions of faith; the later and more familiar title of Confessing Church referred more to the act of confession, which involved determination to remain faithful to Christ as 'confessors' (those who suffered for their faith).

6 On Christian attitudes to the establishment of the state of Israel, see Stephen Sizer, 2004, *Christian Zionism: Road-map to Armageddon?* Leicester: IVP. On Christian–Jewish relations generally, see G. Wigoder, 1988, *Jewish–Christian Relations since the Second World War*, Manchester: Manchester University Press.

16

The Eastern Churches from 1917

This chapter takes up several of the themes which we saw emerging during the nineteenth century. The ambivalent relationship with the West which had been evident before has become much more so, especially since the collapse of Communism in much of Eastern Europe from 1989. The relationship between the quests for political and ecclesiastical independence, which ran in parallel during the nineteenth century, has again become a major factor complicating church life. Forced union, too, which had occurred under the Ecumenical Patriarchate at the behest of the Ottoman sultans, appeared again, this time bringing Orthodox in Communist countries under the Moscow Patriarchate. Although the early decades of Communism saw several small jurisdictions move from Moscow to Constantinople, this was far outweighed by the many Eastern-rite Catholic jurisdictions which were forced to unite with Moscow or other jurisdictions after their territory came under Russian political and military influence. Table 16.1 helps to clarify the details of these developments, allowing the chapter to focus on drawing out broader themes.

Communism and its impact

Marxism was in origin a Western ideology, shaped in part by the experiences of Marx in Germany and Engels in England. However, it was in Eastern Europe and the Chinese sphere of influence that it achieved political dominance during the twentieth century. The Russian Orthodox writer Nicolas Zernov called it 'the last and most radical stage in the process of imitation of the West inaugurated by Peter the Great'.[1] Discussion of the impact of Communist government on church life will focus on Russia and (briefly) China, as these two nations have been the subject of most investigation by researchers and each in its way provided the paradigm for a particular approach to church–state relations. In each case, Communism did not create an entirely new situation but built on certain earlier traditions. In Orthodox countries, traditional conceptions of the church–state relationship proved able to sustain a relationship between the hierarchy and the Communist leadership as they had done under the previous monarchies. Only when the latter

Table 16.1: Developments in Orthodoxy during the nineteenth and twentieth centuries.

CONSTANTINOPLE	Serbia	*1959 Macedonian Orthodox Church (^1967 but not yet recognized as division deemed by EP to be partly political)	
	^1850 Greece (independent 1833)	*1924 Old Calendarists (True Orthodox Church)	*several schisms
		1911 Greek Catholics	
	1861 Bulgarian Catholics		
	#1885 ^1925 Romania	*1924 Old Calendarists	
	^1937 Albania (independent 1922)		
	^1945 (recognition by EP; independent 1870) Bulgaria	*after 1968 Old Calendarists	
MOSCOW	1895 Russian Catholics[1]		
	#1918 Finland (to EP 1923)		
	#Latvia (to EP 1936)	*Latvian Orthodox Church Abroad (in reaction to forced union with Moscow 1940)	
	#Lithuania		
	1920 Russian Orthodox Church Abroad[2]		
	#1923 Estonia (to EP)	*Estonian Orthodox Church Abroad (in reaction to forced union with Moscow 1940)	
	*1927 True Orthodox Church		
	*1929 Exarchate of Western Europe (to EP 1931)		
	1937 Slovakian Catholics[3]		
	#after 1945 Hungary (earlier under EP / Serbia)[4]		
	*1946 Ukrainian Greek Catholic Church)[5]		
	^1948 Poland (independent 1924)		
	^1956 (not yet recognized by EP) China		
	^1970 (not yet recognized by EP) Orthodox Church of America		
	^1970 (not yet recognized by EP) Japan		
	#1990 (not yet recognized by EP) Belarus		

continued

	^1990 Georgia (independent from 1917, recognized by Moscow 1943)	
	^1990 Ukrainian Autocephalous Orthodox Church[6]	
	*1992 Ukrainian Orthodox Church (Kiev Patriarchate)[7]	
	*1992 Ukrainian Orthodox Church (Moscow Patriarchate)	
	^1998 Czech Republic and Slovakia (recognized by Moscow 1951)	
Coptic Orthodox Church	#4th c.; ^1959 Ethiopian Orthodox Church	1961 Ethiopian Catholics
		#1994 ^1998 Eritrean Orthodox
Syrian Orthodox Church	Indians under Syrian Orthodox Church	several schisms, including: *1889 Mar Thoma Church[8] 1930 Syro-Malankara Catholics
		*1889 Malankara Syrian Orthodox Church[9]
Church of the East	*1968 Ancient Church of the East	

NB: The Ecumenical Patriarchate claims the exclusive right to recognize Orthodox jurisdictions as autocephalous; dates for this refer to such recognition unless otherwise stated.[10]

PATRIARCHATES are in upper-case.

Eastern-rite Catholic (also known as Uniat) bodies are underlined.

Key
* originated through schism
# granted autonomy
^ granted autocephaly

Notes
1 Also known as 'Old Believers in Communion with the Holy See'.
2 Also known as Russian Orthodox Church Outside Russia; intercommunion re-established with Moscow Patriarchate 2007.
3 Forcibly united with Orthodox 1950–68.
4 Hungarian Catholics 1912.
5 Resulting from forced union of Greek Catholics with Moscow Patriarchate 1946–90.
6 Forcibly united with Moscow Patriarchate 1930–41, 1945–89; dioceses in the West received into Ecumenical Patriarchate 1996.
7 Briefly co-operated with Ukrainian Autocephalous Orthodox Church.
8 Semi-Reformed, in communion with Anglicans.
9 Also known as Indian Orthodox.
10 Many dates in this table are taken from the online version of Ronald G. Roberson, *The Eastern Christian Churches: A Brief Survey*, 6th edn, at http://www.cnewa.org/generalpg-verus.aspx?PageID=182, accessed 26 June 2005.

mounted an all-out attack on the Church did that relationship break down.

Church and state in Russia, 1917–88

Prospects for the Russian church looked brighter in 1917 than they had done since 1721, when Peter the Great had suppressed the Moscow Patriarchate. Revolution in March had resulted in a far greater degree of religious freedom and ecclesiastical autonomy; a council of the Church was convened in Moscow that autumn, and it elected as Patriarch Tikhon Bellavin (1865–1925), who had been a bishop in the USA. However, the council and the brief opportunity for independence were cut short by the October Revolution, leading to four years of civil war and the seizure of power by the Bolsheviks. Under Communist rule the Orthodox Church was to lose almost all its leaders and thinkers, most being exiled during the 1920s (abroad until 1922, internally thereafter) or killed during the 1930s.[2] Protestant groups, by contrast, enjoyed a few years of hitherto-unknown freedom before they likewise began to feel the full weight of state persecution. We may divide the story of religious persecution into the following time periods: 1918–22, 1922–9, 1929–43, 1943–59, 1959–64, and 1964–88. These correspond to distinct stages or approaches towards religion in the Soviet Union, although at times there is a measure of overlapping between them.

In the first stage of the Communist campaign against religion, the focus was on out-arguing Christianity in debate and on removing the Church's property base: the latter was necessary because in Marxist thought materialist explanations sufficed to account for the dominance of religion. Legislation in 1918 forbade churches to own property, and clergy were prohibited from teaching religion in state schools. In the 1920s Leon Trotsky (1879–1940) directed a campaign of confiscation of church property which he hoped would serve to discredit the Church in the eyes of the masses and so persuade them to adopt atheism. The result was otherwise: thousands were put to death for resisting the campaign, but the campaign also showed that the secret of the Church's strength did not lie in its material wealth. Lenin had wanted the confiscation carried out in a manner which would provoke resistance, but far from discrediting the Church and giving him an opportunity to repress it the campaign demonstrated the strong popular allegiance to Christianity.

It became clear that the government would have to outdo the Church in the area of propaganda if it was to have any hope of converting the masses to atheism. In the second stage, therefore, much more attention was paid to the dissemination of atheist propaganda, as well as attempting to weaken and discredit the Church by dividing it. An Anti-Religious

Commission was established in 1922, with the aims of controlling religious bodies, disseminating atheist propaganda, and infiltrating and dividing the Orthodox Church. Protestant groups were also allowed a greater measure of freedom as it was hoped that this would serve to undermine the position of Orthodoxy, and Baptists and Pentecostals both saw rapid growth in numbers and geographical spread. For a few years a state-sponsored schism from Orthodoxy, the Renovationists or Living Church, dragged out a weak existence, but it soon disappeared.

Nevertheless, schism did occur, resulting in the formation of a temporary jurisdiction, the Russian Orthodox Church Abroad. The Patriarch had urged bishops who were unable to remain in contact with Moscow to set up their own independent jurisdictions in consultation with the local hierarchy, and a meeting of Russian bishops at Constantinople in 1920 had agreed to work towards this. They were invited by the Serbs to Karlovci where at a synod in 1921 formal steps were taken to establish an autonomous jurisdiction, sometimes known as the 'Synod Church'. A majority of those present also agreed that the Church should commit itself to assisting in the restoration of the Russian monarchy, but a minority led by Metropolitan Evlogy of Paris argued that the Church should not be aligned with any one political viewpoint or programme. In 1923 Tikhon disowned the structures which the monarchist majority had created; Evlogy accepted his decision but later separated from Moscow after the church's acting head (Metropolitan Sergei) called on Russian Orthodox abroad in 1927 to affirm their loyalty to the Soviet state (and after Evlogy himself was removed from office in 1930 for participating in an Anglican service of prayer for persecuted Christians in Russia). In 1931 Evlogy was received by the Ecumenical Patriarchate, thus giving rise to three Russian jurisdictions in the West. Perhaps because of the nature of those forming the *diaspora* of the 1920s, which included many of pronounced monarchist views, the Synod Church became noted for its right-wing ethos. It has continued to denounce ecumenism and also 'Sergianism' (that is, the pattern of church–state relations followed by the Moscow Patriarchate from 1927, in which the Church submitted completely to state dictates), although the post-Communist dominance of conservatism in the latter has made it easier for the two jurisdictions to work towards intercommunion and eventual reunion.

The third stage of the onslaught saw widespread persecution in an attempt to deprive the Church by silencing its leaders. The government refused permission for the Church to elect a successor to Tikhon and began a systematic persecution of the hierarchy, arresting and deporting bishops and clergy. From 1929 legislation prohibited religious teaching, especially of children (Sunday schools, which had been popular among Protestants, had been banned in 1921); church activity was restricted to the regular services. The 1930s saw severe persecution and the closure of all but a few hundred of the estimated 46,000 Orthodox churches. At the height of the storm, in the year of 1937, 136,000 clergy were arrested, of whom 85,000 lost their lives. To put this in context, it should be noted that from 1936 to 1939 over 5 per cent of the population of the USSR were arrested, and virtually everyone lived in a state of perpetual apprehension lest they should be next.

Even after the full ferocity of persecution had broken out, most of the population appear to have been believers, and when war returned Stalin recognized that the Church's aid was vital in order to gain the support of the masses for the war effort, the more so because many in Ukraine had welcomed the invading Germans because they allowed churches to be reopened.[3] From 1943, therefore, the Church was once again allowed to elect a patriarch; a limited number of buildings were reopened and certain other freedoms granted. In return, the Moscow Patriarchate became a loyal supporter of Russian foreign policy, continuing to play this role after the war in ecumenical circles. As far as the state was concerned, it was easier to keep watch on a church which had a degree of visible organization than on one which had been driven underground by persecution. Organization entailed centralization, and in 1944 the Baptists and the Evangelical Christians[4] came together in the All-Union Council of Evangelical Christians–Baptists (AUCECB), being joined in the following year by their counterparts in the Baltic republics and by a large minority of the Pentecostals.

However, after Stalin's death in 1953 and an initial increase in freedom for the churches, things began to swing back towards a more oppressive regime. The relative freedom enjoyed by the Church since 1943 had no basis in law, and persecution was renewed under Khrushchev from 1959 to 1964: two-thirds of church buildings were again closed, and those which remained open were subject to increasing restrictions on their activities. This time persecution led to bitter internal division. The Baptists divided, with one group (the Council of Churches of Evangelical Christians–Baptists (CCECB), often known as Reform Baptists or *Initsiativniki*, formally set up in 1965) refusing to accept the limitations on church life entailed by registration of congregations with the government; new statutes had been introduced by the denomination's leadership in 1960 which restricted even further what churches could do by way of outreach. The views of their main spokesman, Georgi Vins, were widely reported in the West. Ironically, state attempts to secure increased control over church life resulted in a loss of control as many congregations chose to remain unregistered and to associate with the CCECB. Since their very existence was illegal, there was no reason for them to hold back on evangelistic activity because they had no privileges to lose.

Once again, therefore, the authorities adopted a 'divide and conquer' policy; from 1963 they began to allow registered congregations more freedoms, while coming down harder on those remaining unregistered. This policy gathered strength after Khrushchev was removed from office in 1964 and replaced by Brezhnev. In essence it remained in place until Gorbachev's 1988 reforms. It was hoped that as a result congregations would be encouraged to register with the authorities, but even the introduction of autonomous registration from the late 1960s, allowing congregations to register without having to join the AUCECB, failed to convince many congregations. They simply felt they had too much to lose, a feeling which owed much to the historic Baptist tradition of congregational autonomy.

From about 1965 signs also emerged of growing Orthodox disquiet. Western media gave extensive coverage to dissidents within the Orthodox Church who criticized both state policy and the perceived compromises of their own hierarchy, although there was never any significant movement of unregistered Orthodox congregations.

The impact on congregational life

State control over the Church was exercised by making the Church answerable to a government department dealing with religious affairs; of course, this was nothing new for the Russians, nor indeed for some of the Balkan states, as restrictions had frequently obtained in pre-Communist days. The impact of Communism on church–state relationships can sometimes be overstated. Only in Albania was religion totally outlawed (from 1967); although in many Communist states it was suppressed by whatever means possible, official policy usually remained that there was, in theory at any rate, freedom of religious practice.

Recognizing that part of the Church's hold on the people was exercised through rites of passage (baptisms, marriages, and funerals), the Soviet state led the way in providing alternative non-religious rites. However, these rarely proved popular even though they were introduced in many Communist states, with the exception of an East German ceremony for young people, the *Jugendweihe*, intended as a replacement for confirmation; by 1983, this was observed by almost all eligible youth.

Russian policy was not always replicated in its sphere of influence, but throughout Eastern Europe the churches were excluded from public life as far as possible, and discrimination against Christians in the fields of employment and education was widespread. As well as restricting church life to church premises, priests and clergy were discouraged from speaking about social or political issues (with the exception of expressing support for the peace movement). However, exclusion was more thorough in some countries than in others. In Czechoslovakia repression was consistent. Romanian Orthodox under Ceauçescu made up the majority of the country's population and enjoyed an unusually high profile in the media, but they were nevertheless persecuted if they attempted to speak out on social issues. The churches had greatest freedom in East Germany, where they remained active in the fields of health, social work, and education (partly because these activities attracted Western financial support, which was welcomed by the state). The East German Evangelical Church remained united with that in the West until 1969, and it drew on lessons learned during the Nazi era to resist state attempts to force it into subservience, adopting a stance of 'critical solidarity'. During the late 1980s it provided the only effective forum for the expression of political dissent, and vigils and prayer meetings on church premises fuelled the changes which resulted in the opening of East German borders and ultimately the downfall of the Communist regime.

One problem resulting from state control arose from Orthodox insistence that bishops had to be drawn from monastic ranks; as monasteries were closed, it became harder to ensure a continuing supply of new candidates and this, with the imprisonment or execution of existing bishops, meant that the church was short of leaders. This in turn meant that it was difficult to ordain candidates for the priesthood, even if such were available. In many areas, therefore, Orthodox practice was restricted to rites which could be performed by laity. To a considerable extent the transmission of Orthodoxy to succeeding generations took place at home, where children were taught the rudiments of the faith and of prayer.

The impact on external relations

By and large, Communist governments discouraged churches from cultivating relations with co-religionists abroad, except for strictly defined purposes such as the promotion of Soviet foreign policy or of a positive image of Communist rule. Catholics of Eastern and Western rites were suspect because of their allegiance to a foreign head, the Pope. Governments and Orthodox hierarchies colluded in forcing Eastern-rite Catholics to unite with Orthodoxy, especially in Ukraine and in the states which became Communist after 1945 (such as Romania). These Christians became a focus in Ukraine for a sense of national identity, since Protestant and Orthodox bodies looked to Moscow for leadership.

China provides an interesting case-study of the way in which Communism affected the external relations of the churches. The main theme emerging from the history of church–state relations in China concerns the way in which the government sought to indigenize the Church and to cut its foreign links. Christianity had been influential in shaping the thought of post-1911 nationalist leaders, and was associated with modernization and Westernization, but this had provoked something of an anti-Christian backlash during the 1920s, after which missionary numbers remained reduced. Even so, when Mao Zedong took control in 1949, there were 4,062 Protestant missionaries and 5,682 foreign Catholic priests and nuns. All had gone by 1959, evicted by the government which was reacting against the earlier tendency to present Christianity as part of a package of Westernizing reform. As a result, some missions had to reinvent themselves: the largest, the China Inland Mission, broadened its focus to other parts of South-East Asia, becoming the Overseas Missionary Fellowship.

Loss of contact with the outside world, and the government's insistence that churches should follow the 'Three-Self' approach rooted in the thinking of Venn and Anderson, as well as locally based exponents Nevius and the high Anglican Roland Allen (1868–1946), resulted in the formation of a Catholic Church independent of Rome from 1957 to 1963 (the 'Open Church'). Protestantism, too, was divided. The officially recognized strand was the Three-Self Patriotic Movement (1951), which continued the earlier tradition of applying Christianity to the sphere of public life as well as giving expression to indigenizing or nationalizing tendencies in the contemporary outlook; by contrast with Eastern Europe, preachers were discouraged from preaching about other-worldly topics and encouraged to focus on the cultivation of those virtues necessary for building the nation; we may detect here an echo of the this-worldly emphasis present in Confucian thought.[5] The unofficial (and larger) strand was an array of evangelical 'house churches' of varying convictions, some with Pentecostal characteristics, which refused to register themselves with the government. During the Cultural Revolution from 1966 onwards, all churches were closed or forced underground, a development which favoured the house churches because of their preference for congregational autonomy and a minimum of organization. After 1980 Rome recognized the ordinations carried out by the 'Open Church', but it remains out of communion with the section which had remained loyal to the Vatican. By 1995, the TSPM had an estimated 10.5 million members, the Catholics 12.3 million, and the 'house churches' almost 30 million.

The Chinese pattern of Communism has also caused problems for Christians in countries as diverse as Albania and North Korea. In both of these, all churches and other religious buildings were closed, and although Albania has seen Christians and Muslims re-establish themselves after the end of Communist rule in 1992, North Korea remains officially churchless apart from two or three show churches in the capital Pyongyang. A Christian community is known to exist there, but contacts with South Korea are erratic and highly secret.

Another aspect of external relations concerns the way in which

Orthodoxy in Russia subsumed other Orthodox jurisdictions as well as attempting to ingest the Eastern-rite bodies. In the same way that the Ecumenical Patriarchate strengthened its leadership as a result of coming under Ottoman rule, the Moscow Patriarchate strengthened its influence in those countries which became Communist after 1945: the Baltic republics, Romania, and Bulgaria in particular. A similar process happened among Baptists in territory annexed by the USSR. In addition, Orthodoxy strengthened its position vis-à-vis other Christian traditions, Orthodox proving able to work with national Communist governments and to provide a focus for nationalist sentiment without becoming too much of a channel for discontent with the state.

What enabled the churches to survive?

Delicate accommodation, even compromise, were crucial to the survival of churches as officially recognized bodies in many countries. Some have even spoken of the sacrifice of Orthodox hierarchs who, knowing that they were 'selling their souls' by reaching an accommodation with Communism, gave up their own hope of salvation in order to ensure that their flocks could continue to practise their faith. Evangelicals too experienced the tension between compromise for the sake of continued freedom and frustration at the prohibitions on aspects of church life which they saw as essential, notably Sunday schools and evangelism. In Czechoslovakia and Hungary there were Roman Catholic clergy who went further in seeking a *modus vivendi* with the Communist state than others thought desirable.

For all the apprehension regarding external contacts, the ecumenical movement is widely thought to have done less than it might have in supporting Christians and churches suffering under Communist rule. The ecumenical movement, while regarded as something of a lifeline by Eastern churches involved in it because of the contacts which it gave them and the desire of their governments to use it in order to project a positive image of themselves to the rest of the world, in fact did relatively little by way of advocacy on behalf of the oppressed Christian communities of Communist countries. Even if the facts became known to WCC officials, they were hamstrung by the public assertion of many church leaders that they enjoyed religious freedom and the concern to avoid the movement being seen as a tool of Western foreign policy. It was to be individuals and independent organizations who from the mid-1960s brought the issue of persecution to the attention of Western media, as was also the case with the contemporary human rights movement. Among individuals who spoke out may be noted the Orthodox Russians Fr Gleb Yakunin (who founded the Christian Committee for the Defence of Believers'

Rights in 1976, a body whose remit extended beyond Christianity to include all forms of religious belief), Fr Dimitri Dudko, and the writer Alexander Solzhenitsyn. Foremost among Western groups active in this field was the Keston Institute, founded in 1965 by the Anglican cleric Michael Bourdeaux.

Post-Communist opportunities and tensions

The increasing openness of the Russian political leadership to reform during the late 1980s (in which, like Stalin, they saw that the Church could play a vital role in influencing public opinion) coincided fortunately with the millennium of Russian Christianity in 1988. Mikhail Gorbachev granted permission for this to be celebrated, and the media were able to give extensive coverage to the celebrations, which assisted the Church in recovering a prominent position in Russian life. Legislation in the 1990s, however, appeared to lean in the direction of privileging Orthodoxy at the expense of other Christian confessions and other faiths, and some at least in the hierarchy appeared to be seeking to turn the clock back to times when the Church enjoyed a privileged relationship with the state. For many smaller groups, the advantage of the Communist era had been that all were treated alike, which made co-operation easier; many had more freedom during parts of that period than they had had when Orthodoxy had influenced state religious policy. In addition, the 'ecumenism of the gulags' from the 1930s even brought Baptists, Catholics, and Orthodox together as nothing else had done or would do, as prisoners for the sake of Christ.

Nationally, some churches benefited from being perceived as principled opponents of state policy. This was especially true of Catholicism in Poland, whose leaders had frequently spoken out against policies which they considered unjust. However, the rapid process of Westernization brought with it far-reaching changes in the moral climate, and the Church lost much of its support within a few years because it was now seen as trying to exercise too much influence in government affairs and in society at large. Other national churches also suffered from being perceived as having compromised with the state: this was true of large Orthodox jurisdictions such as those of Russia, Romania, and Bulgaria, but also of registered Evangelicals, such as the Russian AUCECB. Even where the Church as a whole continued to enjoy widespread public support, its hierarchy might face pressure to resign, as in Ethiopia (under Communist rule from 1974 to 1991). Westernization has caused other problems for the churches, as it has brought to the surface the divergent outlooks of those who had opposed communism on traditional theological grounds and now sympathized with right-wing politicians, and those who had

opposed it on humanitarian grounds and who were now much more willing to work within a politically and religiously pluralist climate. Where
there was strong local support for moves towards a more democratic
political process, churches which failed to support this have forfeited
much public sympathy.

At the local level, the Communist era bequeathed a legacy of mistrust
between those who had co-operated with the authorities and those who
had spoken out (the two Russian Baptist groups remain separate at the
denominational level), tension between different groups laying claim to
the same buildings (especially Eastern-rite Catholics and Orthodox),
and mutual suspicion between conservatives who wished to secure the
position of the Church by legal means and who distrusted ecumenism at home and abroad and progressives who sought to adapt to the
new reality and present the Church's message to outsiders in a pluralist
setting. This fragmentation at the theological level has been matched by
fragmentation at the ethnic level, as Orthodox hierarchies in newly independent nations such as Ukraine and Belarus sought autonomy from
Moscow[6] and Baptists in newly independent states formed their own
unions. Externally imposed unions have unravelled, as between Eastern-
rite Catholics and Orthodox, or between Baptists and Pentecostals. The
potential of Orthodoxy to fragment is often under-estimated, but the
history of the Eastern churches demonstrates that the divisions it has
suffered have often been of major significance and extremely difficult to
overcome.

East and West

Three waves of immigration

One of the main ways in which Eastern Christianity has impacted the
West has been through immigration. It occurred during the nineteenth
century as Eastern Europeans migrated to Western Europe and North
America, and twentieth-century immigration to Western Europe has been
in three waves: post-revolution, post-war, and post-Communism.

With the advent of Communism, many Russians, especially from the
aristocracy and intelligentsia, sought refuge in the West. This was the
Russian *diaspora* of the 1920s. It fell into three groups: right-wing mon-
archists, often belonging to the 'Synod Church'; those who remained
faithful to the Moscow hierarchy; and the group led by Metropolitan
Evlogy of Paris. This last group played a dynamic part in the developing
ecumenical scene of the 1930s and 1940s; it included such luminaries
as Georges Florovsky (1893–1979), John Meyendorff (1926–91), and
Alexander Schmemann (1921–83), all of whom did much to ensure that

Eastern theology became better known in the West, especially in ecumenical circles.

A post-war migration lasting through the late 1940s and 1950s brought not only Orthodox but also Roman Catholics from several countries to the West from Eastern Europe, giving rise in Britain to a considerable Polish population. It included some who had served in the forces in Britain, others who came as 'voluntary workers' on a government scheme, and many who simply wished to flee new Communist regimes in countries such as Hungary.

The post-Communist migration, which began in 1989 and is still continuing, may turn out to be the largest of the three. The expansion of the European Union has given it added impetus, and numbers of Poles, Russians, Romanians, and Bulgarians. It is estimated that there are now over 25 million Orthodox in the West, and the various jurisdictions face the challenge of adapting to a context in which pluralism is far more acceptable than it has been in many traditionally Orthodox areas.

While Orthodox communities in the West have often stressed the need to preserve their ethnic culture, as have Roman Catholics, a significant minority have become assimilated to the extent of using the local language in worship. This has made it much easier for them to reach out to non-Orthodox as well as to reclaim many who had abandoned their religious profession and become thoroughly Westernized.

The Cold War and the churches

No sooner had World War II been ended than the so-called Cold War began. The 'iron curtain' became one of the most fundamental aspects of European political and economic reality. The phrase was drawn from a speech by Winston Churchill in 1946 which portrayed Communism as bent on destroying Christian civilization (this was ironic, given Churchill's own belief that Christianity would in time be proved obsolete and done away with) and the English-speaking world as the prime force for resisting its spread. Christianity (especially Evangelicalism) thus became inextricably interwoven in many minds with Western political anti-Communism – a confusion which was understandable in view of the Communists' explicitly anti-religious stance. In the United States, the 1950s were the era of McCarthyism, the paranoid attempt to root out the reds from under every American bed. But they were also an era of religious resurgence, as typified by the establishment of the Southern Baptist evangelist Billy Graham (b. 1918) as a national figure. The looming sense of international crisis led many to seek peace through religious commitment; one of Graham's best-selling books was entitled *Peace with God* (1953), and it was one of several similar books by Protestant and Catholic authors explaining the integral role of religion in personal wholeness. Church membership in the USA peaked at 62 per cent of the population in 1956, as religion came to be seen as an integral part of the 'American way of life'. As part of that process many Catholic, Orthodox, and ethnic Protestant churches became more American in their ethos. In 1960, for instance, the Standing Conference of Orthodox Bishops in America was founded to facilitate co-operation; ten years later the Orthodox Church in America (OCA) became autonomous from Moscow. The Ecumenical Patriarchate protested against this, considering that the Greek Archdiocese, which was considerably larger, would have made a better basis for establishing a united American jurisdiction; to date most jurisdictions have followed the Ecumenical Patriarchate and have not accorded formal recognition to the OCA, which has seriously hindered the process of establishing one jurisdiction for the whole Orthodox community in the USA.

In 1970s North America, one of the best-selling books was Hal Lindsey's prophetic popularization, *The Late Great Planet Earth*. It and a host of similar works offered an outlook on world events which fitted well with the apprehension of the Cold War era, and appealed to many by virtue of its ability to invest the threat of nuclear warfare with eschatological significance on the basis of a particular interpretation of biblical books such as Daniel and Revelation (thus ensuring its appeal to Fundamentalists), and the hope which it offered that Christians would avoid this by being 'raptured' (caught up to heaven with Christ) and thus missing the seven-year 'Great Tribulation' which would climax in Christ's visible return to destroy his enemies and inaugurate the millennial reign.

It was Roman Catholicism which proved most successful in establishing strong links between West and East. John XXIII inaugurated a sea-change in relationships between the Vatican and Communist governments. While firmly opposing the atheistic aspects of Communism as his predecessors had done, his realism made him aware that the Church had to engage with Communism as a system of government and as a social and economic theory. He secured improved relationships with several governments, including Moscow, enabling him to fill vacant posts in the hierarchy and to secure the participation at the Second Vatican Council of 90 bishops from Eastern Europe. This was capped by the appointment in 1978 of the Polish Cardinal Karol Wojtyla as Pope John Paul II, a development which provoked a horrified reaction in Moscow and put new heart into millions of Eastern Europeans.

Western influences on Eastern churches

Eastern Christians have often found it hard to find much positive to say about the impact of Western Christianity on their churches. One negative aspect of Western influence in the eyes of some conservative Orthodox concerned the calendar used to calculate when the Church's festivals should be observed.[7] An Orthodox council in 1583 had condemned the Gregorian calendar used in the West, and Orthodox churches preferred the Julian calendar, which was 13 days behind the Gregorian. In 1923 a conference chaired by the Ecumenical Patriarch agreed to adopt a revised calendar which was similar to it (the Russians did not do so). The result was a number of conservative schisms, especially from the church in Greece: changing the calendar was seen as compromise with the apostate West, and it was asserted that only an ecumenical council had the right to take such a decision. Since the Old Calendarists' approach is rooted in a deeply conservative mindset, it is not surprising that some see the whole of the rest of Orthodoxy as apostate and its sacraments as invalid. Most Orthodox churches (but not the Russians or Serbians) now use the new calendar for feasts celebrated on fixed dates and the old calendar for moveable ones such as Easter.

The West has, however, left its mark on Orthodoxy in positive ways too. Notable among these is a renewal of preaching which has occurred at various points during the twentieth century in the diverse settings of Greece (through the 'Zoë' movement[8]), Romania (where the strong Baptist community and the 1930s Orthodox renewal movement 'the Lord's Army' have played a part), Russia (where preaching was the only mode of communication left for clergy during much of the Communist era), and the United States. Common to all is the desire to foster preaching which is both anchored in the liturgical context and pastorally and socially relevant.

With the opening up of Eastern borders, Western Christian agencies have flooded into the East. This has added a new dimension to the story of Orthodox involvement in ecumenism. We shall see later that from the start Orthodox offered strong input to Faith and Order, and were also involved in Life and Work. However, the 1990s saw a marked swing to a more suspicious and critical attitude, as evidenced by the Russian Bishops' Jubilee Letter (2000). One of the objections most often voiced against the surge of Western Evangelicals into former Communist countries has been that they seek to draw away Orthodox into their churches, often by underhand means. Even when converts have been to all intents and purposes non-religious, the mere fact that they may have been baptized Orthodox as infants is enough for hierarchs to claim that such people have been proselytized. Complaints are also made about alleged Catholic expansionism, drawing on centuries of mutual distrust in areas where the two traditions have coexisted. Rejection of proselytism has often been based on the idea of 'canonical territory', in which traditionally Orthodox areas (mainly in Eastern Europe) have been seen as already provided for and needing no other religious input. By contrast,

Orthodox in the West have usually been happy to welcome converts from other Christian traditions, and strictly speaking they could be seen as trespassing on the canonical territory of the Patriarch of Rome, who is none other than the Pope, Rome still being recognized by Orthodox as one of the ancient patriarchates. 'The apparent contradiction is resolved, from the Orthodox view, by defining "proselytism" as the drawing away of Orthodox adherents by promises of material gain or reward, while conversion to Orthodoxy is seen as a coming to the truth.'[9] The whole issue remains highly charged, and a joint working group of the WCC and the Roman Catholic Church has produced an important statement on proselytism, *The Challenge of Proselytism and the Call to Common Witness* (1995).[10]

Elsewhere, relationships between Orthodox and Western Christian traditions have been more positive. The Patriarch of Antioch,[11] for example, has been used to the presence of religious diversity in what are now Syria and Lebanon, thanks not only to the Muslim population but also to the longstanding presence of Roman Catholics, and of the Maronites, Eastern-rite Christians who, unusually, have never been out of communion with Rome. This patriarchate has therefore tended to be more outgoing in cultivating ecumenical relationships, as is evidenced by its being the jurisdiction to receive a group of about 2,000 converts from Evangelicalism in 1987, and its receiving many who left the Church of England in the wake of the decision to ordain women as priests. In its own territory, the Patriarchate of Antioch has also re-established communion with the Syrian Orthodox Church, one of the Oriental Orthodox communions.

The churches in the Middle East

Two of the most prominent features of the life of many Middle Eastern churches during the last century have been ethnic cleansing and emigration. Hostilities between Turkey and Greece in the early 1920s, and the accompanying large-scale population exchanges, left the Ecumenical Patriarch with a far smaller flock in his heartland – just a few thousand. The Armenians suffered even more severely; during the 1914–22 violence, a third were massacred and another third forced into exile. Persecution did not end there; from 1922 the territory then became part of the USSR. The Syrian Orthodox lost over 90,000 members, at least a third of their Middle Eastern strength, in the years following 1915. As for the Assyrians of what is now northern Iraq, about a third of them lost their lives during this period. In all these cases, Turkish groups were primarily responsible, and large-scale emigration ensued, with many settling in North America. It is currently thought that half the Syrian Orthodox community now reside in Europe, a development which must have profound consequences for its outlook and sense of identity. Palestine in 1922 had about 10 per cent Christians in its population, but emigration has seen this proportion decline in the modern states of Israel and Palestine to below 1 per cent. More recently, Western media coverage of conflicts in Iraq has tended to overlook both the presence and the problems of the country's significant Christian minority (Baghdad has one of the largest concentrations of Christians in the entire Middle East). Unrest among the Kurds in the north of the country, coupled with a robust military response, resulted in the departure of most of the Christian population: between 1961 and 1995, this declined from a million to just 150,000. At least two-thirds of Iraqi Christians belong to the Chaldean community, East Syrians who are in communion with Rome.

Those who remain in such settings are often prey to growing apprehension at the future of their community and its traditions, while those who leave face the challenge of maintaining their faith in an unfamiliar setting and ensuring that it is handed on to subsequent generations, who are more likely to abandon the *diaspora* mentality for a greater measure of assimilation to Western culture. For example, large-scale emigration from Cyprus to Britain occurred after World War II and again following the partition of the island in 1974, giving the Greek Orthodox community in Britain a marked Cypriot flavour; their sense of exile and longing to return home means that they have often preferred to maintain their distinct identity through such means as Greek schools attached to parishes, rather than seek assimilation into the British community. However, this is likely to change as a generation born in Britain assumes responsibility in the Church.

The minority status of Christianity in much of the Middle East has, however, proved beneficial for ecumenical relationships. One of the most promising aspects of Christian relations in the region has been the growing convergence of Eastern and Oriental Orthodox. Dialogue has been in progress since 1961, and it has been acknowledged in official statements that differences in Christological terminology do not affect the substance of the faith.[12] By contrast, the Church of the East (formerly known as Nestorian), which subscribes only to the councils of 325 and 381, still experiences some resistance to its participation in such dialogue and in ecumenical activities more generally: thus its application to join the Middle East Council of Churches in 1985 was blocked by the Coptic Orthodox.

Many of these minority churches have recognized the vital importance of education in order to ensure that the community remains well-grounded in its traditions and yet able to adapt to the modern world. The Coptic Orthodox Church provides a striking example of this: its Sunday school movement, which owed something to the stimulus provided by

American Protestant missionaries, played a major role in the church's revitalization from the 1940s. Its teachers, to whose training considerable attention is devoted, have provided a rich source of new priests and monks, and a monastic revival has also been under way since the 1950s. Under its current leader, Pope Shenouda III (1971–), the number of monks has increased from 200 to 1,200. In spite of emigration, the church now numbers around 7 million members, about 10 per cent of the population of Egypt.

Questions for thought

1 In the light of what you have read earlier in this book about the status of Christianity and its relations with the governing authorities in Russia and China, in what ways do you see Communist policy towards the Church in these nations as continuing that of earlier rulers?

2 William Temple described Marxism as a Christian heresy. To what extent do you consider this a valid judgement?

3 We have seen that in several cases, allegiance to Orthodoxy became equated with belonging to the nation. This remains a powerful factor in many East European countries (for example, I have heard it said, 'To be Romanian is to be Orthodox'), and a problem for adherents of other Christian traditions. In the West, our first reaction is probably to condemn it. But is there anything to be said in favour of such a link?

4 Discuss the impact on Eastern Orthodoxy of domination by hostile political forces.

5 Compare and contrast the place of child education in nineteenth-century American Protestantism and the twentieth-century Coptic Orthodox Church.

Further reading

Michael Angold (ed.), 2006, *Cambridge History of Christianity*, vol. 5: *Eastern Christianity*, Cambridge: Cambridge University Press, chs 20–4.

John Binns, 2002, *An Introduction to the Christian Orthodox Churches*, Cambridge: Cambridge University Press.

Owen Chadwick, 1992, *The Christian Church in the Cold War*, Penguin History of the Church 7, London: Allen Lane.

Jane Ellis, 1986, *The Russian Orthodox Church: A Contemporary History*, London: Croom Helm.

Peter Hammond, 1956, *The Waters of Marah: The Present State of the Greek Church*, London: Rockliff.

Hugh McLeod (ed.), 2006, *Cambridge History of Christianity*, vol. 9: *World Christianities c.1914–c.2000*, Cambridge: Cambridge University Press, ch. 19.

Michael Rowe, 1994, *Russian Resurrection: Strength in Suffering – A History of Russia's Evangelical Church*, London: Marshall Pickering.

It is also worth browsing through the Keston Institute journal *Religion, State and Society* for articles on the churches under Communism.

Notes

1 Nicolas Zernov, 1964, *The Russians and their Church*, London: SPCK, p. 156.

2 Communism did not have a monopoly on anticlericalism, as was demonstrated by another revolution, that in Mexico from 1910. So antagonistic was it that from 1926 to 1929 the bishops suspended public worship in protest. Here the Church was forbidden to own property and religious ceremonies were allowed only in churches or homes.

3 The German policy also encouraged the setting up of separate Orthodox hierarchies in formerly independent territories, in order to weaken Moscow's hold on these areas.

4 It is worth correcting the widespread misapprehension that such groups are recent American imports; Baptists had been present in Russia since 1867, and the Evangelical Christians from about 1880; both owed their origins to the work of Europeans. A similar point could be made concerning Evangelicals (sometimes known as Neo-Protestants) in other East European countries. This has made for ambivalence in their relations with Western aid and missionary agencies in the post-Communist era, especially where such groups are intent on pushing their own agenda.

5 It is worth noting that Christianity had not exercised the kind of shaping influence on Chinese culture that it had in Russia, and that it was therefore easier for Communism to build on existing cultural traditions in China.

6 In Ukraine, for example, there is the Ukrainian Orthodox Church (Moscow Patriarchate; 10,384 communities in 2004), the Ukrainian Orthodox Church (Kiev Patriarchate; 3,395 communities), whose patriarch had decided to seek independence from Moscow before being deposed in 1992 for disciplinary reasons; the Ukrainian Autocephalous Orthodox Church (1,156 communities), set up locally in 1917 and forcibly united with Moscow from 1930 to 1990; and the Greek Catholics (3,340 communities), also forcibly united with Moscow from 1946 to 1990. The tension between them is all too evident: I recall seeing a poster in one church in Odessa in 2004 warning against sectarians – not, as one might expect, Baptists but other Eastern-rite jurisdictions.

7 Lest we minimize this issue, it is worth remembering the role played by calendar differences in the events surrounding the Synod of Whitby (664).

8 Founded in 1907, this movement, also known as the 'Brotherhood of Theologians', was composed of members who were celibate, held property in common, and devoted themselves to preaching and teaching the Christian faith. It played a major role in the renewal of Orthodoxy in Greece, although it is now declining.

9 James J. Stamoolis, 1986, *Eastern Orthodox Mission Theology Today*,

American Society of Missiology Series 10, Maryknoll, NY: Orbis, p. 160.

10 Reproduced in Jeffrey Gros, Harding Meyer, and William G. Rusch (eds), 2000, *Growth in Agreement II: Reports and Agreed Statements of Ecumenical Conversations on a World Level, 1982–1998*, Faith and Order Paper 187, Geneva: WCC, pp. 892–9.

11 This is the 'Greek' patriarch, i.e. the one who upholds the Christology of the Chalcedonian Definition.

12 For details, see Christine Chaillot and Aleksandr Belopopsky (eds), 1998, *Towards Unity: The Theological Dialogue Between the Orthodox Church and the Oriental Orthodox Churches*, Geneva: WCC.

17

Christianity in the West – Change or Decline?

It is widely asserted that the observance of Christianity has been diminishing in the West. However, there is considerable variation of opinion regarding when this process began, whether it is irreversible, whether it represents a decline in religiosity or merely in public religious observance, and what factors have been involved in provoking or hastening it. This chapter looks at the main developments in Western Christianity during the twentieth century, using the themes of change and decline to give some coherence to what might otherwise be a mixed bag of topics.

Defining our terms

To begin with, it is helpful to clarify our understanding of the position from which this decline began, and in particular what we mean by such concepts as a Christian state or Christendom. Hugh McLeod defines Christendom as 'a society where there were close ties between the leaders of the church and those in positions of secular power, where the laws purported to be based on Christian principles, and where, apart from certain clearly defined outsider communities, every member of the society was assumed to be a Christian'.[1] Owen Chadwick's definition explains how these principles have worked out in practice: a Christian state declares itself to be such in its constitution; it restricts certain high offices to members of the established church, it recognizes its duty to provide Christian instruction as part of the educational system; it claims a voice in the selection of church leaders, who in turn are responsible for influencing public opinion in support of state policies; and it supports the Church financially through the collection of taxes.[2] By these criteria, it can be seen that much of the West has been retreating from a Christendom model of religious practice, but whether this amounts to a decline in religiosity is debated among scholars as well as church leaders.

McLeod further suggests that there are four observable stages in the decline of Christendom: (i) toleration of different forms of Christianity,

(ii) open dissemination of anti-Christian ideas, (iii) separation of church and state, and (iv) loosening of ties between church and society.[3] Applying this to Western Europe, we might conclude that the seeds of decline were present as early as the Peace of Augsburg (1555), which established the principle *cuius regio, eius religio* ('the religion of the ruler shall be that of his subjects'): while that made for unity within a given state, it represented a *de facto* admission that the Holy Roman Empire could no longer be united on a religious basis. Scholars have argued over whether the process of decline began in the eighteenth century with the Enlightenment, the nineteenth with large-scale urbanization and industrialization, or the 1960s. Those who see pluralism as a symptom of decline argue that the seeds of decline were present even while the churches were continuing to grow during much of the modern period. However, many interpreters see decline as a more recent phenomenon, because they understand religiosity primarily in terms of such observable phenomena as church attendance and participation in the churches' sacraments and rites of passage. Our verdict will depend on what we understand by such slippery terms as 'religion', 'church', and 'decline', which is one reason why scholars reach widely divergent conclusions from the same body of evidence. In evaluating the various views on the subject, we must also be careful to distinguish statements concerning what has happened from interpretations of the evidence or assertions driven by what a particular theory of religion says must happen.

It is also important to clarify what is meant by the slippery term 'secularization', although a full discussion is not possible here as it belongs primarily to the discipline of sociology. The term appears to have come into use during the seventeenth century, with reference to the transfer of church lands to the ownership of rulers (as in the Peace of Westphalia in 1648). Put simply, secularization theory argues that the social significance of religion declines in proportion as a society becomes modernized: religion has less of a public role to play in a society dominated by technology and industry, and its explanations of the world have less appeal in a setting where human ability to shape the environment is emphasized. It is also argued that secularization is inherent in the Western religious tradition because the latter has desacralized the world and by tolerating pluralism has undermined the plausibility of all religious structures of thought. Related to this is the claim that the Enlightenment swept away the old supernaturalist view of the world and replaced it with one in which human beings are self-sufficient actors, masters of their context. Although secularization is widely accepted as a description of the fate of religion in the modern West, each aspect of the theory (considered as an attempt to explain, rather than merely describe, what has happened) has come in for severe criticism: religiosity can be seen as changing rather than declining (as people adopt a more privatized form of spirituality), and some modernized societies are still marked by a high level of traditional religious observance (for example, the United States). Even large urban localities are sometimes seeing a resurgence of religious practice. Furthermore, the decline of Christendom should not be simplistically equated with the decline of Christianity: indeed, some would argue that it frees individuals to be Christian on the basis of a personal commitment rather than being legally compelled to conform to the state religion. More recent work has argued that nineteenth-century churches tried so hard to reach out to the wider society by incorporating aspects of contemporary culture into their programmes as a means of attracting people, that they failed to look after their 'core business' of fostering the spiritual development of their members and bringing people to respond to the Christian message. It is also claimed that as the state took over aspects of education and welfare work which had previously been the preserve of the churches, that churches were left trying to reinvent themselves. Some have contended that people stopped believing because they stopped going to church, rather than the other way round, although the picture here is complex: in addition to those who stopped believing and stopped attending, some stopped believing but continued going to church, while others stopped going to church but continued believing. The sociologist Callum Brown has seen the decline of female religious practice as crucial to 'the death of Christian Britain', and others have followed his lead by focusing on gender issues as a factor in the decline of organized Christianity. At present, therefore, there is no general agreement on the reasons for secularization, nor even on its significance. Brown's assertions that it can be dated fairly precisely to the 1960s, that it is irreversible, and that it was unprecedented in affecting the whole of Western Europe, will continue to provoke vigorous debate. Any model which is to be constructed to account for the evidence will have to be as complex as human behaviour itself, and will need to be constructed on a global basis rather than a purely Western one.

The state of the churches

The extent of numerical decline in church membership in Western Europe should not be overstated. Germany is perhaps the closest parallel to Britain, having seen a decline in church membership totals from 50 million in 1970 to 45 million by 1995; in France membership has declined only slowly throughout the twentieth century, from about 31 million (1900) to about 30 million (2000), and in the Netherlands it has increased very slightly since 1970 to just over 7 million. However, it is true that there has been a more marked decline in religious practice, and of course these figures, when set against population growth during the century as a whole, still translate into a decline in membership as a proportion of the population.

Before decline came a brief period when things appeared to be going well for the churches. The late 1940s and 1950s saw Christian Democratic parties, owing much of their inspiration to Catholic social teaching, at the height of their influence in countries such as West Germany (and hence on the formation of the European Economic Community in 1957). Not only were the churches exercising a considerable influence on the political reconstruction of Europe, but they benefited from popular apprehension at the development of the Cold War, as well as experiencing a fresh surge of vigour in outreach. Britain saw a succession of evangelistic campaigns through the late 1940s and 1950s, and although the results of these should not be overestimated, they did help to ensure that Christianity remained a prominent part of the world of public discourse. Similarly, church membership in the USA reached its highest recorded levels during the same period, as mainline churches recovered from the controversies of the 1920s and the depression of the 1930s.

Decline has not affected all churches equally, nor has it affected churches of the same tradition in different countries to the same extent. For example, ethnic minority churches in London are growing even as traditional churches decline (by 1999, half the churchgoers in London were from ethnic minorities); whereas Brethren in Angola, India, and other Majority World countries are growing, in Britain and North America their decline is approaching crisis proportions. Generally speaking, 'state' churches and those which practise infant baptism are declining most rapidly, and churches which require individuals to 'opt in' through baptism as a believer and which have a charismatic or Pentecostal flavour are usually growing. Another factor accelerating numerical decline has been the recent widespread fall in the birth rate in the West; increased economic well-being has played a part in this, as has widespread Catholic rejection of the papal ban on artificial contraception.

In Britain, church membership peaked in 1906 for Baptists, Congregationalists, and Methodists; as for established churches, their high point came in 1932 (England) and 1956 (Scotland). Catholic membership peaked in 1969. Many evangelical or charismatic groups have continued to grow, and Baptists (who in Britain are largely evangelical) have also begun to reverse several decades of decline, especially in Scotland. Taken on its own, Scotland saw membership peaking rather later: 1934 for Congregationalists, 1935 for Baptists, 1955 for the Episcopalians and the United Free Church, 1956 for the Church of Scotland and the Methodists, and 1966 and 1980 for the Catholics.

It should be noted that decline in church attendance is part of a wider cultural shift, from participation in corporate activities to a more privatized lifestyle. Leisure activities and voluntary organizations have all been hit by this. To a considerable extent it is linked with changing settlement patterns: the post-war period saw large-scale migration out of city centres to new estates, both council-owned and private; this decimated inner-city congregations, but it also entailed the weakening of the old social networks. In some ways, the situation may be compared with the nineteenth-century population shift to urban areas. Yet it is also true that for most denominations, their largest congregations are in suburban areas, especially those inhabited mainly by the middle classes. But it was the new lifestyle, which placed great value on the trappings of material prosperity – the car, the television, and the holiday – which presented the biggest problem for the churches. As people retreated behind their garden fences, they withdrew not only from church attendance but also from visiting the cinema, playing sport, or going to the dance hall. Life became more privatized and the social networks which had held together many older-established communities struggled to establish or maintain themselves. Not only did people cease attending church, but they ceased to send their children too. Sunday school attendance, traditionally if not too accurately seen as a major source of recruitment, fell dramatically in Scotland from 325,000 in 1956 to 61,000 in 1994. And the rate at which infant baptisms were eventually converted into adult communicants likewise fell: in Scotland, it dropped from 82 per cent in 1963 to 28 per cent about two decades later.

Politically and socially, churches in the English-speaking world have had to cope with a process of marginalization. Not only have many of their social and philanthropic functions been taken over by the state and by other voluntary bodies, but also religion has come to be seen as a private affair which should not hinder the smooth running of a secular society. Furthermore, from the 1960s a morality which clashed with traditional Christian teaching began to be advocated openly and supported by legislative changes. Many, especially among Evangelicals, had adopted a politically quietist stance for much of the twentieth century before 1970, but since then there has been something of a reaction. Many Christians have become increasingly outspoken against what they see as unjust or immoral government policies, whether it be abortion (the 1973 US Supreme Court ruling in the case of 'Roe vs Wade' was a major stimulus to evangelical and Catholic action) or nuclear armament (the Campaign for Nuclear Disarmament attracted significant support from British churchmen during the early 1960s). Bodies such as the EA in Britain have introduced a strong element of social critique and parliamentary lobbying into their activity (in 2000 the EA relaunched itself as 'a movement to change society'). Yet, for all this, English-speaking Christians have yet to succeed in forming effective political parties (whereas in Europe Catholic social thought helped to inspire the Christian Democrats), and most have not so far articulated a coherent moral vision which has been able to

command widespread attention and respect. Many have focused on issues of personal morality ('family values') but neglected economic and
social issues. Furthermore, their perception of the status of their country
varies significantly; in both Britain and the United States, some regard
their nation as uniquely favoured by God and as having responsibilities
arising from such a relationship, while others see it as liable to imminent
judgement for its tolerance of injustice and moral decay; thus the United
States could be perceived as Israel or as Babylon.

Curiously, church attendance in the USA has held up considerably
better, especially among Protestants, although Canada followed the
European pattern. This has been seen as challenging the notion that
secularization occurs when the truth-claims of all faiths are undermined
by the toleration of religious pluralism, although one might argue that
American pluralism is only skin-deep since American 'civil religion'
underlies a diversity of Christian and Jewish expressions and is the real
focus of allegiance for many. In such an argument, secularization could
occur when the civil religion itself was widely challenged when there was
a change in the nature of civil religion: the latter argument is borne out
by the way in which the status of a broad Evangelicalism as the widely
shared public faith during the mid-nineteenth century gave way first to a
broader Protestantism and then to a consensus which included Catholics
and Jews. Nowadays, although presidents since the 1970s have often
publicly espoused certain evangelical values such as the importance of
the Bible or testimony to a 'born again' experience, public policy is not
usually shaped by religious considerations.[4] It could therefore be argued
that religion has become privatized, a matter of what individuals do with
their spare time, rather than something which offers an all-embracing
worldview; this could certainly be regarded as a form of secularization,
since it implies a retreat of Christianity from the public arena.

Belief has not, however, declined at the same rate; many scholars have
spoken of 'believing without belonging',[5] as surveys indicate that the
index of belief in God, and of self-identification as Christian, is often
higher than those for church membership or attendance. The importance
of this phenomenon should not be overstated, as it is not as new as might
be thought: attendance at Mass was less regular during the medieval
period than it later became, and many working-class Englishmen during
the nineteenth century would have claimed to be Christian even though
they did not attend church. This is one instance of a perceived tendency
on the part of secularization theorists to draw the contrast too sharply
between past and present.

How have churches responded to decline and to the marginalization of
their position in society? Some have lamented it without taking any action.
Some have interpreted it as referring only to those whose church attendance was a matter of social conformity rather than personal conviction,

and welcomed numerical decline as a form of 'clearing the decks'; it has often been argued that religious allegiance is now much less likely to be something imposed from above or by social expectations, and more likely to be a matter of the individual's free and informed choice. Some have interpreted ecumenism, especially in the form of denominational or congregational mergers, as a response to decline along the lines of that adopted in the business world, although it is debatable whether there is any direct correlation between ecumenical openness and experience of decline. Some have attempted to reinvent the Church, its mission, its role in society, and its *raison d'être* as referring to this world rather than the next one; in particular, some in the 1960s urged religion to embrace 'the secular city', calling believers to abandon 'God-talk', an approach which could be caricatured as making a virtue out of necessity.

In France church–state relations improved a great deal after World War I, and the Church made considerable efforts to understand and overcome the alienation between it and working-class men; in 1943 an influential book posed the question *La France, Pays de Mission?* and during the 1940s and 1950s a number of priests took jobs in industry. There were not lacking French theologians with the ability to contribute to debates in the political arena, such as Jacques Maritain and the Protestant Jacques Ellul (1912–94). Yet the impact of all this seems to have been minimal, at least in terms of reversing a decline in Catholic practice.

In the English-speaking world, however, attempts at outreach have formed the most popular response. Even the Church of England has taken this route, as seen in the 1945 report *Towards the Conversion of England* or the current (2007) stress on becoming a 'Mission-Shaped Church'. In particular, many denominations sought to plant new congregations in the post-war decades, and numbers of congregations may in fact have peaked some decades later than numbers of members. For example, the London Baptist Association's highest membership figures were recorded in 1907, but by 1964 it had more churches than ever before. Such figures probably reflect attempts to follow the outward migration from city centres by planting new churches on suburban developments, as well as a change in style: the mega-churches of the Victorian era were becoming as unfashionable as the pulpit oratory of the same period, and indeed the lack of orators was one reason why large congregations were rarely sustainable.

It is worth noting that although Christian practice has declined, to some extent other religious paths have filled the gap. The post-war period saw large-scale immigration, especially to England, France, and Germany. This resulted in the establishment of sizeable communities adhering to other faiths (in addition to the old-established Jewish community). Although relatively few Westerners convert to these faiths, the ethnic groups which practise them have seen considerable demographic growth, ensuring that society takes on a more pluralistic colour, especially in larger urban areas. Moreover, in much of Western Europe alternative spiritualities often grouped together under the 'New Age' umbrella have proved attractive, though whether as passing fads or as enduring lifestyle choices is open to question. Many, too, claim to be interested in spirituality but not in religion. So it seems too early to claim that religion no longer has any significant public presence; in many quarters it appears quite well able to coexist with, and to deploy aspects of, contemporary culture.

Theological developments

Clearly, in such a radically changing social and intellectual context, there was bound to be a measure of theological ferment. In this section we look at some of the main theological trends during the twentieth century not covered elsewhere; some have argued with reference to certain trends that they actually hastened decline, but here we shall confine ourselves to interpreting them as responses to contemporary intellectual, social, or political trends. Some may fairly be seen as attempts to recover the key position of theology as a major intellectual player, and others as attempts to restate the essence of the Christian gospel in a form comprehensible to contemporary outsiders. Some of these trends have exercised their primary influence in the West, and may be seen primarily as aspects of academic theological debate; but others have shaped the way in which the Church has acted in various parts of the world.

Developments in biblical studies

Major developments in biblical studies cannot all be surveyed here,[6] but it is worth noting first the programme of demythologization associated with the German Lutheran New Testament scholar Rudolf Bultmann (1884–1976) as an example of how contemporary philosophical currents have often shaped theology. Bultmann opposed the Quest for the Historical Jesus as impossible (because of the lack of evidence: we can know from history *that* Jesus existed but not *what* he was like), unnecessary (for response to the gospel), and illegitimate (because we are justified by faith, not by history). His programme of 'demythologization' aimed to reinterpret what he saw as the mythical elements of the New Testament in order to allow its message (conceived in terms of a call to personal encounter with Christ and response to him) to stand out; on doing so, the result appeared distinctly like the stress of contemporary existentialist philosophy on the need to act 'authentically', that is, in accordance with one's true self. In the 1950s, however, the 'New Quest' stressed the degree of continuity between the Jesus of history and the Christ of faith, arguing that the Gospels include historical narrative as well as kerygmatic material. It in turn collapsed in the 1960s, to be replaced by a 'Third Quest' which majored on studying the miraculous elements of Jesus' ministry. In spite of the media attention sometimes given to exponents of such views, or to those of the more recent 'Jesus Seminar', it is debatable how much the average church member has been influenced by them.

A more conservative approach to the Bible was adopted by the Biblical Theology movement, which emerged during the 1930s with the work of scholars such as the German Old Testament theologian Walther Eichrodt. This movement encompassed a variety of outlooks, united by the belief that it was possible to regard the Bible as a unity and therefore worthwhile to attempt the reconstruction of the theology found in it as a coherent entity. It was at the height of its influence during the culturally conservative 1950s, and was exemplified by the work of such scholars as the Britons C.H. Dodd (1884–1973) and H.H. Rowley (1890–1969), the Frenchman Oscar Cullmann (1902–99), the Germans Joachim Jeremias (1900–79) and Gerhard von Rad (1901–71), and the American John Bright (1908–95). The importance of this movement lay in its influence on generations of ministerial candidates during their training, and on the wider Christian community through the stream of books coming from its exponents and their role as Bible translators.

Developments in systematic theology

In the field of systematic theology, the beginning of the period was marked by the challenge to liberalism presented by World War I: the optimistic outlook expressed in the belief that humanity was engaged on an upward march of progress became incredible for many, especially in Continental Europe, and some turned to the emergent Neo-Orthodox movement (often known at the time as 'dialectical theology' or 'the theology of crisis'). Nevertheless, the liberal tradition of accommodating Christian theology to modern thought was not thereby extinguished: in England it continued to make significant contributions to Anglican theological debate, thanks to its espousal by occupants of professorial chairs and episcopal thrones. Indeed, the Modern Churchmen's Union (founded in 1898) aroused considerable controversy by the published report of its 1921 conference, which provoked the Church of England to establish a doctrinal commission (the first of several during the century), whose report appeared in 1938 as *Doctrine in the Church of England*. Generally, old-fashioned liberal belief in progress has disappeared; but liberal attitudes to the supernatural, to Christ, and to Scripture have fed into some newer movements of thought. Such attitudes often shape the beliefs of people in the pews, whatever their ministers might preach from the pulpit.

One of the most notorious expressions of theological radicalism was the 'Death of God' school, which attained a brief vogue in the United States during the mid-1960s. Some of its leading lights argued that the Church should abandon talk of God as it was now meaningless (an approach which reflected the distrust of metaphysics shown by the contemporary philosophical movement of Logical Positivism), or that it should seek to do without God in a manner appropriate for 'man come of age' (a phrase taken from Dietrich Bonhoeffer, though whether he was correctly interpreted is still debated). The way was prepared for this approach to theology by Paul Tillich (1886–1965), a philosophical theologian forced to leave Germany for the United States after opposing National Socialist ideology as idolatrous. In his theological method, Tillich advocated the practice of 'correlation', relating the message of theology to the questions thrown up by the contemporary cultural context. For him, God became the 'ground of our being', that is, being as such rather than an entity who exists. Christian conversion (Tillich was something of an evangelist at heart) was interpreted as overcoming the fear of non-being through 'the courage to be' (his interpretation of justification by faith). Tillich's approach was popularized most famously by the Bishop of Woolwich, John Robinson (1919–83), in *Honest to God* (1963). Thanks to a front-page article in *The Observer* on 17 March 1963 entitled 'Our image of God must go', Robinson became a household name overnight. Not all approved of his attempt to make the gospel speak to contemporary people by means of replacing traditional talk of God 'up there' with images of depth and ultimate concern: from the Archbishop of Canterbury downwards, Robinson's hastily constructed book came in for severe criticism. Yet it gave impetus to a renewal of Anglican liberalism which would hit the headlines as a result of the theology of the Cambridge don and Anglican priest Don Cupitt (b. 1934), author of *Taking Leave of God* (1980), who described himself as a 'Christian Buddhist' and the concept of 'God' as a human construction, and again when in 1993 a Sussex vicar, Anthony Freeman, published *God in Us*, arguing for a similarly non-realist approach to theology; for him, God was the name we give to our deepest convictions, and prayer amounted to talking to oneself. Freeman's case hit the headlines as one of the few occasions during the twentieth century when a Church of England cleric has been removed from office for heresy by his diocesan bishop.

Slightly less radical has been Process Theology, an American movement which drew on the philosopher A.N. Whitehead (1861–1947) and was at the height of its influence during the 1970s. It was grounded in the idea that being is dynamic rather than static, and relational and hence open to being affected by others. Applied to God, it resulted in a stress on divine immanence (its worldview has been called panentheistic) and vulnerability and a tendency to reject the idea of divine supernatural intervention in the world.

Reacting to certain liberal emphases but at the same time possibly retreating from public intellectual debate is another North American movement, Postliberalism or Narrative Theology (so called from its extensive use of the biblical narratives). This was centred on Yale Divinity School and arose during the 1970s. It sees religion as concerned with living in a particular community and inwardly appropriating its tradition of thought with a view to becoming a force for the healing of a divided world. Doctrine is regarded as corrective rather than constructive, setting out the boundaries for proper Christian thought and action rather than laying down a system of right beliefs. Key thinkers include George Lindbeck (whose *The Nature of Doctrine* (1984) was a seminal text for the movement), Stanley Hauerwas, and Hans Frei.

Although we shall not deal with Liberation Theology in this chapter, it is important to look at one of its major sources, a German-initiated movement known as Political Theology,[7] which has been seminal for the development of ecumenical thinking about the Church and its mission. Of course there is a long and venerable tradition of theological reflection concerning the Church and its relationship to the social order, going back to Augustine of Hippo's work *The City of God*. The political role of the Church in post-war Germany was seen as a pressing issue, but theologians wished to avoid either identifying the kingdom of God with the prevailing social order (or with any political system) or retreating into the sphere of private religion (as many had done during the 1930s) and failing to address the issue. Political Theology owes much to a Roman Catholic theologian, Johann Baptist Metz (b. 1936). He argues that theology is not merely a discipline addressing the Church's 'in house' concerns, but a mode of social critique in the public arena. Salvation, he contends, is concerned primarily with bodily and corporate (even political) existence, rather than being something reserved exclusively for the future. Thus issues of justice become of crucial importance, for good theology should issue in right practice.

Such themes have been developed further in a broader theological context by the most widely read contemporary Protestant theologian, the Tübingen professor Jurgen Moltmann (b. 1926). Moltmann's theology was decisively shaped by his conversion to Christian faith while a prisoner of war in England from 1945 to 1948, and it has always been marked by a stress on the idea of solidarity with the suffering, whether of God with humanity (as seen in the cross) or that of the Church with the poor. Equally important for Moltmann's 'theology of hope' has been the resurrection of Christ, which he sees as the guarantee of hope for the whole created order. Since there is such a hope, we are called to change in anticipation, and ecological themes have become increasingly prominent in Moltmann's thought, partly in the light of this hope and partly because the relationship of mutuality between humankind and the physical environment is seen as a reflection of the relationship between God and humans, and ultimately of that between the Persons of the Trinity. Such thought has been influential in the ecumenical arena, not only in giving ecology a higher profile but also in the development of a doctrine of the Church based on the concept of *koinonia* ('fellowship'). Eschatology takes centre stage as God's action in the world is conceived in terms of pulling us forward into the new age, and mission comes to be seen as transforming the world in preparation for its arrival. Such thinking was seminal for early liberation theologians, many of whom studied in Europe during the 1960s.

Along similar lines to Liberation Theology and in fruitful dialogue with it, a distinctive 'black theology' began to be articulated in the USA from the 1960s, responding to the Black Power movement's rejection of Christianity as a white religion and affirming black history as theologically significant and Christianity as a black religion. An important statement of this approach was *Black Theology and Black Power* (1969) by James H. Cone (b. 1938). Black churches have drawn on such thinking in becoming more politically active, and on the example provided by the Baptist minister Martin Luther King (1929–68). In 1957, King was involved in founding the Southern Christian Leadership Conference to oppose racial discrimination and segregation, as part of the wider Civil Rights movement of the 1950s and '60s. He based his strategy on the Sermon on the Mount and Mahatma Gandhi's tactic of 'non-violent resistance', his objective being to bring about confrontational situations through peaceful civil disobedience, hoping in this way to mobilize public opinion to call for changes in unjust legislation. His assassination gave him the status of a Christian martyr worldwide, and ensured that his approach would be adopted by many other groups seeking social change.

In Southern Africa, Black Theology took a somewhat different form, thanks to the different context, that of apartheid. Apartheid, the ideology of 'separate development' for different races, was rooted in the theological reflection on experience of the Dutch Calvinist Boers as they colonized Southern Africa and suffered the humiliation of British rule. Many Dutch Reformed churchmen of the 1930s and 1940s had been educated in Nazi Germany and admired the dominant ideology. Their successors came under increasingly heavy fire, and in 1982 the church's membership of the World Alliance of Reformed Churches was suspended, apartheid being deemed a heresy. In 1986 the church formally withdrew its support for apartheid. A landmark statement of South African Black Theology was the *Kairos Document* (1985, revised in 1986), which shows the influence of liberationism and Political Theology in criticizing both 'state theology' which legitimates the existing political order and 'church theology' which fails to address the structures which promote oppression. It challenged the churches to seize the moment and commit themselves to working against the unjust regime. What has been particularly noteworthy about the South African tradition has been its contribution to the reconstruction of the nation after the end of apartheid; the Truth and Reconciliation Commission, whose chief architect was the Archbishop of Cape Town, Desmond Tutu (b. 1931), has worked hard to understand the dynamics of what had gone on and to enable the various racial groups in the country to move forward together.

Feminist or Womanist Theology has sometimes been seen as a variant of Liberation Theology. Like some of the others studied in this chapter, it is perhaps best seen as a family of theologies, all responding to the developing awareness of the ways in which much of the Church's theological tradition had silenced women and legitimated their oppression. The catalysts for their development were the wider feminist movement and the attempt by Catholic women to respond to the pronouncements of the Second Vatican Council. Some more radical theologians, such as the former Catholic Mary Daly and the former Anglican Daphne Hampson, have argued that Christianity is incorrigibly patriarchal and therefore oppressive, and so can never be an acceptable religion for women. Others have asserted that many traditional theological formulations reflect male dominance and need to be rewritten. There are also evangelical feminists, who are happy with traditional theological understandings but who read the Bible as an egalitarian document. Feminist thought has affected the Church in many areas of its life, notably liturgy and Bible translation (through the use of inclusive language and the quest for alternative images of God), ministry (many denominations have moved since the 1960s to begin ordaining women), and ethics (especially in the area of sexuality).

A movement strongly influenced by the growth of interest in ecological issues and alternative spiritualities has been Creation-Centred Spirituality, whose foremost advocate has been the American Dominican turned Episcopalian priest, Matthew Fox (b. 1940). In such works as *Original Blessing* (1983), Fox seeks to move away from what he sees as the dualism of the Western theological tradition resulting from the stress on fall and redemption and leading to alienation between humankind and nature, to a positive affirmation of the created order. The movement has been widely criticized as over-indebted to 'New Age' thinking, but since the early 1980s the questions it seeks to address have been at the forefront of thinking in the WCC, which instituted a programme to respond to issues of 'Justice, Peace, and the Integrity of Creation'.

Developments in evangelical thought

Evangelicalism saw a further episode in the conflict with liberalism. In 1922, the liberal New York Baptist Harry Emerson Fosdick (1878–1969) preached a swashbuckling sermon entitled 'Shall the Fundamentalists Win?' Taking a leaf out of his opponents' book, he had it distributed free of charge to 130,000 Protestant clergy. In 1925, the Scopes trial raised the issue of the legitimacy of teaching evolution in state schools in Tennessee, but the result was a widespread backlash against the teaching of creationism in such a context. Battles raged over control of seminaries, publishing houses, and denominational structures, with Baptists and Presbyterians in the North being particularly affected. The American Fundamentalist movement therefore became increasingly strident and separatist, in reaction to what it saw as a liberal takeover of denominational structures.[8] A network of alternative institutions and Bible schools was founded, one of the best known being the staunchly dispensationalist Dallas Theological Seminary (1924). Everything that a denomination provided was available through such means: training, outreach (for example, by radio), summer conferences, Sunday school curricula, and sound literature. Fundamentalists might have been opposed to what they called 'modernism' (though their own thought is widely seen as tinctured with elements of modernity, such as their stress on rationality), but they led the way in adapting modern publicity methods such as radio broadcasting for church use. By the 1930s explicitly Fundamentalist denominations were appearing (for example, the Regular Baptists in 1932 and the Orthodox Presbyterians in 1936), though they found it hard to comprehend both Dispensationalists and conservative confessional Evangelicals, whose outlook and theology differed significantly. Fundamentalism, perhaps even more so than Evangelicalism, came to rely on the leadership provided by high-profile figures such as T.T. Shields (1873–1955) in Toronto and Ian Paisley (b. 1926) in Belfast. Such men (and they were always men) could also count on an undercurrent of support for their critiques of the churches from disaffected conservatives within mainline denominations.

Theologically similar to Fundamentalism and often sharing its separatism, but adopting cultural forms instead of condemning them, was the Jesus Movement, which originated in Californian counter-culture and owed much to the *Zeitgeist* of the 1960s: informality, spontaneity, refusal to be bound by cultural or ecclesiastical norms, and a sense that society was on the 'Eve of Destruction'.[9] Its laid-back style of worship came to dominate evangelical gatherings in England as well as North America, either directly or through the medium of the Charismatic movement.

After 1945 a reaction set in against Fundamentalist separatism and withdrawal from engagement with the world, in the form of Neo-

Evangelicalism. Among leading exponents of a new, socially engaged outlook in the United States has been Carl Henry (b. 1913), and prominent institutions have included the National Association of Evangelicals (1942) and Fuller Theological Seminary in California (1947). In various parts of the world there has been growth in serious evangelical scholarship, largely in response to the perceived domination of liberal approaches in the field of biblical studies. This trend has helped to ensure that leadership of churches in many parts of the Majority World has been extensively influenced by evangelical thought and priorities. It has also fed into the burgeoning Pentecostal and Charismatic movements, whose development we shall explore in the next chapter.

Questions for thought

1 When do you see the decline of Christianity in the West as beginning, and what reasons would you give for your opinion?

2 It seems likely that Britain has seen a sharper decline in Christian practice than many other countries in Western Europe. As a historian, what factors would you see as having contributed to this? Are they all factors which emerged during the twentieth century, or have some of them been evident for a longer period?

3 Which of the theological trends outlined in this chapter do you consider to have had most impact on church life? What evidence would you offer in support of your verdict?

4 Why did Fundamentalism flourish in the United States but not in Britain?

Further reading

David Ford with Rachel Muers (eds), 2005, *The Modern Theologians: An Introduction to Christian Theology since 1918*, 3rd edn, Oxford: Blackwell.

Robert T. Handy, 1976, *A History of the Churches in the United States and Canada*, Oxford History of the Christian Church, Oxford: Clarendon, chs 11–12.

Hugh McLeod (ed.), 2006, *Cambridge History of Christianity*, vol. 9: *World Christianities c.1914–c.2000*, Cambridge: Cambridge University Press, chs 9, 13, 16–18.

Hugh McLeod and Werner Ustorf (eds), 2003, *The Decline of Christendom in Western Europe, 1750–2000*, Cambridge: Cambridge University Press.

Mark A. Noll, 1992, *A History of Christianity in the United States and Canada*, London: SPCK, part 5.

Notes

1 Hugh McLeod, in McLeod and Ustorf, *Decline of Christendom*, p. 1.

2 Owen Chadwick, 1992, *The Christian Church in the Cold War*, Penguin History of the Church 7, London: Allen Lane, pp. 181–2.

3 Hugh McLeod, in McLeod and Ustorf, *Decline of Christendom*, p. 4. McLeod's introduction to this volume offers an accessible and comprehensive overview of the debate about the decline of religion in the West. Another thought-provoking evaluation of secularization theory, including recent modifications, is: David Hempton, 2005, *Methodism: Empire of the Spirit*, New Haven, CT: Yale University Press, pp. 189–99.

4 One probable exception to this is the pro-Israeli stance of successive United States administrations, though whether this has been adopted as a matter of conviction or as a vote-winner may be debated. Similarly, when President Reagan famously described the Soviet Union as an 'evil empire' during the 1980s, it may well be that he had popular evangelical eschatology in view (it taught the future downfall of Russia), either shaping his thinking or as a language of discourse which his audience would understand and approve.

5 See, for example, Grace Davie, 1994, *Religion in Britain since 1945: Believing without Belonging*, Oxford: Blackwell. In Sweden, however, it would be more appropriate to speak of 'belonging without believing', as most people belong to the state church but a far smaller proportion believe in God or practise Christianity.

6 For surveys of the history of biblical interpretation, see Gerald Bray, 1996, *Biblical Interpretation Past and Present*, Leicester: Apollos; Stephen Neill and Tom Wright, 1988, *The Interpretation of the New Testament 1861–1986*, Oxford: Oxford University Press.

7 An accessible introduction to Political Theology is the article in *NDT*.

8 Britain was less affected by such strife, although some missionary societies divided during the 1920s and the Inter-Varsity Fellowship was founded as a national body in 1927. But the separatist note was rarely heard in most parts of Britain.

9 The title of an album by the American artist Barry McGuire.

18

Pentecostalism and the Charismatic Movement

Until recently, surveys of global church history rarely had much to say about Pentecostalism. Yet the astonishing growth and spread which have marked its first century betoken an ability to contextualize itself which should make it of interest to those working in the field of religious history. The very orality of Pentecostal culture means that much of the movement is sparsely documented, and the section whose history has been recorded in detail (mostly in the Anglo-Saxon world) is not necessarily representative of the movement as a whole. This chapter should therefore be taken as a provisional account, and furthermore one which is angled towards the English-speaking world. A truly global account would pay far more attention to Pentecostalism in Latin America, Asia, and Africa.

Pentecostal development

Internal division

Chapter 12 introduced the Pentecostal movement in North America. Shortly before the First World War, it began to divide over differing understandings of Christian experience: was this to be conceived in terms of two stages or three? The two-stage model, which was rooted in the broader Reformed tradition, saw conversion as followed by baptism with the Holy Ghost; it was sometimes called 'finished work' teaching, because of the belief that the work of Christ on the cross was sufficient not only for forgiveness but also for sanctification, and that the latter was something to be appropriated gradually throughout the Christian life rather than obtained by a crisis experience. The three-stage model, which was more congenial to leaders who had come from the Wesleyan-Holiness tradition, added the experience of entire sanctification between the other two stages.

Within the 'finished work' strand of Pentecostalism, which represented the majority view among white Pentecostals, debate began in 1913 regarding whether baptism should be in the name of the Father, the Son, and the Holy Ghost (as in the 'Great Commission' of Matthew 28), or simply in the name of Jesus (as in Acts), the latter being an extension of the Jesus-centred piety widespread in moderate Holiness circles. The latter was given a theological rationale which stressed the oneness of God (hence the designation 'Oneness Pentecostalism'), Father, Son, and Spirit being seen as successive manifestations of this within the economy of salvation.[1] Rebaptism was widespread of those baptized in the name of Father, Son, and Holy Spirit, and the deepening division was formalized in 1916 when the Assemblies of God adopted a Trinitarian doctrinal statement and evicted those who could not accept it. Trinitarian Pentecostals have usually rejected such teaching as heretical, and there has been little contact between the two wings of the movement outside some scholarly circles. All the same, as many as a quarter of classical Pentecostals may belong to this strand, whose most important groupings include the United Pentecostal Church (USA) and the True Jesus Church (China).

In recent years it has been argued that the divide over models of Christian experience was in part motivated by racial concerns; it is certainly noticeable that black Pentecostals adopted the three-stage model, and the leading white denomination, the Assemblies of God, the two-stage one. However, it is not clear that there is a direct link between these trends. On several other occasions black or white minorities withdrew from Pentecostal denominations to found their own, and it has been argued that race was a bigger factor than church order in the divisions of North American Pentecostalism.

In Britain as in North America, Pentecostal congregations soon recognized the need to band together in order to provide safeguards against excess and error, and so denominations emerged which quickly spread overseas through missionary work. What is now the Elim Pentecostal Church began as a regional grouping in Northern Ireland during 1915, the Apostolic Church in 1916, and the Assemblies of God in 1924. They were distinguished principally by their different approaches to church government: Elim adopted a presbyterian system, Assemblies of God adopted a more congregational approach which gave a large measure of autonomy to local churches, and the Apostolics instituted a church order under the rule of Apostles, with considerable authority also being given to officially appointed Prophets. Elim also differed from the others in denying that speaking with tongues was the 'initial evidence' of having been baptized with the Spirit (as do most Pentecostals worldwide).

Pentecostals and the wider Christian community

We saw that Pentecostals were quickly rejected by Evangelicals and Fundamentalists. As the movement matured in the West, however, most of its leaders frequently sought a measure of respectability by locating themselves within the evangelical spectrum, and even (at the risk of denying significant elements of their own spirituality) to call themselves 'Fundamentalists'; this brought the experiential nature of Pentecostal spirituality into collision with the more cerebral and text-orientated approach of Fundamentalism. Fundamentalists, for their part, have almost always denounced Pentecostalism, as in an official statement by the World's Christian Fundamentals Association in 1928. Elsewhere in the world, Pentecostals have been less concerned about making such identifications; they read the Bible within the context of the local Christian community and in the light of their own experience, hearing it speak to their concerns, rather than as an intellectual exercise involving the construction of a coherent theological system. However, many still prefer to remain apart from ecumenical institutions, in spite of the bridge-building efforts of the South African David du Plessis (1905–87), and the first Assemblies of God body to join its national council of churches was the South Korean, as recently as 1999.

The readiness of Pentecostalism in the Majority World to adopt an independent standpoint has also meant that it has often not followed white Pentecostalism in social quietism, but has been willing to combine Pentecostal spirituality with social action and critique, another factor which may explain its greater readiness on occasion to become ecumenically involved. (A similar openness marks black Pentecostal churches in Britain, North America, and South Africa.) An example of this is the work of Frank Chikane, a minister in the Apostolic Faith Mission in South Africa (which during the apartheid era existed in four racially segregated sections). Deposed from 1981 to 1990 for political involvement, he oversaw the writing of the *Kairos Document*. He also served as general secretary of the South African Council of Churches from 1987 to 1994.

By contrast, South Africa has also been one of the major strongholds of the 'prosperity gospel'. This holds that God's purpose for Christian believers includes their physical and financial as well as spiritual well-being. In some ways it is reminiscent of the 'cargo' or 'adjustment cults' of the Pacific region, and both represent attempts to come to terms with Western economic growth. It may be seen as the obverse of Liberation Theology in its advocacy of prosperity and upward mobility as signs of divine blessing. Prosperity teaching has also proved quite popular in the USA, as well as feeding into the teaching of Pentecostal leaders such as David Yonggi Cho (see below) and the Swede Ulf Ekman.

Why the movement spread

Three key factors may be isolated as contributing to the rapid spread and exponential growth of Pentecostalism.

1 Outreach. The 1920s and 1930s were the era of the 'healing evangelists' in Britain and North America. Pentecostal preachers would visit towns and cities to hold high-profile evangelistic campaigns along Finneyite lines. Their closeness to ordinary people and perceived freedom from clericalism enabled them to secure a ready hearing, but what often attracted most attention was their practice of praying for the sick. Following an evangelistic sermon, or as part of a special service, they would invite all who wished, to come to the front of the auditorium and be prayed for. Newspapers reported remarkable cures in detail, thus providing invaluable publicity both for the evangelists and for their message and virtually guaranteeing crowds at the meetings. In North America, there were a number of well-known healing evangelists, including the flamboyant Aimee Semple McPherson (1890–1944), who founded the first Pentecostal megachurch – Angelus Temple, Los Angeles (1923). Other Pentecostal evangelists included Oral Roberts (b. 1918), who founded his own university, and the Oneness Pentecostal William Branham (1909–65). In Britain the Welshmen George Jeffreys (1889–1962) and his brother Stephen (1876–1943) were effective evangelists, who between the wars secured much publicity for healing campaigns which often resulted in the commencement of new churches. Just as significant were the full-time church-planters, and the movement also developed its own considerable overseas missionary force. The distinctive message of all these people was often summed up in terms of the 'Foursquare Gospel' (a pre-Pentecostal slogan taken over by the movement): Jesus Christ as Saviour, Healer, Baptizer with the Holy Ghost, and Coming King.

2 Pentecostal affirmation of lay ministry, based on belief in the Spirit's ability to gift whomever he wills, has given many Christians a sense of empowerment, and resulted in more contextually appropriate and popular (because emanating from the people rather than a trained leadership caste) forms of Christian expression.

3 Pentecostalism provides a theologically orthodox way of addressing the awareness of the supernatural realm which is a feature of many societies. This has been a major factor in the remarkable growth of Pentecostal-type locally instituted churches in Africa and South America.

The global spread of Pentecostalism

Pentecostalism has spread rapidly on an international scale (its spread before 1914 is noteworthy in this respect, given that communication was not instant like it is now[2]), and any attempt to map the lines of influence would be covered with arrows pointing in many directions from many different sources. Thus we see Latin American movements such as the Universal Church of the Kingdom of God making headway in Western Europe, to give just one example. This section offers snapshots of Pentecostal growth around the world to illustrate the assertion made above regarding its ability to contextualize.

Examples

Even before the events which gave birth to the North American movement, there had been outbreaks of Pentecostal-type phenomena elsewhere in the world. Such outbreaks had occurred from time to time throughout Christian history: the second-century Montanists and the seventeenth-century Jansenists provide two examples of movements marked by such phenomena, while Catholic and Orthodox histories are replete with stories of miracles, visions, and prophecies. However, none of these fed into contemporary Pentecostalism in the way that certain movements of the nineteenth century did. Leaving aside the Catholic Apostolic Church, which English-speaking Pentecostalism tended to dismiss out-of-hand,[3] some of the most significant occurred in India. A Tamil evangelist, J.C. Arulappen (1810–67), who worked among CMS congregations but whose practice bore affinities to that of the Brethren, saw such phenomena attending a revival associated with his ministry during the years after 1860. Even more important was the outbreak of tongues and other charismatic gifts associated with Pandita Ramabai (1858–1922) from 1905.

In Europe, around a quarter of Roma in France and Spain belong to Pentecostal churches. In Italy, by 2000 there were over 300,000 Pentecostal members – twice as many as all other Protestant bodies put together. In Ukraine, by 2003 there may have been as many as 780,000 Pentecostal members, and another 400,000 in Russia.

In Southern Africa, the relationship between Pentecostalism and indigenous churches has been the subject of scholarly investigation for some years. A formative influence on the development of Pentecostal-type churches in Southern Africa was the American John Alexander Dowie (1847–1907), founder in 1895 of the Christian Catholic Apostolic Church, whose headquarters were in Zion City, Illinois (also founded by Dowie). Missionaries from this movement came to South Africa during the Edwardian years, although those they taught rapidly began to assume an independent identity. Dowie had trained for the ministry in Edinburgh, where he may have imbibed aspects of the teaching and ecclesiology of the Catholic Apostolic Church, but he also majored on healing as part of his evangelistic ministry and insisted that his followers must not eat pork – two features, along with the 'apostolic' church order, which would be widely replicated in South Africa because of their fit with local cultures and expectations.

Pentecostal growth in Latin America really began to take off in the 1970s and 1980s. These were decades of political repression and to some extent Pentecostal success may be a response to failed revolutionary hopes, since Pentecostal churches offered an alternative sphere for self-determination.[4] Pentecostalism in the region was often supported by the United States authorities, since it was seen as politically quietist, submitting to whatever government was in power, but while this was true of newer middle-class charismatic congregations, the older and more working-class groupings were more socially active, especially in relation to local issues. In an era of rapid urbanization and modernization, the intimate fellowship of the Pentecostal congregation offers a sense of belonging to replace that lost with the move from the villages; such churches are also often active in providing basic health care, education, or training services where government provision has been unable to keep pace with demand. While some scholars have stressed this side of Latin American Pentecostalism, in some countries it is becoming increasingly middle-class and upwardly mobile.

Pentecostals are by far the most numerous Protestants in Latin America, and in some countries there their membership may soon overtake the number of practising Roman Catholics. There are already more locally born Pentecostal pastors than locally born Catholic priests. By 2000 the Assemblies of God were the largest Protestant body in Latin America, with over 4 million members. New denominations were being founded, such as the Universal Church of the Kingdom of God, whose outreach extended to more than fifty countries. In Colombia, Pentecostals pioneered a new model of church life to remarkable effect. The 'G12' approach was developed by César Castellanos in Bogotá, whose church grew from 8 to 120,000 between 1982 and 2000; it is a variation on the theme of 'cell churches', the cell being the basic unit of membership, meeting, and outreach, offering an interesting parallel to the Catholic base communities. The 1970s and 1980s were also decades of Catholic growth, but such has been Pentecostal growth that the Catholic Church has become extremely concerned at the extent of losses to the new movement, a development which is testing Roman ecumenical credentials to their limits. It may be that the popularity of Pentecostalism represents a response to the conservatism of the Vatican, which could be perceived as lacking sympathy with the local context. Paralleling Pentecostal growth has been that of cults rooted in African religious traditions and of spiritualist groups, especially in Brazil.

Pentecostalism in Korea traces its roots back to a revival which began in 1903 and continued for some years, the 'Korean Pentecost'. This appears to have occurred entirely independently of any similar events elsewhere, and although missionaries were involved it was very much an indigenous-led movement. In fact, it was to be the late 1920s before Pentecostal missionaries arrived in the country, by which time things were well under way in the mainstream Protestant denominations. Nevertheless, Pentecostal denominations have also grown, and the largest church in the world is the Yoido Full Gospel Church in Seoul, led by Paul (later David) Yonggi Cho (b. 1936), an Assemblies of God minister, and founded in 1958 at a time when South Koreans were experiencing extreme economic hardship after the Korean War. Cho's version of prosperity teaching has proved to have mass appeal, as well as offering an excellent example of the ability of Pentecostalism to contextualize its message and thus take root in widely differing cultures (Hollenweger has described him as a Pentecostal shaman[5]); by 2000 his church had over 900,000 members in 50,000 cells. By 1995 Pentecostalism was the third largest Christian communion in South Korea after the Catholics and the Presbyterians (and many in both communions were Charismatics), with nearly 2 million members.

Interpretations

Kay and Dyer list several widely divergent scholarly interpretations of Pentecostalism, some of which we discussed in Chapter 12: a phase of Protestant missionary expansion; an African-instituted movement which embraced Western capitalism; an integrated movement of Christian spirituality which split along racial lines; a collection of spontaneous movements originating independently of one another in various parts of the world; and an expression of 'primal spirituality'.[6] Pentecostals initially saw themselves as a movement of the end-times, the 'Latter Rain' outpouring of the Holy Spirit in preparation for the return of Christ. They lived during the heyday of the evangelical missionary movement, and it can be argued that at first they saw the gift of tongues as supernatural equipment for more rapidly fulfilling the missionary task and so hastening the Parousia (cf. Matthew 24.14). Today they would add further variants to this list: a completion of the eighteenth-century Evangelical and nineteenth-century Holiness movements; an eschatological outpouring of the Holy Spirit to prepare the Church for the return of Christ by purifying it and enabling it to reap a worldwide missionary harvest; and a restoration of the 'New Testament Church'. What is clear is that even if we acknowledge the plurality of origins, the North American form of the movement dominated the Pentecostal story for the first half of the twentieth century; its global expansion in part paralleled the gathering pace of globalization, in which the export of North American culture and lifestyle was an integral part.

More recently, however, the picture has changed. For one thing, the form taken by Pentecostalism when appropriated in various cultural settings did not always correspond to that advocated by Pentecostal missionaries any more than had been the case with the propagation of nineteenth-century Evangelicalism. One factor in this process of trans-lation (which some have regarded as distortion) was the congruity of aspects of Pentecostal spirituality with traditional local spiritualities, the stress on physical healing being a prime example. This has made it very difficult in most of the Majority World to draw a sharp distinc-tion between Pentecostal churches and locally instituted churches. For another, the rapid spread of political independence throughout Africa and Asia after 1945 was paralleled by a move to ecclesiastical independence which affected Pentecostalism as much as it did other communions.

So, what are the distinctive features common to Pentecostal churches? The answer given to this is liable to vary according to the perspective of the writer, Western writers tending to place greater stress on doctrine and often on speaking with tongues as the 'initial evidence' of baptism with the Spirit, although research indicates that only a third of those who iden-tify themselves as Pentecostals have spoken in tongues.[7] Early Western Pentecostals often summarized their message in terms of the 'Foursquare Gospel'. Others define Pentecostalism in terms of its distinctive experi-ences and practices – speaking in tongues, healing, prophecy, and so on. But such definitions are as lopsided as those which focus entirely on doctrines, and any adequate definition needs to take into account both aspects, as well as making room for each group which claims to be historically linked with the Pentecostal family of movements.

At the risk of over-simplifying things, it seems fair to say that Pentecostal churches are marked out by a belief in the activity of the Holy Spirit as something intended to be supernaturally evident both in the life of the individual and that of the congregation. The Spirit's presence is not merely to be affirmed as an article of faith, but to be experienced. As part of that, the whole spectrum of charismatic phenomena (including the high-profile ones of tongues, prophecy, and healing) is regarded as part of God's gift to the Church in each generation, not merely as some-thing which attended its birth in the first century, although the account of the Day of Pentecost in Acts 2 is frequently taken as normative for individual and corporate experience (hence the movement's name). This emphasis on the present activity of the Holy Spirit in all believers is seen as legitimating and empowering the ministry (understood in a broad sense) of each one, whether lay or ordained. Pentecostalism thus serves to empower groups who have often felt marginalized in more traditional churches: lay people, less educated people, women, and youth (though as the movement becomes more institutionalized, these groups often find their roles becoming restricted again[8]). This has created a sense of 'ownership', which when coupled with the testimony to God at work in personal experience has made Pentecostals enthusiastic advocates of their version of Christianity, and so stimulated rapid growth in much of the world because they have been able to address issues which are significant in the local worldview, such as the quest for healing or for protection from malign spiritual forces. In that respect, Pentecostalism in much of the world offers a variety of examples of contextual theology.

The Charismatic movement

Although some movements which could be classified as 'charismatic' emerged before 1960 (for example, in the Reformed Church in France during the 1930s or South African Anglicanism from the 1940s), 1960 is often taken by English-speaking writers as the start-point for the contemporary Charismatic movement. We shall treat it as such but with the proviso that it applies only to the English-speaking world. While sharing the Pentecostal belief in the present activity of the Holy Spirit as conceived in terms of supernatural manifestations, Charismatics have stood apart from existing Pentecostal denominations. Many remained within their existing churches, to the extent that in England the Charismatic movement permeated both Anglicanism and the Baptist community extensively from the 1970s, but others formed independent congregations. In this section we review the origins and development of the Charismatic movement in the English-speaking world.

Origins

In North America the ground was prepared to some extent by the activities of itinerant healing evangelists such as Oral Roberts and T.L. Osborn, as well as the interdenominational Full Gospel Businessmen's Fellowship International (FGBMFI), founded in 1951 by Demos Shakarian (1913–93), an ethnic Armenian Pentecostal whose family had fled Turkey before the genocide of the post-World War I period. It held dinners at which lay speakers shared the gospel or advocated the Pentecostal experience. But the movement's beginnings in North America are usually associated with Dennis Bennett (1917–92), an Episcopal priest in California who was baptized in the Spirit in 1959. His experience sparked considerable controversy, which received national media coverage, and eventually Bennett moved to another parish in Seattle. A neighbouring priest in California, Frank Maguire, was a factor in the movement's developing links with the UK: in 1963 he spoke to a group of evangelical leaders in London and encouraged them to make contact with Larry Christenson. Christenson (b. 1928) was a charismatic leader in Lutheran circles who did much to help the movement's theology catch up with its experience; he was also aware of, and wrote about, historical precedents for the movement such as the Catholic Apostolic Church.

In 1967 the Charismatic movement began to take root in the Roman Catholic Church, and grew rapidly, especially where support structures were put in place at a national level to provide teaching resources and guidance. Such structures acted as a stimulus to other denominations to do likewise, and to relate charismatic experience to their own theological tradition. From the USA Catholic charismatic renewal spread to Britain and Europe, where it was championed by one of the leading figures at Vatican II, the Belgian Cardinal Suenens (1904–96). Charismatic Catholicism has also established itself in large parts of the Majority World, notably Latin America and the Philippines. By 1979, 18 per cent of US Catholics were described as charismatic. Globally, by 2000 there were an estimated 120 million Charismatics, most of them Roman Catholic, well outnumbering the 60 million classical Pentecostals. The middle-class and suburban concentration of charismatic churches is noticeable in Britain (and also, interestingly, in Latin America), although they have shown some signs of establishing themselves in inner-city locations. The sense of shared experience which stimulated the growth of interdenominational charismatic prayer groups in many countries during the 1970s has fulfilled the ecumenical vision of men like Zinzendorf and offers an alternative to the structured approach to ecumenism represented by the WCC.

The 'Third Wave'

The 1990s saw what has been described by Pentecostals and Charismatics as the 'Third Wave' (Pentecostalism and the Charismatic movement being the first and second respectively). Led by the Californian John Wimber (1934–97), it was marked by the abandonment of the concept of a post-conversion baptism in the Spirit as a second-stage experience, sympathy with the thinking of the Church Growth movement,[9] and a greater degree of openness from the beginning to scholarly explanation and exposition of its distinctives. It secured a wide degree of acceptance in mainline churches, partly because it did not insist on the necessity of a post-conversion experience of baptism with the Spirit. Wimber's

Vineyard churches also spread to a number of countries, including the UK, sometimes growing at the expense of older-established charismatic congregations. Paradoxically, it was in this more scholarly stream that the 'Toronto Blessing' emerged in 1994, attracting pilgrims from all over the world to experience a range of phenomena such as helpless laughter, trance-like insensitivity to surroundings, and even animal noises. However this is to be understood, and it excited rather more scholarly debate than with hindsight it appears to have deserved, it was clearly touching something deep in the human psyche. That may also be said of Pentecostalism as a whole and in his seminal work *The Household of God* (1955), the missiologist and ecumenist Lesslie Newbigin (1909–98) referred to the 'Pentecostal' (that is, the emphasis on direct experience of God) as a third strand of Christianity alongside the Catholic and the Protestant.

Questions for thought

1 In writing a global history of Pentecostalism, what steps could be taken to overcome the problems posed by relative lack of evidence for non-Western sectors of the movement?

2 To what extent can the Pentecostal and Charismatic movements be seen as examples of the processes of globalization?

3 Locate copies of two best-selling books published in 1963, *Honest to God* and *The Cross and the Switchblade*. What vision of Christianity does each articulate, and to whom did each speak?

4 What interpretation of Pentecostalism do you find most convincing? How does your own perspective influence your interpretation?

5 How would you account for the rapid growth of the Charismatic movement during the period to 1980?

Further reading

(See also the section on Pentecostalism in the 'Suggested Further Reading' at the end of the book.)

Arnold Bittlinger (ed.), 1981, *The Church is Charismatic*, Geneva: WCC.

Harvey Cox, 1996, *Fire from Heaven: The Rise of Pentecostal Spirituality and the Reshaping of Religion in the Twenty-first Century*, London: Cassell.

Murray W. Dempster, Byron D. Klaus, and Douglas Petersen (eds), 1999, *The Globalization of Pentecostalism: A Religion Made to Travel*, Carlisle: Regnum.

Peter Hocken, 1997, *Streams of Renewal: The Origins and Development of the Charismatic Movement*, 2nd edn, Carlisle: Paternoster.

Walter J. Hollenweger, 1997, *Pentecostalism: Origins and Developments Worldwide*, Peabody, MA: Hendrickson.

William K. Kay and Anne E. Dyer (eds), 2004, *Pentecostal and Charismatic Studies: A Reader*, London, SCM Press.

David Martin, 2002, *Pentecostalism: The World Their Parish*, Oxford: Blackwell.

Hugh McLeod (ed.), 2006, *Cambridge History of Christianity*, vol. 9: *World Christianities c.1914–c.2000*, Cambridge: Cambridge University Press, chs 6–7.

Karla Poewe (ed.), 1994, *Charismatic Christianity as a Global Culture*, Columbia: University of South Carolina Press.

Notes

1 This paralleled the modalism of the patristic era.

2 It has been suggested that the initial rapid spread of Pentecostalism was due to its ability to absorb earlier revivalist movements with similar characteristics which had begun independently (Allan Anderson, in David Ford with Rachel Muers (eds), 2005, *The Modern Theologians: An Introduction to Christian Theology since 1918*, 3rd edn, Oxford: Blackwell, p. 589), but it is debatable whether those movements would see themselves as having been 'absorbed'!

3 An exception was the Apostolic Church's slight debt to it in its thinking about apostleship. Pentecostal suspicion was normally rooted in their dislike of Irving's Christology.

4 Cf. the debate about the causes of nineteenth-century Methodist growth in Britain.

5 Hollenweger, *Pentecostalism*, p. 101 n.

6 Kay and Dyer, *Pentecostal Reader*, pp. xxvii–xxviii.

7 For details, see Hollenweger, *Pentecostalism*, pp. 223–4.

8 An exception is the International Church of the Foursquare Gospel, founded by Aimee Semple McPherson, over 40 per cent of whose ministers were women by 2000. Another factor inhibiting women's ministry was the desire of many white North American Pentecostal groups to build closer relationships with the evangelical community, which had a severely limited understanding of the public ministry of women based on its interpretation of passages such as 1 Corinthians 11.2–16; 14.33–6; and 1 Timothy 2.8–15, through such means as the National Association of Evangelicals.

9 This is rooted in the thinking of the US missionary to India Donald McGavran, who from the 1950s sought to put the study of the factors operative in 'people movements' towards Christianity and the growth of individual churches onto a scientific basis. In North America it became closely associated with the evangelical Fuller Seminary in California and the writings of the missiologist Peter Wagner (b. 1930), who had studied closely the growth of Latin American Pentecostal and Charismatic movements.

19

The Ecumenical Movement

'Ecumenism' is a slippery term, freighted in some settings with negative connotations. At the start of this chapter, then, it will be helpful to consider what we mean by it. The term is derived from the Greek *oikoumene*, often used to refer to the whole inhabited world. The Ecumenical Councils of the patristic era were those whose determinations were recognized as binding on the whole Church. In 1937 ecumenism was defined by Life and Work (see below) as 'the expression within history of the given unity of the church', and in 1951 the WCC's Central Committee defined it as 'everything that relates to the whole task of the whole Church to bring the Gospel to the whole world'. These may be taken as handy summaries, and they indicate that the scope is wider than the institutional ecumenical movement, and so this chapter will also discuss other approaches and attitudes to ecumenism. In recent decades, too, many have seen the ecumenical enterprise in even broader terms, as encompassing not only all Christians but all human beings, and therefore have advocated an ecumenism of faiths, but this chapter will keep to the narrower focus of understanding.

Roots

A surprising variety of roots contributed to nourishing the early ecumenical movement, a fact which may help to explain why tension between differing outlooks and approaches has never been completely absent from it.

Bible societies

Bible societies were arguably one of the first modern manifestations of the ecumenical impulse, since they brought members of different denominations together in support of the distribution of the Scriptures; in time they also developed an ecumenical approach to translation. From one perspective, therefore, they illustrate the contention that the Bible has always been fundamental to the growth of unity as Christians study it together. However, from a historical perspective we must also acknowledge that differences between traditions were highlighted by debate about the work of the Bible societies, as in the controversy which affected the British and Foreign Bible Society during the 1820s regarding the legitimacy of sponsoring editions which included the Apocrypha for use in Roman Catholic areas. Another ongoing disagreement between those churches committed to ecumenical co-operation concerned the relative status of Scripture and Tradition.

The missionary movement

It has often been claimed that ecumenism was a child of the Protestant missionary movement, as missionaries realized the scandal that was presented by the spectacle of divided and competing Christians. But this interpretation tends to overlook the role played by national Christians from the late nineteenth century onwards, who themselves saw no reason to perpetuate divisions which had originated in the West and whose relevance to their cultural settings was dubious, to say the least. What can be said, however, is that the decline of the concept of Christendom helped to pave the way for the growth of ecumenism. The disappearance of much European confessionalism paved the way for less defensive relations with other Christian traditions, emerging Christian communities elsewhere rejected the Christendom model of relations between church and society, and World War I was seen as demonstrating that traditional Christendom was in fact rotten to the core and hence its right to exercise authoritative influence over developing churches was seriously challenged.

Student work

A pioneer in bringing together young people from different church backgrounds was the YMCA, along with its counterpart for young women, the YWCA. Founded in 1844, its first world conference took place in 1855, and although its membership remained restricted to evangelical Protestants until World War I, extension brought significant Orthodox involvement.

More specifically aimed at students were the Student Christian Movement (SCM), whose roots are in groups for Bible study, prayer, and evangelism founded in several British universities from the 1850s; such groups shared a commitment to mission and unity. In 1895 the World Student Christian Fellowship (WSCF) came into being to bring together national SCMs as a federation of autonomous movements.[1] Because of the opportunities they provided for study and leadership experience, and the way in which they encouraged innovative thought, such bodies provided many of the key personnel for the WCC and its national counterparts until recent decades, and they also gave institutional ecumenism a model for doing theology which combined small groups and large conferences and which stressed rigorous Bible study as fundamental. Their great advantage was that whereas official ecumenical bodies were limited by the need to seek approval for their actions from member churches, their unofficial status freed them to experiment and explore, enabling them to function as a kind of ecumenical laboratory. This role was enhanced by the presence of Orthodox students from 1911. Moreover, student work provided the context for a network of personal relationships which was vital to the development of organized ecumenism; the WCC's first general secretary, the Dutchman W. A. Visser 't Hooft (1900–85), was a product of the SCM / WSCF / YMCA network who claimed that the WCC began as a group of friends who decided to do something about the disunity of the churches. This relational emphasis provides a salutary corrective to the widespread tendency to view ecumenical history primarily in institutional terms, and should be kept in mind as we survey the movement's institutional development. However, in time ecumenism became more of a churchly concern than an individual one, and with the movement's growth the networks of personal friendship became less significant and perhaps harder to sustain.

The SCM was itself to experience division. By the Edwardian era it was beginning to move from the earlier nondenominational approach which had been typical of evangelical para-church agencies to a more consciously inter-church one, in which students were encouraged to respect their denominational traditions (most of these were by now less evangelical than formerly). From about 1910 the movement began to divide over the extent to which (i) modern critical methods were valid hermeneutical tools, and (ii) Christian doctrine should be reformulated to meet the challenges of new intellectual trends. The more conservative evangelical student unions formed the Inter-Varsity Fellowship (1927 in Britain), and the International Fellowship of Evangelical Students (1947).

Evangelical Alliances

Much late-nineteenth-century 'ecumenical' co-operation was rooted in the 'ecumenism of the heart' practised by Zinzendorf and many later Evangelicals. The concept of an invisible unity of all true believers had proved especially attractive to Evangelicals because they were found across the spread of denominations, and it facilitated the growth of interdenominational para-church agencies bringing Evangelicals together in support of a particular cause. The revivalism of the period also helped to bring together Evangelicals in the cause of outreach and overseas mission.

Global confessional bodies

Clearly for many national communions of churches, ecumenical contact with bodies of churches from different traditions was a foreign concept. However, to some extent the way could be prepared by the development of global communions of churches sharing the same denominational tradition, often known as 'world confessional families' or (since 1979) as 'Christian world communions'. Many in more conservative communions such as the Baptists and the Lutherans have preferred to work on building relationships with other like-minded churches rather than follow the path of interdenominational ecumenism.

These bodies (and their regional counterparts) have played significant roles in bringing together churches divided by war; for example, from its commencement in 1950 the European Baptist Federation (EBF) provided a forum for the reconciliation of Baptists in Britain and Germany. More often, they have enabled national communions not belonging to the WCC to be ecumenically involved: thus most Baptist communities in Europe supported the EBF even though few belonged to the WCC at first.

The main global bodies are listed below:

1867   Lambeth Conference (Anglican)
1875   World Alliance of Reformed Churches
1891   International Congregational Council (reorganized 1949; merged with World Alliance of Reformed Churches 1970)
1905   Baptist World Alliance
1925   Mennonite World Conference
1930   World Convention of the Churches of Christ (Disciples)
1937   Friends World Committee for Consultation
1947   Pentecostal World Conference
1947   Lutheran World Federation
1951   World Methodist Conference

Such agencies have a wide remit, including the promotion of fellowship between national communions, the development of a global sense of denominational identity, the provision of material and financial aid to communities in need, advocacy of religious liberty and human rights, and strategic planning of mission, extension, and theological training. More recently, they have also taken on the role of dialogue partners, thanks to the renewed openness of Roman Catholicism to other Christian communions: as global bodies representing distinctive theological and ecclesiological traditions, they are the closest counterparts to the Roman church. Dialogue has not only been with Rome, however, but with each other.

Global ecumenical organizations

The three agencies, however, that were the nearest ancestors of the WCC were the International Missionary Council (IMC), Faith and Order, and Life and Work.

The IMC was founded as a result of the Edinburgh 1910 missionary conference, bringing together national councils of Protestant missions in sending countries and councils of churches and missionaries in receiving countries (as they were then regarded). Its secretary until 1938 was J.H. Oldham (1874–1969), whose organizational skills and ability as a networker were matched by an equally strong sense of the need to relate Christianity to public life. The IMC was amalgamated with the WCC in 1961, though not without apprehension on the part of some Evangelicals who feared a loss of voice because missionary societies could no longer be members in a body whose membership was restricted to churches, and some Orthodox who associated Western mission in territories such as the Middle East with proselytism, usually at their expense. After integration a division on World Mission and Evangelism came into being within the WCC, but debate about the Council's stance on evangelism has continued both inside and outside the organization. With the disappearance of the IMC as a freestanding entity, evangelical agencies have related to each other through the Lausanne Committee for World Evangelization, founded as a result of the Lausanne Congress (1974), a global gathering of Evangelicals.

The second agency was known as Faith and Order. Its prime mover was an American Episcopalian bishop, C.H. Brent (1862–1929); at Edinburgh he had called for denominations not merely to shelve their differences in the interests of missionary co-operation, but actively to seek to overcome them. Faith and Order came into being, therefore, as a mechanism enabling churches to explore what divided them in doctrinal terms, and initially it worked by means of comparing and contrasting respective viewpoints with a view to increased mutual understanding. After 1948, Faith and Order continued as a commission within the WCC, and a major change in methodology was inaugurated by the 1952 Faith and Order conference at Lund (Sweden), which also established the principle that churches should do together whatever they could, only acting separately where conscience made that necessary. Since Lund the emphasis has been on convergence rather than comparison: participants went back beyond their own confessional standards to study the teaching of the Bible (and the early Fathers) together, focusing on what they had in common in Christ and with the aim of producing new statements which avoided the use of language associated with marking out positions of division. Such an approach necessitated thought concerning the sources for theology, and so the next conference, at Montreal in 1963, explored the theme of 'Scripture, Tradition and traditions'. It argued that these should not be pitted against one another as so often happened because they belonged together: Scripture was a part of the Tradition, the gospel deposit handed down from one generation to the next in the church and given specific expression in the form of local traditions which in their turn were subject to testing by Scripture.

In 1968 the Roman Catholic Church became a member of Faith and Order, and a number of evangelical and Pentecostal denominations have also joined it; its composition is thus significantly broader than that of the WCC itself, which makes its work all the more valuable. The most influential result of its deliberations so far has been *Baptism, Eucharist and Ministry* (1982), in which participants reached a considerable degree of agreement on hitherto-divisive aspects of these three crucial areas of corporate Christian life.

Life and Work was founded at Stockholm in 1925 by Archbishop Nathan Söderblom (1866–1931) of Uppsala, as an instrument for co-operative response to the social challenges of the day. Söderblom believed that the Church of Sweden, more than any other Protestant church, had maintained a continuity of ministry and worship, and that this enabled it to fulfil a unique role as an ecumenical mediator. He wished to see a league of churches whose engagement with society could provide a basis of co-operation for churches to come together in council to overcome their divisions.

The roots of the movement's rather anti-doctrinal approach, expressed in the slogan 'doctrine divides, service unites' may be traced back to the Quest for the Historical Jesus and to the Social Gospel movement and its European parallels. The early years saw Life and Work deeply divided over the theological question of the relationship between the Church, the world, and the Kingdom of God. The 1930s saw a shift in emphasis, due in considerable measure to Neo-Orthodox influence, from the concept of the Kingdom of God to that of the Church. A similar emphasis in Faith and Order facilitated the convergence of the two movements, and hence the formation of the WCC.

Life and Work did much to raise the profile of the laity in the work of the Church; its conference at Oxford in 1937 emphasized this theme, and it was given influential expression by J. H. Oldham. Aware that ecclesiastics had been liable to criticism for making vacuous pronouncements on issues outside their area of expertise, and concerned to enable the Church to relate to an increasingly secular world, Oldham drew together a range of experts in many fields who met together in an informal group known as the 'Moot' and who contributed to the *Christian News-Letter* which appeared weekly or fortnightly for ten years from the outbreak of war. Concern to equip the laity also lay behind the founding of the Ecumenical Institute at Bossey in 1946.

Table 19.1: Major ecumenical conferences.

Faith and Order 1920	Life and Work 1925	IMC 1921
Lausanne 1927	Stockholm 1925	Jerusalem 1928
Edinburgh 1937	Oxford 1937	Tambaram 1938
↓	↓	Whitby, Ontario 1947
World Council of Churches 1948		↓
	1 Amsterdam 1948	Willingen 1952
	2 Evanston 1954	Accra 1958
	3 New Delhi 1961 ◄──────────┘	
	4 Uppsala 1968	
	1971 ◄──────────── World Council for Christian Education 1889	
	5 Nairobi 1975	
	6 Vancouver 1983	
	7 Canberra 1991	
	8 Harare 1998	
	9 Porto Alegre 2006	

The World Council of Churches

Origins and development

To understand the form and goals of the WCC, it is important to place it in context as one of a variety of expressions of growing global awareness which emerged during the twentieth century. Not for nothing is it based in Geneva, as are many other non-governmental organizations, since it seeks to work closely with them. Indeed, in 1920 Orthodox appealed to the example of the newly formed League of Nations in calling for a 'league of churches' to be formed. Significantly, the Greek term used was *koinonia*, whose New Testament occurrences have usually been translated 'fellowship' (as in Acts 2.42) and which has come to represent an influential contemporary approach to the doctrine of the Church.

The WCC came into being in a provisional form from 1938 with the merger of Life and Work and a somewhat hesitant Faith and Order. In part this represented a holistic response (that is, combining doctrine and practice on a global scale) to the challenge presented by the rise of totalitarian governments subjecting churches to national control. Even this provisional existence proved of value during the war in maintaining links between churches on opposing sides and afterwards in facilitating the distribution of material assistance. Amsterdam in 1948 was the venue for the WCC's formal inauguration with 147 churches from

44 nations becoming founder members (by 2007 there were over 350 member churches from every major Trinitarian tradition except Roman Catholicism). The theme of that first assembly was 'Man's Disorder and God's Design', an emphasis which fitted well with the wider post-war emphasis on reconstruction, as well as the chastened realism concerning human capability for evil which had been nourished by the Holocaust and the atom bomb.

As its secretary until 1966, Visser 't Hooft ensured that theological and ecclesiological questions received high priority in the Council's deliberations. The doctrinal basis was the same as that used by Faith and Order, 'a fellowship of Churches which accept our Lord Jesus Christ as God and Saviour'; at New Delhi in 1961, this was strengthened to read 'a fellowship of Churches which confess the Lord Jesus Christ as God and Saviour according to the Scriptures and therefore seek to fulfil together their common calling to the glory of one God, Father, Son and Holy Spirit'.

In early years, about three-quarters of the WCC's budget was provided by North American churches. This paralleled contemporary economic reality: it was the era of the Marshall Plan, which during the late 1940s and 1950s provided massive financial assistance to enable European economies to rebuild themselves in order to create a thriving global trade network and secure the West of the continent against Communist domination. With the advent of increased prosperity, German and Scandinavian churches assumed a large measure of financial responsibility, but in recent years the decline in revenues accruing from the 'church tax' (paid by citizens of these nations unless they opted out) has necessitated the reduction of the WCC's staff by about a third. At the 2006 Porto Alegre assembly it was agreed that the WCC should concentrate on those aspects of its work which were not being duplicated by others and in which it had most to contribute.

Criticisms

Visser 't Hooft's retirement more or less coincided with an upsurge in student unrest and a growing concern on the part of churches with issues of economic development. It was inevitable, therefore, that there should be something of a shift in the WCC's perceived priorities. This attracted considerable criticism and has been portrayed in terms of the eclipse of theology as WCC thinking shifted from a theological orientation to a more ethical and political one. (Nevertheless, Faith and Order has remained a vital component of the Council's work, and it may be just as accurate to see the shift in terms of a fairly thoroughgoing application of Bonhoeffer's thinking about 'religionless Christianity'.) So the theme for the programme of the fourth assembly (Uppsala 1968) was 'Behold, I make all things new', and its methodology was founded in the idea that the world must set the agenda for the Church. Mission had come to be seen in terms of 'development', and theology as providing the rationale for the process of change which this was deemed to require. On missions as traditionally conceived, calls resulted for a moratorium on the sending of personnel and finance from the West (during this decade many nations had achieved political independence, and frequently developments in national churches followed a similar pattern).

There has also been controversy over specific activities in the Life and Work field, for example, the Programme to Combat Racism, set up in 1969. From 1970 this had a special fund, financed by several European governments, from which it was empowered to make grants to organizations working on behalf of oppressed peoples, and the controversy arose because some of the groups so aided were deemed to engage in terrorist activity. In spite of the WCC's stipulation that the money should not be used for violent ends, the programme touched a raw nerve for many in Western nations then seeking to divest themselves of their colonial burden. Such criticism was not only from separatist groups; the Salvation Army, which had been a founder member of the WCC, entered a more distant relationship from the late 1970s in protest at what it saw as politicization of the gospel, and the Presbyterian Church of Ireland withdrew in 1980. Earlier, the Dutch Reformed Church of South Africa had withdrawn from the WCC during the early 1960s after its own political stance had been condemned.

Orthodox criticisms have focused on a distinctive range of issues. They have often found the predominantly Protestant ethos of the WCC difficult to cope with, not only its bureaucratic methodology and its apparent lack of rootedness in a sense of the holy tradition, but also its alleged excessive accommodation to modern thought. A council in Moscow in 1948 rejected the WCC as a potential centre for political power rather than Christian unity, a conclusion which probably was influenced by apprehension on the part of Communist governments. However, the Ecumenical Patriarchate and the Church of Greece, among others, did become founder members. Orthodox theologians such as Schmemann and Florovsky have had a significant effect in shaping the movement's vision of unity; often this has been couched in terms of a return to the common tradition, as Florovsky explained: 'every local church can contribute its own particular experience, but the Orthodox church's unique contribution is to witness to the common heritage of all Christians, because . . . Orthodoxy is the true, though not perfect, manifestation of the living tradition of the universal church'.[2] Many Eastern bloc Orthodox jurisdictions joined the WCC from 1961 onwards, another decision probably influenced by political considerations. Once Communist governments collapsed, many rejected ecumenism as 'the international activity leading church people had to engage in under communism in order to prove to the world at large that their churches at home enjoyed religious liberty'.[3] At ecumenical gatherings the Orthodox developed the practice of issuing minority statements expressing a dissentient viewpoint, culminating in a refusal to participate in joint worship or to vote at the WCC's Harare Assembly (1998). With the addition to the WCC of many churches from newly independent nations, Orthodox have felt themselves to be in a minority in an organization whose balance has continued to shift towards Protestantism, and some jurisdictions have also withdrawn from membership (for example, Georgia in 1997, motivated in part by political factors). The outcome was the setting up of a Special Commission on Orthodox participation in the movement, to report in 2008. Already the Orthodox have secured a change in the WCC's method of decision-making from 2002, away from the Western parliamentary-style model towards one based on achieving consensus.

One factor in the Orthodox withdrawal from ecumenical contact has been the lead given by the Russian patriarch Alexei II (1990–) and his bishops. Having previously been president of the Council of European Churches, he changed tack and the church's outlook has become far more conservative and even nationalistic (though since the dismemberment of the USSR his jurisdiction now extends over 14 nations). A statement issued by the Russian bishops in council in 2000 portrays ecumenism as a matter of calling on other Christians to return to Orthodoxy.

Criticism has also been directed by Evangelicals at the WCC's perceived loss of evangelistic vision. The direct talking about the Church's evangelistic task which was a feature of early years has given way in considerable measure to a more positive outlook on other religions which stresses dialogue and co-operation in the quest to improve global human existence. Evangelicals remain wary of such developments, while often recognizing the benefits of inter-religious dialogue. More positively, relations with the World Evangelical Fellowship had been facilitated during the 1980s by the WCC process *Confessing One Faith*, an ecumenical investigation of the Nicene Creed, to which the WEF responded positively because of the high priority accorded by Evangelicals to the maintenance of orthodox Trinitarianism.

Finally, we should note a major fundamentalist reason for standing aloof – the belief that the apostasy and downfall of institutional Christendom is foretold in biblical prophecy. Such opinions may seem strange to those who do not share them, but they represent a longstanding tradition within Christian thought: within Roman Catholicism the writings of such men as Joachim of Fiore (1135–1209) have foretold the eschatological apostasy of the Church. A similar strain of thought can also be traced within Russian Orthodoxy: it fuelled the Old Believer schism, and is still present in some popular Orthodox thinking. Worldwide, such views are held by considerable numbers of people but have not often received serious attention within ecumenical circles.

It is hoped that these and other issues can be addressed in the Global Christian Forum. This was founded in 1998 and seeks to bring together the WCC, Pentecostals, Evangelicals, and the Vatican.

Changing conceptions of ecumenism and its goals

Developing thought

The developing self-understanding of the WCC can conveniently be traced by examining key statements on ecclesiology.

A statement issued at Toronto in 1950, *The Church, the Churches, and the World Council of Churches*, addressed the issue of the nature of the WCC. It concluded that the Council was not to be seen as a 'super-church' (though some North American ecumenists had slipped into this way of thinking and fundamentalist critics have been loath to accept the assurance); the marks of unity, holiness, catholicity, and apostolicity did not apply to the WCC *per se*. The Council was not based on any particular understanding of ecclesiology, and membership did not entail or imply recognition of fellow-members as churches in the full sense of the word, only that in them elements of the true Church were present. This statement has proved a vital anchor-point for Orthodox in recent years as they have re-examined their involvement in the WCC, although it may be argued that more recent statements have, by virtue of their increasingly detailed elaborations of the ecumenical vision, compromised the Toronto position somewhat.

New Delhi 1961 produced the first formal exposition of the unity vision:

> We believe that the unity which is both God's will and his gift to his Church is being made visible as all in each place who are baptized into Jesus Christ and confess him as Lord and Saviour are brought by the Holy Spirit into one fully committed fellowship, holding the one apostolic faith, preaching the one Gospel, breaking the one bread, joining in common prayer, and having a corporate life reaching out in witness and service to all and who at the same time are united with the whole Christian fellowship in all places and all ages in such wise that ministry and members are accepted by all, and that all can act and speak together as occasion requires for the tasks to which God calls his people.[4]

New Delhi also strengthened the WCC's doctrinal basis in a trinitarian direction as noted above, thanks in part to the influence of Orthodox theologians. This is not just a matter of affirming a key Christian doctrine, but has also begun to influence ecumenical thinking about the nature of the Church.

Uppsala 1968 portrayed visible unity in terms of a conciliar fellowship reflecting that between the persons of the Trinity. Arising from the emphasis on Trinitarian thought is the idea of the Church as *koinonia* or 'fellowship' (in the sense of participation together in the life of God), which has become a controlling metaphor for ecclesiology since the early 1990s. Conciliar fellowship of local churches at a global level was a key concept in the thinking of Nairobi 1975, which defined the ecumenical task as 'the whole church bringing the whole gospel to the whole person in the whole world';[5] the marks of such a Church included consensus in faith, mutual recognition of sacraments and ministries, and conciliar gatherings and structures for debate and decision.

The most recent major statement on ecclesiology was *Towards a Common Understanding and Vision of the World Council of Churches* (1997). This has sought to take account of the variety of aspects of the Council's work which represent its most significant contributions to church life at the local level; these include not only such controversial programmes as that responding to racism, but also *Baptism, Eucharist and Ministry* and the process addressing 'Justice, Peace and the Integrity of Creation'. It is now customary to see the Church's unity as a means to that of all humanity and of the whole creation.

The chapter so far has shown several models of unity; we may list them (with others) as co-operative service, mutual recognition and intercommunion, corporate or organic union, conciliar fellowship, 'reconciled diversity' (what we might call agreement to differ but in fellowship), a communion of communions, and unity in taking a stance of solidarity with the oppressed. Often several models have coexisted in ecumenical circles in more or less creative tension. But during the movement's second generation, after the initial enthusiasm had cooled somewhat, the vision of organic visible unity came to seem to many remote, impractical, and too inward-looking. In 1991 Konrad Raiser (to become the Council's General Secretary from 1993 to 2003) gave expression to this in *Ecumenism in Transition*; he believed that a new paradigm was required because the old one was proving inadequate.[6] A key aspect of the new paradigm, he believed, was the replacement of visible unity as the goal by that of reconciled diversity, based on the idea of the Church as a fellowship of those who are different from one another, rather than those who are the same. Lively debate continues to explore what the priorities of the churches should be, and as yet no ecumenical paradigm appears to have achieved normative status.

Bilateral and multilateral dialogues

Changing concepts of the nature and goal of ecumenism have also been evident in the field of dialogue between different Christian traditions. This is of two types, multilateral (involving a number of parties) and bilateral (involving just two).

Multilateral dialogues have frequently aimed at organizational reunion. One of the first significant mergers of churches from different denominational traditions occurred in Canada in 1925, when the United Church of Christ brought together Congregationalists, Methodists, and Presbyterians. Around 3,000 'Union Churches' already existed, and it was impossible to maintain separate denominational structures in sparsely populated parts of the country. However, it showed the great hazard associated with such enterprises – the tendency to create more denominations rather than fewer – as a third of Presbyterians preferred to remain apart. Similar mergers took place in Zambia (1965, bringing together Congregationalists, Methodists, and Presbyterians to form the United Church of Zambia) and Australia (1977, involving the same traditions). Traditions practising believer's baptism have usually found it more difficult to join such bodies, with the exception of the Disciples of Christ, who are marked by a strong commitment to ecumenism in all forms.

Multilateral dialogue also resulted in the creation of the Church of South India (CSI) in the year that India gained political independence (1947). It brought together Anglicans, the Basel Mission Church, Congregationalists, Methodists, and Presbyterians. Negotiations had been lengthy, partly because of the difficulties involved in bringing together episcopal and non-episcopal ministries. The new church was not regarded as part of the Anglican communion, non-episcopally ordained ministers were not recognized by the Anglican communion, and those ordained by CSI bishops were not recognized by the English Convocations until 1955. However, from 1998 the CSI has been recognized as a full member of the Lambeth Conference.

Multilateral dialogues have also been conducted with a view to achieving a measure of doctrinal convergence rather than aiming at formal unity. The most important example of this is the 55–year process leading to the WCC Faith and Order document *Baptism, Eucharist and Ministry* (1982). This has been subject to a lengthy and continuing process of reception and response by member churches, and has provided a valuable starting-point for many dialogues between Christian communions.

Bilateral dialogue really came into its own after Vatican II. The Decree on Ecumenism provided a powerful motivation for Catholics to become more ecumenically involved. While the Church as a whole has not joined the WCC (a reason often given for this is that its size would threaten to unbalance the ecumenical boat), at national level it has often been a full member of ecumenical bodies. In 1965 a joint working group of the WCC and the Catholic Church was set up, and from 1968 the church has been a full member of Faith and Order. Since then Catholics have played a major role in bilateral dialogues between confessional families; indeed, much of the motivation for these sprang from the dramatic changes in the ecumenical landscape brought about by the church's new outlook on ecumenical matters.

Among the most important bilateral processes have been the Anglican–Roman Catholic International Commission and the Joint Commission of the Roman Catholic Church and the Lutheran World Federation (from 1996 upgraded to a Commission on Christian Unity). On 31 October 1999 the latter process issued an agreed statement on justification by faith (to strong German opposition, it must be said). Anglicans and Lutherans have also been extensively involved in bilateral dialogue; with Catholics they share a strong sense of historical rootedness and continuity with the Church of past centuries which makes it possible for them to recognize the inheritance which they share with other such churches.

An important motivating factor has been the concept of *koinonia*, which has led many to see that they already possess a real degree of communion, even if this is as yet imperfect. Achieving unity then becomes something towards which gradual steps can be taken rather than something which must be brought from non-existence to full existence in one leap. This undoubtedly made it easier for the Anglican churches in Europe and the Lutheran churches of Scandinavia and the Baltic republics to achieve formal intercommunion at Porvoo (Finland) in 1996. The fruit of seven decades of relationship-building, discussion, and negotiation (in which Söderblom had played a catalytic role), this dialogue established full intercommunion and interchangeability of ministries between the signatory churches.

Inter-faith ecumenism

One of the most contentious issues in discussion about the nature and goals of ecumenism is that of the relationship between Christianity and other religions. Debate about the relationship of Christianity to other faiths and ideologies has always been lively, especially in Asia and Africa, and has rarely commanded a consensus. In some ways for the West the resurgence of such discussion as a result of nineteenth-century mission amounted to a rediscovery of the context of early patristic Christianity, which faced some of the same issues. As before, theologians were not united in their approach. Edinburgh 1910 set the issue in the context of mission (as it did that of church unity), and thereafter much thinking oscillated between positive and negative attitudes towards other faiths.

The positive outlook was seen in Jerusalem 1928 (which regarded other faiths as allies in the stand against secularism) and in a landmark report of 1932, *Rethinking Missions*, edited by the American Presbyterian W. E. Hocking and portraying the task of the missionary not as seeking conversions but as helping adherents of other faiths to discover and live by what was best in their own religious tradition and co-operating with them in reforming society (with the goal of a unified world civilization, in its own way as potent an expression of belief in Western superiority as any refrigerator-toting fundamentalist missionary). A negative approach was evident in the discussions at Tambaram 1938 in which the Dutch missionary to Indonesia, Hendrik Kraemer (1888–1965), played an important role; these were influenced by the exclusivist approach of Neo-Orthodoxy which stressed the discontinuity between Christianity and other faiths.

For many in the movement, inter-faith ecumenism has provided the backdrop to the quest for Christian unity. In many areas dialogue came to replace proclamation as the dominant mode in which Christians related to members of other faiths; indeed, it may be argued that in some parts of the world this was a longstanding tradition, especially where two or more faiths coexisted. One factor behind the growth of this approach in the twentieth century was the shift in the centre of gravity of the Church towards areas in which adherents of different faiths lived side by side and sought to co-operate in the establishment of newly independent nations. Another stimulus to inter-religious dialogue were the attempts of Christians and Jews to reflect together on the significance of the Holocaust and the theological issues which it raised. A programme unit for relations with other faiths was set up by the WCC in 1968, its assemblies included official participants of other faiths from 1975, and guidelines on inter-religious dialogue began to appear in 1979. More recently, some theologians have adopted a pluralist approach, exemplified by the British theologian John Hick, who has called for a move from Christocentricity to theocentricity in theology. Since the collapse of Communism, inter-faith organizations and dialogues have multiplied.

Other approaches to ecumenism

It would be inaccurate to give the impression that the institutional ecumenism of the WCC and its regional[7] and national counterparts represents the only form worth mentioning. One of the most important expressions of the ecumenical impetus has been what is called 'spiritual ecumenism', at the heart of which is the practice of prayer for unity. The best-known expression of this is the Week of Prayer for Christian Unity (18–25 January), which was founded by two Anglicans in 1908;

both converted to Catholicism, and when Rome gave formal sanction to their initiative it was with a view to seeing non-Catholics returning to the fold. From 1935, however, it was substantially reshaped by the French Catholic Abbé Paul Couturier. As he articulated it, the underlying presupposition was that it must be in accordance with God's will for Christians to follow Christ's example (John 17) in praying for unity, and therefore they could be sure that God would in time and in his own way grant their request. No particular form or model was predicated, and so Christians from a variety of traditions were able to participate so far as their own churches allowed. In 1949, the Vatican in *Ecclesia sua* gave official blessing to the week. From 1966 material for use during this period has been prepared jointly by the WCC and the Catholic Church.

Such prayer receives permanent expression in the context of ecumenical communities such as Taizé in France. This was founded in 1940 by a Swiss Reformed pastor, Roger Schutz (1915–2005), and from the 1960s it attracted increasing numbers of young people to its gatherings. Another example would be Corrymeela in Northern Ireland, which brings together Protestants and Catholics. A number of such communities sprang out of the Charismatic movement during the 1970s.

More generally, the Charismatic movement and the rise of 'post-denominationalism' (the perceived irrelevance of defining one's Christian identity in denominational terms, coupled with a readiness to switch denominations when moving to a new area or seeking to meet one's personal spiritual wants) provide a contemporary version of the 'ecumenism of the heart'. Such 'unofficial ecumenism' is rooted in the sense of shared experience of God which Zinzendorf talked about in the eighteenth century. It expresses itself primarily in worship and the sharing of personal testimony; shared Bible study is present, but not as prominent. The prevalence of such an outlook has resulted in the worship styles of many churches of different denominations converging, and in cross-denominational interest in events such as Spring Harvest.

Ecumenical co-operation is also the norm in the fields of Bible translation and liturgical revision (for example, from around 1970 through the International Consultation on English Texts, which has sought to produce versions of liturgical texts acceptable to Protestants and Catholics). The United Bible Societies came into being in 1946 and bring together scholars from around the world and from all the major Christian traditions.

Many of these manifestations find local expression in what is sometimes called 'grass roots ecumenism': the sense of many Christians that co-operation with Christians from other congregations is natural because what unites them is greater than what divides them. Often this has been perceived as running ahead of denominational leaderships, and in some quarters impatience with the hierarchy has been the result. This was a major factor in the decision of the British Council of Churches (BCC) to metamorphose into what is now known as Churches Together in Britain and Ireland (1990), a transformation which has been widely replicated at the local level in the United Kingdom. Clearly, while the paradigm with which the WCC began its formal existence has been found increasingly inadequate in many quarters, the impetus to unity is very much alive. In the next chapter we shall explore the changes in twentieth-century Catholicism which have done so much to shape the vision of many in the ecumenical movement.

Questions for thought

1 In what ways are the various roots still evident within the Ecumenical movement? What tensions continue to be evident between them?

2 How would you evaluate the argument that ecumenism and the reunion of churches is a response to decline?

3 What role has been played in the history of the WCC by Neo-Orthodox thinking?

4 Which of the criticisms of the WCC do you consider has most validity? How do you think your own standpoint influences your answer? If you were an East European Christian under Communism, or a development worker in a predominantly non-Christian country, how might your answer differ? How might you respond to the Western input to the WCC and its activities?

5 Why do you think it has been so difficult for ecumenists to agree on what unity is?

6 Review the history of Christian relationships with other faiths during the period covered by this book. What factors outside the churches have influenced the ways in which these relationships have developed?

7 What historical factors have helped to bring about a crisis in institutional ecumenism?

Further reading

Robert S. Bilheimer, 1989, *Breakthrough: The Emergence of the Ecumenical Tradition*, Grand Rapids, MI, and Geneva: Eerdmans and WCC.

John Briggs, Amba Oduyoye, and Georges Tsetsis (eds), 2004, *A History of the Ecumenical Movement*, vol. 3: *1968–2000*, Geneva: WCC.

Harold E. Fey (ed.), 1970, *The Ecumenical Advance: A History of the Ecumenical Movement*, vol. 2: *1948–1968*, London: SPCK.

Jeffrey Gros, Eamon McManus, and Ann Riggs, 1998, *Introduction to Ecumenism*, Maryknoll, NY: Paulist (from a Roman Catholic perspective).

Michael Kinnamon and Brian E. Cope (eds), 1997, *The Ecumenical Movement:*

An Anthology of Key Texts and Voices, Geneva and Grand Rapids, MI: WCC and Eerdmans.

Hugh McLeod (ed.), 2006, *Cambridge History of Christianity*, vol. 9: *World Christianities c.1914–c.2000*, Cambridge: Cambridge University Press, ch. 4.

Ruth Rouse and Stephen Neill (eds), 1954, revised 1986, *A History of the Ecumenical Movement 1517–1948*, Geneva: WCC.

Mary Tanner, 'Ecumenical Theology', ch. 32 in David Ford with Rachel Muers (eds), 2005, *The Modern Theologians: An Introduction to Christian Theology since 1918*, 3rd edn, Oxford: Blackwell.

Marlin VanElderen and Martin Conway, 2001, *Introducing the World Council of Churches*, 2nd edn, Geneva: WCC.

W.A. Visser 't Hooft, 1982, *The Genesis and Formation of the World Council of Churches*, Geneva: WCC.

Useful websites

Ecumenical News International, www.eni.ch, produces a useful digest of global Christian news.

Global Christian Forum, www.globalchristianforum.net.

Week of Prayer for Christian Unity, www.weekofprayer2008.org.

World Council of Churches, www.oikoumene.org, gradually replacing www.wcc-coe.org.

Notes

1 On the SCM and the WSCF, see: Robin Boyd, 2007, *The Witness of the Student Christian Movement: Church ahead of the Church*, London: SPCK.

2 Quoted in: 'Florovsky, Georges (1893–1979)', in Ken Parry *et al.* (eds), 1999, *The Blackwell Dictionary of Eastern Christianity*, Oxford: Blackwell, p. 204.

3 Philip Walters, in *CHC*, vol. 9, pp. 359–60.

4 Quoted in Fey, *Ecumenical Advance*, p. 149.

5 This built on and elaborated the definition adopted by the WCC Central Committee in 1951.

6 This is another example of the use of the concept of 'paradigm shifts' in theology, a concept which was first formulated by the philosopher of science Thomas S. Kuhn.

7 Regional conferences of churches include those for the Middle East (1927; exclusively Protestant until 1964), East Asia (1949/50), Europe (1959/64), Africa (1958/63), the Pacific (1966), the Caribbean (1973), and Latin America (1982)

20

Twentieth-Century Roman Catholicism

If the story of the nineteenth-century papacy could be summed up in terms of the attempt to create an alternative society, the twentieth century might with equal accuracy be described in terms of its struggle to engage with an increasingly secular world. This chapter begins by surveying the relations between the papacy and the civil powers, moving on to outline developments in Catholic social teaching. We then consider the revolutionary impact of Vatican II, concluding with an examination of the turbulent period which it inaugurated.

Papacy, church, and state

Looking at the period as a whole it is noticeable that the stress on diplomacy which marked the approach of Benedict XV (1914–22), Pius XI (1922–39), and Pius XII (1939–58) has given way to a readiness to be more outspoken, especially when moral issues are to the fore.

The popes since 1914:

Benedict XV (1914–22)	Maintained neutrality during World War I; issued encyclical *Maximum Illud* on missions (1919).
Pius XI (1922–39)	Cultivated relationships with right-wing governments but issued encyclicals against Fascism and Communism (1937). Strong supporter of missions.
Pius XII (1939–58)	Began to roll back the restrictions on Catholic biblical scholarship. Infallibly defined the doctrine of the bodily assumption of Mary (1950). Strongly opposed to Communism.
John XXIII (1958–63)	Called Vatican II.
Paul VI (1963–78)	Sought to implement Vatican II; in spite of his generally progressive approach, *Humanae Vitae* (1968) caused fierce controversy and resulted in diminished authority for the papacy as a teaching office.

John Paul I (1978)   His humility showed in his refusal to be crowned as pope.

John Paul II (1978–2005)   First Slav pope; worked for religious freedom but as a theological conservative sought to limit radical application of Vatican II.

Benedict XVI (2005–)   Has continued a theologically conservative strategy.

The political context of the inter-war years was one which saw the rise of totalitarian governments of various political shades throughout much of Europe as nations tried to come to terms with the impact of world war on the old political order. Perhaps the most significant aspect of papal political strategy during this period was its support of the right-wing dictatorships which appeared in Italy (1922), Spain (1923), Poland and Portugal (both 1926), Yugoslavia (1929), Germany (1933), and Austria (1934), among others. The perceived godlessness of both Communism and socialism, coupled with the Church's innate tendency to conservatism and the feeling of Pius XI that Fascism was preferable to Communism, made such a development all but inevitable. Such regimes appeared more likely to recognize the Church's position in national life and to support it. In Italy, for example, Catholics found the Fascism of Mussolini a welcome change from the anti-clericalism of liberal politicians. Care was taken to ensure that the 1929 accord between the Vatican and the Italian leader Mussolini safeguarded the Church's privileged position in Italian society as the established faith:[1] the Vatican recognized the legitimacy of the Italian state, which in turn recognized papal sovereignty over the Vatican and guaranteed financial compensation for the loss of the Papal States. When in the Spanish Civil War (1936–9) 13 bishops, over 4,000 priests, and 2,600 religious lost their lives, the Church's conservatism was strengthened all the more.

Yet there were recurrent misgivings at a fairly high level. The German bishops had been issuing warnings regarding the dangers of Nazi ideology during the 1920s. During the mid-1930s they became aware that Hitler's professed support for the Church was not what it seemed and that he was not prepared to abide by the 1933 concordat, and in 1936 they petitioned the Vatican for an encyclical. The following year, the papacy achieved a remarkable coup when it distributed, under conditions of total secrecy, copies of *Mit Brennender Sorge* (drafted by Cardinal Faulhaber of Munich and, unusually, issued in German rather than Latin) to every parish in Germany, where it was read out at Mass the following Sunday. A few days later it was balanced by an encyclical condemning Communism, *Divini Redemptoris*.

With the expansion of Communism after 1945, the Church sought to ally itself with Western liberal democracies; this brought it face-to-face with the question of the need to tolerate religious pluralism. Relations were good with many governments, especially in Western Europe, and a number of high-ranking politicians were practising Catholics. More recently, however, there are signs that the papacy has taken a more independent line; it has not been afraid to criticize Western intervention in Iraq from 2003, for example.

Social and ethical thought before Vatican II

Catholic social teaching continued Leo XIII's attempt to elaborate a middle way between capitalism and socialism, and this approach has remained fundamental to the outlook of post-war Christian Democratic parties in Western Europe. Along these lines, in 1931 Pius XI marked the fortieth anniversary of *Rerum Novarum* with another encyclical, *Quadragesimo Anno*. It encouraged the application and outworking of social teaching by the laity through Catholic Action, organized social, educational, and institutional reform work under clerical direction; this offered the opportunity for lay involvement in the calling given to the hierarchy to bring society back to its Christian basis. Organizations for Christian workers appeared in several countries, such as the Legion of Mary (Ireland, 1921) and the Jocists (*Jeunesse Ouvrière Chrétienne*; Belgium, 1925). The latter group spread to France and the United States, and encouraged members to win work colleagues to the faith as well as applying Catholic values to their work. A similar movement developed in 1930s Italy as a means of encouraging the laity to apply Catholic social principles in public life. Catholic Action caught on not only in Europe but also in Latin America, where it had a more pronounced lay and radical ethos.

A radical clerical counterpart to Catholic Action was the 'worker priest' movement; during the years following World War II over a hundred French and Belgian priests sought jobs in the industrial sector as a way of evangelizing in a sphere perceived as being in dire need of mission. The experiment received high-level French support but the Vatican regarded it as compromising the priestly calling and from 1954 began to clamp down on it.

In spite of growing awareness that the masses were in many Western countries alienated from the Church, the dream of Christendom was slow to disappear; indeed, it experienced a resurgence in Latin America from the 1930s to the 1950s, under the influence of the French Thomist philosophical theologian Jacques Maritain (1882–1973). Maritain acknowledged that adherents of different worldviews could agree on certain fundamental values essential to the functioning of a just society, but he criticized the idea that such a society could be built on secular principles. For him, its ultimate foundation must be on the values of natural law (a Thomist concept referring to 'the imprint of God's eternal law on human beings'[2]), which Christians would see as deriving from teaching, though he insisted that church and state must be separate.

The seventieth anniversary of *Rerum Novarum* was commemorated in 1961 by the encyclical *Mater et Magistra*. As well as continuing and clarifying discussion of the role of the state in the promotion of a just and prosperous society, this pronouncement showed a new concern for the developing field of human rights; no longer could it be said that the Catholic Church was only concerned for the rights of the faithful. It also acknowledged that there were good elements in communist teaching, an admission which represented a fairly significant concession by the Church.

Pacem in Terris (1963) was addressed to those outside the Church. The papacy was reinventing itself as a focus for attempts to secure world peace and justice, and this document offered a comprehensive presentation of social teaching applied to the international as well as the national scene. As part of its elaboration of human rights and responsibilities, the encyclical affirmed religious liberty as a fundamental human right, something which the papacy had never done before.

By Vatican II, therefore, the Catholic Church was heir to a rich body of social and ethical teaching, grounded in careful consideration of the nature of the modern world and the need for the Church to demonstrate the universal relevance of its principles, often by appeal to the concept of natural law.

Vatican II

When the elderly John XXIII became Pope in 1958, few expected his pontificate to do much more than mark time. Yet it was the occasion for the most dramatic changes to affect the Catholic Church (and arguably Protestantism also) since the sixteenth century. Pope John was convinced that the Church needed to adopt a more open attitude towards the contemporary world, shedding the fortress mentality which had characterized it since the French Revolution; his term for the process of opening up, *aggiornamento*, soon passed into the theological dictionaries. Accordingly he called a church council to begin in 1962.

A little background may be helpful at this point. Vatican I had not finished its work because it had been hastily adjourned due to the worsening political climate. The Church had therefore been left with a lopsided approach to ecclesiology in which the exposition of papal authority had not yet been balanced by a commensurate degree of consideration of the respective roles of the bishops, the clergy, and the laity. Since then considerable thought had been expended on the role of the laity in the modern world, and on the theological principles underlying a just society. Now it was time for other areas of church life to be brought up to date: the religious life, worship, biblical studies, ecumenism, and inter-faith relations, to name but a few.

No fewer than 2,500 hierarchs and monastics were present during the Council, supported by hundreds of canon lawyers and theologians. In addition, there were a number of invited observers present from non-Catholic communions, as well as Catholic laity. In spite of the attempts of the Curia to ensure that proceedings remained in safely conservative hands, the assembled hierarchs refused to be guided by it in such matters as the draft statements which it had produced or the choice of members for the commissions dealing with particular topics.

We turn now to examine the constitutions (that is, statements on matters relating to the essence of the Church) and some of the main decrees and declarations (statements applying fundamental teaching to specific situations or concerns), and to explore how their teaching has been worked out in post-conciliar Catholic history.

The Dogmatic Constitution on the Church (*Lumen Gentium*) marked a shift from a fairly hierarchical understanding of the Church towards a more organic one, stressing the idea of the Church as the People of God. In addition, it did not simply equate the Church of Christ with the Roman Catholic body, but affirmed that the Church 'subsists in' the Catholic Church, a nuance which made it possible to acknowledge the work of God beyond its boundaries.

From 1943, Catholic biblical scholarship had undergone a measure of renewal, thanks to the encouragement offered by the encyclical *Divino Afflante Spiritu*. The Council greatly accelerated this process when it issued a Dogmatic Constitution on Divine Revelation (*Dei Verbum*) which affirmed the value of critical scholarship. This document excited considerable interest because it rejected the 'two source' theory of revelation (Scripture plus Tradition) in favour of an approach which stressed their common origin in God's self-revelation.

On the Sacred Liturgy, the Council issued a Constitution (*Sacrosanctum Concilium*) drawing upon the insights of the Liturgical Movement. This began before World War I as an attempt to encourage the laity to pray with the liturgy during services rather than engaging in their own private devotions. Liturgy was to be the prayer of the people rather than the offering of the priest alone, and should form the basis of personal piety and social renewal. The movement influenced Anglicanism from the 1930s, and to a lesser extent English-speaking Nonconformity, but its main impact was within Roman Catholicism. Crucial to Vatican II's application of this approach was the decision that the Mass should henceforth be celebrated entirely in the vernacular, and that the whole congregation should be actively involved. From the late 1960s a rush of translations began to appear, but the suddenness and extent of change disorientated many faithful; from 2006, therefore, a wider use of the Latin Mass was authorized. Among other major changes introduced by the Constitution were the extension of communion in both kinds to the laity, the introduction of vernacular congregational hymnody as part of the liturgy itself rather than an extra-liturgical addition, the renewal of biblically based preaching, and the restoration of the adult catechumenate.

The longest document issued by the Council was the Pastoral Constitution on the Church in the Modern World (*Gaudium et Spes*). This offered a full theological rationale for the social teaching which had been developed through the succession of encyclicals since *Rerum Novarum*, rooted in reflection on the context of the Church's ministry. Covering issues as diverse as work, marriage, peace, and nuclear weapons, it was to exercise a determinative influence on the course of Catholic moral and ethical thought.

A Decree on the Catholic Eastern Churches (*Orientalium Ecclesiarum*) set out a new and more positive mode of relating to Eastern Catholic bodies, not merely as 'rites' but as fully-fledged churches. It makes clear that these bodies do not, however, represent the whole Christian community in the East, an implicit acknowledgement of the status of the Orthodox jurisdictions. Uniatism has now given way to dialogue as the main way in which Rome relates to Orthodox churches, although suspicion of Roman intentions has continued to colour Eastern Christian perceptions of Vatican activity. National memories also die hard; for example, a factor complicating the situation in the Balkan republics has been the forced conversion of Serbs from Orthodoxy to Catholicism under Croatian rule from 1942, and the killing of as many as 350,000 who would not submit. Nevertheless, it was highly symbolic that at the Council's conclusion in 1965 Pope Paul VI lifted the anathemas which had been in force since 1054, a move which was reciprocated by the Ecumenical Patriarch, Athenagoras.

But what about relations with Protestants and Anglicans? In spite of the papal condemnation of Anglican orders in 1896 as 'absolutely null and utterly void', and the prohibition of ecumenical activity in the 1928 encyclical *Mortalium Animos*, a few visionaries on each side had met from time to time, and a series of conversations between Catholics and Anglicans took place at Malines (Belgium) from 1921 to 1926. Yet there was little practical change until in 1960 John XXIII set up the Secretariat for Promoting Christian Unity; this played a major role in Vatican II, to which non-Catholic observers (who were consulted by the fathers and thus able to influence Catholic policy) were invited. In 1964 the Council issued a Decree on Ecumenism (*Unitatis Redintegratio*) setting out the Church's new approach. No longer were Protestants seen as heretics who should be urged to return to the one true fold of Christ, but as brethren in whose communities certain marks of the Church were visible. Fellowship thus began to replace proselytism as the dominant mode of Catholic relations with Protestants, and the orientation shifted from the past to the future, in the awareness that the Church was not yet complete or perfect. The importance of this decree can hardly be overstated, and is illustrated by the volume of documents which have been appearing ever since, applying its principles to a range of situations and needs. Most notable among these are the *Directory for the Application of Principles and Norms on Ecumenism* (1993) and the encyclical *Ut Unum Sint* (1995). On the other hand, in 2007 the Vatican issued a document denying that Protestant churches were so in the full sense of the word, to the dismay of many in the WCC and elsewhere. So it would appear that the pendulum continues to swing between inclusive and exclusive positions.

The Council did not restrict its consideration to relationships with other Christian bodies, but issued a Declaration on the Relation of the Church to Non-Christian Religions (*Nostra Aetate*), on which the thinking of the Jesuit Karl Rahner (1904–84) had been influential. It argued that salvation was available even to those who did not have any conscious knowledge of God, even atheists. Rahner had formulated the inclusivist concept of 'anonymous Christianity', arguing that adherents of other faiths were 'anonymous Christians' because they were saved through Christ even though unaware of him: divine grace was at work in everyone to make them aware of the transcendent, and all religions could serve as vehicles of saving grace until the point at which the gospel was proclaimed in a particular culture. It therefore affirmed what was good in each of the major world faiths. Particular attention was paid to relationships with the Jewish community, and the Declaration explicitly repudiated the antisemitic aspects of Catholic theological tradition. In 1964 a Secretariat for Non-Christians was founded, which has engaged in interreligious dialogue; individual theologians have also sought to engage with other religious traditions, such as Raimon Panikkar (b. 1918), whose explorations of the relationship between Christianity and Hinduism have followed a pluralist line, seeing each as vehicles for the presence of the Christ.

A Declaration on Religious Liberty (*Dignitatis Humanae*) recognized it as a fundamental human right and grounded the relationship of the Church with the civil power in the idea of freedom rather than that of privilege: what mattered was not that the government should uphold Catholic teaching but that the Church should be free to follow its calling. This declaration contributed to the process of improving relations with Protestants and with East European governments. Its appearance was all the more significant given that persecution of Protestants had continued into the 1950s in countries such as Spain and Colombia, and its teaching has taken time to percolate down through the layers of government:

discrimination against non-Catholics still occurs occasionally at local government level.

Clearly the significance of the Council has been tremendous, and not only for Catholics. Yet so radical were some of its suggested changes and the applications of its norms in succeeding decades that the Church has in fact become deeply divided between progressives and conservatives, each interpreting the Council's statements in different ways.

In his conduct of the Council, it could be argued that Paul VI was trying to steer a course between the twin dangers of rigid reassertion of traditional positions and unthinking accommodation to modern ideas. While making many major changes, he refused to allow the Council to debate the contentious issues of contraception and priestly celibacy. He set out traditional views on the former topic in the encyclical *Humanae Vitae* (1968), which was issued in the face of the recommendations of a panel of medical advisers appointed by John XXIII and confirmed in office by Paul himself. Although it was not declared a mortal sin to disobey it and the acceptance of the faithful was 'invited' rather than insisted upon, Paul's reassertion of the ban on contraception pleased conservative Catholics, but many of them would have been less happy with part of the rationale for it, which was that advocating contraception represented an attempt by rich nations to secure their position by limiting population growth in the Third World, rather than addressing the challenge of poverty by committing themselves to a fairer distribution of wealth and resources. Western responses to *Humanae Vitae* provide the most striking example of the rise of 'pick and mix' Catholicism, in which members feel free to dissent from particular aspects of the Church's theological or ethical teaching. Traditional perspectives on issues of sexual ethics were reaffirmed in *Veritatis Splendor* (1993), but again there is vocal questioning of the Church's condemnation of artificial contraception and homosexual practice, for example.

The Church since Vatican II

Theological ferment

Some conservatives must have felt that Vatican II was opening a Pandora's box of new and radical opinions, and one result of the openness inaugurated by the Council has been a heightened degree of theological ferment more openly expressed than has usually been the case hitherto. One example of this has been the Church's handling of Liberation Theology.

Liberation Theology uses a distinctive methodology and social analysis to read the Bible in a manner somewhat similar to that of Black Theologians in the United States and 'Political Theology' in Western

Europe. It involves critical reflection on the experience of the poor, especially experience of oppression, informed by Marxist analysis of the socio-economic context; a key element of this has been the idea of 'dependency', that Latin American nations are locked into an economic system which perpetuates their dependence on former colonial rulers in Europe, a system which is loaded in favour of European nations and against the Majority World. The Bible is read with a focus on the motifs of exodus and liberation, and the Christian calling is seen as participation in the liberation process through identification with the oppressed; such action is termed 'praxis' and includes the forthright criticism of social structures which are perceived as unjust and as institutionalizing violence against the oppressed. Truth is something to be done before it can be understood. Controversially, fundamental Christian beliefs and ecclesiastical structures are evaluated first and foremost in the light of the experience of the poor rather than the teaching of the Church.

The background to such thinking is the years after 1945, when fear of Communism helped to drive the Church into the arms of military dictatorships following the doctrine of national security, which saw such government as the necessary counter to Marxists and other subversives. The Church was co-opted to legitimize these regimes and so its hierarchy (though not the priesthood or the missionary force) was perceived as resistant to social change. Thus it faced tremendous obstacles in seeking to relate to the vast majority of its membership.

However, Vatican II's stress on opening up to the modern world came at the right moment to inspire the bishops in their leadership of the struggle for the Church's ideological independence and prophetic status. A key moment came with the conference of Latin American bishops (CELAM) at Medellín, Colombia (1968), which considered how the norms established by Vatican II should be applied in their continent. The bishops declared that whereas the Church had hitherto sided with oppressive regimes and upheld the Christendom model of church–state relations, it would henceforth side with the poor.

The movement's most visible impact was in the tens of thousands of 'base communities' which appeared in Brazil and elsewhere from the 1960s. A longstanding shortage of priests in Brazil, which had given Catholicism a pronounced lay ethos, facilitated their emergence. These communities combined worship in fairly small neighbourhood-based groups with attempts to respond to local socio-economic challenges, and sought to make lay people aware of their situation and their rights.

Perhaps the classic statement of Liberation Theology was *A Theology of Liberation* (published in Spanish in 1971, revised in 1988) by the Peruvian Gustavo Gutiérrez (b. 1928). Other key thinkers include the Spanish Jesuit Jon Sobrino (b. 1938) in El Salvador, the Argentinian Protestant José Miguez Bonino, and the Brazilian Franciscan Leonardo

Boff (b. 1938). It is noteworthy that liberationism is primarily a Catholic movement, perhaps because Protestant churches had not participated in the unjust power structures against which it was protesting. Another possible reason may be that the Protestant churches established on the continent in the nineteenth century had tended to attract middle-class liberals, and so the call to do theology from the perspective of the poor had less attraction for their memberships. However, some Protestant liberation theologians have emerged, and its concerns have informed Latin American evangelical theology.

From the early 1970s liberationism began to develop links with other similar movements (often largely Protestant) elsewhere in the world: Black Liberation Theology in South Africa, Minjung theology in Korea, and Dalit theology in India, to name just a few. All stress the need for theology to arise from particular concrete situations as reflection in the light of the Scriptures on the struggle for liberation. Furthermore, they teach that God chooses to side with the oppressed of this world, and that the poor have been granted special insight into his purposes. Such thinking has, as may be evident, become influential in WCC circles as much as Catholic ones.

Intense debate has been provoked by Liberation Theology; in particular, critics have asked whether it is a theology *from* or *for* the poor? Initially, it seemed to be the latter, as theologians trained in the West set out intellectual expositions of their views; however, the proliferation of base communities has assisted a shift towards the former, as theologians such as Gutiérrez have come to regard themselves as listening to the poor and then articulating their thinking.

Much of the criticism has come from within the Catholic Church. Not all national hierarchies were enthusiastic; the Colombians in particular expressed consistent opposition. From the early 1970s CELAM tended to espouse an anti-liberationist line. In 1985, John Paul II (whose background would have made him well aware of Marxist thought) actually condemned Liberation Theology in Lima, warning its exponents against reducing the Christian message of liberation from sin to one of political and economic freedom, and the Vatican has followed a policy of appointing conservative bishops. However, some who were already in office proved forthright defenders of the priority of the poor; notable examples were Dom Helder Câmara (1909–99), Archbishop of Recife in Brazil, who insisted on the need to identify with the poor by adopting a simple lifestyle and not merely to defend them; and Oscar Romero (1917–80), who had adopted liberationist ideas after his appointment as Archbishop of San Salvador, and who was assassinated while saying Mass.

In spite of the efforts of liberation theologians, other movements have often proved more attractive to members of the Church: some focus on personal spirituality, such as the Pentecostal and Charismatic movements, whose forms of church life affirm the gifts of each member and thus serve to empower the poor in the religious sphere; others major on applying a highly conservative version of Catholicism to public life, such as Opus Dei, half of whose global membership was in Latin America by the 1990s.

One question raised by the high-profile controversies over theology is whether the papacy has changed, or whether it still pursues an essentially conservative theological line. Perhaps it, of all the components of the Church, has changed the least. It is true that since Paul VI successive popes have engaged in a hectic routine of world travel in an attempt to establish the Vatican as a key player in world diplomacy, but the Holy Father remains a focus for Catholic devotion in a manner reminiscent of Pio Nono. Authority appears to have become more centralized once again from John Paul II (1978–2005) onwards. Furthermore, in certain respects papal policy does seem to have swung back to a more conservative position. Papal ethical pronouncements have remained robustly and even controversially conservative. This is likely to remain the case under Benedict XVI, who as Cardinal Ratzinger, Prefect of the Congregation for the Doctrine of the Faith, did much to ensure that conservative bishops were appointed in Latin America and elsewhere, and to withdraw the Church's sanction of controversial theologians such as Boff (who, having been silenced for a year, eventually left the Franciscans and became a layman in 1992 in order to be freer to speak out) and the German theologian, apologist, and ecumenist Hans Küng (b. 1928), an adviser at Vatican II who lost his licence to teach as a Catholic theologian in 1979 as a result of challenging the Church's teaching on such issues as papal infallibility.

Decline in vocations

One of the most serious challenges facing the Catholic Church is the sharp decline in vocations to the priesthood and the religious life. Among the factors precipitating this are the affirmation of the mission of the laity as part of the Church, opposition to continuing papal insistence on priestly celibacy in a world which places a premium on the right to sexual self-expression, and reluctance of many to commit themselves to a lifestyle of austerity in societies of plenty.

Numbers in religious orders had been rising through the century, but the new climate in the Church following Vatican II, which gave powerful affirmation to the laity seeking to live Christian lives in the world, precipitated a reversal in many countries, especially in the West.

The changing social, cultural, and moral climate, coupled with the rise in the number of sexual scandals involving Catholic clergy and the publicity now given to such crimes, has provoked frequent calls for re-examination of the requirement of clerical celibacy. Other factors inducing this have included inability to accept the degree of isolation involved in priestly ministry. In 1970 the Dutch Catholic Pastoral Council expressed formal disagreement with the requirement, which has come under increasing fire ever since. The period since Vatican II has therefore seen a catastrophic decline in vocations to the priesthood in some areas. In many countries there has developed a severe shortage of clergy; lay people act frequently as eucharistic ministers using pre-consecrated elements. Indeed, some parishes are in effect pastored by lay people, and in countries such as France and the Netherlands, and even in parts of Latin America, these may be women, often religious or trained pastoral workers. As a general rule, the more liberal or secular the society, the faster the decline in the number of priests. So from 1975 to 1995 numbers increased by 39% in Poland, but decreased by 32% in Belgium, 30% in France, and 26% in Holland. By 2000, Europe and North America had 35% of the world's Catholics but 68% of its priests; by contrast, Latin America had 42% and 20% respectively. In Brazil by the 1980s, there were more Protestant pastors than Catholic priests. Many priests in Latin America were European missionaries, evidence that indigenization of the priesthood had not always progressed: indeed, whereas in 1901 82% of clergy in Peru were locals, by 1973 the figure had actually fallen, to 39%. While the roots of this lay in a post-war influx of missionary priests and religious to counter the twin threats of Marxism and Protestantism, the consequence was to make the priesthood more remote from the people. However, by 2000 there were over a million catechists in the continent; educated and locally born, they were well-equipped to assist the Church in the process of indigenization.

The new emphasis on the role of the laity, including the 'New Evangelization' of once-Christian Europe, has continued to be affirmed. In 1976, a Pontifical Council for the Laity was set up, in response to the growth of lay bodies such as charismatic prayer groups, tertiary orders, and associations such as Opus Dei which aim to foster lay Catholic involvement in society. The enforced laicization of the Church is likely to lead to further radical changes, but at a popular level Catholic devotion has often remained surprisingly conservative. Thus Marian apparitions have continued to play a significant role, the most notable being that at Medjugorje (then in Yugoslavia) in 1981, which continued the rather apocalyptic strain of many such occurrences.

In the next chapter we shall explore the fluctuating fortunes of British Catholicism during the twentieth century, a narrative which will illustrate many of the themes touched on here; what we shall see is that certain aspects of it are in common with the story of British Protestantism.

Questions for thought

1 Why do you think the papacy saw right-wing governments as natural allies?

2 Why did Catholic social teaching have a greater depth to it than that emanating from Protestant sources?

3 With reference to their respective contexts, assess the relative significance of the First and Second Vatican Councils.

4 Compare and contrast the relation between Scripture and experience in Liberation Theology and Pentecostalism.

5 What comparisons would you make between Catholic and Protestant attempts during the last half-century to deal with the problems presented by theological diversity?

6 What longstanding historical causes are there for the shortage of clergy in Latin American Catholicism?

Further reading

Nicholas Atkin and Frank Tallett, 2003, *Priests, Prelates and People: A History of European Catholicism since 1750*, Oxford: Oxford University Press, chs 5–6.

Frank J. Coppa, 1998, *The Modern Papacy since 1789*, Longman History of the Papacy, Harlow: Longman, chs 10–17.

J. Derek Holmes and Bernard Bickers, 2002, *A Short History of the Catholic Church*, with a postscript by Peter Hebblethwaite and final chapter by Peter Doyle, London: Burns & Oates, ch. 7.

Hugh McLeod (ed.), 2006, *Cambridge History of Christianity*, vol. 9: *World Christianities c.1914–c.2000*, Cambridge: Cambridge University Press, chs 3, 10, 20.

Websites

'Vatican II: Voice of the Church', www.vatican2voice.org.

Notes

1 The church was disestablished in 1984.

2 Brendan Sweetman, in Trevor A. Hart (ed.), 2000, *The Dictionary of Historical Theology*, Carlisle: Paternoster, p. 355.

21

The British Churches

The years from 1918 to the present have been a period of almost unparalleled change for the British churches, and there is no sign of any slowing in the pace of change. Whereas the churches began at the centre of British society, shaping its worldview, influencing its legislation, and dominating its institutions, they ended the period somewhere out towards the margins, their worldview seen as deviant by the secularized majority, their influence on legislation minimal, and their institutional status inexorably declining. Out of the many issues which could be discussed, this chapter focuses on those affecting all the churches rather than tracing the history of specific denominations (with the exception of new ones such as Pentecostalism). Beginning with some discussion of the changing status of the churches in society, it goes on to explore institutional, ecumenical, and liturgical changes, as well as introducing some new and significant expressions of Christian faith.

The churches and society

In sharp contrast with the mid-Victorian era, churches found themselves increasingly marginalized from the 1920s: not only did the state take over many of the welfare functions of voluntary bodies, but churches also lost their role as providers of adult education, as bodies such as the Workers' Educational Association developed. The social and sporting activities which churches had laid on were provided elsewhere, and often at times which clashed with church services. So Nonconformists in particular found themselves back where they had been at the start of the nineteenth century, their remaining roles being more explicitly spiritual. The lessening of controversy over education (the 1944 Act making Religious Education and daily school worship compulsory was passed with little protest, unlike the legislation of 1870 and 1902) is indicative not only of the fact that there was less dissatisfaction with the system on the part of Nonconformists but also that churches were becoming less important as educational providers. Nevertheless, aspects of the Christendom model remain: the established status of the Churches of England and Scotland;

Timeline: Events in Britain, 1914–2007

1916	Easter Rising in Dublin
1920	Church in Wales disestablished
1922	Irish Free State comes into being
1924	Conference on Politics, Economics and Citizenship (COPEC)
1929	Union of United Free Church and Church of Scotland
1933	Union of Wesleyan Methodists with United Methodist Church and Primitive Methodists
1942	British Council of Churches (BCC) formed
1944	Education Act makes Religious Education and daily worship compulsory in schools
1953	First congregation of NT Church of God founded
1954	Billy Graham's first large-scale mission in Britain
1963	*Honest to God* published
1964	BCC conference at Nottingham pledges itself to church union by 1980; Fountain Trust founded
1969, 1972	Anglican–Methodist unity proposals fail to secure acceptance
1972	United Reformed Church formed in England from merger of Congregationalists and Presbyterians
1980	Fountain Trust wound up
1985	Commission appointed by the Archbishop of Canterbury publishes *Faith in the City*
1990	Council of Churches for Britain and Ireland (later Churches Together in Britain and Ireland) replaces BCC
1992	Church of England finally approves the ordination of women to the priesthood

the popularity of Christian rites of passage, the provision for religious education in state schools and the continued state support for church schools, and the role of religious leaders (not just Christians) as the national conscience.

In the realm of social thought the churches have continued to expend considerable energy on study and pronouncement; though it may be questioned how far state policy has been affected, the importance for particular social groups of the feeling that the Church was speaking for them (not that all groups have always felt this) should not be underestimated. In the years following World War I many of these pronouncements were marked by a moderate collectivist tone, criticizing a *laissez-faire* approach to economic issues in a manner similar to that of the Social Gospel movement. Perhaps the high point of this approach was the interdenominational Conference on Politics, Economics and Citizenship (COPEC) held at Birmingham under the chairmanship of William Temple in 1924. This was designed to feed in to the Life and Work conference at Stockholm the following year, and it provided the churches with a body of social teaching on which they could draw.

Not all Christians were enamoured of the emphasis on social comment: during the inter-war period most Evangelicals considered it a distraction to discuss social issues; the world was headed for destruction, and their task was simply to rescue as many as they could by proclaiming the gospel. The Nonconformist Social Gospel was regarded as a substitute for the message of the Bible. This was both a reaction against perceived overemphasis before the war on social issues, and a recognition of the increasingly marginal position which Evangelicals held in church life, and which churches held in society generally. Evangelical attitudes began to change after 1945, as a more positive estimate of social and cultural involvement which initially owed much to the Reformed theological tradition gained ground in British evangelical circles. As in North America, it was issues of 'family' and personal morality which attracted much evangelical attention; the Festival of Light (1971) marked the reappearance of publicly expressed evangelical concern. But within a few years some were moving to more radical social critique: David Sheppard, the Anglican Bishop of Liverpool, published *Built as a City* (1974), which examined the problems of decaying urban society, and the magazine *Third Way* began to appear in 1977.

As for British Catholicism, an organization named Sword of the Spirit was founded by Cardinal Hinsley in 1940 to promote justice in war and peace. Basing his approach on the Catholic understanding of natural law, Hinsley was supported by Anglican and Nonconformist leaders. Predictably, in 1941 Rome forbade non-Catholics to become full members, and so the latter founded a parallel body known as Religion and Life, which co-operated closely with Sword of the Spirit. However, both petered out after a few years, possibly victims of a growing preoccupation with institutional ecumenism at the expense of task-orientated co-operation.

It was during the Thatcher years (1979–90) that radical economic change provided the catalyst for the reappearance of equally robust ecclesiastical critique. In 1985 the Church of England published a report provoked by the widespread inner-city rioting of 1980–1, *Faith in the City*. It was not well received by the Conservative government because of its trenchant criticism of official economic policy, but it did put the Church's involvement in inner-city areas in the spotlight. Often the Anglicans were the only remaining Christian presence in such localities, and the Church of England set up the Church Urban Fund to fund church-linked projects there.

Apart from far-reaching social and economic changes such as the introduction of the package of changes known as the Welfare State in the 1940s and the ever-rising standard of material well-being (for most, at any rate), churches found themselves having to respond to changing moral standards, the 1960s representing a watershed in this respect.

Many believed that moral standards were slipping further and further away from Christian ones. Abortion and homosexual practice were both legalized in 1967; divorce became widespread, especially after legislation in 1969 made it easier and widened the grounds on which it could be sought; and the culture of integrity and public service gave way in many quarters to a materialistic outlook. Churches were divided in their responses: some hankered after the old days in which they believed that, outwardly at least, Britain had been a country governed by a broadly Christian morality; others such as John Robinson called for Christian ethics to accommodate themselves to changing social thought. So rapid has been the shift, and the associated decline in church attendance, that Callum Brown has written of *The Death of Christian Britain*, an event which he pinpoints to 1963.[1] At the same time, new issues have become the subject of extensive thought on the part of the churches: overseas aid, nuclear armaments, debt reduction, and now environmental stewardship have each in turn come under the theological spotlight, contrasting with the tendency at the beginning of the century to focus on matters of personal lifestyle such as sexual morality, temperance, and gambling.

One result of the rapid decline of the size and standing of the churches in society has been a renewed emphasis on evangelism. In 1945 the Archbishops commissioned a report entitled *Towards the Conversion of England*, which affirmed the need for and legitimacy of such activity, in order to meet the spiritual hunger evident in the post-war period. The 1950s saw the 'Tell Scotland' campaign, which sought to stimulate ongoing lay evangelism at the parish level by the Church of Scotland. But the biggest impact was made, not by any official denominational venture or publication, but by the visit of Billy Graham to London in 1954. His 'crusade' at Harringay Stadium (and follow-up visits in 1955, 1956, 1961, 1966, 1984, and 1989) showed British church leaders a model of evangelism with which they had become unfamiliar (though in essentials it was simply a technologically updated version of that espoused by Moody and Sankey). Suddenly evangelism was on the map once again, and that provoked a vigorous and at times heated debate in the media from 1955 about the phenomenon of 'Fundamentalism' which has never quite died down. Nevertheless, with each return visit Graham's support base widened, and those who have not felt able to support his missions have found themselves constrained to think about how to commend the Christian faith to those outside the churches. Even Robinson's *Honest to God* could, in a sense, be seen as an evangelistic work in its concern to overcome the church's inability to communicate with such people. Ecumenically based ventures such as the Nationwide Initiative in Evangelism (1980) and denominational ones such as the Church of England's Decade of Evangelism (the 1990s) have not, however, been distinguished by their success. More influential on church practice have been models of evangelism such as the 'seeker services' developed by Willow Creek Community Church (near Chicago) in the 1980s, one of a succession of models of church life and outreach exported across the Atlantic to British Evangelicals. One of the most important factors, however, making for the maintenance of evangelical numbers has been the attention they have given to work among children and young people through organizations such as Scripture Union (founded in 1867 as the Children's Special Service Mission and now an international organization) and British Youth for Christ (founded in the late 1940s), taking over from bodies such as the YMCA and YWCA. In this they followed and developed the older Free Church tradition, which was largely evangelical during the nineteenth century. Evangelical churches have thus been markedly more successful than others in reaching young people from unchurched backgrounds and retaining many who had been brought up within the churches. A surprising number of leading theologians and clergy experienced an evangelical conversion during their teens, although some such as the philosopher of religion John Hick, the biblical scholar James Barr, and the theologian and former Bishop of Durham David Jenkins have subsequently moved a long way from these theological roots.

In many parts of the country, church attendance is now primarily a suburban and small-town phenomenon: the Church of England's adherence to the parish system has allowed it to maintain a presence in inner-city and rural areas after other denominations have withdrawn, albeit at the cost of amalgamation of benefices and an increasing reliance on the work of non-stipendiary clergy and readers. For a much larger proportion of the population, 'believing without belonging'[2] describes their approach, as a succession of opinion polls asking questions about religious belief have testified. However, with the decline of Christian-based religious education in schools and the collapse of Sunday school attendance, it is questionable how much longer such a tradition of residual belief can continue.

Institutional developments

An instructive contrast may be drawn between Catholicism and Anglicanism in terms of their respective relations with society, which may be summarized in the terms assimilation and marginalization. The Catholic Church had worked fairly successfully during both world wars at demonstrating its essential patriotism and thus seeking to overcome both its own tendency to isolationism and residual suspicions of Catholicism as an exotic foreign import. However, growing confidence after 1945 was soon followed by increasingly rapid decline from the 1960s. By 1980, two-thirds of English Catholics were marrying a non-Catholic; the community was no longer as clearly distinguishable from mainstream society as it had been; and the impact of ecumenism and the Charismatic movement, along with the general climate of pluralist tolerance which contrasted with Rome's insistence on maintaining traditional positions, had lessened the commitment of many Catholics to their church. Furthermore, in England and Wales especially it was about to suffer a serious fall in clerical and religious vocations, in common with much of the Western world.

As for the Church of England, its position at the heart of national rites of passage has not gone unchallenged during the twentieth century, although the critics this time were less likely to be Nonconformists and more likely to be either Anglicans themselves or non-Christians. There have been recurrent calls for it to be disestablished (since 1977 it has been the only established Anglican church in the world) but nothing on the scale of the bitter nineteenth-century Nonconformist campaigns. In practice, as it has become the church of a minority, it has also taken on more of the feel of a gathered church; at the same time, lay involvement in its ministries and government has increased dramatically, thus substantially lessening the difference between it and most Nonconformist denominations. This has been accompanied by something of a turn inwards to a greater emphasis on internal affairs. However, it remains distinctive in having a much larger 'penumbra' or circle of nominal adherents than most other denominations, making it the church to which many still turn for rites of passage (the Nonconformist penumbra of former Sunday scholars largely disappeared between the wars, as evidenced by emptying chapel galleries).

All denominations have felt the impact of the decline in clerical vocations. Numbers of Church of England clergy halved from 20,000 in 1900 to 10,000 in 1984, and have continued to decline since, although numbers of evangelical ordinands have risen steadily in recent decades, a trend which is indicative of changes in the nature of English Christianity. Similarly, Scottish Presbyterians (of all types) saw the numbers of their ministers decline from 3,600 in 1900 to 2,950 in 1950 and 1,450 in 1990. The decline among the Free Churches has been steepest in the most theologically liberal denominations such as the Unitarians and the bodies which now comprise the United Reformed Church (URC), but less so in more evangelical denominations such as the Baptists. Perhaps more significant for the next few decades is the changing age profile of ministers: as a body they are older now than at the start of the twentieth century, not least because many are entering the ministry after ten or twenty years in another career. The aging of the clergy is most marked among the Catholic priesthood; although numbers actually increased in England and Wales from 2,300 in 1900 to 6,200 by 1970, a catastrophic decline in vocations means that many who are now active will shortly retire, and the church will face a similar challenge to that facing it over recent decades in parts of South America.

In Britain as elsewhere, the ordination of women has been one of the most contentious ministry-related issues of the century. The Salvation Army had always had women officers, and encouraged husband and wife teams. The Congregationalists and Baptists first ordained women in 1917, the Church of Scotland in 1969, Methodists in 1945 (and under less stringent conditions from the 1970s), and the Anglicans from 1989 (Ireland), 1992 (England), 1994 (Scotland), and 1996 (Wales). As a result of these decisions, several hundred Anglican clergy converted to Rome (including many married clergy, which itself has had a knock-on effect on Catholic pressure to abandon the insistence on priestly celibacy), and others joined one of the Orthodox jurisdictions. Among less ecumenically inclined bodies, Elim and Assemblies of God both had women pastors from the earliest days, although their numbers declined as the movements took on more of an institutional form and grew closer to other Evangelicals.

Sometimes seen as a response to decline along the lines of the business world, there have been several major denominational mergers, though the success of these at staving off decline is dubious. In Scotland, 1929 saw the union of the United Free Church (which stood for the separation of church and state) with the (established) Church of Scotland, a merger which had been facilitated by an act of 1921 granting the Kirk effective autonomy. The Church of Scotland had lost its civil functions over preceding decades but was to remain established in the sense of being accorded national recognition, but free to determine all aspects of its doctrine, government, and worship.

Among the Wesleyans, 1907 saw the creation of the United Methodist Church by the merger of the Bible Christians, the Methodist New Connexion, and the United Methodist Free Church (itself a mid-nineteenth-century merger of several breakaway Wesleyan groups). In 1932 this merged with the Primitive Methodists and the original Wesleyan Methodists to form the Methodist Church, though at the local level it was often extremely hard to persuade congregations in the same village to unite and give up one of their buildings. More recently English Congregationalists and Presbyterians came together to form the United Reformed Church (URC) in 1972, later adding many congregations from the Churches of Christ and in 2000 taking many Scottish Congregationalists under its wing. In spite of this successful record, the URC has declined faster numerically than other Nonconformist denominations, giving rise to some anguished questioning about the relevance of ecumenism for declining churches.

Ecumenism

The event which symbolized the commencement of serious British attempts at cross-denominational ecumenism was the 'Appeal to all Christian People' issued by the Lambeth Conference of Anglican bishops in 1920, to which war had been a stimulus. It urged churches to try a new approach based on regarding unity as something which already existed and needed only to be made visible, rather than something which did not exist and therefore had to be created. But the task of making unity visible was challenging enough, involving as it did the areas of faith, sacraments, and ministries. Its basis (as in the Lambeth Quadrilateral of 1888) was to be the Scriptures, the Nicene Creed, the sacraments, and the historic threefold pattern of ministry (bishops, priests, and deacons). Many Nonconformists greeted it somewhat coolly, but a striking exception was the secretary of the Baptist Union of Great Britain and Ireland (which in spite of its name was almost entirely made up of English churches), J.H. Shakespeare (1857–1928). A committed and far-sighted ecumenist in a denomination which was often wary of letting slip its distinctive beliefs and practices in the process of interdenominational co-operation, he was even prepared to countenance some form of episcopacy as part of a united church. However, in this his denomination refused to follow him, and the Baptist constituency has remained the most ambivalent of all the historic denominations regarding ecumenism, in spite of producing noted ecumenists such as Ernest Payne (1902–79). Another appeal from Lambeth was heard in 1946, when Archbishop Fisher of Canterbury sought to restart discussions by calling on the Free Churches to 'take episcopacy into their system'. He had correctly located the most difficult issue, and one which shipwrecked Anglican–Methodist reunion negotiations in 1969 and 1972.

Organizationally speaking, ecumenism in England began with the Free Churches. The National Council of Evangelical Free Churches (1896) and the Federal Council of Evangelical Free Churches (1919) were merged as the Free Church Federal Council in 1939. (This became the Free Churches Group of Churches Together in England in 2001, reflecting the trend to downsizing of ecumenical bodies as much as a decreasing sense of Free Church distinctiveness vis-à-vis the established church.) The British Council of Churches (BCC) was inaugurated by sixteen denominations in 1942. Its first chairman was the newly enthroned Archbishop of Canterbury, William Temple, who regarded unity not as an end in itself but as a means to service and mission. His sudden death in 1944 was a severe blow to the movement, but he had succeeded in envisioning it in a way which was to last for several decades.

The idealism (perhaps linked with the contemporary stress on post-war reconstruction) which had brought the BCC into being ran into choppy seas from the late 1950s. Conversations between the Church of England and the Church of Scotland foundered several times on the rock of episcopacy (the most serious being in 1957), opposition to which was long-standing and deeply rooted north of the border. Although most British Protestant churches committed themselves at a conference in Nottingham in 1964 to achieving visible unity by 1980, a scheme for Anglican–Methodist union was twice rejected, in 1969 and 1972; the formation of the URC saw significant numbers of Congregational churches opting to remain outside it; and a Covenant for Unity involving Anglicans, Methodists, Moravians, and United Reformed, which was intended to secure intercommunion and mutual recognition of ministries, failed in 1982, although a later Anglican–Methodist version came into force from 2003. (By contrast, such a covenant had been successfully inaugurated in Wales in 1975, bringing together the Church in Wales, the Presbyterian Church of Wales, the Union of Welsh Independents, and the Methodists.) Coupled with the fact that Christians were enjoying increasing informal contact with one another in such settings as charismatic prayer groups and co-operative evangelism, and the increasing mobility of Christians between denominations (partly as brand loyalty gave way to religious consumerism), it seemed to many that institutional ecumenism had had its day in an era of what some have called 'post-denominationalism'.

An extensive process of reflection and reshaping resulted. The Inter-Church Process, *Not Strangers but Pilgrims*, began in 1985, and the following year a million people participated in an ecumenical Lent course, *What on Earth is the Church For?* It became evident that many Christians felt held back by their denominational leaders, and that a new approach was needed in order to channel their enthusiasm. Such an approach could also take account of both the increasing level of religious pluralism and of irreligion, as well as the changes in the church scene which had resulted from the appearance of dynamic bodies of black majority churches and independent charismatic churches (often known as 'house churches' or 'new churches'), which were not at ease with traditional ecumenical structures and ways of doing things, and the involvement of Catholics in local ecumenical bodies from the 1970s (the first of these had been founded in 1917; by 1965 there were about 500, and by 1992 there would be over 1,100, an indication that local ecumenism had certainly not run out of steam). In consequence, 1990 saw the replacement of the BCC with an array of new 'ecumenical instruments' including the Council of Churches in Britain and Ireland (later Churches Together in Britain and Ireland) and its national counterparts, known by the acronyms CTE (England), ACTS (Scotland), CYTUN (Wales), and ICC (Ireland). These reflected an approach to ecumenism which gave priority to local initiatives ('grass-roots ecumenism') rather than national ones, and which was less exclusively committed to the goal of visible denominational unity. The new approach also made it easier for Catholics to participate at a national level, as well as churches from ethnic minorities and the evangelical and Pentecostal sectors.

Although the aspirations of Nottingham 1964 for full denominational unity were not, by and large, to be realized, the conference did result in the introduction of Local Ecumenical Projects, by which congregations in a locality could come together on a formal basis. Since 1994 these have been renamed Local Ecumenical Partnerships, and they come in several forms: local covenants between separate congregations, congregations sharing a building but holding separate services, sharing of worship and pastoral ministries, and mutual recognition of members. The range of denominations involved varies from place to place, but it is significant that in a number of cases it includes the Roman Catholic Church.

A factor which has deeply affected the ecumenical scene has been the renaissance of Evangelicalism. Between the wars it was insular and tended to eschew academic theological study; it has been said that the best evangelical brains were all abroad on the mission field. However, with the war came a rediscovery of Reformed theology which paralleled (and was to some extent influenced by) the rise of Neo-Orthodoxy on the wider scene; this helped to provoke a shift from pietistic anti-intellectualism to a more intellectually orientated approach. Early fruit of this was the founding in 1943 of Tyndale House in Cambridge as a research centre for Biblical Studies, and the London Bible College (now London School of Theology) in 1946 as an institution designed to provide a theological education which was fully up to contemporary academic standards. Evangelical student work, too, has experienced periods of growth, whereas the SCM's work suffered a dramatic collapse during the 1970s from which it has recovered only slowly and partially. Over succeeding decades Evangelicals established a reputation for solid biblical scholarship, and with that came a renewed sense of confidence on the part of evangelical churchmen. Whereas they had for several decades tended to have as little as possible to do with denominational hierarchies, they now sought actively to play a part in wider church affairs, and with that came a growing willingness on the part of many (though by no means all) to become more involved in ecumenical activities. In turn, ecumenical bodies have become more open to Evangelicals, though it is hard to say whether this is grounded in theological conviction or simply a matter of pragmatism and the recognition that most churches which are growing are evangelical. Evangelicalism has also undergone considerable theological diversification, especially in England; for example, conditional immortality, the belief that the unrepentant cease to exist after the judgement rather than suffering eternal conscious punishment, has gained ground, in part due to its espousal by leaders of the calibre of John Stott (b. 1921), and so there are now a range of views on the afterlife held openly by Evangelicals. The Evangelical Alliance has found its boundaries tested on several occasions and in recent decades has adopted a more open approach to institutional ecumenism; a watershed for this was a public disagreement in 1966 between Stott and the Welsh-born minister of London's Westminster Chapel, Martyn Lloyd-Jones (1899–1981); the latter (who had been involved in some discussions between Evangelicals and the BCC in the early 1950s, and was influential in the development of evangelical student work) called on Evangelicals to withdraw from denominations which were compromising the gospel. Interestingly, as many in mainstream denominations have moved towards a more pragmatic and 'invisible' approach to unity, the EA has placed increasing emphasis on its role as a fellowship of churches, and not merely of individuals. Linked with the growing profile of Evangelicals has been the growing emphasis on evangelism. Churches have gradually begun to realize that in what is effectively a non-Christian society, what unites them is far more significant than what divides them. From the 1980s, therefore, a growing sense of a common faith and a common calling has been apparent.

New traditions

As older traditions have declined in numbers and influence, new ones have emerged to take their places. We shall examine Pentecostalism, the Charismatic movement, and Restorationism, as well as the black majority churches; attention could also have been given to the exponential growth of Eastern Orthodoxy in Britain during the century, although this has tended to be accompanied by a somewhat lower measure of interaction with other Christian traditions.

Pentecostalism[3]

It seems that a Pentecostal meeting was established in London as early as 1906, but we saw earlier that the main early platform for the new movement was provided by Alexander Boddy in Sunderland. Significantly, the first formal Pentecostal organization was a missionary society, the Pentecostal Missionary Union (1909). Soon afterwards Pentecostal congregations began to come together to form denominational groupings. Negatively, this was in reaction to the fierce opposition experienced from the churches (especially from Evangelicals); positively, it enabled them to act together, to plan for outreach, and to establish doctrinal safeguards and sanctions against heresy. Elim is now the largest of them in Britain, partly because a sixth of its members in 2000 were linked with one church – Kensington Temple (now London City Church). From the mid-1950s large-scale immigration from the West Indies introduced another Pentecostal denomination, the New Testament Church of God: this is part of a North American denomination, the Church of God (Cleveland, Tennessee), but here it has become a black-majority grouping, its best-known leader being Joel Edwards, General Secretary of the Evangelical Alliance. From the 1970s, further Pentecostal denominations have taken root here, such as the Redeemed Christian Church of God (originating in West Africa and now with over 300 congregations in the UK) and the Universal Church of the Kingdom of God (Brazil). Some of the growth of these newer denominations has been due to immigration, but in more recent decades much of it has been due to decisions by denominational leaders elsewhere to establish a presence in Britain.

During the 1960s many British Pentecostals were suspicious of the Charismatic movement, not least because it managed to hold onto denominational respectability whereas they had been forced out of their churches. This gave rise to suspicion that Charismatics were theologically and ecumenically compromised, but during the 1970s this gave way to widespread acceptance of much of the resources (such as songs, books, and teachers) being produced by Charismatics. Not surprisingly, this left many Pentecostals wondering whether they had anything distinctive to offer any more, and whether their day had passed. They faced an 'identity crisis'.

The Charismatic movement

A number of independent charismatic congregations and groups had emerged in Britain during the 1940s and 1950s, often stressing prayer for healing, but their activity was not widely known, and they had few links with the Pentecostal churches. During this period, British Evangelicalism was also marked by a hunger for revival, with meetings and conferences for prayer being widespread. It was an Anglican, Michael Harper (b. 1930), who did much to lay the foundations for the phenomenal growth of charismatic Christianity in Britain. A curate to the evangelical leader John Stott in London, he was baptized in the Spirit in 1962 and began to draw interested church leaders together, as well as networking with other Charismatics. Harper founded the Fountain Trust in 1964 as a service agency for charismatic renewal, and the following year began publishing the influential magazine *Renewal*. Stott soon made clear his opposition to talk of a post-conversion baptism in the Spirit, providing a theological rationale for many Evangelicals who were unhappy about the new movement and its claims, and Evangelicalism became deeply divided over the charismatic issue.

At first, most Charismatics were drawn from evangelical ranks, Baptists and Anglicans being the denominations most affected. Before long, however, a substantial number were drawn from high Anglicanism, and even more from Roman Catholicism. As for the considerable tension between Charismatics and mainstream Evangelicals, this began to ease during the late 1970s, aided by reports such as the Anglican joint statement *Gospel and Spirit* (1977). Perhaps the best-known British leader was David Watson (1933–84), an Anglican clergyman and evangelist. He built a model charismatic congregation at St Michael-le-Belfrey in York, and wrote a number of books expounding charismatic thinking in an irenic manner which helped to gain acceptability for the movement in denominational circles. Furthermore, in the wake of denominational investigations, renewal groups were being founded within the main denominations, such as the Baptist group Mainstream (1979), and some hoped that entire denominations would thus become charismatic; the Fountain Trust was wound up in 1980 in the belief that its mission to see renewal permeate the mainstream churches had been fulfilled. As part of the process of accommodation, many Charismatics dropped the idea of a post-conversion baptism with the Spirit, or else adapted it to fit with their belief in infant baptism (for example, by renaming it 'release of the Spirit' and seeing it as entering into what had been given by God at baptism).

More recently, leading charismatic centres in England have been St Aldate's, Oxford, during the ministry of Michael Green; Holy Trinity, Brompton, from whence the Alpha course originated and whose espousal of the 'Toronto Blessing' did much to make it popular for a few years in the mid-1990s; St Andrew's, Chorleywood, which had been led by men with a wider teaching ministry such as David Pytches and Mark Stibbe; and Millmead Baptist Church, Guildford, under the ministry of the ex-Methodist David Pawson. Large independent charismatic churches have also appeared, such as the black-led Kingsway International Church in Hackney, London (now moving to Rainham in Essex). Several large Pentecostal congregations have left their denominations to throw in their lot with the newer charismatic churches.

Perhaps the most influential charismatic initiative has been the Alpha course, developed in the early 1990s at Holy Trinity, Brompton, as a way of introducing enquirers to the foundational truths of Christian faith and life as seen from a charismatic evangelical perspective. It has been taken up by most shades of churchmanship except the more liberal, and by most denominations except the Quakers and the strongly Reformed. Apart from its cultural 'fit' (the format of a meal followed by discussion is one which would be familiar to many, especially in the middle classes), its mode of operation parallels the widespread business practice of franchising. Like other contemporary franchises, it has become well-known in much of the world, the course materials having been translated into many languages. However, it is perhaps too early to offer any definitive estimate of its success worldwide in reaching the unchurched (as opposed to the churches' fringe adherents).[4]

By now, Charismatics represent the dominant form of Evangelicalism in England, but are considerably less influential in Scotland, Northern Ireland, and Wales, in part due to the inheritance of Reformed theology which remains in those countries. It appears that charismatic Evangelicals are growing faster than non-charismatic Evangelicals, although this is likely to be because their style of worship is a closer reflection of contemporary culture, rather than for theological reasons. Andrew Walker suggests that the charismatic emphasis on experience appeals to the late-modern concern with the self and with finding fulfilment.[5] Yet some are questioning whether the movement in Britain has run out of steam. This may be related to the interest shown in the 'Toronto Blessing' and other similar phenomena: it seems that there is a continual hunger for something new, and a readiness to follow in the footsteps of the early Pentecostals by going on pilgrimage to find out more. In reaction, some sought a home in more traditional forms of Christianity. For example, Michael Harper became Orthodox in 1997, and the Restorationist leader David Tomlinson became an Anglican.

Restorationism[6]

By the late 1970s it seemed as if the Charismatic movement had arrived, but a new challenge was already emerging – Restorationism. Independent Pentecostal-type congregations had been appearing since the 1940s but in increasing numbers from the 1970s. The 1970s saw the appearance of a number of networks of independent churches with roots in the Charismatic movement as well as in classical Pentecostalism. The most controversial was Christian Growth Ministries, based in Fort Lauderdale, Florida, which emphasized the concepts of discipleship and shepherding and, for a while at least, pursued a strongly authoritarian approach to church leadership which influenced the development of Restorationism. Leaders in these networks such as Gerald Coates (b. 1945) and Bryn Jones (1940–2003) began to pursue a course which took them in a rather different direction from denominationally orientated Charismatics. Often influenced by Brethren thinking, they believed that God had finished with denominations and that the only thing to do was to start afresh; the key distinctive of restorationist thought was their belief that God intended to restore New Testament church life and structures, including ministries listed in Ephesians 4.11 (apostles, prophets, evangelists, and pastor-teachers), as a means of bringing about the final great outpouring of the Spirit. In particular, the ministries of apostle and prophet are seen as fundamental, and initially at least other churches tended to be seen as defective because they lacked them.

Restorationists have tended to reject the 'eschatology of defeat' which they saw as marking Western Pentecostalism. This was heavily influenced by Dispensationalism, and its prognosis for the world was gloomy. By contrast, Restorationism sought to recover something of the sense of optimism and hope which marked earlier postmillennialist thought (Jonathan Edwards has sometimes been drawn on to legitimate such thinking). The restoration of the Church according to the New Testament pattern is seen as enabling it to engage in an ingathering of souls to an extent hitherto unparalleled in church history. In preparation for the return of the Church, history was seen as a succession of preparatory rediscoveries of neglected truths: justification (Luther), believer's baptism (the Baptists), assurance of salvation (Methodism), mission (Carey), every-member ministry (the Brethren), and spiritual gifts (the Pentecostals).

Although American writers were seminal in the development of the movement's thought, it has been in England that it has proved most successful. From about 1980, a number of individuals and churches left their denominations for Restorationism; Baptists were especially hardhit. A major bone of contention was the strongly authoritarian approach of many such churches. The theological and ecclesiological radicalism of these churches has not usually been matched by a social radicalism; indeed, their greatest strength seems to lie in suburbia, and among younger middle-class professionals. In this they were not alone in British Evangelicalism.

Relations between 'house churches'[7] and the older denominations have not always been harmonious: sweeping condemnations and insensitive church-planting by the former, and allegations of sheep-stealing and refusals of fellowship by the latter (as in blocking the entry of such churches to local ecumenical bodies) have made things difficult. However, as Restorationism has matured, several of its initiatives have become part of the Christian mainstream, such as the Marches for Jesus (1989) and the Jubilee Campaign. Convergence in worship styles and a downplaying of the newer groups' distinctives (especially in the area of leadership) have also facilitated the process, as has the measure of healing which has come as memories of old hurts have subsided.

Black majority churches[8]

Significant waves of immigration occurred from the Caribbean in the late 1950s and early 1960s (in response to labour shortages) and from Africa during the 1970s. Each resulted in the appearance of a number of denominations not previously present in Britain, partly because of the experience of rejection by white churches but also because Christians from these areas wished to worship in a manner rooted in their culture. For example, 1953 saw the planting of the first British congregation of the New Testament Church of God. Many such denominations are Pentecostal in theology; others reflect that of the Wesleyan or Baptist traditions; among newer arrivals, a number belong to the category of African-instituted churches. From the 1980s, some West African denominations have begun to plant churches in Britain as part of a planned strategy which enhances their credibility at home and ensures their growth in Britain through providing for members who have moved here and evangelizing non-members; an example would be the Nigerian Pentecostal denomination, the Redeemed Christian Church of God, which arrived in 1989. The entrepreneurial vision of those involved in planting such churches fitted well the spirit of the later Thatcher years, as did the openness to prosperity teaching, and these factors may have facilitated their success.

It should be noted that English is the predominant language used in the worship of such congregations, and that they often have a vision to reach out into the wider community as opposed to merely seeking to preserve a particular ethnic form of Christianity. Indeed, some churches have successfully reached out to other ethnic groups; for example, the Church of God of Prophecy has established itself among Spanish- and Greek-speaking communities. In recent years, too, black and Asian Christians have been appointed to high-profile positions within traditional bodies, such as John Sentamu as Archbishop of York (2004), and Kate Coleman as president of the Baptist Union (2006).

Changes in worship

It is not possible to do more in this section than indicate major areas of change, but because worship provides, from one perspective, the rationale for church history in that without it there would have been no reason for the church to exist, certain key trends not previously mentioned should be highlighted. Changes during the century have affected the architecture and layout of buildings, clerical (and congregational) attire, music, the order and language of services, and the Bible translations used. Increasingly there is a convergence of style evident in many Protestant traditions, as they sing similar hymns and songs and conduct services in a similar, usually informal, way. Elements of this are even evident among Roman Catholic congregations. Factors underlying this convergence include the influence of the Charismatic movement, the increase in ecumenical contact, and the shared debt to a growing corpus of biblical and liturgical scholarship.

However, the most significant occurrence during the early part of this period was the controversy over the spread of 'ritualism' in the Church of England. This culminated in the 1927–8 debate surrounding a proposed revision of the Prayer Book which would have sanctioned such practices as prayer for the dead. Although it secured approval by the three houses of the Church Assembly (bishops, clergy, and laity) and by the House of Lords, lobbying by Evangelicals and Anglo-Catholics ensured that the Commons twice rejected it, motivated in part perhaps by a lingering sense of Protestant national identity which Free Churchmen shared with many Anglicans. These events provoked questions regarding the nature of the relationship between church and state in England, but in practice the bishops had the last word, as they allowed clergy to deviate from the Prayer Book if following the lines of its 1928 revision. The result of the debacle was to strengthen the trend towards what might be called 'liturgical anarchy' as clergy of various shades felt increasingly free to modify the services in ways which expressed their distinctive beliefs. With the introduction of modern-language liturgies from 1965, choice has received a new degree of official sanction. More recently, however, many congregations have adopted forms of service (if 'forms' can be called the right term) which are heavily influenced by evangelical exaltation of the sermon or charismatic spontaneity; in some churches, one would have to look hard for evidence that a liturgy was being followed.

(This phenomenon has not been nearly so evident in Welsh or Scottish Anglicanism.) At the other end of the liturgical spectrum Anglo-Catholic congregations have sometimes adopted the English Missal instead of an Anglican service book.

Worship was one area over which high churchmen became increasingly divided; for one thing, should they attempt to express their Catholicism by imitating the liturgical practice of twentieth-century Catholicism, or by re-enacting the worship of medieval Catholicism? The nineteenth-century divide between theological conservatives and those who favoured a measure of accommodation to the contemporary world also persisted, and indeed deepened; one of the most contentious issues in this respect has been that of women's ministry: of the two main Anglo-Catholic organizations, 'Affirming Catholicism' contains many clergy who are happy to accept the ordination of women to the priesthood, while 'Forward in Faith' encourages parishes to opt into the system of alternative episcopal oversight provided by the Church of England for those unable to accept this development. Such internal division may be one reason why high churchmanship has lost the dominance which it exerted over the Church of England during the 1920s and 1930s.

Nevertheless, one emphasis congenial to high churchmen has become part of the worship of Anglicans of almost all shades: the central position accorded to the Eucharist. In the years after 1945, the Parish and People movement did much to apply the insights of the Catholic Liturgical Movement to Anglican congregational life, with the result that a parish Eucharist replaced matins as the main Sunday morning service in most churches. Even Evangelicals adopted this, although since the 1980s they have begun to move away from it, often motivated by a concern to introduce non-eucharistic services which will be attractive to the unchurched. They have pioneered the introduction of family and 'seeker-friendly' services, while charismatic congregations have been among those willing to experiment with 'alternative services' making full use of all five senses and drawing on an eclectic mix of spiritual traditions.

Some aspects of these trends have been evident among Catholics, especially the move towards making the Eucharist far more the action of the whole congregation and not that of the priest(s) alone. More of them have shaped most Nonconformist worship, which in any case lacks any official requirement to follow a particular liturgy. As for Presbyterian worship practice in Scotland, this has converged with Anglican and Catholic practice in its move towards greater observance of the liturgical calendar and more frequent celebration of communion. Paradoxically the old 'communion seasons', whose significance we noted earlier, have more or less completely died out, with the demise of the preparatory and thanksgiving services.

Questions for thought

1 Is Callum Brown premature to speak of the 'death of Christian Britain'? What evidence would you offer for your opinion?

2 What historical factors have enabled Evangelicals to resist decline more successfully than other traditions?

3 In what ways does the course of ecumenism in Britain reflect wider ecumenical developments?

4 What earlier movements, in your view, offer parallels to Restorationism in being eschatologically motivated? Do you notice any common factors about their organization or goals?

5 What challenges are presented for historians by the task of recording and analysing changes in worship? What types of evidence are available, and what pitfalls are associated with each one?

Further reading

Callum G. Brown, 1997, *Religion and Society in Scotland since 1707*, Edinburgh: Edinburgh University Press, chs 6–8.

David Butler, 1996, *Dying to be One. English Ecumenism: History, Theology and the Future*, London: SCM Press.

Horton Davies, 1996, *Worship and Theology in England: The Ecumenical Century, 1900 to the Present*, Grand Rapids: Eerdmans.

Duncan Forrester, 'Worship since 1929', in Duncan Forrester and Douglas Murray (eds), 1995, *Studies in the History of Worship in Scotland*, 2nd edn, Edinburgh: T. & T. Clark.

Adrian Hastings, 2001, *A History of English Christianity, 1920–2000*, London: SCM Press.

Kenneth Hylson-Smith, 1998, *The Churches in England from Elizabeth I to Elizabeth II*, vol. 3: *1833–1998*, London: SCM Press, chs 4–10.

G.I.T. Machin, 1998, *Churches and Social Issues in Twentieth-Century Britain*, Oxford: Clarendon.

Edward Norman, 1986, *Roman Catholicism in England: From the Elizabethan Settlement to the Second Vatican Council*, Oxford: Oxford University Press, ch. 6.

Alan P.F. Sell and Anthony R. Cross (eds), 2003, *Protestant Nonconformity in the Twentieth Century*, Studies in Christian History and Thought, Milton Keynes: Paternoster.

David M. Thompson (ed.), 2006, *Protestant Nonconformist Texts*, vol. 4: *The Twentieth Century*, Aldershot: Ashgate.

Websites

Churches Together in Britain and Ireland, www.ctbi.org.uk.

Notes

1 Callum Brown, 2001, *The Death of Christian Britain*, London: Routledge.

2 Cf. Grace Davie, 1994, *Religion in Britain since 1945: Believing without Belonging*, Oxford: Blackwell.

3 On British Pentecostalism, see: William K. Kay, 2000, *Pentecostalism in Britain*, Carlisle: Paternoster; James Robinson, 2005, *Pentecostal Origins: Early Pentecostalism in the Context of the British Isles*, Studies in Evangelical History and Thought, Milton Keynes: Paternoster.

4 On Alpha, see Stephen Hunt, 2004, *The Alpha Enterprise: Evangelism in a Post-Christian Era*, Aldershot: Ashgate.

5 In Stephen Hunt, Malcolm Hamilton and Tony Walter (eds), 1997, *Charismatic Christianity: Sociological Perspectives*, Macmillan: Basingstoke, p. 32. This statement needs to be qualified in the light of the strongly communal emphases of groups such as the Jesus Fellowship, which grew out of the Baptist congregation at Bugbrooke near Northampton from the late 1960s.

6 'Restorationism' is used in North America to denote the movement back to New Testament Christianity which was linked with the creation of the Disciples of Christ. This, while sharing some characteristics with twentieth-century British Restorationism, is not historically linked to it. Restorationism in Britain was often known as the 'house church movement' (although most soon outgrew their members' living-rooms), and more recently as the 'new churches': the latter designation invites confusion with the Swedenborgian New Church, as well as obscuring the fact that not all newly emerging denominations or groups of churches share the emphases which distinguish Restorationism, such as the priority of apostles and prophets. For a valuable discussion of the movement as it stood in the mid-1990s, see Nigel Wright, 'The Nature and Variety of Restorationism and the "House Church" Movement', in Hunt, Hamilton and Wright, *Charismatic Christianity*, ch. 3.

7 On this movement, see Peter Hocken, 1997, *Streams of Renewal*, rev. edn, Carlisle: Paternoster; Andrew Walker, 1998, *Restoring the Kingdom: The Radical Christianity of the House Church Movement*, rev. edn, Guildford: Eagle.

8 On black Christianity in Britain, see Joe Aldred, 2005, *Respect!*, Peterborough: Epworth; Mark Sturge, 2005, *Look what the Lord has Done! An Exploration of Black Christian Faith in Britain*, Bletchley: Scripture Union.

22

Global Christianity

Christianity, while often seen as a European religion, was not so in its origins and has only been so in terms of numbers since about 1500. At some point around 1980 the balance of Christian population shifted from the West to the Majority World, and the imbalance will probably become more pronounced as Christianity declines in the West and grows elsewhere. This chapter attempts to open up some lines of enquiry relating to the global nature of Christianity. The statistics quoted are in all cases open to question; different sources use different methods of calculation; different denominations have different criteria for counting individuals as participant members; and in many cases the figures are based on estimates rather than comprehensive records. Nevertheless, they are sufficiently accurate to enable a grasp of the overall picture.[1]

The shift in the centre of Christian gravity away from the post-Christian West

It is clear from Figures 22.1–2 that most Christians are now to be found outside the West. Furthermore, one sector which has shown striking growth is that of locally instituted churches (although denominations which have their roots in Western mission have also grown rapidly, that is offset by decline in the West). These have often grown because of their close cultural 'fit' at points where Western forms of Christianity were perceived as culturally alien, for example in their dismissal of the reality of the demonic. However, it is probably best to view locally instituted churches in any part of the world on a spectrum ranging from the thoroughly 'exotic' (to Western observers) to the barely indistinguishable from older denominations which originated in the West. The following discussion focuses primarily on African examples, but it would be possible to illustrate many of the same themes by examining other areas, such as China or the Philippines.

By contrast with older churches, many African instituted churches (AICs) have additional sources of revelation (often to the founder, but also to current members); they have come to stress healing and prophecy

Figure 22.1: Christians by continent, 1900 and 2000 (figures in millions).

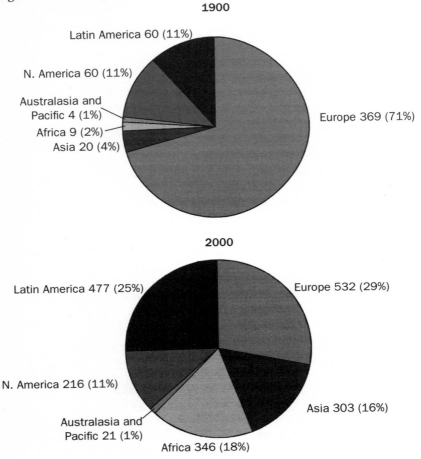

1900

Latin America 60 (11%)

N. America 60 (11%)

Australasia and Pacific 4 (1%)

Africa 9 (2%)

Asia 20 (4%)

Europe 369 (71%)

2000

Latin America 477 (25%)

Europe 532 (29%)

N. America 216 (11%)

Asia 303 (16%)

Australasia and Pacific 21 (1%)

Africa 346 (18%)

(thus connecting with concerns prevalent in society), and some allow polygamy. Ritual plays a major role in their gatherings, but scholars disagree over whether this represents an appropriation of indigenous religious traditions or a conscious counterbalance to them. Perhaps the answer is slightly different in each case; Chidester, who teaches in South Africa, writes of 'complex local negotiations with traditional religion'.[2] Usually Zionist churches were more obviously African than Ethiopian ones, and in some cases combined aspects of Christianity with aspects of African traditional religions in a manner which has been regarded as syncretistic but now is more often seen in terms of inculturation. They

Figure 22.2: Christians by communion, 1900 and 2000 (figures in millions).

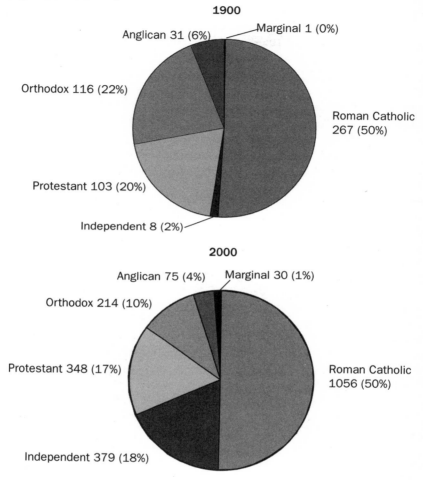

1900

Anglican 31 (6%)

Marginal 1 (0%)

Orthodox 116 (22%)

Roman Catholic 267 (50%)

Protestant 103 (20%)

Independent 8 (2%)

2000

Anglican 75 (4%)   Marginal 30 (1%)

Orthodox 214 (10%)

Protestant 348 (17%)

Roman Catholic 1056 (50%)

Independent 379 (18%)

tended to emphasize healing and prophecy, and to practise pilgrimage to sacred sites.

Not infrequently they also adopted dietary prohibitions similar to those found in the Pentateuch. Their roots may have been in the American Dowie, but they were quite clear that the promised land was located on South African soil. Such an emphasis distinguishes them from more recently founded (post-1980) charismatic congregations, which adopt Western technology with enthusiasm for spreading their message and appeal to the younger Westernized sectors of society.

By 1990 South Africa was home to as many as 5,000 Zionist denominations, to which about 30 per cent of the population adhered. Such churches were also widespread in West African countries, especially Ghana and Nigeria. By contrast, they were largely absent from East Africa, apart from Kenya. This may be partly due to the dominance of Roman Catholicism in that area. It may have had a highly centralized authority structure, but it has usually proved more sympathetic than Protestantism in accommodating local variations of Christian thought and spirituality; furthermore, it did not place the same emphasis on Bible translation and thus avoided placing into local hands a tool which could be used to critique the missionary enterprise.[3]

Easily the largest African-instituted body, with 9 million members by 2005, is the *Église de Jésus Christ sur la terre par le prophète Simon Kimbangu*, whose founding in Congo may be dated to the early 1920s. Kimbangu, a Baptist, began to see healings attending his ministry; deemed to be a potentially anti-colonial force, he was imprisoned by the Belgian colonial authorities from 1921 until his death thirty years later, but the movement has grown in spite of (or perhaps because of) persecution and large-scale deportation, securing official recognition in 1959, just prior to independence. Although its founding depended in part on Kimbangu's visionary experiences, it is markedly less charismatic than most African-instituted churches, although such phenomena are not rejected. It has adopted a stance of radical opposition to traditional religion, and has also upheld the practice of monogamy.

Some AICs have joined the WCC, such as the Church of the Lord (Aladura) in 1975, and the Kimbanguists in 1969. Their applications occasioned considerable debate, the Kimbanguist view of their founder as an intercessor with God along traditional African lines (you do not approach an eminent person except through the proper intermediary) causing some problems, but their desire to participate in the WCC as an expression of their belief in the catholicity of the Church doubtless ensured their ultimate acceptance. Related to this was the Kimbanguist refusal to celebrate the sacraments on the basis that these cannot be the preserve of any one denomination but are rites of the whole Church; while they have introduced a form of communion since their acceptance into the WCC, they still do not baptize with water, stressing instead the inner baptism of the Spirit. The growth and increasing ecumenical acceptability of many AICs has meant that in some countries what was formerly regarded as marginal Christianity has now become mainstream, while the churches which formerly represented mainstream Christianity risk becoming marginalized. In Botswana, for instance, it is estimated that by 2000 almost two-thirds of Christians belonged to one of the locally instituted churches.

One reason why such congregations are attractive is the mismatch between leadership and membership in 'historic' churches. This may be in terms of nationality, as in the late colonial era, but it may also be a matter of social class or of caste. In India, for instance, 150 out of 156 Catholic bishops in 2000 were from the higher castes, yet 75 per cent of the Christian population are Dalits (formerly known as Harijans or 'untouchables'), which compares with about 25 per cent of the population. Here, denominations which were divided in the West by theology have found that a more significant division relates to caste, so that since the nineteenth century particular denominations have been seen as catering to particular castes. Some locally instituted movements have sought to overcome this, such as the independent assemblies deriving from the ministry of Bakht Singh (1903–2000), and the Dalits themselves have developed a version of Liberation Theology, but the problem remains.

Another reason for the growth of locally instituted churches may be the roles accorded to women. Feminist theologians in the Majority World are now beginning to examine not only traditional forms of Christianity but also other faiths which have shaped their culture and to isolate those elements which are seen as having contributed to the oppression of women. Many locally instituted churches have been in advance of such developments, however, according key roles to women: among them have been founders, apostles, prophetic visionaries, local leaders, and healers. This may relate to the emphasis on the 'charismatic' as opposed to the 'institutional' side of church life, in which gifting by the Holy Spirit is what alone counts and biblical restrictions on women are seen as overridden in specific cases, set aside in the present day, or not applicable locally. Furthermore, the highly participatory nature of worship in many of these churches allows women to contribute in a variety of ways, just as men may do, including such things as dance, testimony, and prayer.

Some non-indigenous movements have also experienced remarkable growth. A prime example would be the New Apostolic Church, founded in Germany in 1863 as a schism from the Catholic Apostolic Church and still dominated by German-speaking leaders. While it is now declining in its homeland (admittedly from a position of strength), it has grown exponentially in Africa (especially former British colonies) and now has 11 million members worldwide.

Having considered the way in which locally originated forms of Christianity have grown, we need to ask what has happened to those forms which are more obviously the fruits of the missionary enterprise. It is often asserted that Christianity is a Western religion, and its heralds have been condemned as agents of American expansionism. The truth is more complex than this, and it is no more accurate to say that late-twentieth-century missionaries were agents of American colonialism than nineteenth-century ones had been of European colonialism. While North America did provide the driving force for much post-war Christian mission, it must be recognized that Majority World peoples took determinative shaping roles in the process of appropriation, and that what they produced was, more often than not, something rather different from what had been exported to them. At Tambaram in 1938 it was asserted that mission must have as its goal the creation of indigenous churches. That conference sounded the death-knell of the division of the world into (Christian) sending nations and (heathen) receiving ones, replacing it with the idea of global partnership between older and younger churches. In recent decades, therefore, the Christian communities of countries such as Brazil, India, and South Korea have rapidly assumed roles as major 'sending nations', as they have grown in maturity and as numbers of 'Western' missionaries declined (in qualification it should be noted that this trend is further advanced in Protestantism than in Roman Catholicism).

One phenomenon which is becoming more noticeable is that whereas many Western churches have tended towards relatively liberal positions on a range of ethical issues, churches from the Majority World have usually maintained more traditional stances, and done so in a more outspoken way. Western attempts to impose liberal perspectives have been construed as the latest version of Western cultural imperialism, as well as being blamed for the decline of Christianity in the West. A prime example of this type of reaction has been the debates concerning homosexuality within the Anglican Communion, in which churches such as the US Episcopalians have moved to ordain and affirm practising homosexuals, in the face of fierce condemnation from provinces such as Nigeria and Singapore. Some conservative American parishes have therefore sought alternative episcopal oversight from bishops in such provinces, and it seems possible that the issue will do more to split the Anglican Communion, and provinces within it, than previous major contentions over slavery or the ordination of women. Such divergence of opinion is evident in some other world communions but has not had the same effect, perhaps because Anglicanism has both a powerful body of supporters of a more liberal approach in some provinces and a vocal group of provinces opposed to what they see as moral compromise. Elsewhere one side or the other is usually much weaker, and thus an open conflict cannot be sustained at the highest levels of the communion's governing or consultative structures.

Most of the main Christian World Communions (CWCs) have become truly global in nature. Again, an example is the Anglican communion. As late as 1960, the majority of Anglican bishops worldwide were English, but during succeeding decades that has changed. At Lambeth in 1998, out of 736 bishops present, 316 were from North America and Europe, 224 from Africa, and 95 from Asia. There are now 38 provinces, which are effectively self-governing, the Archbishop of Canterbury retaining only a primacy of honour. The largest national Anglican churches are now those in Nigeria (17.5 million) and Uganda (9.6 million). One factor in the East African growth of the communion was the *Balokole* movement of the 1930s and 40s, which grew out of the work of the conservative Ruanda Mission of the Church Missionary Society. This represented a religious revival in the classic evangelical tradition fused with aspects of the local religious context. It responded to the indigenous focus on the spirit world and emphasized traditional ideals of community solidarity, but was strongly opposed to any kind of syncretistic accommodation with indigenous religion, and became known for a stress on the unity of black and white, missionary and lay believer. The movement spread through Uganda, Kenya, Rwanda, Burundi, and Tanzania. While often highly critical of the existing churches, it stopped short of schism, opting instead to supplement the regular diet of worship and instruction by its own group meetings and large-scale conventions. Strongly pietistic in tone, it was inclined to stereotype the expected pattern of Christian experience and to adopt a legalistic approach to ethical issues; however, in its second generation it produced some notable leaders such as Archbishop Janani Luwum who was killed in 1977.

The most truly international CWC (if it may be so described), the Roman Catholic, has nevertheless been somewhat slow to adapt to its changing centre of gravity: in 1900, 77 per cent of Catholics lived in Europe and North America; this figure had fallen by 1990 to just 30 per cent. The development of an indigenous priesthood and episcopate has been a priority in many areas for much of the twentieth century (though it has not always been achieved), and the College of Cardinals ceased to have a majority of Italians under Pius XII, but to date no pope has come from a non-European country, and John Paul II was the first non-Italian occupant of the chair of St Peter since 1523. Nevertheless, many areas have seen territorial hierarchies replace the system of government by vicars apostolic, reflecting their transition from mission field to fully-fledged church, as in West Africa (1950), Southern and British East Africa (1951), and French Africa (1955).

Of the other CWCs, the Baptists are not untypical in seeing a move from Western domination to a more extensive exercise of leadership by non-Westerners. The recent withdrawal of the Southern Baptists is likely to facilitate this process, since they were probably the largest national body in the Baptist World Alliance. The Lutherans are probably the most eurocentric: in 2001 there were an estimated 64,000,000 worldwide, of whom 37,000,000 were in Europe and 8,500,000 in North America; yet even they could boast a church of 3,300,000 in traditionally Orthodox Ethiopia, the Evangelical Church Mekane Yesu.

The churches and national identity

The twentieth century has not only been an era of unprecedented Christian expansion, but also one in which the Western empires were dismantled and many modern nation states came into being. In many nations political and ecclesiastical independence came at about the same time. This section explores some of the different patterns of relationship between church and nation.

In Korea Christianity benefited from being associated with the struggle for national self-determination. The principles outlined by Nevius operated successfully when the 'Korean Pentecost' swept vast numbers of converts into the churches, especially the Presbyterians. From 1910 to 1945 Korea was under Japanese domination and Christianity, especially in its Protestant form, came to be seen as highly compatible with Korean nationalism. As a result up to 40 per cent of South Korea is now Christian. Before partition Christianity had been stronger in the North than the South, but its current strength in North Korea is unknown.

China's long Confucianist tradition stressed the importance of co-operation and social harmony, and we have already seen how in the nineteenth and early twentieth centuries Christianity was seen as having a substantial contribution to make towards the process of social reconstruction (seen as involving Westernization), especially after the Empire became a republic in 1912. The idea of Christianity as a social force was given a new spin by Communism as churches in the Three-Self Patriotic Movement were discouraged from preaching on 'spiritual' themes and urged to inculcate support for the work of national reconstruction.

The Orthodox world has often stressed the importance of Christianity becoming rooted in national culture, though not to the extent of becoming identified with national interests to the exclusion of any wider vision. We have seen the role it played in several East European nations as they struggled for independence from Ottoman rule. Orthodox Christianity continued to portray itself as an essentially patriotic force under Communism, and since 1990 that self-understanding has been strengthened, at times to the point of offering spiritual legitimation of national aspirations, as has perhaps been the case in Russia, which is once more aspiring to imperial greatness and seeking to regain its position as a world power.

The South African churches played a key role in the dismantling of the apartheid system and in enabling the country to move forward. Desmond Tutu, who had been general secretary of the South African Council of Churches from 1978 and then Archbishop of Cape Town from 1986, was instrumental in the creation of the Truth and Reconciliation Commission: this sought to establish the truth behind the events of the apartheid era, getting those involved to face up to their responsibility for their actions, but it also tried to apply the Christian virtue of forgiveness in the national sphere. While this has been criticized as an inappropriate mode of procedure for such a body, it has proved fairly effective in practice.

The Catholic Church in Latin America had, in its alliance with conservative nationalism during the immediate post-war years, connived at the use of force to suppress religious dissent. In Colombia, for instance, 116 people were killed during the decade 1949–59 on account of their Protestant faith (Protestantism was at this stage widely associated with political liberalism). In the 1970s and 1980s there was another wave of conservative regimes throughout Latin America, most of whom used force to repress critics and dissidents. This time those who suffered included large numbers of priests and religious, as well as lay Catholics, and Protestants generally were exempted (partly because some such governments enjoyed substantial financial and logistical support from the USA, which looked kindly on Protestantism as a pacifying force). Here we see the Church acting as an opposition force, albeit one whose opposition to the state was rooted in its commitment to the well-being of the nation.

What many of these examples show is that churches have given considerable thought to their role in national life and have rarely restricted their concerns to the realm of the 'spiritual'. Problems have arisen when the Church has either chosen to identify itself too closely with state interests or else been forced into upholding them uncritically. Rulers have frequently seen the Church as a thorn in their side, as most recently in Zimbabwe in 2007, where President Mugabe has made clear his antagonism towards the Catholic hierarchy and national ecumenical leaders on account of their severe criticisms of the human rights abuses perpetrated under his rule.

The growth of regional theologies[4]

It is not possible to survey the whole range of regional theologies which have begun to be developed over the last fifty years and which have become widely disseminated thanks to the increase in global communication through agencies such as the WCC. I will simply take two examples, from Korea and Africa, to illustrate some of the issues thrown up by many of these theologies.

After the end of Japanese occupation in 1945 and the war which resulted in the country's partition (1950–3), Koreans endured severe poverty. To this was later added the experience of repressive military rule, even in the South. The theological expression of opposition to the military rule of the 1970s became known as Minjung theology, *minjung* being a Korean term for the poor and oppressed, the 'crowds' of the Gospels. Minjung

Theology represents a distinctive form of Liberation Theology, as Korean Christians have reflected on their own experience of oppression. Among other things, it sees Jesus as the one who embodies the experience of the oppressed, and it seeks to address the problem of unresolved anger which in traditional Korean religious thought finds expression in the concept of *han*, the unresolved anger and grief felt by the spirits of those who have died unjustly, to whose voice the living must listen in order to rectify the injustice. Such theology found controversial utterance in a speech by Chung Hyun Kyung at the WCC Assembly in Canberra in 1991; she was accused of syncretism, and Evangelicals and Orthodox in ecumenical circles discovered hitherto-unrecognized common ground as they articulated their responses. The influence of Minjung Theology at home, however, is not universal: Protestant growth has paralleled and perhaps been assisted by the country's economic boom, and versions of 'prosperity theology' have not infrequently proved more attractive to the upwardly mobile.

The big issue in African theology concerns the relationship of Christianity to the traditional religions of various parts of the continent: where was God in the African past? The idea that these acted as a preparation for the gospel has a long pedigree going back to second-century Greek thought, but it has been seen as patronizing by some in the same way that the idea of Christ as the fulfilment of the religious quest expressed in other world faiths has been seen as patronizing. Another issue is that of accounting both for the rapid spread of Christianity and for the proliferation of African-instituted Churches. It is important to note that 'theology' in this context, as elsewhere in the world, is not so much something which is reduced to writing but something which is dramatized in ritual, sung, prayed, and acted out in life. Even in the West, the thinking of many Christians is influenced far more by what they sing or what they do in church than by what they read. Conversely, there have always been theologians who have recognized this and who have sought to 'translate' their ideas into other modes such as song, liturgy, and even drama. The globalization of the Church thus poses with renewed force major questions about the way theology is done in traditionally Christian nations.

From missions to mission[5]

In all this, what has happened to Christian missions? In 1919, Benedict XV issued the encyclical *Maximum Illud*, which set out the agenda for resurgent Catholic mission. Opposing the intrusion of national interests into the sphere of mission, it established the goals of an indigenous clergy and hierarchy, and urged missionaries to adopt a more positive attitude to local cultures. Building on this, Pius XI set about consecrating bishops

from newly Christianized countries – 48 of them by the end of his pontificate in 1939. At Vatican II, 800 of the 2,300 bishops present were from
younger churches in Africa, Asia, and Oceania, though many of them
would have been Westerners. The Decree on the Church's Missionary
Activity (*Ad Gentes*) spoke of mission in terms of proclamation, presence, and dialogue, and from the 1960s Catholic understanding of the
nature of mission has developed fairly significantly, with a much greater
emphasis on dialogue (we have seen already the approaches to other
faiths advocated by key thinkers such as Rahner and Panikkar).

Protestant circles too saw an ongoing debate concerning the nature
of mission and its relationship to the Kingdom of God. Many Anglo-
Saxon practitioners, influenced by the same optimism which helped to
fuel the Social Gospel movement, believed that it was possible to bring
in, or at the very least prepare for, the Kingdom through working to
right social injustice. However, Continental Europeans, especially from
the German theological tradition, were wary of this and insisted that
the Kingdom was an eschatological entity which only God could bring
to visible manifestation on earth; for them, Anglo-Saxon missiology
was too activist and lacking in substantial theological basis. From the
evaluations of Anglo-Saxon thinking offered by the founding father of
Protestant missiology, Gustav Warneck (1834–1910), through to the
years following World War II, such debates continued to bedevil attempts at co-operation. They were fuelled by the rise of Neo-Orthodoxy,
which denied both that human agency could bring in the kingdom and
(in its thoroughgoing expressions) the existence of any 'point of contact'
between the gospel and human religious cultures. In practice, however,
the Anglo-Saxon approach seems to have won out. Increasing emphasis
on the 'horizontal' aspects of mission (such as education, health care,
or economic development) and developing thinking concerning the relationship between Christianity and other faiths have meant that in some
quarters the task of the missionary is no longer seen as winning non-
Christians to Christ but as bearing witness to their own faith, seeking
to build bridges with adherents of other faiths, and working with all to
build a just society. An early expression of this was the report edited by
Hocking, which resulted from a thorough enquiry into the state of North
American mission around the world. However, Evangelicals have continued to stress traditional priorities in mission: preaching, Bible translation,
and church-planting, although recent decades have seen a more holistic
approach become fairly widespread. They have also been trenchant critics of the trend in ecumenical circles during the 1960s to reconceptualize
mission in terms of enabling people to become fully human, a trend which
found expression at the 1968 Uppsala assembly of the WCC, with its slogan 'the world sets the agenda'. Responses to it included a declaration
issued at Frankfurt in 1970 which was intended to parallel that made at

Barmen and which likewise protested against what it saw as distortions of the Christian faith. But the enduring legacy of evangelical concern has been the Lausanne organization; this has sponsored research into various aspects of missiology as well as providing an alternative forum to the WCC for Evangelicals to co-operate in mission. The WCC itself saw something of a retreat from missiological radicalism in the 1970s although the idea of mission as humanization remains dominant.

Although World War I did result in a decline of recruits through agencies such as the SVM, the number of Protestant missionaries actually increased fourfold during the twentieth century to 1958; that year, two-thirds of them were from the United States, many serving with non-denominational societies (from the 1920s, liberal theology had exercised increasing influence on denominational mission boards, and most Evangelicals therefore preferred to serve with nondenominational societies).[6] However, from the 1940s missionaries began to be expelled (as in China) or to find that they could only enter a country if deemed to be carrying out work which was to the national benefit (as in India). As for the European missionary force, this has long been in decline as churches gained independence. But a striking development has been the growth in numbers of missionaries from the Majority World, some coming to the West. The largest missionary agency in the world may well be an Indian body, Gospel for Asia, which has about 14,000 workers. Perhaps that is a suitable point at which to conclude our discussion of the globalization of Christianity. In the final chapter we shall attempt to draw together some of the threads which have run though this narrative.

Questions for thought

1 How would you compare locally instituted churches of the twentieth century with the new Nonconformist bodies of the nineteenth? How far are the impulses at work in their emergence comparable?

2 How successful have Majority World churches been at finding alternative models for church–state relationships to the Christendom model?

3 What other regional theologies are you aware of? How popular has their appeal been in their countries of origin?

Further reading

Philip Jenkins, 2007, *The Next Christendom: The Coming of Global Christianity*, 2nd edn, New York: Oxford University Press (a provocative assessment of what the future might hold).
Ogbu Kalu (ed.), 2007, *Interpreting Contemporary Christianity: Global Processes*

and Local Identities, Grand Rapids, MI: Eerdmans.

Hugh McLeod (ed.), 2006, *Cambridge History of Christianity*, vol. 9: *World Christianities c.1914–c.2000*, Cambridge: Cambridge University Press, chs 5, 22–5, 27.

Stephen Neill (revised by Owen Chadwick), 1986, *A History of Christian Missions*, The Pelican History of the Church 6, Harmondsworth: Pelican, chs 12–13 (these chapters are not in the earlier edition).

Craig Ott and Harold A. Netland (eds), 2006, *Globalizing Theology: Belief and Practice in an Era of World Christianity*, Grand Rapids, MI: Baker.

Lamin Sanneh and Joel A. Carpenter (eds), 2005, *The Changing Face of Christianity: Africa, the West and the World*, New York: Oxford University Press.

Notes

1 Many of the statistics are taken from volume 1 of WCE. As well as comprehensive survey tables, it has sections dealing with each nation which include statistics, a brief history, and a bibliography.

2 David Chidester, 2001, *Christianity: A Global History*, London: Penguin, p. 467.

3 For a stimulating discussion of the earlier phase of African-instituted Christianity, see Adrian Hastings, 1994, *The Church in Africa 1450–1950*, Oxford History of the Christian Church, Oxford: Clarendon, ch. 11. One of many more recent overviews is: John S. Pobee and Gabriel Ositelu II, 1998, *African Initiatives in Christianity: The Growth, Gifts and Diversities of Indigenous African Churches – a Challenge to the Ecumenical Movement*, Geneva: WCC. Fuller coverage is offered by Allan Anderson, 2001, *African Reformation: African Initiated Christianity in the Twentieth Century*, Trenton, NJ, and Asmara: Africa World Press.

Ironically, it was in Kenya that the largest secession from Catholicism occurred, the Legion of Mary (1963). Inculturation could on occasion go too far for the Vatican, as in the case of Emmanuel Milingo, Archbishop of Lusaka, Zambia, who was removed from office in 1983 because of his controversial emphasis on healing and exorcism and his portrayal of Christ as the greatest of the spirits of the dead with us today.

4 For a readable introduction to contemporary regional theologies with useful suggestions for further reading, see: David Ford with Rachel Muers (eds), 2005, *The Modern Theologians: An Introduction to Christian Theology since 1918*, 3rd edn, Oxford: Blackwell, chs. 27–30.

5 On the development of various theologies of mission during the twentieth century, see Timothy Yates, 1994, *Christian Mission in the Twentieth Century*, Cambridge: Cambridge University Press. No up-to-date history of mission has yet appeared to replace Stephen Neill's work, but specific topics are covered by the volumes in the series Studies in the History of Christian Missions, appearing from Eerdmans.

6 Some have seen a link between this and the Cold War, missions being encouraged as an antidote to Communist advance. This was explicitly acknowledged by the Vatican in its appeal to North American Catholics.

23

Conclusion

The fact that modern church history is still continuing to unfold makes it very difficult to being this narrative to any definitive conclusion. It is valuable to explore the historical roots of contemporary religious realities but dangerous to see history teleologically, that is, in terms of 'how we got to be where we are today', as if our present state represents some kind of goal or terminus for the journey. In addition, our understanding of many of the processes currently at work is incomplete and lacks the advantage of temporal distance from the events. Even so, it is worth revisiting the key themes which we listed in the introduction, to see what has emerged in the course of the last three and a half centuries.

Changing patterns of mission: at the beginning of this period mission was something done by Christian countries to 'heathen' ones, as far as possible in association with the civil and colonial powers. By the end, it had become a global network in which most countries with any sizeable Christian population are both senders and receivers, and the links with the civil powers had been cut. In spite of claims that the day of mission is past, there is no sign of it coming to an end. As for the approach and goals of mission, these have always included the establishment of a worshipping Christian community. However, what has changed is the emphasis on enabling such communities to stand on their own feet rather than remaining dependent on the churches of the sending country. Furthermore, the concept of mission has broadened to include such fields as development work, health care, and education. For many engaged in mission, conversions to Christian faith remain a key objective; but for others, this is no longer the case. The agencies for mission in the seventeenth century were the Catholic religious orders; now, these and their Protestant counterparts, career missionaries, continue to play vital roles, but mission has become a task incumbent on the whole church.

Global expansion and a shift in the centre of gravity of the Christian population: population has increased exponentially since 1648, especially in the Majority World, although the West has seen the least increase. Changing demographics have played a role in the shift in Christianity's centre of gravity from the West to the South, but so have other processes, notably the decline in religious practice in areas which were tradition-

382

ally Christian. This can be seen as exemplifying a recurrent pattern in Christian history in which Christianity flourishes in a particular area but then declines to the point of extinction, being saved by successful trans- plantation elsewhere. In the early centuries, Christianity flourished in North Africa but then disappeared almost completely (except in Egypt), having transplanted to Europe.[1]

The relationship between religion and national identity: often religion has acted as a bearer of national identity, whether it is Romanian Orthodoxy or English Anglicanism. However, there have been religious groups who have sought to distance themselves from such a link because they believe that the Church should subsist independently of all earthly powers and loyalties. Nineteenth-century Catholicism offers another pattern of relationship in which loyalty to the papacy supersedes all other allegiances, with the Church being seen as an alternative society. Related to this is the variety of relationships between religion and local cultures: should the churches seek to inculturate their message and practice as far as possible, or to present a conscious contrast to them?

Church–state relations: it is noticeable that the main turning-points of this book were associated with war: the end of the Thirty Years' War and the Peace of Westphalia (1648), the French Revolution (1789), and the outbreak of the First World War (1914). These are times when churches are particularly aware of the challenge of relating rightly to the civil powers. At one end of the spectrum of relationships is the idea that the Church should offer uncritical support to the state, and at the other is the idea that the Church must stand apart from it and proclaim its imminent destruction. A more recent challenge to church–state relations has been the growing awareness that in many parts of the world various religions and ideologies have to coexist; should the state express a preference for one, treat them all alike, or seek to replace them with an ideology of its own which claims ultimate loyalty?

The churches' response to modernity: the realm of Christian theology has seen a continuing debate about the extent to which the Christian message should be adapted to fit new ways of thinking. Debates between progressives and traditionalists have been occurring throughout church history, and this period has provided plenty of examples: the Deist attempt to recast the essentials of religion in a non-supernatural form, nineteenth-century liberal Protestantism and Catholic Modernism; and contemporary movements such as the Non-realist theology of Don Cupitt and others. Modernity has affected every area of the Church's life: worship, ministry, spirituality, ethics, biblical interpretation, and mission, although not all have been covered in equal detail in this book. But underlying this is the basic question: how far is modernity inimical to religion *per se*, as opposed to any particular form of it? And is that so much the worse for religion, or for modernity?

The process of secularization: linked with the advance of modern ways of looking at the world has been the process of secularization. However we interpret this, and whether or not we see it as inevitable or irreversible, it remains true that religion has retreated from public life in the West, partly under the influence of new forms which lay greater stress on private commitment than communal allegiance. The historian's task in the secularization debate involves clarifying not only the facts but also the relationships between them; so, for example, how far was the individualism of Evangelicalism an accommodation to secularization and how far was it a catalyst for it?

The quest for a meaningful and relevant spirituality: quite apart from the technological aspects, it would be hard for Christians of 1648 to recognize some of the forms of Christian spirituality now widespread. In addition, such a religion has been related to local contexts in myriad different ways, from the growth of local saint cults in post-Tridentine France to the incorporation of local holy places into the theology and practice of some African-instituted churches. Yet the quest for a 'religion of the heart' has continued to be central to the history and development of Christian spirituality.

Changing patterns of believing: in the seventeenth century, it was usually made fairly clear by church leaders what Christians were expected to believe, even if the presentations differed between Orthodox, Catholic, and Protestant. Only at the fringes were there a few who questioned some of the doctrines enshrined in the ancient creeds. Now, the picture is different: not only are certain doctrines questioned in public by leading churchmen, but also the very idea that religion includes acceptance of a particular body of truths, which offer an accurate presentation of the way the external world is, is widely challenged. With reference to the Church of England, some have spoken of a shift in emphasis from belief to believing evident in official reports. Other writers have argued that there has been a 'turn inward', with religion coming to focus more on personal experience than on claims to possess objective truth.[2]

What surprises might the next act in the story hold? The sheer complexity of the changes under way at present makes it hard to tell, though many have tried. Some commentators have predicted the demise of institutional Christianity in the West within the next century, but such a view seems somewhat extreme. In any case, the West continues to see a significant degree of interest in spirituality, as is evident from the mushrooming of 'New Age' thinking. It is therefore unlikely that the West will become an exclusively secular society. But even if it does, history shows us a pattern in which Christianity dies out or declines dramatically in one area, only to flourish elsewhere. It has proved highly translatable in terms of its ability to take root in a variety of cultures; this looks set to continue, and new forms will emerge which are as unfamiliar to us as today's forms were when they first emerged. My personal assessment is that Christianity is not dead yet!

Notes

1 This is worked out in Andrew F. Walls, 2002, *The Cross-Cultural Process in Christian History: Studies in the Transmission and Appropriation of Faith*, Maryknoll, NY: Orbis; *idem*, 1996, *The Missionary Movement in Christian History: Studies in the Transmission of Faith*, Maryknoll, NY: Orbis.

2 For an example of this approach, see Linda Woodhead, 2004, *An Introduction to Christianity*, Cambridge: Cambridge University Press.

Glossary

Absolution: the formal declaration of forgiveness issued by a priest to those who confess their sins in penitence and faith.

Adventism: the expectation of Christ's imminent return to earth; more particularly, the body founded by Ellen G. White in 1861, drawing on the teachings of William Miller, and known as Seventh-Day Adventism.

Anabaptists: (literally 'rebaptizers') a renewal movement in sixteenth-century Europe which stressed the nature of Christian faith as a voluntary commitment; from this followed the separation of church and state (since the Church was a body for individuals to join of their own free will), the practice of believer's baptism (since an infant could not make such a faith-commitment infant baptism was not valid and those baptized as infants needed to be baptized as believers), and the idea of the Christian life as one of imitating Christ, even to the point of bearing the cross in martyrdom. Almost all Anabaptists were pacifists because of their belief that the use of force was precluded by the ethical teaching of Jesus. Among the best-known Anabaptist groupings are the Mennonites, named after their founder Menno Simons (1490–1561), and the Hutterites, named after their founder Jakob Hutter (d. 1536).

Anathema: a formal pronouncement of complete exclusion from the Church, which was used from the fourth century against those whose teaching was deemed heretical.

Anticlericalism: opposition to the perceived influence of the clergy.

Antinomianism: the belief that the Christian is not under obligation to obey the law of God. Most antinomians upheld a moral lifestyle, some arguing that the Holy Spirit replaced the law as the believer's rule of life, but a minority argued that the believer could not commit sin, or else was free to flout accepted moral norms.

Apologetics: the defence and commendation of the Christian faith to non-believers as intellectually trustworthy.

Apostolic succession: the belief that the ministerial authority bestowed on the apostles by Christ has been handed down through successive generations of bishops to clergy duly ordained by them.

Asceticism: the practice of denying the body certain needs (such as food or sleep) in order to master physical appetites and grow spiritually.

Autocephaly/autonomy: in Orthodox usage, an autocephalous jurisdiction has the right to self-government in all aspects of its life, including the selection of its head; an autonomous jurisdiction is under the control of its mother church in selecting a head and occasionally in other respects.

Baptism: the rite by which an individual is initiated into the community of Christians through being sprinkled or immersed in the name of the Father, the Son, and the Holy Spirit as a sign that they have been washed from sin and have begun a new life.

Baptists: a religious tradition which began among English Separatists early in the seventeenth century and which stressed personal faith, believer's baptism, and the separation of church and state. Scholars debate the extent to which this was due to Anabaptist influence.

Benediction: a Roman Catholic service of prayer which culminated in the blessing of the congregation by the priest using the monstrance, an ornamented container in which the Blessed Sacrament (the consecrated bread and wine, believed to be the body and blood of Christ) is displayed for veneration by the faithful.

Bull: a written papal mandate.

Canon law: the body of legislation concerning matters of faith, morals, ministry, and ecclesiastical procedure accepted by a particular Christian tradition (usually Orthodox, Catholic, or Anglican) as authoritative.

Catechumen: one who is receiving a formal course of instruction with a view to being baptized.

Chalcedon: in 451, the Council of Chalcedon defined the relationship between the two natures, divine and human, of Christ as being 'without confusion, without change, without division, without separation'. The Oriental Orthodox churches, while upholding Christ's divinity and humanity, did not accept the definition, partly on political grounds and partly because they preferred to speak of 'the one nature of the incarnate Word' (i.e. Christ).

Charismatic: theologically speaking, those who affirm that the gifts of the Holy Spirit mentioned in the New Testament writings are all available to the Church today and should be deployed in church life and worship.

Christendom: those parts of the world in which Christianity has historically been recognized as the foundation for national life.

Communion: (1) a service of remembrance of Christ's death which involves the consumption of bread and wine by the faithful (also known as the Eucharist, Lord's Supper, or Mass); (2) one of the Christian traditions (usually Protestant) such as the Lutherans or Methodists (also known as Confessions).

Concordat: a bilateral agreement between the Vatican and a particular state regulating such issues as church–state relations and education.

Confessionalization: the process whereby post-Reformation Protestant churches defined themselves with increasing precision over against others by such means as doctrinal statements and expositions.

Confraternity: a voluntary organization, usually locally based, providing practical assistance (e.g. sickness benefits and funerals) and spiritual support (especially through the saying of masses) for its members; these agencies were particularly popular during the later medieval period, but have continued to exist until the present.

Consistory: an ecclesiastical court.

Conversion: the turning of an individual from following their own path in life to following the will of God. Protestants often understood this as crystallized in an event in which the individual repented of their sin and placed their faith in Christ; Catholics have preferred to stress conversion as a lifelong process.

Curia: the Vatican bureaucracy charged with governing and administering the Roman Catholic Church.

Diaspora: from the Greek word translated 'dispersion' in the New Testament; used then of Jews living outside Palestine. In modern church history, it refers primarily to Orthodox living outside traditionally Orthodox areas.

Dispensationalism: a hermeneutical system which divides salvation-history into a number of periods known as 'dispensations' each marked by a distinctive conceptualization of the divine–human relationship. Popularized by the early Brethren, it was marked by a profound pessimism, asserting that each dispensation ended in human failure and the ruin of the people of God in their visible and institutional expression. Its stress on parallel tracks in God's purposes for Israel and the Church has influenced United States attitudes towards Israel and hence the former nation's foreign policy in the Middle East.

Donatism: a fourth-century North African movement which began as a protest against the involvement in the consecration of bishops of those bishops who had compromised the faith under persecution by handing over biblical and liturgical texts; it argued that sacramental acts performed by such clergy were invalid. Its doctrine did not differ materially from that of the mainstream Church but the two were out of communion and its limited geographical spread told against it.

Ecclesiology: the doctrine of the nature, purpose, and order of the Church.

Ecumenical Councils: seven councils held during the early centuries which are seen as laying down the main lines of Christian belief concerning the Trinity and the person of Christ, and called 'ecumenical' because their decisions came to be universally received as binding on all the faithful. They were: Nicaea (325), Constantinople (381), Ephesus (431), Chalcedon (451), Constantinople II (553), Constantinople III (680–1), and Nicaea II (787).

Encyclical: a circular letter sent out by the pope to the whole Catholic Church; also used of the letters issued by Anglican bishops gathered in conference at Lambeth.

Erastianism: from the Swiss theologian Thomas Erastus (1524–83); denotes the belief that the state has authority over the Church in ecclesiastical as well as civil matters.

Eschatology: the doctrine of the 'last things'. Traditionally, the major aspects of this were death, judgement, and the afterlife, but it also includes the doctrine of the Second Coming of Christ and associated events.

Excommunication: the exclusion of a Christian from communion and from exercising ministerial functions, though not from membership.

Hermeneutics: the study and process of interpretation; primarily used in theology with reference to the Bible, it has also been applied in recent ecumenical thought to liturgies and agreed statements.

Hesychasm: from the Greek *hesychia*, 'silence'. It denotes a type of spirituality influential in Chalcedonian Orthodox churches, authoritatively formulated during the fourteenth century, which stresses that we can know God's energies (i.e. his operations in relation to the created order), but not his essence.

Heterodox: the opposite of orthodox; those who are seen as believing something other than the truth.

Jurisdiction: in Orthodox usage, a particular (national) hierarchy possessing a measure of self-determination as autonomous or autocephalous; may be used by extension of the territory in which that hierarchy exercises authority.

Justification: the declaration by God that an individual is accepted as righteous. Luther, and much Protestant thought after him, taught that this occurred 'by faith alone': the believer is justified on account of their faith in Christ as the one who died in their place, and not on account of any good works they have done or will do. Such teaching was condemned by the Roman Catholic Council of Trent (1545–63), although it tended to understand 'faith' as equivalent to 'intellectual assent' rather than 'trust'.

Lollards: an English movement brought into being by the teaching of John Wyclif (c.1330–84); in its developed form it was a clandestine Bible-reading movement which denied the efficacy of physical sacraments, condemned what it saw as the superstition and image-worship of contemporary Catholicism, and stressed the invisibility of the true Church.

Nestorian: from Nestorius (d. 451), Patriarch of Constantinople, who allegedly taught that there were not merely two natures but two persons in Christ (whether he taught this is highly debatable).

Panentheism: the belief that the material universe exists in God, but that God is greater than it and thus not simply to be identified with it, as is the case in Pantheism.

Pentateuch: the books from Genesis to Deuteronomy in the Hebrew Bible.

Presbytery: the next tier of Presbyterian government above the local congregation. Churches in a particular area appointed representatives (including lay people) to the presbytery, which was responsible for such matters as ordination and ministerial discipline. (In Roman Catholicism, the presbytery is the house where the parish priests live, but this usage does not appear in this book.)

Puritanism: a movement within the Elizabethan Church of England which sought a fuller measure of ecclesiastical reform on the basis of a Calvinist understanding of theology and ecclesiology. It became known for its deep spirituality and its concern to apply Christian principles to all areas of life. After the restoration of the monarchy in 1660 Puritans were forced out of the Church of England into Dissent.

Reformed: those churches which are rooted in the theology of the Swiss reformers Jean Calvin (1509–64) and Huldrych Zwingli (1484–1531). They have usually been marked by a more negative attitude to tradition than that shown by Anglicans and Lutherans, and by a thoroughgoing application of the doctrine of the authority of the Bible to all areas of church life.

Regeneration: the implantation of spiritual life in an individual by the agency of the Holy Spirit. In many Christian traditions this was associated in some way with baptism.

Reserved sacrament: that portion of the consecrated bread and wine reserved for use with the sick and dying; in Catholic spirituality it has often been the focus of specific devotional observances.

Rigorism: in ethics, the preference for the strictest application of moral principles; it characterized the early Jansenists.

Rosary: a late-medieval Western form of prayer involving multiple repetitions of the Lord's Prayer, the Hail Mary, and the Gloria, each set being counted off on a special string of beads.

Sacrament: traditionally defined in the West as 'an outward and visible sign of an inward and spiritual grace', sacraments are rites believed to have been instituted by Christ. The Quakers do not observe any sacraments; Protestants generally observe two – baptism and communion – and some prefer to call them 'ordinances' to stress that they are observed in obedience to Christ's command; Roman Catholics observe seven: baptism, confirmation, the mass (communion), confession (also known as penance), marriage, ordination, and extreme unction (anointing of the dying); Orthodox have sometimes spoken in terms of seven sacraments but usually prefer not to limit the number, although they observe them all. Debate concerning the sacraments continues: Are they merely signs of an inward change, or do they make what they promise a reality in the life of the recipient? What is the relationship between the sacraments and the Word of God? Who has the right to celebrate them? Who may be admitted to them?

Sanctification: the process by which a Christian becomes increasingly holy in order to be fit to enter heaven.

Separatists: initially used of a sixteenth-century movement within Puritanism which withdrew from the Church of England on the basis that adequate reform was impossible and the only course was to start afresh. Separatists formed churches to which individuals were admitted on giving a testimony of personal faith in Christ. In the seventeenth century they became known as Independents and later as Congregationalists, from their belief that each local church is independent of any higher authority except Christ himself and that the whole membership has a voice in church affairs. More recently the term has been used of those who advocate separation from existing churches because of perceived doctrinal or ethical laxity.

Stations of the Cross: a series of 14 visual representations of incidents during Christ's journey from the house of Pontius Pilate to the cross and the tomb. They are usually found around the walls of Catholic churches, or else outside them. A popular devotion is to walk round them, pausing to pray and meditate at each one.

Syncretism: the attempt to combine ideas or practices which do not belong together; nowadays usually refers to attempts to incorporate aspects of the thought or practice of non-Christian faiths into Christian theology or worship.

Third orders: associations of Catholic (and now some Anglican) laity (known as 'tertiaries') following the religious life but in the world, in affiliation with a particular religious order, most notably the Franciscans. Traditionally, the 'first order' of a given tradition was that of male religious, and the second that of females.

Tithes: from 'tenth', the proportion laid down in the Pentateuch as due to God for the maintenance of the Jewish priesthood. In Britain, they were payable to the Church, and included produce as well as profits. Some churches still encourage members to give such a proportion of their income.

Typology: a system of biblical interpretation in which events and individuals in the Old Testament were seen as corresponding to and foreshadowing the coming of Christ and events in the New Testament era.

Uniat (often spelt Uniate; nowadays the preferred term is 'Eastern-rite Catholic'): a jurisdiction which follows the Byzantine liturgy used by Eastern Orthodox and retains Orthodox practices such as the veneration of icons, the reception of the wine as well as the bread at communion ('communion in both kinds') and the married priesthood, but acknowledges the pope as the head of the Church and submits to his leadership. Almost all Uniat jurisdictions began as schisms from Orthodoxy.

Unitarianism: denial of the doctrine of the Trinity.

Suggested Further Reading

In many cases, the works cited here contain their own bibliographies which will lead the reader to many further sources of material. I have not attempted to duplicate their contents here. For additional works on particular themes, see the relevant chapter bibliographies.

Reference works

David B. Barrett, George T. Kurian and Todd M. Johnson (eds), 2001, *World Christian Encyclopedia: A Comparative Survey of Churches and Religions in the Modern World*, 2nd edn, 2 vols, New York: Oxford University Press (important statistical resource).

F.L. Cross and E.A. Livingstone (eds), 2005, *Oxford Dictionary of the Christian Church*, 3rd edn revised, Oxford: Oxford University Press (indispensable).

Franklin H. Littell, 2001, *Historical Atlas of Christianity*, 2nd edn, London: Continuum.

General websites

Paul Halsall, 'Internet Modern History Sourcebook', www.fordham.edu/halsall/mod/modsbook.html (comprehensive coverage of Roman Catholicism and of cultural history, but selection of other material is tendentious).

Alister McGrath, 'Theology and Religion Resources', www.blackwellpublishing.com/religion/page2.asp#history.

'Wabash Center Internet Guide', www.wabashcenter.wabash.edu/Internet/front.htm. (In my opinion this is the most useful; worth exploring for any theology-related topic, it includes useful pages listing links for many modern theologians and denominations. If I have given no website references for any individual or movement, see what this site offers.)

Good collections of relevant primary source material include:

'Christian Classics Ethereal Library', www.ccel.org (covers the whole of church history; includes many writings by Jonathan Edwards and John Wesley, though inevitably in older editions because of copyright restrictions).

'St Pachomius Library', www.voskrese.info/spl/index.html (wide range of Orthodox documents).

Major collections of Roman Catholic documents are located at: www.papalencyclicals.net and www.vatican.va/offices/index.htm.

Serious attempts at global coverage

Stewart J. Brown and Timothy Tackett (eds), 2007, *Cambridge History of Christianity*, vol. 7: *Enlightenment, Reawakening and Revolution 1660–1815*, Cambridge: Cambridge University Press.

Sheridan Gilley and Brian Stanley (eds), 2006, *Cambridge History of Christianity*, vol. 8: *World Christianities c.1815–c.1914*, Cambridge: Cambridge University Press.

Hugh McLeod (ed.), 2006, *Cambridge History of Christianity*, vol. 9: *World Christianities c.1914–c.2000*, Cambridge: Cambridge University Press.

Adrian Hastings (ed.), 1999, *A World History of Christianity*, London: Cassell.

Jonathan Hill (ed.), 2007, *Lion Handbook: The History of Christianity*, Oxford: Lion.

The history of Christianity in each continent

Africa

Adrian Hastings, 1994, *The Church in Africa 1450–1950*, Oxford History of the Christian Church, Oxford: Clarendon.

Adrian Hastings, 1979, *A History of African Christianity 1950–1975*, Cambridge: Cambridge University Press.

Elizabeth Isichei, 1995, *A History of Christianity in Africa*, London: SPCK.

Bengt Sundkler and Christopher Steed, 2000, *A History of the Church in Africa*, Cambridge: Cambridge University Press.

Asia

R. Goh, 2005, *Christianity in South East Asia*, Singapore: Institute of Southeast Asian Studies.

Samuel Hugh Moffett, 2005, *A History of Christianity in Asia*, vol. 2: *1500–1900*, Maryknoll, NY: Orbis.

Scott W. Sunquist *et al.* (eds), 2001, *A Dictionary of Asian Christianity*, Grand Rapids, MI: Eerdmans.

The significance of the Christian communities in several Asian countries justifies inclusion of some useful titles relating to them:

Daniel Bays (ed.), 1996, *Christianity in China from the Eighteenth Century to the Present*, Stanford, CA: Stanford University Press.

Robert E. Buswell and Timothy S. Lee (eds), 2006, *Christianity in Korea*, Honolulu: University of Hawai'i Press.

Cyril B. Firth, 2005, *Introduction to Indian Church History*, rev. edn, Delhi: ISPCK.

Alan Hunter and Kim-Kwong Chan, 1993, *Protestantism in Contemporary China*, Cambridge: Cambridge University Press.

Bob Whyte, 1988, *Unfinished Encounter: China and Christianity*, London: Fount.

C.-S. Yu (ed.), 2002, *Korea and Christianity*, Berkeley, CA: Asian Humanities Press.

Australasia

Ian Breward, 2001, *A History of the Churches in Australasia*, Oxford History of the Christian Church, Oxford: Clarendon.

Europe

Curiously, an up-to-date general history of Christianity in Europe does not exist in English, although certain volumes of the Oxford History of the Christian Church are devoted to particular areas:

Nicholas Hope, 1995, *German and Scandinavian Protestantism 1700–1918*, Oxford: Oxford University Press.

John McManners, 1998, *Church and Society in Eighteenth-Century France*, 2 vols, Oxford: Oxford University Press.

North America

Sydney E. Ahlstrom, 1972, *A Religious History of the American People*, New Haven, CT: Yale University Press.

Edwin S. Gaustad (ed.), 1982, 1983, *A Documentary History of Religion in America*, 2 vols, Grand Rapids, MI: Eerdmans.

Robert T. Handy, 1976, *A History of the Churches in the United States and Canada*, Oxford History of the Christian Church, Oxford: Clarendon.

Mark A. Noll, 1992, *A History of Christianity in the United States and Canada*, London: SPCK.

Mark A. Noll, 2002, *The Old Religion in a New World: The History of North American Christianity*, Grand Rapids, MI: Eerdmans.

Daniel G. Reid *et al.* (eds), 1990, *Dictionary of Christianity in America*, Downers Grove, IL: Inter-Varsity.

South America

Enrique Dussel, 1981, *A History of the Church in Latin America: Colonialism to Liberation (1492–1979)*, translated and revised by Alan Neely, Grand Rapids, MI: Eerdmans.

Enrique Dussel (ed.), 1992, *The Church in Latin America 1492–1992*, Tunbridge Wells: Burns & Oates.

H.M. Goodpasture (ed.), 1989, *Cross and Sword: An Eyewitness History of Christianity in Latin America*, Maryknoll, NY: Orbis.

The global history of particular Christian traditions

Anabaptist

H.S. Bender (ed.), 1955–9, *Mennonite Encyclopedia*, 3 vols, Scottdale, PA: Herald Press (a fourth volume was added in 1990).

Anglican

Kevin Ward, 2006, *A Global History of Anglicanism*, Cambridge: Cambridge University Press.

Baptist

H. Leon McBeth, 1987, *The Baptist Heritage: Four Centuries of Baptist Witness*, Nashville, TN: Broadman.

Church of the East

Wilhelm Baum and Dietmar W. Winkler, 2003, *The Church of the East: A Concise History*, London: RoutledgeCurzon.

Lutheran

Eric W. Gritsch, 2002, *A History of Lutheranism*, Minneapolis, MN: Fortress.

Methodist

Kenneth Cracknell and Susan J. White, 2005, *An Introduction to World Methodism*, Cambridge: Cambridge University Press.

Orthodox

Michael Angold (ed.), 2006, *Cambridge History of Christianity*, vol. 5: *Eastern Christianity*, Cambridge: Cambridge University Press.
Ken Parry *et al.* (eds), 1999, *The Blackwell Dictionary of Eastern Christianity*, Oxford: Blackwell.

Pentecostal

Allan Anderson, 2004, *An Introduction to Pentecostalism*, Cambridge: Cambridge University Press.
S.M. Burgess and E.M. van der Maas (eds), 2002, *Dictionary of Pentecostal and Charismatic Movements*, 2nd edn, Grand Rapids, MI: Zondervan.

Walter Hollenweger, 1972, *The Pentecostals*, London: SCM Press.

Walter J. Hollenweger and Allan H. Anderson (eds), 1999, *Pentecostals after a Century: Global Perspectives on a Movement in Transition*, Sheffield: Sheffield Academic Press.

Reformed

Donald K. McKim (ed.), 1992, *Encyclopedia of the Reformed Faith*, Louisville, KY: Westminster/John Knox.

Roman Catholic

J. Derek Holmes and Bernard Bickers, 2002, *A Short History of the Catholic Church*, with a postscript by Peter Hebblethwaite and final chapter by Peter Doyle, London: Burns & Oates.

Richard P. McBrien (ed.), 1995, *The HarperCollins Encyclopedia of Catholicism*, New York: HarperCollins.

Index of Names and Subjects

Africa 41, 216, 236, 241, 242, 243, 249, 251–2, 256n, 309, 313, 331, 335n, 364, 373; East Africa 233, 372, 375, Central Africa 4; North Africa 4, 241, 383, 388; West Africa 41, 199, 234, 247, 252, 360, 364, 372, 375

African-instituted churches (AICs) 251, 364, 369–72, 378

African religious traditions 78, 247, 312, 370, 378, 384

Alaska 53, 111, 203

Albania 45, 271, 276, 278

Alexander I, Tsar 111–12

All-Union Council of Evangelical Christians-Baptists (AUCECB) 275, 276, 280

Alpha course 361, 362

American Board of Commissioners for Foreign Missions (ABCFM) 115–16, 207, 237, 244

Americanism 202–3

Anabaptists 44, 206, 386

Ancestors, veneration of 39, 40, 126

Anderson, Rufus 244, 248, 278

Anglicanism 35, 59, 61, 64, 67, 69, 88, 155, 159–73, 182, 183, 189, 226, 238, 266, 314, 330, 331, 352, 354–5, 361, 374, 387, in Africa 234, 242, 251, 255n, 374–5, ethics and social thought 222–6, 227, 374, high

Anglicanism 62–3, 87, 361, Tractarianism; mission 234, 237–8, 244, 251, theology 91, 95, 97–9, 165, 298–9, 390, worship 67, 165, 177, 261, 340, 365–6 see also Church of England, Anglo-Catholicism, high churchmanship, Oxford Movement, Ritualism

Anglo-Catholicism 161, 163, 253, 261, 365, 366, see under Anglicanism

Angola 41, 236, 293

Anti-Catholicism 61, 125, 157, 193, 225

Antichrist 50, 52, 171

Anticlericalism 21–3, 34, 59, 80, 121, 122, 124–7, 128, 288n, 386

Antinomianism 74, 92, 386

Antioch 45, 47, 285

Antisemitism 143, 263–7, 342

Apartheid 301–2, 308, 376

Apologetics 23, 139, 167, 204, 206, 238, 240, 386

Apostolic succession 161, 162, 163, 386

Apparitions, Marian 133–5, 267, 347

Architecture 29, 67, 164, 365

Arianism 68–9, 189

Armenia 45, 55, 113, 115–16, 117, 285

Arminianism 13, 25n, 90, 92, 99, 166, 217n

Arndt, Johann 14, 15, 48
Arnold, Gottfried 15
Asbury, Francis 95, 201
Asceticism 13, 51, 62, 387
Asia, 242, 243, 249, 313, 331,
    East and South-East Asia 38,
    42, 126, 266, 278, 335n
Assemblies of God 307–8, 311,
    355
Atheism 142–3, 273–4, 342
Austria 10, 31–2, 127, 131–2,
    337, Austro-Hungarian
    Empire 114, 117
Australia 235, 330
Azariah, V. S. 253

Balokole movement 375
Baltic 18, 44, 275, 279, 331
Baptist Missionary Society 156,
    247
Baptist World Alliance 321, 375
Baptism 14, 47, 52, 100–1, 102,
    163–4, 186, 221, 252, 256n,
    264, 276, 284, 293, 294,
    306–7, 330, 372, 386, 387,
    390, 391
Baptism, Eucharist and
    Ministry 323, 329, 330
Baptist Union of Great Britain and
    Ireland 356, 365
Baptists 13, 66, 68, 69, 71, 76,
    79, 102–3, 111, 151, 173,
    181–2, 193, 195n, 199, 201,
    205, 208, 223, 247, 274,
    275–6, 279, 280, 281, 284,
    293, 303, 314, 321, 355, 356,
    361, 363, 364, 387, General
    Baptists 69, 70, 71, 82n, 83n,
    99, New Connexion 99, 156,
    Particular Baptists 67, 68,
    69, 70–1, 74, 82n, 99, 173,
    Seventh-Day Baptists 69, 82n,
    Southern Baptists 223, 375,
    Spiritual Baptists 247

Barmen Declaration 264,
    379–80
Barth, Karl 141, 262–3, 264
Base communities 311, 344, 345
Baur, F. C. 146
Bebbington, David 85–6
Belgium 122, 132, 137n, 338,
    347
Benedict XIV 28, 36
Benedict XV 260, 261, 267, 336,
    378
Benedict XVI 337, 346
Benediction 134, 387
Bengel, J. A. 18–19
Berridge, John 98
Bible 18, 132, 133, 141, 143,
    240, 295, authority of 69,
    85, 140, 143, 204, 211, 213,
    215, 390, interpretation of 22,
    63, 168, 205, 210, 298, read-
    ing of 36, 91, 101, 111, 210,
    231–2n, 302, 308, 343–4, 390,
    study of 14, 213, 319–20, 322,
    333, translation of 18, 53, 78,
    88, 111, 112, 116, 239, 240,
    243, 302, 333, 365, 372, 379,
    see also Hermeneutics
Bible Christians 176, 184, 187–8,
    318, 356
Bible societies 111, 112, 130,
    207, 318–19
Biblical criticism 22, 23, 143–8,
    165, 166, 167–8, 204, 205, 263
Biblical Theology movement 298
Bishops, role of 34, 38, 95, 161,
    277, 339, 356, 386
Black churches 78, 198–9,
    208, 216, 301, 307, 308, in
    Britain 358, 360, 362, 364–5,
    Black Theology 301–2, 343,
    345
Boehme, Jakob 15
Bohemian Brethren 10, 16, see
    also Moravians

Bonhoeffer, Dietrich 265, 299, 325
Book of Common Prayer 163, 170, 176
Booth, William 174, 228
Bossuet, J.-B. 29, 31
Brazil 126, 312, 344, 347, 360, 374
Brethren 150–1, 181, 189, 190, 193, 195n, 205, 211, 226, 260, 293, 363, 388
British Council of Churches (BCC) 333, 350, 357–8, 359
British and Foreign Bible Society 151, 222, 240, 319
Broad churchmanship 167–9, 225–6
Brown, Callum 292, 352
Bulgaria 55, 115, 271, 279, 280, 282
Bultmann, Rudolf 263, 297
Bunting, Jabez 170, 176
Bushnell, Horace 209
Butler, Joseph 23, 68
Buxton, Thomas Fowell 222–3, 246

Calvinism 7, 8, 9, 10, 12, 13, 46, 73, 76, 87, 92–3, 97, 99, 150, 166, 185, 203–4, 208, 237, 266, high Calvinism 67, 70, 74, 99, see also Reformed tradition
Calixtus, Georg 8
Calvinistic Methodism 89, 92, 172, 182
Camisards 9–10
Camp meetings 176, 207–8
Campbell, John McLeod 192
Campbell, R. J. 229
Campbell, Ted 13, 86
Campbellites 211, see also Disciples of Christ
Canada 41, 51, 78, 80, 198,

236, 295, 330, see also North America
Canonical territory 48, 284–5
Canonization 27, 29
Capitalism 84, 139, 152, 197, 219, 224, 338
Carey, William 78, 236–7, 243, 253
'Cargo cults' 235, 308
Caribbean 335n, 364, see also West Indies
Caste 38, 373
Catechists 38–9, 235, 242, 250, 347
Catherine the Great 10, 44, 46, 53
Catholic Action 338
Catholic Apostolic Church 141, 151, 190, 231, 310, 311, 315, 373
Catholic Modernism 132–3, 147, 383
Consejo Episcopal Latino-Americano (CELAM) 344, 345
Celibacy 39, 50, 288, 343, 346–7, 355
Cell churches 311, 316
Census of Religious Worship (1851) 172, 175, 181–3, 191
Chaldean Christians 45, 113, 286
Chalmers, Thomas 191, 224
Charismatic movement 293, 304, 311, 312, 314–16, 333, 345–6, 354, 357, 360–2, 365–6, 371, 387
Charity 10, 34–5, 37, 218, 219, see also Philanthropy
Charity schools 65–6, 222
Charles II 66, 72, 77, 104n
China 4, 38, 39–40, 53, 127, 233, 238–9, 246–8, 271, 277–8
China Inland Mission (CIM) 238–9, 247, 255n, 278, 307, 376

Chinese Rites controversy 28, 40–1
Cho, David Yonggi 308, 312
Christian World Communions (CWCs) 322, 374, 375
Christendom 4, 12, 87, 101, 245, 290–1, 319, 338, 344, 349, 387
Christian Democrats 293, 294, 338
Christian Science 213
Christian Socialism 225–6, 229
Christology 70, 82–3n, 146, 148, 389, see also Jesus
Church of the East 44, 45, 53, 115, 116, 272, 286, see also Nestorians
Church of England 61–4, 68, 77, 80, 95, 98, 159–69, 183, 186, 188, 214, 226, 296, 298–9, 352, 353, 354–5, 365, 366, 384, 390, 391, see also Anglicanism
Church of Ireland 95, 162, 188–9, 193, 355
Church of Scotland 59, 73–4, 179n, 190–2, 193, 246, 293, 349, 352, 355, 357, General Assembly of 74, 190, 191, 246
Church of South India 330
Church of Sweden 323
Church in Wales 173
Church discipline 64, 68, 71, 101, 133, 175
Church, doctrine of the, see also Ecclesiology 68, 100, 170, 301, 324
Church government 64, 77, 176, 307
Church Growth movement 315
Church Missionary Society (CMS) 116, 235, 237, 239, 242, 251, 255n, 375
Church and state 4, 10–11, 12, 30–4, 52, 74, 80, 114,

123, 124, 125, 126–7, 128, 130, 132, 148–50, 155, 159, 165,191, 197–8, 202, 207, 219, 270, 273–6, 277, 291, 296, 336, 339, 344, 365, 383, 386, 387
Churches of Christ 190, 193, 321, 356
Churches Together in Britain and Ireland 334, 357, 358
City missions 184, 230
Civil religion 79, 295
Civil War, American 199, 205–6, 223
'Clapham Sect' 222–3, 224, 237
Clergy 19, 20, 22, 27, 34–5, 49, 52, 77, 93, 95. 134, 160, 182–3, 339, 346, 347, 354, 355, see also Priesthood
Coke, Thomas 95, 255n
Cold War 282–3, 293, 381n
Colenso, J. W. 168
Coleridge, S. T. 167–8, 209, 225
Colombia 126, 311, 342–3, 345, 377
Colonization 12, 19, 21, 37, 38, 41, 111, 117, 139, 246–50, 252, 255n, 301
Comity 238–9, 243
'Common Sense' philosophy 80, 204
Communion 47, 49, 66, 76, 91, 95, 101, 163, 175, 227, 341, 366, 372, 387, 391, 392, see also Eucharist, Lord's Supper, Mass
Communion seasons 76, 89, 90, 191, 207, 366–7
Communism 54, 127, 220–1, 265, 267, 268, 270, 273–83, 284, 325, 326–7, 337, 339, 344, 376, 381n
Conference on Politics, Economics and Citizenship (COPEC) 351

Confessing Church 264, 265, 267
Confessionalization 8–9, 11, 388
Confirmation 61, 276, 391
Confraternities 36, 134, 388
Confucianism 39, 40, 126, 278, 376
Congo 41, 372
Congregationalism 77, 100–1, 173, 198, 201, 203, 330, 355, 356, 391, see also Independents
Conscientious objection 260, 265–6
Constantinople 45, 47, 48, 54–5, 114–16, 270, 271, 274, 389, see also Ecumenical Patriarchate
Coptic Orthodox Church 45, 117–18, 272, 286–7
Council of European Churches 327
Council of Churches of Evangelical Christians-Baptists 275
Council of Trent 27, 29, 31, 35, 38, 41, 61, 210, 389
Countess of Huntingdon's Connexion 92–3, 94
Covenanting tradition 74, 89–90
Creation-Centred Spirituality 302
Creationism 303
Creeds 64, 70, 76, 384
Croatia 267, 341
Crowther, Samuel Ajayi 234, 251
Cupitt, Don 299, 383
Curia 236, 340, 388
Cyprus 45, 286
Czechoslovakia 271, 276, 279

Dalits 345, 373
Darwin, Charles 133, 138–9, 168, Darwinism 251
Deaconesses 151, 188, 220
'Death of God' theology 299
Deism 19–23, 79, 198, 201, 383
Denmark 151, 221

Denominations 17, 76, 79, 155, 161, 173–4, 197–8, 243, 296, 303, 321, 330, 333, 357, 358, 363
Devotion 17, 27, 29, 35–7, 73, 110, 134–5, 158, 167, 340, 346, 347, 390, see also Piety, Spirituality
Dialogue 286, 321, 330–1, 341, inter-faith 241, 267–8, 327, 332, 342, 379
Diaspora (Orthodox) 274, 281, 286, 388
Disciples of Christ 201, 210–11, 321, 330, 368n
Dispensationalism 204–6, 268, 303, 363, 388
Dissenters 35, 62, 64, 66–72, 76, 99, 100, 102, 155, 159, 169, 181–4, 186, 228, 246, 390, in Scotland 75, 190, 193, in Switzerland 151, dissenting academies 68, see also Free Churches, Nonconformists
Doddridge, Philip 99
Dominicans 40, 210
Doukhobors 51
Dowie, John Alexander 310–11, 371
Dutch Reformed churches 220, 301, 326, 347

Eastern-Rite Catholics 45–7, 55, 117, 270, 271–2, 281, 341, 392, see also Greek Catholics
Ecclesiology 16, 67, 94, 95, 98, 163, 175, 311, 321, 325, 328–9, 339, 363–4, 389, see also Church, doctrine of the
Ecology 301, 302
Ecumenical Councils 44, 54, 130, 284, 389
Ecumenical Patriarchate 45, 54, 55, 112–13, 114–15, 117,

118, 270, 272, 274, 279, 283, 284, 285, 326, 341, *see also* Constantinople

Ecumenism 16, 17, 55, 84, 113, 118, 197, 198, 211, 253, 265, 267, 274, 275, 279, 280, 281–2, 284, 285, 286, 296, 300, 301, 308, 311, 315, 318–35, 340, 341–2, 352, 353, 354, 356–9, 364, 365, 372, 378, 379, 389

Edict of Nantes 9, 30

Edinburgh conference (1910) 253, 322, 331

Education 10, 35, 47, 68, 112, 113, 118, 124, 125, 150, 155, 157, 161, 183–4, 191, 199, 209, 214, 216, 219, 224, 228, 276, 277, 286, 290, 292, 311, 338, 349, 351, 354, 358, controversy over in Britain 171, 226, in missionary work 18, 113, 116, 241, 246, 249, 250, 379, 382, theological 47, 54, 112

Edwards, Jonathan 78, 89, 101–2, 184, 203, 209, 223, 237, 255n, 393

Egypt 4, 115, 117–18, 123, 233, 287, 383

Elim Pentecostal Church 307, 355, 360

Eliot, John 77–8

England 3, 9–10, 12, 20, 23, 35, 59, 61–73, 74, 78, 84, 88, 89, 90–100, 132, 140, 155–80, 181–8, 227, 255n, 270, 293, 295, 296, 298, 304, 314, 354, 355, 356, 357, 359, 361–2, 363, 365

Enlightenment 19–24, 51, 53, 67, 73, 80, 85, 121, 122, 140, 210, 223, 233–4, 291

Episcopalianism, in Scotland 73, 75, Scottish Episcopal Church;

in the United States 200–1, 252, 374; *see also* Anglicanism, Church of England

Equiano, Olaudah 223

Erastianism 64, 164, 389

Erskine, Ralph and Ebenezer 74, 89

Essays and Reviews 168

Eschatology 12, 18, 115, 122, 147, 166, 169, 179n, 197, 205–6, 221, 224, 235, 238, 239, 241, 268, 283, 301, 305n, 312, 327, 363, 379, 389, *see also* Prophecy, biblical

Ethics 16, 22, 32, 34, 40, 79, 141, 146–7, 221, 228, 230, 256n, 302, 325, 338–9, 341, 343, 346, 352, 374, 375, 383, 386, 390, *see also* Morality

Ethiopia 4, 251–2, 255–6n, 272, 280, 375

'Ethiopian' churches 252, 370

Eucharist 54, 164, 167, 169, 347, 366, 388, *see also* Communion

Europe 4, 8, 11, 30, 36, 48, 73, 86, 98, 124, 140–1, 143, 148, 150, 161, 206–7, 213, 219, 267, 282, 293, 294, 298, 319, 325, 335n, 337, 347, 375, 379, 383, Central Europe 4, 8, 76, 151, Eastern Europe 4, 7, 8, 151, 267, 270, 276, 284, 288n, 376, Northern Europe 4, 7, 21, 126, 174, Southern Europe 4, 126, South-East Europe 54–5, 113, Western Europe 4, 35, 281, 291–2, 297, 310, 338, European Union 282

Evangelical Alliance (EA) 172, 198, 223, 294, 359, 360

Evangelical Christians 111, 275, 288n

Evangelicalism 59, 64, 70, 80, 84–106, 111, 116, 151, 165,

169, 170–3, 182, 185, 188, 189, 190, 192, 215, 234, 245, 267, 278, 279, 280, 282, 288, 293, 303–4, 308, 320, 322, 323, 327–8, 351, 353, 355, 358, 361, 362, 364, 366, 375, 378, 384, in the Church of England 97–9, 163–4, 165–7, 168, 170, 172, 214, 222–5, 227, 237, 355, 365, in the Church of Scotland 74, 190–1, in North America 100–3, 192, 198, 206–7, 214, 223–4, 285, 295, mission 233–4, 236–7, 238, 239–40, 244, 246, 247, 284, 320, 322, 379, 380, social thought 214, 222–5, 229, 230, 294, 351, theology 37, 76, 85–8, 91, 92, 96, 98–9, 100, 122, 139, 163, 165, 166, 167, 186, 204, 206, 214, 224, 229, 233–4, 237, 240, 302, 303–4, 327, 345, 358–9

Evangelical Revival 66, 68, 73, 84, 85, 88–94, 97

Evangelical Union 192

Evangelism 67, 70, 98, 161, 166, 167, 173, 184, 187, 207–8, 228–9, 230, 244, 309, 314, 322, 327, 352–3, 357, 359, *see also* Revivalism

Evlogy, Metropolitan 274, 281

Faith and Order 284, 322–3, 324, 325, 330–1

Farquhar, J. N. 241

Fascism 265, 336, 337

Febronianism 31

Federal Council of Churches of Christ in America 198

Feminist Theology 302, 373

Fénelon, François 29, 37

Feuerbach, Ludwig 142–3

Finland 151, 271, 331

Finney, Charles 185, 203–4, 207, 208, 210, 214, 230

Fisher, Archbishop 356

Florovsky, Georges 281, 326

Fountain Trust 361

'Foursquare Gospel' 309, 313

France 9–10, 20, 21, 22, 23–4, 28, 29, 30–1, 32–6, 37–8, 76, 112, 120–5, 126, 132, 134, 135–6, 140, 150–1, 200, 246, 249, 260, 292, 296, 310, 314, 338, 347, 384

Franciscans 40, 210, 392

Francke, August Hermann 16, 17, 18

Free Churches 169–70, 353, 355, 356–7, 365, *see also* Dissenters, Nonconformists

Free Church of Scotland 191, 192

Freemasonry 21, 111, 130

Frelinghuysen, T. J. 100

French Prophets 10, 33

French Revolution 85, 120–3, 157, 169, 236, 237, 383

Friedrich Wilhelm I 15, 17

Friends, Society of 99, 321, *see also* Quakers

Full Gospel Businessmen's Fellowship International 314–15

Fuller Theological Seminary 304, 317n

Fundamentalism 205, 206, 215, 268, 283, 303–4, 308, 327–8, 353

Gallicanism 28, 30, 34, 36, 123

George III 75, 188

George IV 157

Georgia 45, 272, 327

'German Christians' 263, 264, 265

Germany 3, 7, 8, 10–11, 13, 18–19, 20, 23, 24, 31, 34, 35, 76,

122, 125, 128, 131, 132, 140, 141, 148, 149–50, 151, 152, 161, 174, 185, 186, 188, 215, 219–21, 237, 249, 259–61, 262, 263–5, 267, 292, 300, 321, 325, 331, 337, 373, 379, East Germany 276, 277, West Germany 293

Ghana 252, 255n, 372

Global Christian Forum 328

Globalization 313, of Christianity 2, 3, 378, 380

'Glorious Revolution' 61, 74, 75, 169

Gorham Controversy 163–4

Gospels 22, 145–7, 213, 298, 377

Graham, Billy 208, 282, 353

Great Britain 3, 11, 12, 13, 20, 38, 60, 76, 77, 78, 80, 87, 95, 96, 100, 116, 122, 123, 124, 141, 150–1, 152, 155–96, 208, 209, 214, 215, 222–9, 236, 236, 242, 246, 249, 259–61, 266, 282, 286, 292–5, 305n, 307–9, 315, 334, 349–68, 392, see also England, Ireland, Scotland, Wales

'Great Awakening' 100–3; 'Second Great Awakening' 207–8

Greece 55, 56, 112–13, 114, 115, 117, 271, 284, 285, 326

Greek Catholics 45, 46n, 117, 119n, 271, 288n, see also Eastern-Rite Catholics

Greenland 12, 18

Gregory XVI 128, 236

Habsburgs 7, 8, 10, 13, 46, 86

Hackney Phalanx 161

Halévy, Elie 84

Half-Way Covenant 100–1, 102

Halle 16, 18, 48, 65, 91, 141

Harnack, Adolf 147, 260

Harper, Michael 361, 362

Harris, Howell 89

Harris, William Wadé 252

Healing 29, 36, 141, 192, 213, 215, 256n, 309, 311, 313–14, 361, 369, 371, 372, 373, 381n

Health care 113, 116, 311, 379, 382, see under Mission

Hegel, G. W. F. 142–3, 145–6

Helvetic Consensus 9

Hermeneutics 23, 168, 205, 320, 388, 389, see under Bible

Hick, John 332, 353

High churchmanship 62–3, 84, 90, 161–5, 167, 168–9, 226, 366, mission 237–8, 244, see under Anglicanism

Hinduism 18, 117, 235, 243, 342

Hocking, W. E. 332, 379

Holiness tradition 96, 208, 214, 215, 216, 302, 307

Holland 7, 12, 13, 33, 76, 100, 149, 150, 151, 347 Netherlands 9, 185, 236, 292, 347

Holocaust 265–8, 325, 332

Holy Roman Empire 7, 18, 30, 291

House churches 278, 358, 364, 368n

Hughes, Hugh Price 228, 229

Huguenots 9, 10, 76

Humanae Vitae 343

Hungary 44, 271, 272, 279, 282

Hutterites 10, 386

Hymns 11, 19, 67–8, 88, 89, 92, 95–6, 97, 167, 186, 341, 365

Inculturation 245, 370, 381n

India 4, 12, 18, 38, 45, 116–17, 185, 216, 233, 235, 236, 238, 241, 242, 243, 245, 246, 247, 272, 293, 310, 330, 345, 373, 374, 380

Independents 66, 68, 69, 71, 74, 99, 100, 182, 391, *see also* Congregationalists
Industrialization 65–6, 140, 197, 219, 224, 229, 246, 291
'Inner Mission' 152, 174, 220–1, 229
Innocent XI 28, 37
International Missionary Council (IMC) 253, 263, 322
Inter-Varsity Fellowship 305n, 320
Iraq 115, 285, 286, 338
Ireland 60, 75–6, 88, 95, 96, 135, 150, 156, 157, 162, 179n, 180n, 188–9, 208, 228, 231–2n, 246, 338, 350, 358, Northern Ireland 307, 333, 362, *see also* Ulster
Irving, Edward 167, 192, 223n, 238, 317n
Islam 54, 55, 112, 240–1, *see also* Muslims
Israel, biblical 139, 144, 168, 205, 211, 264, 388, modern 205, 268, 286, 305, 388
Italy 29, 35, 122, 125, 131, 151, 310, 337, 338, 375

Jacobitism 60, 72, 75, 82n, 85, 193
Jamaica 199, 247
James II 61, 63, 66, 72, 75
James VI/I 76, 90
Jansenism 14, 28, 32–4, 40, 86, 132, 310, 390
Japan 126–7, 248, 267, 271
Jehovah's Witnesses 213–14
Jerusalem 45, 47, 324, 332
Jesuits 28, 31, 32, 33–4, 37, 39–41, 42, 46, 47, 55, 78, 123, 126, 210, 236
Jesus 22, 85, 133, 141, 230, 235, 264, 298, 309, 325, 378, *see also* Christology
Jesus Movement 303
Jews 12, 79, 116, 120, 150, 172, 194, 205, 241, 263–5, 266–8, 295, 296, 332, 342
John XXIII 283, 339, 341
John Paul II 283, 345, 346, 347
Jones, Griffith 65
Joseph II 31–2
Judaism 13, 86, 264, 268

Kairos Document 302, 308
Kant, Immanuel 20, 141, 142, 145, 146
Keble, John 162
Kenya 372, 375, 381n
Keston Institute 280
Keswick Convention 214, 239, 249, 251
Kierkegaard, Søren 151, 263
Kimbanguists 372
King, Martin Luther 301
Kirchentag 152, 220
Koinonia 301, 324, 329, 331
Korea 39, 126, 248–9, 312, North Korea 278, 376, South Korea 312, 345, 374, 376, 377–8
Kraemer, Hendrik 332
Kulturkampf 125, 149
Küng, Hans 12, 346

Laity 27, 36, 39, 77, 122, 135, 160, 164, 176, 189, 201, 277, 309, 314, 323, 338, 339–41, 344, 346–7, 354, *see under* Preaching
Lambeth Conferences 161, 168, 321, 330, 356, 374
Latin America 39, 41, 125–6, 243, 245, 311, 315, 335n, 338, 344–6, 347, 377, *see also* South America
Latitudinarianism 62–4, 73, 167

Latter-Day Saints, *see* Mormons

Lausanne Committee for World Evangelization 322, 380

Law, William 63, 90

League of Nations 262, 324

Lebanon 115, 285

Leibniz, G.W. 9, 52

Leisure 140, 148, 174, 186–7, 188, 293

Leo XIII 117, 125, 132, 133, 202, 218

Lessing, G. E. 22, 145

Li Tim Oi (Florence) 266

Liberalism: ethical 374, political 124–6, 128–30, 134, 149, 150, 219, 228, 264, 337, 345, theological 133, 140–1, 147–8, 177, 209, 230, 262–3, 298–9, 300, 303–4, 355, 362, 377, 380, 383

Liberation Theology 301, 302, 343–5, 373, 378

Liberia 199, 242

Life and Work 265, 284, 318, 323–4, 326

Liguori, Alphonsus, 29, 210

Lindsey, Hal 283

Literacy 11, 18, 225

Lithuania 35, 127, 271, *see also* Baltic

Liturgical Movement 340, 366

Liturgy 38, 40–1, 46, 49, 54, 111, 164–5, 167, 302, 333, 340–1, 365–6, 378

Livingstone, David 246

Locke, John 20, 21, 86, 91, 102

Loisy, Alfred 133, 147

London Missionary Society (LMS) 237, 242

Lord's Supper 211, 388, *see also* Communion

Louis XIV 9, 28, 30, 31, 33

Louis XVI 120, 121, 169

Low churchmanship 165

Low Countries 33, *see also* Belgium, Holland

Luther, Martin 11, 12, 14, 19, 31, 91, 149, 263, 264, 389

Lutheranism 7–8, 10–11, 12, 14, 19, 35, 46, 76, 148, 149, 150, 161, 201, 221, 242, 255–6n, 265–6, 321, 331, 375

McLeod, Hugh 152, 186, 290–1

McPherson, Aimee Semple 309, 317n

Madagascar 240

Majority World 293, 304, 308, 315, 344, 369, 373, 374, 380, 382

Malines conversations 341

Mar Thoma Church 117, 272

Maria Theresa 31, 46

Maritain, Jacques 296, 338–9

Maronites 45, 47, 285

Marx, Karl 143, 220–1, Marxism 139, 220–1, 270, 273, 344–5, 347

Mass 41, 188, 255n, 295, 340–1, 388, 391, *see also* Communion

Maurice, F. D. 167, 225–6

Melkites 45, 47, 113

Mennonites 10, 76, 82–3n, 111, 150, 321, 386

Mercersburg theology 209

Methodism 70, 84–5, 87, 91, 93–7, 99, 100, 170, 172, 173, 174, 175–6, 181, 185, 189, 293, 321, 330, 355, 356, 357, in North America 79, 201, 208, 223, 227, societies 89, 91, 93–4, 95, 96, *see also* Calvinistic Methodism, Primitive Methodism, Wesleyanism, Wesleyan Methodism

Methodist New Connexion 174, 176, 356

Mexico 126, 200, 288n

Middle East 4, 113, 115, 117, 203, 241, 285–7, 322
Middle East Council of Churches 286, 335n
Millennialism 122, see also Amillennialism, Postmillennialism, Premillennialism
Millennium 12, 169, 175, 179n, 205
Millet system 54, 55, 113, 116, 117
Minjung Theology 345, 377–8
Miracles 21, 23, 33, 133, 146, 213, 298, 310
Mission halls 159, 184, 187, 195n
Mission, overseas 113, 165, 233, 241, 242–50, 326, 332, 374, 378–80, 382, agencies/ societies 12, 18, 78, 111, 113, 115–16, 150, 161, 207, 235–41, 242–3, 244, 245, 246, 249, 253, 278, 288n, 305n, 322, faith missions 238–9, 250, medical mission 39, 224, 239, 240, 250, see also Health care
Missionaries 3, 13, 18, 39, 165, 184, 199, 233, 235, 239, 240, 241, 242, 244, 245, 247–8, 249, 250, 263, 373, 374, 380, training of 18, 38, 111, 238–9
Missionary orders 41, 135, 158, 235–6, 382
Moderatism 73–4, 190, 246
Modern Churchmen's Union 298
Mogila, Peter 47, 52
Molokans 52, 111
Moltmann, Jürgen 300–1
Monasticism/monasteries 32–3, 35, 50, 51, 52, 53, 56, 109–10, 114, 120, 124, 125, 126, 236, 277, 287

Monophysites see Orthodox, Oriental
Moody, D. L. 185, 209, 230, 242, 353
Morality 13, 16, 21, 36, 63–4, 68, 228, 229, 231n, 294, 295, 351, 352, see also Ethics
Moravians 17, 18, 19, 76, 88, 91, 97, 105n, 150, 151, 220, 240, 357
Mormons 175, 182, 211–12
Mott, John R. 253
Mount Athos 53, 56, 114, 117
Müller, George 238
Muslims 7, 44, 55, 113, 116, 117, 241, 278, 285, see also Islam

National Association of Evangelicals 304, 317n
Nazism 261, 263–5, 266–7, 277, 301, 337
Neo-Orthodoxy 262–3, 298, 323, 332, 358, 379
Nestorians 116, 233, 390, see also Church of the East
Nevius, John L. 239, 248, 278, 376
New Age 297, 302, 384
New Apostolic Church 267, 373
New England 79, 90, 102, 201, 207
'New Haven theology' 203–4
New Martyrs 54
New Measures 203, 208, 210
New Testament Church of God 360, 364
Newman, John Henry 130, 133, 162–3
Newton, John 97
Niemöller, Martin 264, 267
Nietzsche, Friedrich 143, 260
Nigeria 364, 372, 374
Nikon, Patriarch 49–50

Noll, Mark A. 87, 102–3, 200–1
Nonconformists 161, 169–77,
    182–7, 226–9, 237, 259, 260,
    261, 340, 349, 354, 356, 366,
    Nonconformist conscience 228,
    see also Dissenters, Free
    Churches
Non-Jurors (England) 63, 64
Non-realism 299, 383
Non-Subscribing
    Presbyterians 69, 189
North America 4, 9, 12, 13, 38,
    60, 76–80, 88, 96, 100–3, 113,
    149–50, 198, 200, 205, 206,
    208, 210, 211, 213, 214, 215,
    216, 220, 229–30, 237, 244,
    263, 281, 283, 285, 293, 304,
    307, 308, 309, 313, 314, 325,
    328, 347, 373, 375, *see also*
    Canada, United States
Norway 151, 266
Nostra Aetate 268, 342

Old Believers 45, 48–51, 111,
    112, 119n, 327
Old Calendarists 271, 284
Old Catholics 33, 131–2
'Old Dissent' 66
Oldham, J. H. 322, 323
Opus Dei 346, 347
Ordination 35, 61, 62, 93–5, 163,
    172, 193, 238, 314, 330, 374,
    386, 390, 391, of women 188,
    266, 302, 355, 366
Orthodox Church in America 283
Orthodoxy, Eastern 4, 7, 44–58,
    109–19, 124, 310, mission 4,
    53, 110–11, 116, 117, 203,
    251, relations with Roman
    Catholicism 46–7, 117, 131,
    theology 47–8, 54, 109, 110
Orthodoxy and nationalism 55,
    113–15
Orthodoxy, Oriental 44, 47

Other faiths 4, 19, 21, 241, 296,
    331–2, 342, 379; *see under*
    Dialogue
Ottoman Empire 4, 46, 54–5,
    112–18, 241, 270
Oxford Movement 161, 162,
    177, *see under* Anglicanism

Pacific 233, 235, 242, 243, 308,
    335n
Pacifism 260, 265–6, 386
Palestine 268, 286
Panikkar, Raimon 342
Papacy 27–9, 31, 122, 123, 124,
    126, 127, 128, 130, 134, 157,
    169, 236, 240, 336–8, 339,
    346, 383
Papal States 123, 124, 125, 128,
    129, 337
Para-church agencies 161, 320
Paraguay 41
Parham, C. F. 215, 216
Parish missions 29–30, 209–10
Pascal, Blaise 33
Pastoral care 62, 63, 73, 94, 166,
    183, 188, 191
Patronage (in parishes) 34, 74,
    98, 190, 192
Paul VI 341, 343, 346
Paulist Fathers 202
Peace of Augsburg 7, 291
Peace of Westphalia 4, 7, 18, 86,
    291, 383
Penn, William 77
Pentateuch 144, 168, 371, 390
Pentecostalism 2, 96, 185, 213,
    214–16, 260, 274, 275, 278,
    281, 293, 306–17, 321, 323,
    328, 345, 349, 358, 359–60,
    362, 363, 364; Oneness
    Pentecostalism 307
Persecution 10, 15, 16, 31, 33,
    40, 46, 49, 54, 67, 112–13,
    119n, 121, 122, 126, 127, 170,

240, 248, 273–6, 277, 279–80, 285, 342, 372,

Peter the Great 10, 50, 52–3, 114, 270

Petite Église 123

Phanariots 54–5

Philanthropy 64, 161, 183, 188, 220, 224–5, 294

Pietism 12, 13–19, 32, 47–8, 77, 87, 88, 100, 141, 151, 206, 220, 221, 237, 245

Piety 11, 16, 19, 37, 49, 100, 133–6, 174, 307, 340, *see also* Devotion, Spirituality

Philippines 38, 39, 243, 245, 249, 252, 315

Philosophes 22, 34

Phyletism 115

Pilgrimage 122, 129, 134–5, 362, 371

Pius IX 125, 128–30, 131

Pius X 125, 132

Pius XI 264–5, 336, 337, 338, 378–9

Pius XII 265, 267, 336, 375

Pluralism, clerical 61–2, 159–60, 189

Pluralism of religions 295, 297, 332, 342, 358,

Poland 10, 35, 36, 44, 46, 48, 127, 271, 280, 337, 347

Political Theology 300, 302, 343

Polynesia 233, 235

Portugal 28, 30, 37, 38, 41, 125–6, 135, 249, 337

Postliberalism 300

Postmillennialism 12, 363

Preaching 29–30, 49, 61, 63, 67, 74, 78, 87, 88, 95, 100, 101–2, 111, 176, 207, 208, 263, 284, 341, lay preaching 89, 93, 94, 96, 98, 172, 173, 180n, 192, 193, 195n, 227, open-air preaching 89, 92, 93, women

as preachers 93, 175, 187–8

Premillennialism 169, 205, 238, 239

Presbyterian Church of Wales 172, 357

Presbyterianism 64, 66, 67, 68, 69, 71, 73, 75, 99, 101, 144, 177, 182, 190–3, 307, 312, 366, 376, 390, in Ireland 76, 90, 189, 326, 330, 355, 356, in the United States 201, 205, 208, 223, 303

Priesthood 39, 44, 93, 95, 134, 161, 164, 338, 343, 346–7, 356, 375, *see also* Clergy

Priestley, Joseph 23, 169

Primitive Methodism 176, 181, 184, 185, 187, 227, 350, 356

Princeton theology 204, 206

Process Theology 299–300

Propaganda (Sacred Congregation for the Propagation of the Faith) 38, 39, 41, 202, 236

Prophecy, biblical 21, 23, 163, 167, 204–5, 206, 212, 231n, 241, 246, 268, 283, 327

Prophecy, charismatic 10, 141, 192, 307, 310, 313, 363, 369, 371, 373

Proselytism 17, 46, 116, 117–18, 184, 189, 284, 285, 322, 342

Protestantism 7–26, 42, 44, 46, 66, 87, 238, 339, 374; mission 4, 11–13, 18, 77–8, 117–18, 151, 233, 236–7, 238, 242, 248, 319, 320, 322, 379–80, 382, relations with Roman Catholicism 8, 9, 86–7, 117, 341–2, theology 8–9, 11–12, 16, 18, 21–4, 37, 101–2, 133, 140–2, 224, 236–7, 240, 262–3, 345, 372, 379, 383, 391

Prussia 9, 10, 14–15, 16, 19, 28, 32, 76, 112, 116, 121, 123,

124, 125, 127, 141, 149–50
Puritanism 12, 13, 14, 59, 63,
    64, 67, 77–8, 79, 85, 86, 87,
    91, 97, 98, 102, 159, 197, 230,
    240, 390
Pusey, E. B. 162, 165

Quakers 51, 66–7, 69, 71, 79,
    99, 172, 175, 182, 187–8, 201,
    223, 260, 362, 391, *see also*
    Friends, Society of
Quest for the Historical
    Jesus 145–8, 262, 297, 323
Quietism 26n, 28, 29, 36, 91

Racism 301, 307, 326, 329
Rahner, Karl 342
Ramabai, Pandita 216, 310
Rationalism 8, 19–21, 23–4, 51,
    67, 80, 130, 140, 145, 167,
    198, 201, 204, 206, 215, 303
Redeemed Christian Church of
    God 360, 364
Redemptorists 29, 35, 202, 210
Reformed tradition 9, 10, 13–14,
    35, 67, 70, 73, 74, 149, 193,
    201, 204, 263, 306, 351, 358,
    362, 390, *see also* Calvinism
Religion of the heart 13, 30, 32,
    86, 384
Rerum novarum 218–19, 338–9,
    341
Restorationism 363–4
Revelation, divine19–23, 40, 69,
    127, 131, 141, 168, 211, 213,
    263, 340, 369
Revelation, book of 122, 163,
    205, 283
Revival 86, 89–90, 99–100, 103,
    138, 150, 169, 172, 184–5,
    187, 189, 191, 203, 207–9,
    216, 223, 312, 361, 375
Revivalism 30, 100, 103, 151,
    174–5,176, 185, 189, 192,

197, 199, 206–10, 211, 320,
    in Catholicism 30, 134, 158,
    209–10
Ritschl, Albrecht 146, 147, 221,
    230
Ritualism 161, 165, 365, *see
    under* Anglicanism
Roberts, Oral 309, 314
Robinson, John 299, 352, 353
Roman Catholicism 3, 9, 27–43,
    120–37, 150, 234, 244, 310,
    315, 323, 331, 336–48, 375,
    383, devotion 35–6, 133–5,
    158, 346, 347, ecumenism 30–
    1,321, 323, 333, 341–2, 358,
    mission 4, 28, 35–6, 37–42,
    44, 46, 55, 78, 117, 126, 128,
    135, 158, 202, 235–6, 244,
    347, 378–9, theology 24, 37,
    127–32, 218–19, 268, 293,
    294, 327, 330–1, 338–46, *see
    also* Eastern-Rite Catholics,
    Rome
Romania 44, 46, 114–15, 271,
    276–7, 279, 280, 284
Romanticism 24, 71, 133, 140–1,
    143, 149, 162, 164, 201, 238
Rome 8, 28, 31, 33–4, 36, 38,
    39–40, 44, 45, 46–7, 49, 59,
    86, 117, 122, 123, 125–35,
    157, 158, 163–4, 202, 218,
    251, 267, 278, 285, 286, 321,
    333, 341, 351, 354, 355, *see
    also* Roman Catholicism
Rosary 36, 134, 158, 391
Rowland, Daniel 88–9
Russia 28, 44, 46, 48–53, 56,
    109–12, 117, 123–4, 127, 140,
    270–81, 282, 284, 310, 327,
    376

Sabbath 89, 186
Sacraments 24n, 32, 37, 50, 51,
    62, 95, 101, 134, 151, 172,

175, 209, 291, 329, 356, 372, 391, reserved sacrament 36, 164, 390; *see also* Baptism, Communion

Sacred Heart, devotion to 36, 134, 158

Saints 28, 29, 36, 122, 384

Salzburg 8, 10, 76

Salvation Army 174–5, 187, 195n, 326, 355

Scandinavia 151, 174, 215, 220, 325, 331

Scepticism 22, 132, 133, 147, 238

Schleiermacher, F. D. E. 141–2, 154n

Schweitzer, Albert 146–7

Science 11, 133, 135, 138–40, 142, 167, 168, 202

Scotland 20, 60, 64, 73–5, 76, 88, 89–90, 99, 149, 184, 186, 187, 189. 190–3, 263, 293, 294, 355, 357, 362, 366

Scottish Episcopal Church 75, 80, 190, 193, 200, 293, 355, 366

Secession Church (Scotland) 74, 75, 90

Secularization 2, 8, 113, 133, 138, 140, 152, 291–2, 295, 384

Seminaries 28, 31, 35, 47, 53, 93, 112, 125, 160, 303

Separatism 13, 391

Serbia 45, 115, 271, 284

Sermons 11, 14, 64, 96, 101, 112, 133, 309, 366

Seventh-Day Adventism 212, 386

Seymour, W. J. 215, 216

Shaftesbury, Lord 166, 224

Siberia 53, 111, 233

Sierra Leone 79, 199, 223, 242

Silesia 15, 76

Simeon, Charles 166

Slavery, slave trade 13, 18, 41, 78, 199, 209, 222–4, 242, 246, 247, 374

Slavophils 110

Slovakia 267, 271, 272

Smith, William Robertson 144, 192

Social Gospel movement 146, 220, 229–30, 245, 323, 351, 379

Socialism 125, 150, 218–19, 221, 225–6, 229, 337, 338

Society for the Promotion of Christian Knowledge (SPCK) 12–13, 65, 237

Society for the Propagation of the Gospel (SPG) 12–13, 65, 90, 237

Socinianism 68–9

Söderblom, Nathan 323, 331

South Africa 18, 197, 199, 250, 251, 302, 308, 310–11, 314, 326, 345, 371–2, 375, 376–7

South African Council of Churches 307, 376

South America 41, 126, 253, 309, 355, *see also* Latin America

Spain/Spanish 7, 13, 28, 29, 30, 36, 37, 38, 39, 41, 122, 125–6, 135, 151, 310, 337, 342–3

Spener, Philip 14, 15, 16

Spiritualism 71, 261, 312

Spirituality 11, 16–19, 56, 62, 73, 86, 87, 91, 95, 97, 99, 109, 110, 135, 151, 185, 199, 213, 216, 239, 291, 297, 302, 308, 312, 313, 372, 383, 384, 389, 390, *see also* Devotion, Piety

Spurgeon, C. H. 170, 171, 174

Sri Lanka, *see* Ceylon

Stations of the Cross 36, 134, 391

Stone, Barton W. 211

Stott, John 359, 361

Strauss, D. F. 145–6

Student Christian Movement (SCM) 319, 320

Student Volunteer Movement for

Foreign Missions (SVM) 242, 249, 250, 256, 380
Stundists 111
Sunday schools 65–6, 183–4, 274, 279, 286–7, 294, 354
Sweden 11, 151, 305n
Swedenborg, Emmanuel 71
Switzerland 7, 9, 150–1
Sword of the Spirit 351–2
Syllabus of Errors 130
Syncretism 8, 40, 245, 247, 370, 375, 378, 391
Syria 115, 272, 285

Taizé 333
Tanzania 244, 375
Taylor, Jeremy 62, 90
Taylor, Nathaniel 203–4
Temperance 175, 210, 227, 228
Temple, William 268, 351, 357
Textual criticism 9, 18
'Third Rome' 48, 49, 50, 110
Third orders 36, 391
'Third Wave' 315–16
Thirty-Nine Articles 66, 68, 69, 162, 225
Thirty Years' War 4, 7, 383
Thomas Christians 38, 116–17
Thomism 133, 218, 338–9
Thompson, E. P. 84, 227
Three-Self Patriotic Movement 278, 376
Tillich, Paul 299
Tillotson, Archbishop 63–4
Tithes 67, 160, 392
Toleration 8, 10, 20, 22, 32, 54, 62, 66, 72, 75, 76, 77, 116, 117, 120, 130, 150, 157, 171, 193, 290, 291, 295, 338, 354, Toleration Act 66, 69, 70, 95, 159
Tongues, speaking in 10, 33, 141, 192, 215–16, 307, 310, 312, 313

'Toronto Blessing' 315, 361, 362
Tractarianism 161, 163, 170, 226, *see under* Anglicanism
Tradition 91, 140, 319, 323, 326, 340, 390
Training for ministry 35, 47, 70, 98, 134, 160, 166, 187, 195n, 298
Transcendentalism 201
Transylvania 8, 10, 45, 46, 114
Tutu, Desmond 302, 376
Typology 23, 392

Uganda 234, 374, 375
Ukraine 10, 44, 48, 51–2, 111, 117, 127, 271–2, 273, 277, 281, 288n, 310
Ulster 69, 76, 90, 184, 187, 189, 207, *see also* Ireland, Northern
Ultramontanism 30, 123, 127–30, 135, 157, 158, 247
Unitarians 66, 68, 69, 70, 71, 82n, 99, 102, 105n, 169, 177, 182, 198, 201, 209, 355, 392
Unitatis Redintegratio 330, 341–2
United Bible Societies 333
United Free Church of Scotland 192, 293, 355
United Kingdom, *see* Great Britain
United Reformed Church 355, 356, 357
United States 197, 200, 201, 202–3, 209–10, 283, 295, Declaration of Independence of 79, 200, Middle Colonies 78, 102–3, Southern states 78, 102–3, 199, 200, 223–4, *see also* New England, North America
Universal Church of the Kingdom of God 310, 311, 360
Universities' Mission to Central Africa 238, 246
Urbanization 65–6, 140, 152,

159, 172, 184, 193, 219–20,
291, 311

Vatican 28, 29, 39, 117, 129,
130, 132, 134, 218, 267, 283,
311, 328, 333, 337, 338, 341,
342, 345, 346, 381n, 388
Vatican I 125, 130–1
Vatican II 37, 130, 268, 283,
330, 336–7, 339–43, 344, 346,
347, 379
Venn, Henry (1725–97) 98
Venn, Henry (1796–1873) 239,
244, 251, 278
Vicars apostolic 33, 38, 39, 158,
375
Vietnam 38–9, 126
Visser 't Hooft, W. A. 320, 325
Voltaire 20

Wales 65, 70, 88–9, 92, 95, 100,
155, 170, 172–3, 182, 184–6,
187, 195n, 355, 357, 358, 362,
366
Walls, Andrew 87, 234
Ward, W. R. 86–7, 88
Warfield, B. B. 204, 206
Watts, Isaac 67, 68, 101
Week of Prayer for Christian
Unity 332–3
Wellhausen, Julius 144
Wesley, Charles 88, 92, 95
Wesley, John 19, 37, 59, 64, 84,
88, 90–1, 92, 93–7, 99, 170,
175, 176, 187, 222, 223
Wesleyanism 93, 96, 97, 169,
171, 176–7, 182, 187, 190,
214, 215, 226, 227, 306, 350,
356, 364, see also Methodism

Westminster Confession 69, 73,
74, 100, 144, 189, 192, 211
West Indies 13, 18, 38, 247, 360,
see also Caribbean
White Fathers 234, 236, 240
Whitefield, George 88, 90–3, 99,
100, 102
Wichern, J. H. 152, 220, 221
Wilberforce, William 222, 224
William III 61, 63, 75
Wimber, John 315–16
Woolman, John 78, 223
World Alliance of Reformed
Churches 301, 321
World Council of Churches
(WCC) 252, 263, 285, 302,
318–35, 342, 345, 372, 378,
379–80
World Student Christian
Fellowship (WSCF) 319–20
World War I 148, 259–61, 298,
319, 336, 380, 383
World War II 265–7
Worship 41, 47, 67, 70, 141,
161, 164–5, 167, 169, 170,
174, 177, 195n, 261, 282,
302–3, 333, 362, 364–7, 373,
383

Young Men's Christian
Association (YMCA) 198, 319,
320, 353
Yugoslavia 115, 337, 347

Zambia 330
von Zinzendorf, Nikolaus
Ludwig 16–18, 19, 48, 315,
320, 333
Zionist churches 252, 370–2